AAUSC Issues in Language Program Direction

Internet-mediated Intercultural Foreign Language Education

Julie A. Belz
Steven L. Thorne

Editors

HEINLE
CENGAGE Learning™

Australia • Brazil • Japan • Korea • Mexico • Singapore • Spain • United Kingdom • United States

HEINLE
CENGAGE Learning

AAUSC Issues in Language Program Direction: Internet-mediated Intercultural Foreign Language Education
Julie A. Belz, Steven L.Thorne

Executive Editor: Carrie Brandon

Senior Development Editor:
Joan M. Flaherty

Assistant Editor: Arlinda Shtuni

Editorial Assistant: Morgen Murphy

Technology Project Manager:
Sacha Laustsen

Production Director: Elise Kaiser

Marketing Manager:
Lindsey Richardson

Marketing Assistant:
Marla Nasser

Advertising Project Manager:
Stacey Purviance

Manufacturing Manager:
Marcia Locke

Compositor: GEX Publishing
Services

Project Manager: GEX
Publishing Services

407
I 61

For product information and technology assistance, contact us at **Cengage Learning Customer & Sales Support, 1-800-354-9706**

For permission to use material from this text or product, submit all requests online at **www.cengage.com/permissions**
Further permissions questions can be emailed to **permissionrequest@cengage.com**

Library of Congress Control Number: 2005935615

ISBN-13: 978-1-4130-2992-5

ISBN-10: 1-4130-2992-2

Heinle
20 Channel Center Street
Boston, MA 02210
USA

Cengage Learning is a leading provider of customized learning solutions with office locations around the globe, including Singapore, the United Kingdom, Australia, Mexico, Brazil, and Japan. Locate your local office at **www.cengage.com/global**

Cengage Learning products are represented in Canada by Nelson Education, Ltd.

To learn more about Heinle, visit **www.cengage.com/heinle**

Purchase any of our products at your local college store or at our preferred online store **www.cengagebrain.com**

Printed in the United States of America
2 3 4 5 6   17 16 15 14 13

Contents

Acknowledgments

The 2005 volume of the annual *AAUSC Issues in Language Program Direction* series is the product of much hard work on the part of numerous individuals. First, we are thankful to the members of the AAUSC Editorial Board who provided many suggestions and valuable feedback in the developmental stages of the volume. Second, we are indebted to the series editor, Sally Sieloff Magnan, for her generous assistance throughout the editorial process.

We are very grateful for the expertise and efforts of our referees beyond the editorial board members who provided timely, detailed, and careful reviews of the submissions for the volume: Matthew Carlson, Meredith Doran, Carolin Fuchs, Paula Golombeck, Michael Legutke, Glenn Levine, Robert O'Dowd, Emily F. Rine, J. Scott Payne, Jonathon Reinhardt, D. Bryan Smith, Julie Sykes, Nina Vyatkina, and Paige Ware. Special thanks go to our colleague at Pennsylvania State, editorial board member Celeste Kinginger, who provided reviews above and beyond the call of duty.

We also wish to acknowledge Heinle, Cengage Learning for its continued support of the AAUSC annual series. In particular, we are grateful to Carrie Brandon, Executive Editor for World Languages, Elise Kaiser, Production Director, and Jennifer Roehrig, Project Manager for GEX Publishing Services, for their help in bringing this volume to press. The volume contributors deserve special thanks for their willingness to engage in, and explore, the time-consuming, challenging, frequently tense, but persistently rewarding enterprise of Internet-mediated intercultural foreign language education.

Finally, we wish to thank those department heads, administrators, and language program directors who recognize the long-term educational and humanistic value of interaction with persons from other cultures and therefore encourage the establishment of networked foreign language and culture exchanges in their units. We hope the intercultural experiences reported in this volume will not only encourage enhanced conditions for language learning, but also highlight the capacity for foreign language education to foster dialogue between members of different cultures at a point in time when such dialogue is greatly needed.

Julie A. Belz and *Steven L. Thorne*
Editors

American Association of University Supervisors, Coordinators, and Directors of Foreign Language Programs

Issues in Language Program Direction
A Series of Annual Volumes

Series Editor

Sally Sieloff Magnan, *University of Wisconsin-Madison*

Editorial Board

Style Sheet for AAUSC Series

Beginning with the 2006 volume, this publication will follow the style of the *American Psychological Association* (APA), latest edition.

Issues in Language Program Direction
AAUSC Annual Volume Series

Series Editor: Sally Sieloff Magnan, University of Wisconsin–Madison
Preceding Volumes from Heinle, Cengage Learning

2004:   *Language Program Articulation: Developing a Theoretical Foundation*
Editors: Catherine M. Barrette and Kate Paesani

2003:   *Advanced Foreign Language Learning: A Challenge to College Programs*
Editors: Heidi Byrnes and Hiram H. Maxim

2002:   *The Sociolinguistics of Foreign Language Classrooms: Contributions of
the Native, the Near-native, and the Non-native Speaker*
Editor: Carl Blyth

2001:   *SLA and the Literature Classroom: Fostering Dialogues*
Editors: Virginia M. Scott and Holly Tucker

2000:   *Mentoring Foreign Language Teaching Assistants, Lecturers,
and Adjunct Faculty*
Editor: Benjamin Rifkin

1999:   *Form and Meaning: Multiple Perspectives*
Editors: James Lee and Albert Valdman

1998:   *Research Issues and Language Program Direction*
Editor: L. Kathy Heilenman

1997:   *New Ways of Learning and Teaching: Focus on Technology and
Foreign Language Education*
Editor: Judith A. Muyskens

1996:   *Patterns and Policies: The Changing Demographics of Foreign
Language Instruction*
Editor: Judith E. Liskin-Gasparro

1995:   *Redefining the Boundaries of Language Study*
Editor: Claire Kramsch

1994:   *Faces in a Crowd: The Individual Learner in Multisection Courses*
Editor: Carol A. Klee

1993:   *The Dynamics of Language Program Direction*
Editor: David P. Benseler

1992:   *Development and Supervision of Teaching Assistants in Foreign Languages*
Editor: Joel C. Walz

1991:   *Assessing Foreign Language Proficiency of Undergraduates*
Editor: Richard V. Teschner

Introduction:

Internet-mediated Intercultural Foreign Language Education and the Intercultural Speaker

Julie A. Belz
Steven L. Thorne

> Despite what our political and corporate leaders want us to believe, the educational bridge to the 21st century will not ultimately be found in the ever-increasing technological cleverness of school graduates. The quality of life in the new millennium will depend much more on the capacity of human beings to find ways to resist the draw of victimizing and brutalizing others, and the seduction of joining those who build their sense of identity and value on the indignity of others (Shapiro 2002, p. 64).

Internet-mediation and the Intercultural Perspective in Foreign Language Education

When we first began work on this volume, it became clear to us that there was the potential for its purpose to be misconstrued as an explication of the use of technology and, more specifically, the Internet, in foreign language (FL) learning and teaching. This is a reasonable conclusion, of course, because the adjective "Internet-mediated" occurs in its title as a modifier of the phrase "foreign language education." Such a perception might be supported further by the fact that an engagement with technology seems to permeate contemporary foreign language education (FLE) with respect to pedagogy, curricular design, and research (e.g., Beatty 2003; Chapelle 2003; Fotos and Browne 2004; Levy 1997; Muyskens 1997; Warschauer 1996a; Warschauer and Kern 2000). These three areas of inquiry have been at the heart of the professional mission of the *American Association of University Supervisors, Coordinators, and Directors of Foreign Language Programs* since its inception in 1980.

The stated present-day preoccupation of FLE with technology is evidenced by the number of publications focusing on technology-related research and pedagogy in generalist journals in our field such as *The Modern Language Journal* and *Applied Linguistics*, the existence of specialist journals devoted to issues of technology and language learning (e.g., *CALICO Journal, Language Learning & Technology, ReCALL,* and *System: An International Journal of Educational Technology and Applied Linguistics*), the high number of conference presentations and symposia in which technology constitutes a key component, the ubiquity of required coursework on technology and language teaching in many graduate degree programs in the FLs and applied linguistics, as well as the sheer volume of recently coined terms and acronyms to index the intersection of technology and language learning (e.g., computer-assisted language learning [CALL], technology-enhanced language learning [TELL], network-based language teaching [NBLT], networked collaborative interaction [NCI], tandem learning, and telecollaboration, to provide only a partial list).

The attention paid to technology in FLE circles and in education in general (e.g., Cuban 2001; Cummins and Sayers 1995; Tomei 2003) is derivative of the attention that it attracts, for better or for worse, in other facets of modern life, where it has been heralded variously (and oppositionally) as the democratizing force *par excellence*; the hemlock of higher education; the new mediator of human identity and social activity; the death of meaningful human relations; one of the primary tools advancing socio-economic, linguistic, and cultural globalization; and the medium that enables resistance to the crushing forces of global capital toward convergence (see, for example, Brabazon 2002; Brennan 2003; Cameron and Block 2002; Castells 1996; Feenberg 2002; Hiltz and Turoff 1993; Lanham 1993; Rheingold 1993; Sproull and Kiesler 1991; Tella 1996; Turkle 1984, 1997; Warschauer 1996b).

As pervasive and alluring as the role of technology in FLE might be, we do not view the adjective "Internet-mediated" to be the most important word in the title of this volume and, correspondingly, this volume is not primarily about the use of technology in FL learning and teaching. Instead, the emphasis for us lies on the adjective "intercultural" and the potential for FLE to serve as a site for the complexification of the self on linguistic, social, cultural, and ethical planes through lived experiences of communicative interaction with persons from other cultures in both additional and native languages. As a result, Internet-mediated intercultural foreign language education (ICFLE) fundamentally is predicated on what Istvan Kecskes (2004), in the inaugural editorial of *Intercultural Pragmatics*, refers to as the "intercultural perspective." Language-related inquiry from the intercultural perspective takes the phenomenon of intercultural communication (Scollon and Scollon 2001a) as its primary object of investigation. *Intercultural* communication differs from *cross-cultural* communication in that the latter "is usually considered a study of a particular idea(s) or concept(s) within several cultures that compares one culture to another on the aspect of interest, [while the former] focuses on interactions among people from different cultures" (Kecskes 2004, pp. 1–2). Scollon and Scollon further observe that intercultural communication involves "the study of distinct cultural or other groups *in interaction with one another*" (italics in the original). In the cross-cultural paradigm, on the other hand, "the members of the distinct groups do not interact with each other . . . but are studied as separate and separable entities" (2001b, p. 539).

There are two analogies to be drawn here. The first regards the similarity of cross-cultural communication and traditional classroom-based FL instruction where learners study the language and the culture of a different group but typically do not interact with members of that group during instructional periods. The second analogy concerns the parallels between intercultural communication in general and ICFLE in particular where interaction with members of the studied culture forms the leading classroom activity. Just as the intercultural perspective on communication brings "a multilingual angle into . . . overwhelmingly monolingual research paradigms," directs special attention to the "dynamic nature of meaning and culture," and investigates "the construction of culture by interactants with different national, ethnic, and racial backgrounds" (Kecskes 2004, p. 2), the linkage of different cultural groups in ICFLE shifts the focus of tutored FLE away from monolingual norms (Firth and Wagner 1997), static depictions of culture, and monolithic target-language identities (Davies 2003) toward the quotidian realities of multilingualism (Belz 2002a; Blyth 1995; Danet and Herring 2003) and the multiplicity of meaning and identity (Norton 2000; Rampton 1990, 1995).

As the above discussion makes clear, the hallmark of ICFLE, as defined in this volume, is the inclusion of living, breathing human representatives of the languages and cultures under study in classroom-based FL instruction (Kinginger 2004, p. 103). The Internet serves as the mediator of this inclusive process, but it is not the object of investigation *per se*; instead, it is the means by which educators may bring together those who represent various national, ethnic, socio-economic, social class, and faith-based viewpoints via classroom practices generally termed "telecollaborative" in a supportive environment and in pedagogically sound ways to develop what Byram (1997) has described as "intercultural competence" (see also Ager, Muskens, and Wright 1993; Bausch, Christ, and Krumm 1997; Bennett 1998; Corbett 2003; Freinet 1992; Kramsch 1993) as well as grammatical and pragmatic FL competencies.

To repeat a definition that by now has been learned by rote by many FL educators, particularly those who regard FLE as a curricular pillar of the humanistic tradition, Byram characterizes intercultural competence (IC) as "a readiness to suspend disbelief and judgment with respect to others' meanings, beliefs and behaviours" and as a "willingness to suspend belief in one's own meanings and behaviours, and to analyse them from the viewpoint of the others with whom one is engaging" (1997, p. 34; see Müller-Hartmann, this volume, for a more detailed explication of Byram's formulation of IC). Byram likens this process to the ability to decenter, an advanced aspect of psychological development, which is necessary for understanding other cultures and may culminate in the dismantling of an individual's "preceding structure of subjective reality and [its reconstruction] according to new norms" (1997, p. 34). As is evident in this focus on culture, identity, behavior, and meaning, Byram does not view the development of FL linguistic competence as the sole or, indeed, as the most important outcome of FLE, although he does refer to such development as "central" (p. 22). Instead, Byram argues that "the more desirable outcome [of FLE] is a learner with the ability to see and manage the relationships between themselves and their own cultural beliefs, behaviors and meanings . . . and those of their interlocutors" (1997, p. 12).

A person who possesses such abilities is referred to as an "intercultural" or sometimes "multicompetent" speaker (Belz 2002a; Cook 1992). According to Kramsch (1998, pp. 27–30), a pedagogy of the intercultural speaker in FL classrooms would involve efforts to make classroom discourse itself more explicitly intercultural by identifying and examining the various social and cultural voices present in the class (see Belz, this volume, for a discussion of varying social class backgrounds in the classroom) or by capitalizing on the multiple languages that may be present in the FL classroom (Belz 2003; Blyth 1995). Kramsch further explains that "an increase in the quantity and quality of contacts between learners across national borders through student exchanges" (1998, p. 25) can result in a FL pedagogy wherein intercultural competence is fostered. Although Kramsch does not explicitly mention the role of Internet-mediated contacts in the implementation of an intercultural pedagogy, the essays in this volume (as well as other studies on telecollaboration) amply demonstrate their potential to contribute to the goals of intercultural education (e.g., Cononelos and Oliva 1993; Donath and Volkmer 1997; Eck, Legenhausen, and Wolff 1995; Fischer 1998; Kern 1996, 1998; Kinginger, Gourvés-Hayward, and Simpson 1999; Tella 1991), particularly for persons living in more culturally and ethnically homogenous regions, who may otherwise have limited opportunities to participate in prolonged intercultural communication.

In ideologically monolingual cultures (see Train, this volume), where educational achievement is often measured in terms of the attainment of skills and the possession of facts and figures, there is the danger that the development of the interpretive expertise characteristic of the intercultural or multicompetent speaker may be underappreciated or, worse yet, overlooked as an educational and/or life goal. In such contexts, intercultural speakers may be misunderstood, devalued, marginalized, oppressed, or even despised, often by virtue of their membership in multiple communities, and as they move with artful poise and linguistic grace in the interstices and in the inlands of their own interpretive repertoires. Kramsch's use of the word "privilege" (1998, p. 16) to index the state of being an intercultural speaker is an attempt to remedy this injustice, among other things.

Individual Contributions to the Volume

The chapters in this volume fall into three categories: 1) the pedagogy of ICFLE; 2) research on ICFLE; and 3) new developments in ICFLE. The volume is framed with opening and concluding chapters by Steven L. Thorne and Robert Train, respectively. In Chapter 1, which functions as a prologue, Thorne argues for the relevance of a shift from communicative competence to intercultural competence and outlines the role of ICFLE in this process. Aimed primarily at the concerns of FL instructors and language program directors, Thorne provides a detailed description of ICFLE pedagogical frameworks, a select review of research, and a discussion of the cultural variability of Internet communication tools used to mediate ICFLE partnerships. In Chapter 9, which serves as an epilogue, Train offers a critical appraisal of the ways in which key ideologies of FLE, such as the Native Speaker and the Native Standard Language, are either reproduced or challenged in the telecollaborative partnerships reported here. Concrete examples from each chapter are examined with a view to creating meta-discursive awareness of the ideologies and conceptual metaphors that underpin both research and practice in Internet-mediated intercultural foreign language education.

Above and beyond this organizational taxonomy, the chapters in this volume can be distinguished according to whether or not they investigate primarily the development of intercultural or linguistic competence in telecollaboration. In the chapters by Beth Bauer, Lynne deBenedette, Gilberte Furstenberg, Sabine Levet, and Shoggy Waryn (Chapter 2), Robert O'Dowd (Chapter 4), and Jeffrey Schneider and Silke von der Emde (Chapter 7), the primary emphasis lies on the development of intercultural competence. FL researchers and practitioners, however, have also recognized the potential of telecollaborative instruction for the development of linguistic and/or pragmatic competence (e.g., Belz and Vyatkina 2005; Kinginger 2000; Kinginger and Belz 2005). Studies in this vein generally vary according to the ways in which the native-speaking keypals and the process of intercultural communication itself are conceptualized. In those studies that espouse the interactionist hypothesis as their guiding theoretical framework, the foreign partners typically are conceptualized as L2 "input providers," while the action of Internet-mediated intercultural communication is seen as a cost-effective means for learners to obtain exposure to comprehensible input that, in turn, can provide opportunities for the negotiation of ideational meaning and the subsequent acquisition of L2 structures. In contrast, the foreign partner is generally understood as a person embedded in particular socio-historical contexts and settings who exercises agency for specific, personally meaningful reasons, while the electronic interactions in which they engage are viewed as dynamic sites for the interpersonal construction and contestation of identity in and through language in those investigations that are underpinned by sociocultural, semiotic, or linguistically critical theoretical commitments. The contributions to this volume that focus on the ways in which ICFLE affords linguistic or pragmatic development, Dussias (Chapter 5), Lee (Chapter 6) and Belz (Chapter 8), span the range of theoretical possibilities described above.

Bauer *et al.* (Chapter 2) provide an updated report on the *Cultura* Project, one of the most widely recognized and exemplary pedagogical projects incorporating telecollaborative practices for the purposes of ICFLE. *Cultura* is based on the premise that FL students can and should develop critical perceptions of both their own as well as another's culture through the structured juxtaposition of texts and images, the creation and interrogation of lexical and semantic networks, and the sharing of interpretations of these data by participants in intercultural exchanges. The authors detail the development of the project since its start in French language courses at the *Massachusetts Institute of Technology* in 1997 to include new techniques and technologies, additional institutions, new topics and issues, and the instruction of less commonly taught languages. In particular, Bauer and her colleagues describe the adaptation of the principles and techniques of *Cultura* to two new socio-institutional settings: 1) a Russian-English exchange between intermediate students of English at the *University of Petrozavodsk* in Russia and second and third-year students of Russian at *Brown University*; and 2) a Spanish-English exchange between third-year students of English enrolled in a course called "Intercultural Comparisons" at the *Universidad de las Américas* in Puebla, Mexico, and third-year students of Spanish in a course on Hispanic Populations in the United States also at *Brown University*. While the Russian-American exchange illustrates the pressures of the digital divide and the operation of socio-institutional constraints on the execution of a specific intercultural collaboration, the Mexican-American partnership highlights how a *Cultura*-based pedagogy can foster an increasingly complex sense of national identities and cultural heterogeneity in language learners. Because the authors focus explicitly on the challenges associated with the expansion of the project to new institutions and languages, the chapter provides practical advice as well as instructional inspiration for FL teachers, language program directors, and other administrators who are contemplating involvement with ICFLE.

Andreas Müller-Hartmann (Chapter 3) is also concerned with the development of intercultural competence via telecollaborative activity. His contribution to the volume is unique, however, in that it examines the potential of Internet-mediated intercultural language and culture learning partnerships to foster IC in pre- and in-service FL and English as a Foreign Language (EFL) teachers rather than in language students (see also Fuchs 2005). Relying on an empirically robust data set of five years of German-American telecollaborative exchanges between the *Pädagogische Hochschule Heidelberg* in Germany and *The Pennsylvania State University* in the United States, Müller-Hartmann demonstrates how the processes of reflective practice and model learning contribute to the construction of teacher knowledge bases with respect to critical media literacy, the design, execution, and management of international telecollaboration projects, and the development of intercultural competence via participation in such projects. Qualitative evidence for student-teachers' emerging knowledge bases in these areas is found in the pages of their cumulative course portfolios, in retrospective interviews and surveys, and in the micro-interactional details of their electronic interactions. Müller-Hartmann's description of his two-tiered instructional configuration involving a transatlantic pairing of two graduate-level teacher education/applied linguistics seminars, the members of which observed and discussed the intercultural interactions of a second pair of undergraduate language courses as they engaged in telecollaborative activities, will be of particular interest to those language program directors who wish to integrate technology-enhanced experiential intercultural learning into their FL teacher education programs.

Robert O'Dowd (Chapter 4) explores the use of "hands-on" ethnographic protocols by students in telecollaboration as a means of developing intercultural competence, including the operation of the skills of discovery in real time. Third-year English students at the *University of Essen* in Germany and undergraduate students in a Communication Studies course at the *University of Columbus* in Ohio received training in the use of typical ethnographic interviewing techniques such as descriptive or grand tour questions and creative listening. These techniques were later utilized by the same students in classroom-based interactions with their foreign keypals in the media of both e-mail and videoconferencing in order to construct thick descriptions of their keypals' culture from an *emic,* or insider's, perspective. O'Dowd's project is of import to the field of ICFLE because it is one of the few studies in which the influence of both text and image-based Internet communication tools is examined. In addition, the stipulation that project participants maintain an ethnographic stance in their intercultural interactions raises important questions about both the possibility and desirability of "objective talk" and "neutral observation" in intercultural communication, and their relationship to the development of critical cultural awareness. Drawing on richly detailed excerpts from videoconference transcripts, the chapter provides practicing FL teachers with valuable information on the pedagogy of intercultural video-conferencing in FLE.

In Chapter 5, Paola E. Dussias asks whether text-based, Internet-mediated intercultural communication has measurable consequences for the development of face-to-face oral communication. She compares two sets of L2 learners, all enrolled in fourth-semester university-level Spanish courses, but who were assigned to either an experimental group that engaged in an ICFLE partnership with native speakers in Spain or to a control group that also participated in Internet-mediated activity but with one another in intra-class electronic discussions. Both groups engaged in synchronous and asynchronous computer-mediated communication (CMC) interaction. The focus of the study is a comparative linguistic analysis carried out on transcriptions of pre- and post-semester ACTFL Oral Proficiency Interviews. Her findings indicate that relative to learners in the control group, students in the experimental group demonstrated an increased capacity to attend to linguistic form, such as control over the use of overt-null subjects in Spanish, a finding that Dussias associates with awareness of NS discourse strategies made possible by the intercultural CMC discussions. Another student showed decreases in hesitations, pauses, and lexical interference from his L1 (English). While expressing caution about generalizing these finding to other populations of learners, her conclusion is that the experimental group benefited from the NS-NNS interactions and that language learning mediated by the use of synchronous and asynchronous Internet communication tools appears to readily transfer to spontaneous oral language production.

Working within the well-established tradition of the interactionist approach to Second Language Acquisition (SLA), Lina Lee (Chapter 6) reports on a study of networked collaborative interaction (NCI) that examined the relationships among error type, feedback types, and responses in synchronous communication between native teachers and nonnative speakers of Spanish. The participants engaged one another using two tasks—an open-ended question and a goal-oriented activity. Confirming the results of other studies, Lee found that for both the NS and NNS groups, lexical rather than syntactical errors were the main triggers for negotiation moves. Differences between the groups included the proportional use of particular moves, in particular that the NS group exhibited the strong tendency to provide corrective feedback using recasts. The NS use of recasts was successful in focusing the NNSs' attention to errors in form as indicated by the high rate of NNS repairs. Lee notes that CMC provides a form of "written visual communication" that may have also facilitated the NNS response to corrective feedback. Her conclusions are that NCI empowers learners to become active and effective language users, supports a variety of interaction types, and promotes negotiation of meaning.

Jeffrey Schneider and Silke von der Emde (Chapter 7) address the issue of conflict emerging within intercultural partnerships. The participants in the study were students participating in what has been a long-standing exchange between the German Studies Department at *Vassar College* and the English Department at *Universität Münster*. Synchronous interactions were carried out using a German-English MOO called *MOOssiggang*, based at *Vassar*. The topic for the exchange was to discuss two school shootings, one at *Columbine High School* in Littleton, Colorado, and the other in Germany at the *Johannes Gutenberg Gymnasium* in Erfurt. A significant conflict occurred during their interactions. In response, rather than proposing strategies to either deal with or avoid conflict, Schnieder and von der Emde report on the development of a dialogic paradigm that reframes the tensions of intercultural communication as valuable sites for intercultural exploration and learning. As part of their approach, they suggest a shift away from the term *communication*, encumbered by its long association with communicative language teaching, and toward the Bakhtinian conception of dialogue, which characterizes language not as a unified system or resource for maintaining *status quo* semantics, but as a site of struggle. Their approach also involves situating telecollaborative partnerships in explicitly academic discourse that includes having students read ICFLE research. A student in their course reported that the academic framing of the interpersonally challenging intercultural tensions provided her with conceptual tools to better understand the situation. Schnieder and von der Emde conclude that building intercultural knowledge helps ensure that students continue to learn about the language and culture they are studying, even in the face of conflict.

Julie A. Belz (Chapter 8) presents one of the very first discussions of the ways in which ICFLE and contrastive learner corpus analysis mutually inform one another with respect to the data-driven development of L2 linguistic/pragmatic competence and critical language awareness. In her essay, Belz introduces the 1-million-word *Telecollaborative Learner Corpus of English and German* or *Telekorp*, a bilingual contrastive learner corpus of diachronic, Internet-mediated, NS-NNS interactions with built-in NS control corpora. *Telekorp* was constructed using the process data produced by more than 200 learners who participated in German-American telecollaborative partnerships between the *Pädagogische Hochschule Heidelberg* and *The Pennsylvania State University* from 2000 to 2005. Based on learner and NS concordance lines extracted from *Telekorp*, Belz demonstrates how FL teachers can capitalize on the blended quality of telecollaborative pedagogy in conjunction with the results of contrastive learner corpus analysis to convey an understanding of L2 competence that is rooted in frequency of use as well as grammatical accuracy, to construct quantitative profiles of learners' linguistic development over time, and to design individualized, corpus-based pedagogical interventions for underused or misused features. The results of two such pedagogical interventions are discussed for the focal learner in the study with regard to her socio-cultural history as ascertained via an array of ethnographic data, also archived in *Telekorp*. One of the most important points in this chapter is the fact that *Telekorp* provides a longitudinal, quantitative look at individual learner's L2 development (see Ortega and Iberri-Shea 2005) since telecollaborative partnerships typically span two to three months and the entirety of all telecollaborative interactions have been archived in the corpus.

Underexplored Aspects of Internet-mediated Intercultural Foreign Language Education

Despite the fact that a great deal of attention has been paid to ICFLE from both pedagogical and theoretical perspectives, many areas remain underexplored, while other aspects are unexplored. In this section, we provide a brief and selective discussion of some of the more neglected areas in an effort to encourage future investigation.

Intercultural Tensions in ICFLE

At the outset of research on ICFLE, researchers and practitioners in FLE seemed to imagine that language learners would benefit unconditionally and automatically from contact with NSs, if one could just get them together. More recently, FL researchers and practitioners have recognized and documented the fact that ICFLE is not without its challenges (e.g., Belz 2001, 2005; Ware 2005), especially in text-based media bereft of paralinguistic meaning signals, just as researchers in inter-group contact, sociology, and conflict resolution have discovered time and time again that simply "getting people together does not work" (Tal-Or, Boninger, and Gleicher 2002, p. 89; see also Allport 1954; Pettigrew 1998).

In response to the occurrence of intergroup tension in ICFLE, Schneider and von der Emde (this volume) recommend a dialogic telecollaborative pedagogy in which one should "teach the conflicts." However, in the current geopolitical climate, it may be more productive to spin the enterprise of ICFLE in terms of "capitalizing on the rich points" (Belz 2005, p. 29). Lakoff (2004) reminds us of the importance of choosing the right metaphors in his discussion of the discursive framing of the 2004 U.S. presidential race. As the consumerization of the academy increases, administrators may be reluctant to schedule those courses that they perceive to be predicated on confrontation, not least of all because they are under institutional pressures to achieve "customer satisfaction" in their units. In any case, more research is called for on the types of tensions that arise in ICFLE, the ways in which such "sweet" or perhaps "sour" tensions may facilitate or impede learner development, and on the outcomes of a telecollaborative pedagogy that takes "conflicts" or "rich points," as the case may be, as a point of departure.

Less Commonly Taught Languages

Aside from the discussion of Russian in Bauer *et al.* (Chapter 2), there are no partnerships involving less commonly taught languages reported in this volume, despite the fact that such studies constituted the number-two item in our 12-point call for papers. There is, however, an emerging body of literature on Japanese-English ICFLE in which researchers focus on the development of grammatical (Azuma 2003; Chapman 1997), pragmatic (Gray and Stockwell 1998), and "cultural" competence (Itakura 2004; Stockwell and Stockwell 2003; Torii-Williams 2004) as well as a few publications involving other less commonly taught languages (e.g., Chung, Graves, Wesche, and Barfurth 2005; Meskill and

Rangelova 2000; Sakar 2001). A forward-looking study by Vick, Crosby, and Ashworth on Japanese-American interactions using chat, *CUSeeMe*, and *Cooltalk* has as its goal the "development of advanced oral and written communication skills in Japanese" for non-Japanese participants and the "cultivation of a sense of international citizenship" for Japanese participants (2000, p. 204; see also Osler and Starkey 2005; Penttilä 2005; Starkey 2005). Nevertheless, the majority of ICFLE studies on less commonly taught languages seem to connect members of what Phillipson (1992) terms core English-speaking countries with members of periphery English-speaking countries. We feel that dialogue between all types of groups is valuable and potentially transformative and call for increased implementation and investigation of telecollaborative partnerships involving other less commonly taught languages (e.g., Arabic), interactions between periphery English-speaking groups, and interactions that do not involve English at all (e.g., a Hebrew-Arabic exchange).

Peace educators Tal-Or, Boninger, and Gleicher (2002, pp. 103–105) describe a program of contact encounters between Israeli Jews, Palestinians, and Jordanians called the *NIR School of the Heart* in which 60 high school students (20 from each group), all interested in medicine, met for a two-week period in Israel and Jordan (one week in each location) and used English to collaborate with one another on health-related projects. In addition to the mastery of specific content, one of the goals of the project was to foster intercultural understanding and to reduce prejudice and stereotypes through contact (Kadushin and Livert 2002). "Unfortunately," the authors write, "the program is faced with enormous obstacles because the supportive environment in which it once existed has fallen apart . . . unrest has again returned to the area, leading to a breakdown in the peace process and a nearly complete loss of public enthusiasm for programs such as this one" (2002, p. 105). Internet-mediated intercultural communication may be a less threatening and less risky way forward for the *NIR School of the Heart* for the time being.

At the time of this writing, Nancy Kerranen at the *Universidad Iberoamericana* in Puebla, Mexico, and Yasemin Bayyurt at *Bosphorus (Boğaziçi) University* in Istanbul, Turkey, are experimenting with telecollaborative interaction in English among pre-service English teachers and adult learners of English in a course on intercultural communication, respectively. We proffer that such partnerships foster intercultural competence in the teachers who guide them as well as in the learners. Nader Morkus is in the process of designing and implementing synchronous and asynchronous collaborations between American students of Arabic at the *University of South Florida* and Egyptian learners of English at the *Arab Academy for Science, Technology, and Maritime Transport* in Alexandria, Egypt. In Morkus' exchanges, keypals answer online surveys (see Furstenberg, Levet, English, and Maillet 2001) that are designed to throw into relief important intercultural "rich points" (Agar 1994; see Thorne, this volume) such as dress, marriage, care of the elderly, and hospitality. While these efforts and others like them begin to push the boundaries of research on Internet-mediated intercultural interaction in new directions, further research in other contexts, using new and innovative configurations (see the two-tiered exchange reported in Müller-Hartmann, this volume) and new and emerging technologies (Thorne and Payne 2005) are required.

Critical Perspectives on Technology Use in ICFLE

Technology is not neutral; technologies and our uses of them are positioned by discursive, cultural, economic, and geographical systems of power (van Dijk 2005; Warschauer 2003). In this sense, global communication technologies are cultural artifacts that are produced by and productive of socio-historically located subjects. As a result, Internet information and communication tools accrue significance, value, and robust patterns of preferred and unpreferred uses from the human activities they mediate and the meanings that communities create through them (see Kramsch and Thorne 2002). While Internet communication tools carry the historical residua of their uses across time, patterns of past use do not determine present and future activity, just as nation-state affiliation, gender, or social class do not determine present and future activity. Rather, the cultures-of-use framework provides another axis along which to perceive and address intercultural variation and similarity (Thorne, this volume). When cultures-of-use do not align minimally, workable levels of intersubjectivity may be difficult to achieve in ICFLE. The reciprocal, however, is also possible, where proficiency with a digital vernacular, perhaps only at the level of style and affect, may form a bridge to support initial and then continuing interaction that could lead to the development of additional communicative repertoires. To date, relatively little work has been done on cultures-of-use of Internet information and communication tools and the ways in which varying cultures-of-use may influence the stated goals of ICFLE (e.g., Thorne 2000, 2003, 2005).

Socio-institutional Affordances
and Constraints Operative in ICFLE

To date, research on ICFLE has revealed that the varying socio-institutional affordances and constraints operative on each end of an exchange will exert an influence on the ways in which the partnership is executed and on the ways in which learners react to the words and behaviors of their keypals (e.g., Belz 2002b; O'Dowd 2005). Scholars have explored the influence of such diverse factors as technological know-how, institutional layout, technological access, and societal valuations of particular FLs on the processes of ICFLE at the micro-interactional level from the perspectives of both the learners and the teachers. These explorations have occurred in a limited range of contexts for a limited range of languages, however. Further investigations of additional contexts, settings, and learning configurations are needed in order to ascertain best practices for a pedagogy of the intercultural speaker.

Persistent Records of ICFLE

A significant problem with the teaching of culture is that its more visible aspects, such as overt behaviors, material culture, and special events, while interesting and important, may require only modest explication or mediation to notice and potentially appreciate. On the other hand, the historically structured resources (i.e., culture) that inform everyday communication can remain difficult to access without the adequate time and perhaps also the expert assistance necessary for reflection. This is especially the case for face-to-face encounters.

Computer-mediated communication, on the other hand, provides a number of affordances in this area because most CMC environments produce a digital record that has been described as the "scriptialization of speech" (Sandbothe 1998, no pag.) or as "persistent conversation" (Erickson 1999).

The persistence of (relatively) spontaneous language production is useful for FL learning on at least two levels. The first is the immediate re-representation of a message that has been typed and submitted to a synchronous or asynchronous forum. A second and more profound level of persistence is that transcripts can be intensively studied after the fact. If we understand language use as a form of social action (Heritage 1984), computer-mediated communication makes these actions visible and durative. This opens up significant opportunities for reflection and analysis that would otherwise not be possible. Nevertheless, the persistent quality of CMC and the opportunities that it may afford for meta-pragmatic awareness over traditional forms of classroom-based FL instruction is an area that begs for more elucidation (see Belz, this volume).

The Negotiation of Language and Identity in ICFLE

One of the primary praxiological issues that teachers and learners in ICFLE must resolve is when to use what language and for what purposes in the course of Internet-mediated interactions with foreign keypals. Some researchers have ascribed a "deficiency" interpretation to the use of the L1 by learners in telecollaboration (see Train, this volume, for discussion); others have explicitly advocated L1 use in order to provide keypals with "accurate" models of the languages they are studying (see Bauer et al., this volume). To a large extent, however, researchers have not investigated the electronic discourse of ICFLE partnerships from the sociolinguistic, sociological, and social psychological perspectives of code-switching and bi-/multilingualism in which the relationship between language choice and speaker identity often takes center stage, although some studies are beginning to emerge (e.g., Kötter 2003; Lam 2003, 2004; Thomas, Liao, and Szustak 2005). Communication researchers are also beginning to investigate the multilingual nature of the Internet in general (Danet and Herring 2003), the processes of language selection in bi-/multilingual Internet-mediated communities, and the relationship of language choice and (group) identity in Internet-mediated communities (e.g., Paolillo 2001). In ICFLE, some researchers have also examined the ways in which medium-contigent aspects of CMC as well as the non-traditional nature of telecollaborative classrooms may encourage learners to engage in creative and innovative forms of electronically mediated, multilingual language play (Belz and Reinhardt 2004). The digital and persistent nature of CMC in general in conjunction with the inherently bi-/multilingual nature of FLE in particular (i.e. speakers of at least one language learning another language) make ICFLE a research site par excellence for the investigation of multiple language use and its relationship to issues of identity and self-presentation (in text). The recent compilation of meticulously archived corpora of bilingual telecollaborative discourse (see Belz, this volume) represent an invaluable (and largely unprecedented) resource for the exploration of code-switching (from both functional and syntactic perspectives) and multiple language use in Internet-mediated environments, especially if the electronic communication has been archived in association with a number of learner variables. We envision the investigation of multiple language use and its relationship to issues of identity to be an area of robust future research in ICFLE.

Blended Instruction and ICFLE

The persistent quality of Internet-mediated interaction has much to offer in the service of the meta-pragmatic, meta-discursive, and linguistically critical goals of ICFLE in the form of blended instruction (see Belz, this volume). In its essence, blended instruction involves the integration of technology-mediated teaching with traditional forms of instruction such face-to-face discussion. To date, very little research has been conducted on the interplay of technology-mediated and non-technology-mediated instruction and the relationship of various configurations to learner development (e.g., Schultz 2000). This is an area that is ripe for further exploration, particularly with respect to the development of pragmatic competence.

References

Agar, Michael. 1994. *Language Shock: Understanding the Culture of Conversation.* New York: William Morrow.

Ager, Dennis, George Muskens, and Sue Wright, eds. 1993. *Language Education for Intercultural Communication.* Clevedon, UK: Multilingual Matters.

Allport, Gordon W. 1954. *The Nature of Prejudice.* Reading, MA: Addison-Wesley.

Azuma, Shoji. 2003. Business Japanese Through Internet-Based Videoconferencing. *Global Business Languages* 8: 108–119.

Bausch, Karl-Richard, Herbert Christ, and Hans-Jürgen Krumm, eds. 1997. *Interkulturelles Lernen im Fremdsprachenunterricht.* Tübingen, Germany: Gunter Narr.

Beatty, Ken. 2003. *Teaching and Researching Computer-Assisted Language Learning.* New York: Pearson.

Belz, Julie A. 2001. Institutional and Individual Dimensions of Transatlantic Group Work in Network-Based Language Teaching. *ReCALL* 13(2): 129–147.

———. 2002a. Second Language Play as a Representation of the Multicompetent Self in Foreign Language Study. *Journal for Language, Identity, and Education* 1(1): 13–39.

———. 2002b. Social Dimensions of Telecollaborative Foreign Language Study. *Language Learning & Technology* 6(1): 60–81. *http://llt.msu.edu/vol6num1/BELZ/default.html*

———. 2003. Identity, Deficiency, and First Language Use in FL Education. In *The Sociolinguistics of Foreign-Language Classrooms: Contribution of the Native, the Near-Native, and the Non-Native Speaker,* edited by Carl Blyth, 209–248. Boston, MA: Thomson Heinle.

———. 2005. Intercultural Questioning, Discovery, and Tension in Networked Language Learning Partnerships. *Language and Intercultural Communication* 5(1): 3–39.

Belz, Julie A., and Jonathon Reinhardt. 2004. Aspects of Advanced Foreign Language Proficiency: Internet-mediated German Language Play. *International Journal of Applied Linguistics* 14(3): 324–362.

Belz, Julie A., and Nina Vyatkina. 2005. Learner Corpus Analysis and the Development of L2 Pragmatic Competence in Networked Intercultural Language Study: The Case of German Modal Particles. *Canadian Modern Language Review/Revue canadienne des langues vivantes* 62(1): 17–48.

Bennett, Milton J. 1998. Intercultural Communication: A Current Perspective. In *Basic Concepts of Intercultural Communication: Selected Readings,* edited by M. J. Bennett, 1–34. Yarmouth, Maine: Intercultural Press.

Block, David. 2003. *The Social Turn in Second Language Acquisition.* Washington, D.C.: Georgetown University Press.

———. 2004. Globalization, Transnational Communication, and the Internet. *International Journal on Multicultural Societies* 6(1): 22–37.

Blyth, Carl. 1995. Redefining the Boundaries of Language Use: The Foreign Language Classroom as a Multilingual Speech Community. In *Redefining the Boundaries of Language Study,* edited by Claire J. Kramsch, 145–184. Boston, MA: Thomson Heinle.

Byram, Michael. 1997. *Teaching and Assessing Intercultural Communicative Competence.* Clevedon, UK: Multilingual Matters.

Brabazon, Tara. 2002. *Digital Hemlock: Internet Education and the Poisoning of Teaching.* Sydney, Australia: University of New South Wales Press.

Brammerts, Helmut. 1996. Language Learning in Tandem Using the Internet. In *Telecollaboration in Foreign Language Learning,* edited by Mark Warschauer, 121–130. Honolulu: Second Language Teaching & Curriculum Center.

Brennan, Teresa. 2003. *Globalization and its Terrors.* London and New York: Routledge.

Castells, Manuel. 1996. *The Rise of the Network Society.* Cambridge, MA: Blackwell.

Chapelle, Carol. 2003. *English Language Learning and Technology: Lectures on Applied Linguistics in the Age of Information and Communication Technology.* Amsterdam: John Benjamins.

Chapman, David. 1997. Computer Mediated Communication and Japanese Immersion: Investigating the Potential. *On-Call* 11(1): 12–18.

Chung, Yang-Gyun, Barbara Graves, Mari Wesche, and Marion Barfurth. 2005. Computer-Mediated Communication in Korean-English Chat Rooms: Tandem Learning in an International Languages Program. *Canadian Modern Language Review/ Revue canadienne des langues vivantes* 62(1): 49–86.

Cononelos, Terri, and Maurizio Oliva. 1993. Using Computer Networks to Enhance Foreign Language/Culture Education. *Foreign Language Annals* 26(4): 527–534.

Cook, Vivian. 1992. Evidence for Multicompetence. *Language Learning* 42(4): 557–591.

Corbett, John. 2003. *An Intercultural Approach to English Language Teaching.* Clevedon, UK: Multilingual Matters.

Cuban, Larry. 2001. *Oversold and Underused: Computers in the Classroom.* Cambridge: Harvard University Press.

Cummins, Jim, and Dennis Sayers. 1995. *Brave New Schools. Challenging Cultural Literacy Through Global Learning Networks.* New York: St. Martin's Press.

Danet, Brenda, and Susan C. Herring, eds. 2003. *The Multilingual Internet: Language, Culture, and Communication in Instant Messaging, E-Mail, and Chat.* A special issue of the *Journal of Computer-mediated Communication* 9(1). *http:// jcmc.indiana.edu/vol9/issue1/*

Davies, Alan. 2003. *The Native Speaker: Myth and Reality.* Clevedon: Multilingual Matters.

Donath, Reinhard, and Ingrid Volkmer, eds. 1997. *Das Transatlantische Klassenzimmer.* Hamburg: Koerber-Stiftung.

Eck, Andreas, Lienhard Legenhausen, and Dieter Wolff. 1995. *Telekommunikation und Fremdsprachenunterricht: Informationen, Projekte, Ergebnisse.* Bochum: AKS-Verlag.

Erickson, Thomas. 1999. Persistent Conversation: An Introduction. *Journal of Computer-Mediated Communication* 4(4). *http://jcmc.indiana.edu/vol4/issue4/ ericksonintro.html*

Feenberg, Andrew. 2002. *Transforming Technology*. Oxford: Oxford University Press.

Firth, Alan, and Johannes Wagner. 1997. On Discourse, Communication and (Some) Fundamental Concepts in SLA. *The Modern Language Journal* 81(3): 277-300.

Fischer, Gerhard. 1998. *E-Mail in Foreign Language Teaching. Towards the Creation of Virtual Classrooms*. Tübingen, Germany: Stauffenburg Medien.

Fotos, Sandra, and Charles Browne, eds. 2004. *New Perspectives on CALL for Second Language Classrooms*. Mahwah, NJ: Lawrence Erlbaum.

Freinet, Celestin. 1994. *Oeuvres Pédagogiques*. Paris: Editions du Seuil.

Fuchs, Carolin. 2005. The Potential of Computer-Mediated Communication (CMC) in Task-Based Language Teacher Education. In *Aufgabenorientierung im Fremdsprachenunterricht–Task-Based Language Learning and Teaching*, edited by Andreas Müller-Hartmann and Marita Schocker-von Ditfurth, 299-308. Tübingen, Germany: Narr.

Furstenberg, Gilberte, Sabine Levet, Kathryn English, and Katherine Maillet. 2001. Giving a Voice to the Silent Language of Culture: The *Cultura* Project. *Language Learning & Technology* 5(1): 55-102. *http://llt.msu.edu/vol5num1/furstenberg/default.html*

Gray, Robert, and Glenn Stockwell. 1998. Using Computer Mediated Communication for Language and Culture Acquisition. *On-CALL* 12(3): 2-9.

Heritage, John. 1984. *Garfinkel and Ethnomethodology*. Cambridge, UK: Polity Press.

Hiltz, Starr Roxane, and Murray Turoff. 1993. *The Network Nation*, 2nd ed. Cambridge, MA: MIT Press.

Itakura, Hiroko. 2004. Changing Cultural Stereotypes through E-Mail Assisted Foreign Language Learning. *System: An International Journal of Educational Technology and Applied Linguistics* 32(1): 37-51.

Kadushin, Charles, and David Livert. 2002. Friendship, Contact, and Peace Education. In *Peace Education: The Concept, Principles, and Practices Around the World*, edited by Gavriel Salomon and Baruch Nevo, 117-126. Mahwah, NJ: Erlbaum.

Kecskes, Istvan. 2004. Lexical Merging, Conceptual Blending, Cultural Crossing. *Intercultural Pragmatics* 1(1): 1-4.

Kern, Richard. 1996. Computer-Mediated Communication: Using E-mail Exchanges to Explore Personal Histories in Two Cultures. In *Telecollaboration in Foreign Language Learning: Proceedings of the Hawaii Symposium*, edited by Mark Warschauer, 105-109. Honolulu: Second Language Teaching & Curriculum Center.

———. 1998. Technology, Social Interaction, and FL Literacy. In *New Ways of Learning and Teaching: Focus on Technology and Foreign Language Education*, edited by Judith Muyskens, 57-92. Boston, MA: Thomson Heinle.

———. 2000. *Language and Literacy Learning*. Oxford: Oxford University Press.

Kern, Richard, Paige Ware, and Mark Warschauer. 2004. Crossing Frontiers: New Directions in Online Pedagogy and Research. *Annual Review of Applied Linguistics* 24(1): 243-260.

Kinginger, Celeste. 2000. Learning the Pragmatics of Solidarity in the Networked Foreign Language Classroom. In *Second and Foreign Language Learning through Classroom Interaction*, edited by Joan Kelly Hall, 23-46. Mahwah, NJ: Erlbaum.

———. 2004. Communicative Foreign Language Teaching Through Telecollaboration. In *New Insights Into Foreign Language Learning and Teaching*, edited by Oliver St. John, Kees van Esch, and Eus Schalkwijk, 101-113. Frankfurt: Peter Lang.

Kinginger, Celeste, and Julie A. Belz. 2005. Socio-cultural Perspectives on Pragmatic Development in Foreign Language Learning: Microgenetic Case Studies from Telecollaboration and Residence Abroad. *Intercultural Pragmatics* 2(4): 369-422.

Kinginger, Celeste, Alison Gourvés-Hayward, and Vanessa Simpson. 1999. A Tele-Collaborative Course on French-American Intercultural Communication. *The French Review* 72(5): 853–866.

Kötter, Markus. 2003. Negotiation of Meaning and Code-Switching in Online Tandems. *Language Learning & Technology* 7(2): 145–172. *http://llt.msu.edu/vol7num2/kotter/default.html*.

Kramsch, Claire J. 1998. The Privilege of the Intercultural Speaker. In *Language Learning in Intercultural Perspective: Approaches through Drama and Ethnography*, edited by Michael Byram and Michael Fleming, 16–31. New York: Cambridge University Press.

———. 1999. Global and Local Identities in the Contact Zone. In *Teaching and Learning English as a Global Language,* edited by Claus Gnutzmann, 131–143. Stauffenburg Verlag.

———. 2002. In Search of the Intercultural. *Journal of Sociolinguistics* 6(2): 275–285.

Kramsch, Claire J., and Steven L. Thorne. 2002. Foreign Language Learning as Global Communicative Practice. In *Globalization and Language Teaching,* edited by David Block and Deborah Cameron, 83–100. London: Routledge.

Lakoff, George. 2004. *Don't Think of an Elephant! Know Your Values and Frame the Debate.* White River Junction, VT: Chelsea Green Publishing.

Lam, Wan Shun Eva. 2003. *Second Language Literacy and Identity Formation on the Internet: The Case of Chinese Immigrant Youth in the U.S.* Unpublished doctoral dissertation, The University of California, Berkeley.

———. 2004. Second Language Socialization in a Bilingual Chat Room: Global and Local Considerations. *Language Learning & Technolgoy* 8(3): 44–65. *http://llt.msu.edu/vol8num3/lam/default.html*

Lanham, Richard A. 1993. *The Electronic Word: Democracy, Technology, and the Arts.* Chicago: University of Chicago Press.

Levy, Michael. 1997. *Computer-Assisted Language Learning: Context and Conceptualization.* Oxford: Oxford University Press.

Little, David, and Helmut Brammerts, eds. 1996. A Guide to Language Learning in Tandem via the Internet. Centre for Language and Communication Studies, Occasional Paper 46. Dublin: Trinity College.

Meskill, Carla, and Krassimira Rangelova. 2000. Sociocollaborative Language Learning in Bulgaria. In *Network-Based Language Teaching: Concepts and Practice,* edited by Mark Warschauer and Richard Kern, 20–40. New York: Cambridge University Press.

Muyskens, Judith A., ed. 1997. *New Ways of Learning and Teaching: Focus on Technology and Foreign Language Education.* Boston, MA: Thomson Heinle.

Norton, Bonny. 2000. *Identity and Language Learning: Gender, Ethnicity, and Educational Change.* New York: Longman.

O'Dowd, Robert. 2005. Negotiating Sociocultural and Institutional Contexts: The Case of Spanish-American Telecollaboration. *Language and Intercultural Communication* 5(1): 40–56.

Ortega, Lourdes, and Gina Iberri-Shea. 2005. Longitudinal Research in Second Language Acquisition: Recent Trends and Future Directions. *Annual Review of Applied Linguistics* 25: 26–45.

Osler, Audrey, and Hugh Starkey, eds. 2005. *Citizenship and Language Learning: International Perspectives.* Sterling, VA: Trentham Books.

Paolillo, John. 2001. Language Variation on Internet Relay Chat: A Social Network. *Journal of Sociolinguistics* 5(2): 180–213.

Penttilä, Tuula. 2005. Intercultural Learning: Connecting Young Citizens Through ICT. In *Citizenship and Language Learning: International Perspectives*, edited by Audrey Olsar and Hugh Starkey, 103-112. Sterling, VA: Trentham Books.

Pettigrew, T. F. 1998. Intergroup Contact Theory. *Annual Review of Psychology* 49: 65-85.

Phillipson, Robert. 1992. *Linguistic Imperialism*. Oxford: Oxford University Press.

Rampton, Ben. 1990. Displacing the "Native Speaker": Expertise, Affiliation, and Inheritance. *ELT Journal* 44: 338-343.

———. 1995. *Crossing: Language and Ethnicity Among Adolescents*. London: Longman.

Rheingold, Howard. 1993. *Virtual Community: Homesteading on the Electronic Frontier*. New York: Addison-Wesley.

Sakar, A. 2001. The Cross-Cultural Effects of Electronic Mail Exchange on the Turkish University Students of English as a Foreign Fanguage (EFL). *CALL-EJ Online* 3(1). *http://www.clec.ritsumei.ac.jp/english/callejonline/6-1/sakar.html*

Sandbothe, Mike. 1998. Media Temporalities on the Internet: Philosophy of Time and Media with Derrida and Rorty. *Journal of Computer-Mediated Communication* 4(2). *http://www.ascucs.org./jcmc/vol4/issue2/sandbothe.html*

Scollon, Ron, and Suzanne Wong Scollon. 2001a. *Intercultural Communication: A Discourse Approach*. Malden, MA: Blackwell.

———. 2001b. Discourse and Intercultural Communication. In *Handbook of Discourse Analysis,* edited by Deborah Schiffrin, Deborah Tannen, and Heidi E. Hamilton, 538-547. Malden, MA: Blackwell.

Schultz, Jean Marie. 2000. Computers and Collaborative Writing in the Foreign Language Curriculum. In *Network-Based Language Teaching: Concepts and Practice,* edited by Mark Warschauer and Richard Kern, 121-150. New York: Cambridge University Press.

Shapiro, Svi. 2002. Toward a Critical Pedagogy of Peace Education. In *Peace Education: The Concept, Principles, and Practices Around the World*, edited by Gavriel Salomon and Baruch Nevo, 63-72. Mahwah, NJ: Erlbaum.

Sproull, Lee, and Sara Kiesler. 1991. *Connections: New Ways of Working in the Networked Organization*. Cambridge, MA: MIT Press.

Starkey, Hugh. 2005. Language Teaching for Democratic Citizenship. In *Citizenship and Language Learning: International Perspectives*, edited by Audrey Olsar and Hugh Starkey, 23-40. Sterling, VA: Trentham Books.

Stockwell, Esther Seonghee, and Glenn Stockwell. 2003. Using E-mail for Enhanced Cultural Awareness. *Australian Language Matters* 11(1): 3-4.

Tal-Or, Nurit, David Boninger, and Faith Gleicher. 2002. Understanding the Conditions and Processes Necessary for Intergroup Contact to Reduce Prejudice. In *Peace Education: The Concept, Principles, and Practices Around the World*, edited by Gavriel Salomon and Baruch Nevo, 73-88. Mahwah, NJ: Erlbaum.

Tella, Seppo. 1991. *Introducing International Communications Networks and Electronic Mail into Foreign Language Classrooms: A Case Study in Finnish Senior Secondary Schools*. Helsinki: Yliopistopaino.

———. 1996. Foreign Languages and Modern Technology: Harmony or Hell? In *Telecollaboration in Foreign Language Learning*, edited by Mark Warschauer, 3-18. Honolulu: Second Language Teaching and Curriculum Center.

Thomas, Joshua, Jianling Liao, and Anja Szustak. 2005. The Use of L1 in a L2 Online Chat Activity. *Canadian Modern Language Review/Revue canadienne des langues vivantes* 62(1): 161-182.

Thorne, Steven L. 2000. Beyond Bounded Activity Systems: Heterogeneous Cultures in Instructional Uses of Persistent Conversation. In *The Proceedings of the Thirty-third Hawaii International Conference on Systems Science*. New York: IEEE Press.

Thorne, Steven L., and J. Scott Payne. 2003. Artifacts and Cultures-of-Use in Intercultural Communication. *Language Learning & Technology* 7(2): 38–67. *http://llt.msu.edu/vol7num2/thorne/*

———. 2005. Epistemology, Politics, and Ethics in Sociocultural Theory. *The Modern Language Journal* 89(3): 393–409.

———. 2005. Evolutionary Trajectories, Internet-mediated Expression, and Language Education. *CALICO Journal* 22(3): 371–397.

Tomei, Lawrence, ed. 2003. *Challenges of Teaching with Technology across the Curriculum.* Hershey, PA: Information Science Publishing.

Torii-Williams, Eiko. 2004. Incorporating the Use of E-mail into a Language Program. *Computer Assisted Language Learning* 17(1): 109–122.

Turkle, Sherry. 1984. *The Second Self: Computers and the Human Spirit.* New York: Simon and Shuster.

———. 1997. *Life on the Screen: Identity in the Age of the Internet.* New York: Touchstone.

van Dijk, Jan A. G. M. 2005. *The Deepening Divide: Inequality in the Information Society.* London: Sage.

Von der Emde, Silke, Jeffrey Schneider, and Markus Kötter. 2001. Technically Speaking: Transforming Language Learning Through Virtual Learning Environments (MOOs). *The Modern Language Journal* 85(2): 210–225.

Vick, Rita M., Martha E. Crosby, and David E. Ashworth. 2000. Japanese and American Students Meet on the Web: Collaborative Language Learning through Everyday Dialogue with Peers. *Computer Assisted Language Learning* 13(3): 199–219.

Warschauer, Mark. 1996a. *Virtual Connections: Online Activities and Projects for Networking Language Learners.* Honolulu: Second Language Teaching and Curriculum Center.

———, ed. 1996b. Comparing Face-To-Face and Electronic Discussion in the Second Language Classroom. *CALICO Journal* 13(2): 7–26.

———. 2003. *Technology and Social Inclusion: Rethinking the Digital Divide.* Cambridge, MA: MIT Press.

Warschauer, Mark, and Richard Kern, eds. 2000. *Network-Based Language Teaching: Concepts and Practices.* Cambridge, UK: Cambridge University Press.

Part One

The Pedagogy of Internet-mediated Intercultural Foreign Language Education

Chapter 1

Pedagogical and Praxiological Lessons from Internet-mediated Intercultural Foreign Language Education Research

Steven L. Thorne

Abstract

This essay describes research findings, pedagogical methods, and theoretical frameworks emerging from and contributing to Internet-mediated intercultural foreign language education (ICFLE). ICFLE emphasizes participation in intercultural dialogue and development of the linguistic and meta-communicative resources necessary for doing so. Various models of ICFLE are described and ICFLE studies that address processes of intercultural communication from linguistic, interpersonal, and developmental perspectives are reviewed. A number of exigent dimensions of ICFLE are also presented, in particular the challenges of implementing successful ICFLE projects, issues of cultural contestation, and variability in the cultures-of-use of Internet communication tools used to mediate ICFLE interaction. Throughout, the aim of this chapter is to introduce ICFLE to new audiences and specifically to address the concerns of language program directors and instructors. In conclusion, a case is made for the potential of ICFLE to re-orient foreign language education from a focus on communicative competence to a focus on intercultural competence.

Introduction

The start of the twenty-first century is an exciting, if not tumultuous, era in which to be a language educator. Discourses and material effects associated with globalization, itself a contested construct (Giddens 1999; Harvey 2000), have come to inform applied linguistics (Canagarajah 1999; Pennycook 2001), foreign language education (Cameron and Block 2002), and the use of global communication networks for foreign language learning (Kramsch and Thorne 2002). Within affluent regions of the world, and more generally for Internet users everywhere, everyday communication and information practices are markedly different today from those of even a decade ago. There now exists a plethora of established, as well as emerging, genres of Internet-mediated communicative activities, many of which vary substantially from pre-digital epistolary conventions (e.g., Crystal 2001; see also Goodwin-Jones 2005; Thorne 2003a; Thorne and Payne 2005, pp. 381–387).

This chapter and volume focus on the use of Internet information and communication tools to support intercultural dialogue, debate, collaborative research, and less structured social interaction between (typically) internationally dispersed groups of learners who are members of different linguistic and cultural groups. Rather than imposing an existing label onto the diversity of approaches in this area, which could be seen as biased toward one model or unrepresentative of others, the non-sectarian umbrella term used in this chapter (and as the title of this volume) is Internet-mediated intercultural foreign language education (hereafter ICFLE).[1] The rationale for this choice has three components. The first is that while other labels already exist for Internet-mediated intercultural FL projects, such as "tandem learning" and "telecollaboration," and relevant studies are also described more generically as "network-based language teaching" or "computer-mediated communication," each of these terms leaves unmentioned the *intercultural* aspect of the approach advanced in this volume (see Belz and Thorne, this volume). The second is "tandem learning," "telecollaboration," and "intercultural communication" alone do not reflect a focus on foreign language education *per se*. Lastly, the decision to end "ICFLE" with the word "education" indexes a broader humanistic tradition than would alternatives such as "teaching," "learning," or "acquisition" (see Kramsch 2000).

The use of Internet technologies to encourage dialogue between distributed individuals and partner classes proposes a compelling shift in second (L2) and foreign language (FL) education, one that ideally moves learners from simulated classroom-based contexts toward actual interaction with expert speakers of the language they are studying. As Kinginger (e.g., 1998, 2004) notes, the most salient element to ICFLE is the inclusion of other people. The conceptualization and use of FL learning as foremost a process of intercultural communication, in both online and offline contexts, has received significant attention in recent years (e.g., Belz 2002; Brammerts 1996; Byram 1997; Furstenberg *et al.* 2001; Kinginger 1998; Kinginger, Gourvés-Hayward, and Simpson 1999; Kramsch 1998; O'Dowd 2003; Sercu 2004; Tella 1991; Thorne, 2003b). ICFLE-related articles now regularly appear in prestigious venues such as *The Modern Language Journal* (e.g., Belz and Müller-Hartmann 2003; Kinginger 1998; von der Emde, Schneider, and Kötter 2001; Ware and Kramsch 2005), in journal special issues (e.g., *The CALICO Journal* volume 23 issue 3; *The Canadian Modern Language Review/La Revue canadienne des langues vivantes* volume 62 number 1), and in a journal special issue focused solely on this topic (*Language Learning & Technology* volume 7 issue 2). A review of this research will show that the goals of ICFLE projects are diverse, but generally include aspirations of linguistic and pragmatic development as well as increasing awareness about one's own cultural background, those of one's interlocutors, and the processes involved in carrying out extended, productive, and ultimately meaningful intercultural dialogue. While correspondence with expert speakers of the language of study is a pedagogical method with a long history, the recent surge in pedagogical and research efforts in this area suggest that ICFLE is beginning to exert a significant and broad-based influence on the character, processes, and perhaps even goals of mainstream foreign language education (FLE).

As we are well into the second decade of Internet-mediated language learning activity, there has been the suggestion that interculturally oriented "distance collaborations" constitute a "second wave" of L2 pedagogy (Kern, Ware, and

Warshauer 2004, p. 243). This second wave of computer-mediated L2 learning, according to Kern, Ware, and Warshauer (2004), emphasizes three major shifts, which I liberally interpret and build upon in this review article: 1) an emphasis on embedding discrete language learning within the frameworks of intercultural competence and pragmatics; 2) a broadening of the context of instructed language learning from classroom-based, local activity to inter-community and international interaction; and 3) a problematization, or perhaps complexification, of conceptualizations of communication and culture within L2 pedagogy and research. Like a complex Venn diagram, ICFLE research and pedagogy have many overlaps and adjoining borders with other areas of language research such as pragmatics, intercultural communication and communication theory, computer-mediated communication, critical theory and cultural studies, and, of course, second language acquisition and language pedagogy. While research and theory are explicitly addressed in this chapter, its main purpose is to distill significant pedagogical implications from the ICFLE research literature and to describe a set of praxiological lessons aimed primarily at the concerns of FL instructors, coordinators, and program directors working in institutional and instructed FLE contexts.

ICFLE History and Contemporary Foci

Internet-mediated intercultural communication used to promote L2 learning has antecedents in earlier traditions, perhaps the most direct being the educational model developed early in the twentieth century by French educator Célestin Freinet (1994). Freinet's pedagogy included presciently modern methods such as cooperative group work, service learning, inquiry-based learning, and encouraging students to publish their work in the form of classroom journals and school newspapers; each of these methods would be quite innovative even by contemporary standards. Freinet's particular insight, however, was to recognize the power of embedding the entirety of learning processes in correspondence activities with other school children in France and around the world. The school newspapers ("*Les Journal Scolaire*"), for example, were exchanged among participating elementary schools first in France and later internationally. What is now known as the *Freinet Movement* remains vibrant to this day and has directly influenced some ICFLE projects (see Lomicka 2001).[2]

Contemporary ICFLE research is premised on the notion that dialogue and other forms of interaction can foster productive, and perhaps even necessary, conditions for developing intercultural communicative competence. ICFLE emphasizes the use of Internet communication tools to support dialogue, debate, collaborative research, and social interaction among geographically dispersed participants. But the goal is loftier than social interaction *per se* and builds on the hypothesis, developed by communication researcher Joseph Walther (1992, 1996), that Internet-mediated relationships have the potential to be as, and sometimes more, intensely personal than those which occur in face-to-face settings.

This potential of computer-mediated communication (CMC) lies at the heart of most ICFLE projects — the aspiration for participants to develop meaningful relationships with one another and to use the language they are studying to do so. Although ICFLE can produce tension and frustration (e.g., Belz 2003, 2005; Kramsch and Thorne 2002; Schneider and von der Emde, this volume; Ware 2005) as well as camaraderie and intimate friendship (Thorne 2003b), embedding the learning of a new language in the larger context of significant relationship development has demonstrated considerable learning outcomes, especially in the areas of pragmatics and critical reflexivity (Belz 2005; Kinginger and Belz in press).

Foundational to ICFLE pedagogy is the desire to cultivate conditions for the development of intercultural competence. In the following section, the term "intercultural competence" is unpacked and references to relevant research are provided.

Intercultural Competence (and Why We Should Care)

According to the *Council of Europe* (2001), communicative competence alone is no longer adequate as the sole goal of FL learning. Rather, the "objective of foreign language teaching is now . . . 'intercultural competence'" (Sercu 2004, p. 115). Sercu continues by noting, "[s]een from the intercultural perspective, it can be said that what a foreign language learner needs to learn in order to attain communicative competence is not how to adapt to any one of the foreign cultures present, and forget about his/her own cultural identity. Rather, the task of the participants in such an intercultural situation will be to negotiate, by means of implicit or explicit cues, a situationally adequate system of (inter)cultural standards and linguistic and pragmatic rules of interaction" (2004, p. 116). Whether explicitly referenced or implicitly foundational, much (though not all) of North American ICFLE benefits from prior research in L2 pragmatics (Kasper and Rose 2002), intercultural communication theory (e.g., Scollon and Scollon 2001), and/or research that describes language and culture as essentially inseparable and mutually constructive phenomena (e.g., Agar 1994; Kramsch 1993, 1998). These perspectives will be synoptically conjoined in the following discussion.

As Kramsch has argued, language is the principle means through which we conduct our social lives; communication is a social practice that expresses, embodies, and symbolizes cultural realities (Kramsch 1998, p. 3). Further, language enables and evokes the collaborative construction of partially shared realities (what is sometimes termed "intersubjectivity," see Rommetveit 1974; Thorne 2000a). There has been considerable scholarship establishing linkages between language and human meaning making that is highly relevant to L2 development. To list a few, these include expositions on the interdependence of language, ideology, and consciousness (Bernstein 1996; Volosinov 1973), language and its relation to thought (Gumperz and Levinson 1996; Lakoff 1987), and Vygotskian treatments of L2 language development (Lantolf and Thorne 2006; Thorne 2005).

Of particular relevance to ICFLE is Michael Agar's notion of "languaculture," a term he acknowledges is an "awkward" but also "inevitable" invention that brings together language and culture into a dialectical unity (1994, p. 60). The "langua" in "languaculture" extends beyond words and sentences[3] to discourse (see also Scollon and Scollon 2001). Agar helps us to understand that utterances are always produced and interpreted in relation to historically formed cultural practices and speech situations. For FL learners, perhaps especially those at more advanced levels, the growing realization of the subtle and obvious differences between their own and others' languacultures produces what Agar (1994) terms "rich points." In application to FLE, rich points can be glossed as opportunities— the opportunities to collaboratively forge a heightened awareness of self and other that is fueled by the contestations and confusions that arise during communication (explicitly "intercultural" and otherwise). Various responses to communicative breakdown are possible, such as ignoring the problem or projecting deficiency onto the interlocutor or the self. "Or," writes Agar,

> you can wonder—wonder why you don't understand, wonder if some other languaculture isn't in play, wonder if how you thought the world worked isn't just one variation on countless themes. If you wonder, at that moment and later as well, you've taken on culture, not as something that "those people" have, but rather as a space between you and them, one that you're involved in as well, one that can be overcome (1994, p. 106).

Confronting oneself, as well as having others doing the confronting, as described in more detail below, is not a smooth process for many students (see also Schneider and von der Emde, this volume). Kramsch describes FL learning as the process of seeing the world through another's eyes but not losing sight of oneself, a process that may involve both "elation" and "deeply troubling" emotions (1993, p. 234). In direct reference to intercultural dialogue, Agar moves culture from the status of object to that of a process and provides the following formulation: "[c]ulture happens when a problem in language has to do with who you are" (1994, p. 48). A "problem" in the sense meant by Agar (see also Belz and Müller-Hartmann 2003) is not something to avoid or ignore; it is a resource. As has been suggested by practitioners of activity theory (Engeström 1987, 1999; Leont'ev 1981; Thorne 2004, 2005), development itself emerges from the resolution of contradictions, which in turn create conditions for future, perhaps more complex contradictions. As the research described below shows, differing languacultures and the rich points made visible through their contact have the potential to create potent conditions for learning.

In specific reference to the FL arena, Byram and Zarate (1997) describe intercultural competence as the capacity to mediate multiple cultural identities and situations. Sercu extends this characterization and suggests that "intercultural speakers are committed to turning intercultural encounters into intercultural relationships" (2004, p. 117). Of course, the outstanding problem is how conditions for developing a capacity, and perhaps even a hunger, for the challenges presented by intercultural communication can be inculcated in instructed FL settings. The discussion of ICFLE models described below cannot address this question directly, but as with other pedagogical innovations, developing a clear and contingency-responsive pedagogical infrastructure marks a solid starting point.

Models of ICFLE

As discussed above, ICFLE is referred to in various ways in the literature and there exist numerous models that make use of Internet-mediated interaction between learners interested in one another's expert language. International class-to-class partnerships within institutionalized settings, often termed "telecollaboration"[4] (Belz 2003; Kern 1996; Kinginger 2004; Kinginger, Gourvés-Hayward, and Simpson 1999; Warschauer 1996), is the model best known to North American language educators. By definition, telecollaboration occurs within instructed FL settings and offers a wide range of interactional possibilities such as pair work, small-group work, and whole class exchanges. Telecollaborative projects generally involve intensive coordination that can include aligning partner class syllabi around shared information and media (literature, films, scholarly texts) and collaborative interpretive and investigative activities. For university language program directors, instructors, and students, the telecollaboration model has a number of strengths, such as institutional support for the technologies used, the expert guidance and interpretive assistance an instructor can provide as students negotiate tasks in intercultural partnerships, and the collective generation of components of the syllabi for each partner class. This said, the high level of coordination and institutional location of telecollaborative exchanges present challenges as well. These include finding appropriate partner classes, the need for substantial pre-interaction negotiation between class instructors (see Belz and Müller-Hartmann 2003), and often a limited interaction window due to the lack of alignment in the academic calendars of partner classes. Belz notes additional constraints such as differences in socio-institutional cultures, one example of which is high-stakes end-of-year testing (the situation in Germany) versus low-stakes and frequent "evaluation scenes" such as quizzes, small projects, and homework (the American model); these differences have been linked to tensions in collaborative transatlantic working groups (see Belz 2001, p. 227–228). Accepting that all pedagogical innovations come with challenges, for language program directors wishing to instigate ICFLE projects, the telecollaboration model's institutional character makes it a reasonable choice. Scalability and implementation across multiple sections is still relatively uncharted terrain, but local teaching assistants and instructors can share general orientation sessions, syllabi and activity planning can be ameliorated over successive iterations, and, with a tolerance for mutability, the ICFLE experience can be engineered to align with curricular goals. Specific examples of telecollaboration projects are described at length in the following sections.

A second model (used extensively in Europe) is tandem learning, the pairing of individuals in complementary dyads where each is interested in learning the other's language (e.g., Appel 1999; Brammerts 1996, 1999, 2003; Cziko 2004;

Kötter 2002, 2003; O'Rourke 2005). Tandem learning is most associated with non-institutional learning configurations and usually requires partners to negotiate discussion topics and the balance between overt pedagogical and conversational activity. Support for finding partners, initiating a tandem learning relationship, and structuring the partnerships is extensive (e.g., Brammerts' *eTandem* project).[5] Tandem learning is reported to serve numerous communities and purposes such as seniors wishing to learn a new language or maintain one learned earlier in life; young people interested in learning and/or using foreign languages before travel or study abroad experiences; and students wishing to use a foreign language in an informal, non-institutional environment. In the context of North American FLE, tandem learning would make an ideal companion to self-paced FL study and to FL distance education programs where students have limited or minimal interaction with an instructor or other students.

Along with the notion of reciprocity (mutual benefit), tandem learning is built on the concept of learner autonomy. Learner autonomy has a significant presence in FLE in Europe and is based on principles of self-direction and intrinsic motivation (e.g., Dam 1995; van Esch and St. John 2003). In the tandem learning framework, learner autonomy is both a prerequisite for successful partners as well as a capacity that can be enhanced by the tandem learning experience. The ideal of autonomous learning is attractive with its emphasis on independence, critical thinking, and self-reliance. Of course, many teacher-facilitated instructional settings would also claim similar objectives. The significant difference between tandem learning and instructed varieties of ICFLE revolve around the perceived usefulness and function of expert guidance in the intercultural communication process. While it is beyond the capacity of this chapter to engage this issue in significant detail, researchers working within the telecollaboration model have suggested that teacher-mediation plays a critical role in facilitating more sophisticated understandings of self and other in intercultural interaction (e.g., Belz and Müller-Hartmann 2003; O'Dowd and Eberbach 2004). Further, developing an awareness of the complex relationships between culture and its linguistic expression have proven extremely challenging even with expert-teacher mediation, examples of which include varying expected genres of communication (Kramsch and Thorne 2002), exposing and working through cultural stereotypes (O'Dowd 2005), and differences in directness and pragmatics that are expressed in subtle aspects of language use (e.g., Belz, this volume). These studies would suggest that for certain types of learning goals, such as building meta-communicative awareness or performing fine-grained linguistic analyses to better understand and constructively engage in intercultural communication, tandem learning may have significant limitations. However, a reciprocal argument can also be made that generating intrinsically motivated and "authentic" activity on the part of learners is a problem within instructed educational environments. Tandem learning is predicated on the idea that the participants are genuinely invested in the process. Using tandem learning in an institutional context (see also O'Rourke 2005), Kötter presents both arguments: tandem partners may not address repeated and significant linguistic errors, and if they do, they may not be capable of providing productive explanations. At the same time, dyadic relationships generally provide more attention than would a whole class situation, and since each participant occupies the role of both expert and learner, there is an "atmosphere of confidence and trust" (2002, p. 147) that might support the risk taking, creative expression, and unhindered negotiation that formal educational environments may stifle.

Based on a number of studies that self-describe as "telecollaboration" or "tandem learning," however, ascertaining absolute differences between the two approaches is problematic. Kötter (2003) and O'Rourke (2005), for example, both label their approaches as "tandem learning," but in each case, participants are students in instructed FL courses that include explicit instruction and *post-hoc* discussion of tandem learning activity. Additionally, the students in Kötter's (2003) study were partnered with students taught by Schneider and von der Emde, both proponents of significant teacher mediation in intercultural FLE (see Schneider and von der Emde, this volume). In conclusion, the goals and processes of tandem learning and telecollaboration differ at their points of greatest divergence. In the intervening areas of the continuum, however, between fully autonomous learning and significant teacher mediation and intervention, these two approaches overlap and, in certain instances, may be functionally indistinguishable from one another.

A third and emerging ICFLE configuration is to link together local expert speakers, such as diaspora, immigrant, and heritage language populations, with FL students in organized partnerships. Blake and Zyzik (2003), to describe one example, used synchronous chat to connect Spanish heritage language students in a university language course with Spanish FL learners on the same campus. Benefits were reported for both groups. The FL learners gained access to interaction with more advanced speakers of Spanish while the heritage speakers, many of whom had expressed insecurity about their Spanish language ability, by saying that it was "not good enough" (Blake and Zyzik 2003, p. 540), occupied expert roles that helped to affirm their cultural and linguistic backgrounds. Blake and Zyzik suggest that for both groups, Internet mediation decreased anxieties about negative appraisals of their linguistic performance and, correspondingly, that such "non-inhibiting" situations "may tend to increase language output" for both groups (2003, p. 540). While many institutions and regions include populations possessing heterogeneous linguistic and cultural backgrounds, these intra-community resources remain largely untapped in FLE.

A final approach to FLE that utilizes the Internet to access expert speakers is to encourage (or require) learners to participate in established and non-educationally oriented Internet communities, such as discussion forums associated with newspapers such as *Le Monde* (see Hanna and de Nooy 2003, discussed in detail below; see also Tudini 2003). While other possibilities exist for online multilingual and intercultural communication, such as informal keypal partnerships and participation in Internet-based "massive multiplayer online games,"[6] these configurations are currently less amenable to the needs associated with instructed language education.

Pedagogical Approaches to ICFLE

In this section, two key elements common to many ICFLE approaches are described. The first is the use of parallel texts to structure discussion and provide overall themes and goals for the partnerships. The second element concerns systems for sharing the use of the L1 and FL within intercultural collaborations. Two project types are discussed that provide concrete illustrations of successful and continuing class-to-class intercultural interaction (the "telecollaboration" approach). The first is a composite model[7, 8] that has been described in the work of Belz (2002, 2003), Belz and Kinginger (2002, 2003), Müller-Hartmann (2000), and Thorne (2003b). The second example is the *Cultura* project (see also Bauer *et al.* this volume). Note that this section is intentionally descriptive rather than evaluative as it attempts to present a coherent framework for developing successful ICFLE projects. However, as O'Dowd (2005) recently described, local conditions, expectations, and learning goals make simple adoption of an existing model problematic. The descriptions that follow are meant to be generative orientations, not prescriptive declarations.

Parallel Texts, Concrete Activities, and Phase Sequences

The primary concern in telecollaborative language learning is what to have students do and how to orient them to the invariably serendipitous process of doing it. Having students engage with parallel texts has been particularly productive and many telecollaborative projects explicitly reference Kramsch (1993) as the source for this pedagogical inspiration (e.g., Kinginger *et al.* 1999; Kinginger 2004; Müller-Hartmann 2000a). The use of parallel texts can involve literature, film, children's stories, fairy tales, or other genres of textual and media expression. Kinginger (2004) and Belz (2002) emphasize themes of childhood, adolescence, young adulthood, family life, and university life and education that include the following parallel texts and media. For French, students on both sides of the Atlantic read, analyze, and contrast a number of *dessins animés* "graphic novels" such as *La Grande Traversée*, *The Little Mermaid*, and *Pépé le Pew*. Students are also given the choice of analyzing a variety of films and their remakes, such as *Trois Hommes et un Couffin* (1985)—*Three Men and a Baby* (1987), *Neuf Mois* (1994)—*Nine Months* (1995), and *Les Compères* (1983)—*Father's Day* (1997), among others. For German, Belz and her partner instructor Müller-Hartmann, use Grimm and Disney versions of the *Aschenputtel/Cinderella* tale, two juvenile literature novels *Ben Liebt Anna* by Peter Härtling (1997) and *If You Come Softly* by Jacqueline Woodson (1998), and two films depicting young adulthood in contemporary middle-class families, *Nach fünf im Urwald* (1995) and *American Beauty* (1999). For both the French and German courses, parallel texts provide the primary content for the dialogue and collaborative work the partner classes carry out together.

One of the more striking intercultural interventions within FLE is that created by Furstenberg and her colleagues (Bauer *et al.* this volume; Furstenberg *et al.* 2001; Furstenberg 2003). *Cultura* is noteworthy for its significant infrastructural development of Web-based materials and activities (see *http://web.mit.edu/french/culturaNEH/)*. Students utilize CMC for asynchronous interaction (see discussion in the section "Approaches to Language Sharing," below), but also engage one another through Web-based questionnaires in which they make word associations (creating semantic networks), sentence completions, and provide responses to culturally specific situations and circumstances (examples are available on the *Cultura* Web site, above). The responses that students produce then form the data that each partner class analyzes in an effort to notice similarities and differences and to hypothesize possible reasons for these convergences and divergences. Public opinion polls are also made available so that students can discover where their analyses align within the larger context of population-wide national-level trends and beliefs. Increasingly over the semester, students are presented with a diverse set of parallel texts, including films (e.g., French films and their American remakes), French and American newspaper articles on the same topic but that represent divergent cultural positions, and diverse academic and literary texts. The *Cultura* project's constructivist approach supports active engagement on the part of students and instructors alike. As anthropologists have noted for decades, most of what matters in culture operates at subtle levels that are difficult to capture or even to recognize. These facets of culture are "essentially elusive, abstract, and invisible. Our challenge [with *Cultura*] was to make them visible, accessible, and understandable" (Furstenberg *et al.* 2001, p. 56). The development of multiple heuristics, material artifacts, pedagogically progressive activities, and the use of Internet information and communication technologies make the *Cultura* project particularly noteworthy as a model for instructed FL learning. *Cultura* Web materials, as well as archives of previous exchanges, are available for use by interested classes and institutions.

In a detailed overview of the telecollaborative pedagogical processes he uses in the classroom, Müller-Hartmann (2000) describes a set of overlapping and iterative phases (based in part on Candlin 1989) that provide a tested framework for putting into practice telecollaborative language learning. Note that Müller-Hartmann also uses the parallel texts approach and regularly engages in telecollaborative partnerships with colleagues in the United States and elsewhere. As it is described here, Müller-Hartmann's phase sequence is slightly modified and combined with the system used by one of his American collaborators (Belz 2002).[9] In the first phase, generally beginning prior to actual telecollaborative exchanges, students construct a personal cultural identity through the production and exchange of introduction letters (or links to texts and images posted on the Web or in blogs) that act in part as cultural autobiographies (Kern 1996). A variant or complement to individual letters is to have students, typically in groups or as a whole class, construct Web sites that represent their local campus and home community experiences. The explicit goal at this stage is to tailor these compositions to anticipate the projected interests and questions of partner class peers as well as to reflect upon, and perhaps to begin to see differently, the everyday cultural settings and processes at home.

Phase two begins with an emphasis on building a foundation of personal rapport and then moves into substantive dialogue focused on the parallel texts. Müller-Hartmann (2000) places particular emphasis on the teacher's role in helping students to understand key themes in the FL texts as well as to facilitate reflection on their own personal and collective worldviews (see also Fuchs 2004; O'Dowd and Eberbach 2004). As an aid to this process, reading journals should be kept for recording questions and insights that subsequently can be brought up in local class discussion before being shared with the partner class. Müller-Hartmann comments that by "[m]oving into the literary text in this way, learners started working collaboratively, trying to come to terms with their partners' and their own identities and culture(s) in the process" (2000, p. 138). Building on this individual and intra-class preparation, students then share their perceptions, challenges, and analyses with members of the partner class.[10] Recommended group size for phase two interactions are dyads and smaller clusters of three to five students to allow for interpersonal relationship building and the exchange of ideas. During their five-year (and continuing) collaboration, Müller-Hartmann and Belz have found that proper pairing of students is crucial and, through experience, have developed a procedure that balances teacher control and student initiative. On the American side, students are placed into initial dyads based on the teacher's knowledge of their background and experience with them in class over the first six weeks of the semester. Once the telecollaboration begins, two or three German students chose an American dyad based on their Web-biographies. Within these transatlantic groups of four to six, each American can select one or two "special correspondents" with whom they might develop a more personal relationship. This procedure establishes a stable social infrastructure but one that is open to student initiative, a quality that may amplify personal investment in the telecollaborative process.

The third and final phase involves, in Müller-Hartmann's words, "coordinating perspectives" (2000, p. 142). Belz provides a detailed description of what she had her students do during the third phase of telecollaborative interaction,[11] including the measures she employed for evaluating their final products:

> The task during phase [three] was for each group to develop a Web site . . . which contained a bilingual essay pertaining to the parallel texts and a bilingual discussion of a cultural construct (e.g., "racism," "beauty," "family") from multiple perspectives. In addition to discrete-point grammar, discourse grammar . . ., and content, students were evaluated on their demonstration of electronic literacy . . . as evidenced by the appropriate integration of images, video, sound, and topic-related informational hyperlinks into their Web sites (2002, p. 64).

In this excerpt, we see the culmination of approximately eight or nine weeks of age-peer interaction in the form of collaborative essays made available via the Web. Müller-Hartmann (2000) notes that the final phase can often feel rushed and incomplete. Under ideal conditions and with tight adherence to the scheduling of tasks, such as that described by Belz above, final and finished looking collaborative products should represent convergences and agreements as well as articulate ongoing differences and debates. If time is short, as often happens toward the close of the semester, it is also possible to attain some of the closure and summative clarity a more formal project may provide by convening a series of intra-class discussions oriented toward having students express, in academic and personal terms, the significance they gleaned from the telecollaborative experience (see Müller-Hartmann, this volume, for a discussion).

Approaches to Language Sharing: Which Language When?

In most ICFLE projects, electronic discussions are intended to be bilingual in nature so that each participant has ample opportunity to use both their expert language as well as the FL they are learning. Often, however, partner classes have a relative imbalance in communicative expertise, where the FL competence of one group is substantially higher than the FL competence of the other. In U.S.–Europe telecollaborations, for example, it is often the case that the European partners have a higher competence in English than the American students do in the FL (this has also been reported in Ireland–German tandem partnerships, see O'Rourke 2005). Whatever the desired balance between L1 and FL use, the language-use protocol should be explicitly presented to all participants. Additionally, partners should be encouraged to discuss and confirm language-use practices with one another during their first exchanges. If appropriate, participants can also be made aware of different approaches for language sharing. One orientation is to encourage students to produce messages in an "any code" contract, mixing languages as they wish at the clause, sentence, or paragraph levels. A second approach is to suggest that they attempt to sustain their language choice for longer discourse units, for instance to write the first half of an e-mail in French and the second half in English. There are potential benefits to both systems. Any code contract may provoke creative language use and mediate a more complex level of discourse as gaps in FL communicative capacity can be filled in with L1 words or utterances. On the other hand, promoting code-specific periods or units of activity, especially during synchronous CMC sessions, has the advantage of encouraging "pushed output" that has been hypothesized to contribute to syntactic development and which may foreground for the learners gaps in their communicative repertoires that can later be explicitly addressed (Swain 1985; Swain and Lapkin 1998).

In sharp contrast to a language-sharing approach, the *Cultura* guidelines propose that all CMC interaction, as well as responses to the Web-based questions and prompts, be produced in the participants' L1. The rationale given for this controversial pedagogical decision is that the benefit of rich input (from the partner class producing in their L1) outweighs the potential disadvantages of not having the experience of using the FL for age-peer interaction (see Bauer *et al.*, this volume). Recent ICFLE research would indicate that there are significant challenges to this method, particularly in the area of developing pragmatic competence (relevant studies are reviewed below). FL classes have many virtues, but fostering conditions that even distantly reflect the pragmalinguistic context of interaction with expert speakers is not one of them. In a study of U.S.–Spain telecollaboration that utilized a modified version of the *Cultura* model, and after a period of negotiation with the American partner class instructors (who supported the *Cultura* model), O'Dowd (2005) developed a three-part approach that involved all students using

English for some discussions, Spanish for others, and in the third, following the *Cultura* guidelines, students would write to one another only in their L1. In an assessment of each condition, O'Dowd (2005) found that there was no significant change in participation levels associated with language choice. Additionally, both student groups reported a preference for writing and reading in their FL, though they also found other of the formats satisfactory. O'Dowd (2005) notes that students involved in telecollaboration expect to be able to use their FL even when the rationale for culturally oriented L1–L1 exchanges is explained. The principle of reciprocity that informs tandem learning and most varieties of telecollaboration makes available both input from expert speakers using their L1 as well as opportunities to use the FL in situated, interpersonal dialogue. Based on the evidence available and the needs and desires of most FL student participants, a language-sharing approach would seem the superior choice for most ICFLE projects.

ICFLE Research

Part One: From Propositional Content
to Intercultural Communication

More than a decade ago and still prophetic today, Kramsch suggested that FL teaching should be built on a philosophy of conflict, one that affirmed fault lines, engendered a tolerance for ambiguity, and where "understanding and shared meaning, when it occurs, is a small miracle" (1993, p. 2). Those working in the area of ICFLE have discovered the truth value of this formulation many times over. While small miracles do occur, Agar's (1994) contestation-invoked opportunities for development—"rich points"—appear as or more frequently than do the small miracles of smooth interaction (e.g., Schneider and von der Emde 2003; Ware 2005; Ware and Kramsch 2005). In the discussion to follow, I will describe briefly two telecollaboration case studies that focus on disjuncture between discourse systems and then will suggest broader implications for the role of the instructor in ICFLE projects.

Motivated by the awareness that intercultural communication is certainly made more rapid and convenient by global communication networks, Kramsch and Thorne (2002) stress that characterizations of face-to-face communicative competence (e.g., Breen and Candlin 1980; Savignon 1983) may require substantial revision in the context of Internet-mediation. This study of French-American telecollaboration (see also Kern 2000) follows intra-class interaction among the Americans using synchronous CMC and then analyzes the inter-class e-mail exchanges that followed. The results illustrated that the French and American students were operating within, and expecting from the other, differing genres of communication. The French students employed a largely factual, impersonal, and dispassionate genre of writing that included supporting their positions with examples and argument building logical connectors ("for example," "however," "moreover"). By contrast, the American students expected the telecollaborative interactions to result in peer solidarity and mutual trust building. Especially in early phases of the project, the phatic style of the American postings, full of question and exclamation marks (and other message elements seeking to build relations rather than exchange information), suggested a high degree of affective involvement and personal-emotional investment that, in the end, did not convert well to contentious academic argumentation. In a post-telecollaboration interview, one of the American students explained his experiences in the partnership in the following way:

> **Interviewer:** It seemed like you all would ask questions, right? Didn't you get responses?
>
> **Eric:** Sometimes we'd get long. . . . but it's true we didn't get, *it seems true that they weren't doing the same thing we were.* It seemed like, you know, we had a task. And they, it seemed like, *I didn't know what they were doing* [laughs]. . . . When we [Americans] were talking to each other, it was debate and agreement and process. But with the French, we'd ask a question and receive a statement . . . (Kramsch and Thorne 2002, p. 97)

As Eric intimates, the two partner classes were operating on the different and orthogonal axes of communication as information exchange versus communication for personal engagement, forming what Bernstein (1996, p. 44) has termed a "potential discursive gap" that marks an opportunity for alternative possibilities and understandings. In the instance of this telecollaborative exchange, this gap was not adequately recognized until after the fact and so was not explored by students or instructors during the course.

In a study that imparts a complementary perspective on the issue of divergent communication styles, Belz (2003) presents a linguistic analysis of telecollaborative exchanges between one American and two German participants. Belz utilizes a variety of Hallidayan analysis called appraisal theory, a specialized approach used to analyze the linguistic elements at play in the development, negotiation, and maintenance of social relationships. Appraisal theory provides tools to examine epistemic modality and other linguistic resources that communicators use to display and negotiate feelings, judgments, and valuations (see Martin 2000).[12]

Belz produces a quantitative analysis of linguistic features in the asynchronous CMC interactions that illustrate that while overall rates of appraisal were similar for the three participants, there were marked differences in the distribution of positive and negative appraisals between the Germans and the American. To summarize, Belz demonstrates with fine-grained linguistic analysis that Anke and Catharina, the German partners, showed a tendency toward "negative appraisal, categorical assertions, and intensification [that] may be reflective of broader German interactional patterns of directness, explicitness, and an orientation toward the self" (2003, p. 91). In contrast, Eric, the American, exhibited "patterns of self-deprecating judgments, positive appreciation, and the upscaling of positive evaluations [that] may index broader [American] communicative patterns of indirectness and implicitness" (Belz 2003, p. 91). Belz clearly states that these differences dialectically interrelate with cultural and institutional communicative patterns but that languacultural norms do not determine discourse in any absolute fashion. Rather, historically established languacultural systems represent social semiotic resources that inform interactional preferences.

Based on the distinctive and shared qualities of these two cases of inter-cultural communication, the question is, how might instructors help students to capitalize on these opportunities for intercultural learning? One method, drawing on Belz and appraisal theory, is to revisit "rich points" as they develop in intercul-tural dialogue and then to help students to see how the minutia of lexical choice and subtle linguistic cues create social realities that influence the flow of commu-nication and the qualities of relationship development (see also Todoya and Harrison 2002).[13] Building on Byrnes (1986), the pedagogical implication to be drawn is not that students need necessarily change their discourse preferences, but that intercultural communicators would benefit from greater awareness of their own interactional style(s) and the development of heightened attunement to the communicative preferences of their interlocutors, perhaps even choosing, as a result, to occupy a position of hybridity that may complexify their interpretive capabilities as intercultural speakers. The instructor has multiple roles in this process, such as acting as a critical mediating resource and sounding board to facilitate consciousness raising and modeling what Kramsch describes as an inter-cultural stance (1999; Ware and Kramsch 2005). Belz provides the following description of the role of the ICFLE educator: "The teacher in telecollaboration must be educated to discern, identify, explain, and model culturally-contingent patterns of interaction in the absence of paralinguistic meaning signals, otherwise it may be the case that civilizations ultimately do clash—in the empirical details of their computer-mediated talk" (2003, p. 92–93). Put another way, the role of the FL teacher is "to prepare students to deal with global communicative practices that require far more than local communicative competence" (Kramsch and Thorne 2002, p. 100). This is, of course, a tall order for many language educators. If ICFLE contin-ues to increase its market share in FLE, future approaches to instructor preparation will increasingly involve explicit methods (such as that used by Belz 2003) for helping students to interpolate between the familiar and the unexpected in global as well as local learning environments. Productive treatments of ICFLE-specific teacher roles and functions can be found in O'Dowd (2005) and O'Dowd and Ederbach (2004) while Müller-Hartmann (2000, this volume) and colleagues (Legutke, Müller-Hartmann, and Ditfurth in press) have come to place Internet-mediated intercultural communi-cation at the center of their teacher-training program.

Part Two: Interpersonal Mediation and Language Development

This section includes an overview of a case study illustrating interpersonal mediation as it contributes to language learning, a set of research findings addressing pragmatics, and issues of presentation-of-self in the educational uses of non-pedagogical Internet environments. While the studies reviewed here reflect generally positive outcomes, I do not wish to explicitly contrast them to the above research that described tensions and challenges in telecollaboration. Rather, what

I want to emphasize here are specific instances of language development and the contributions of intercultural social relationships to this process.

As Ray McDermott (1977) has argued, people create environments for one another. Interpersonal relationships have the potential to move a student from feelings of alienation to inclusion and vice versa, with significant implications for language learning (see Thorne 2005). This was the case for Kirsten,[14] a university student in a fourth-semester French grammar course participating in an ICFLE exchange with university students in France.[15] In a post-semester interview, the student described a transition that began with frustration over the slow start to the relationship with her keypal:

> I was really upset when I didn't hear from him [French key-pal] at first. …I was like …"he didn't respond, I didn't talk to him, I'm really disappointed, I went and cried," and now I'm like "wow!", within a week I went from completely despondent and being like "I hate this, grrrrr," to "wow, love it! Love it!" (Thorne 2003b, p. 47)

In the latter part of this excerpt, Kirsten is referring to a one-week period of extended and prolific dialogue with Oliver, her French partner, which began with an e-mail exchange but then quickly moved to another Internet communication tool, America Online Instant Messenger (IM). She reports that their first IM interaction went on for nearly six hours and included the use of both English and French. Subsequent to this, they continued interacting in 20- to 30-minute sessions, often twice or three times per day. Two issues are relevant here; the shift to IM, which is the clear communication tool of choice for peer interaction among university-aged youth in the United States, and the subordination of French language study as an educational activity to the use of French (and English) for the building of a personally meaningful relationship. Not discounting the importance of their blossoming (and flirtatious) friendship, Kirsten reported that her linguistic and pragmatic performance in French showed significant shifts. Through interaction with and goading from Oliver,[16] Kirsten eventually gained command of appropriate *tu/vous* (hereafter T/V) pronoun use, a facility that had eluded her throughout years of French study (see also the discussion of T/V use in Belz and Kinginger 2002, 2003, below). More dramatically, Kirsten had always thought of herself as "horrible" at French grammar and had little confidence in her capacity to carry out meaningful communication in the language. When asked about the specific linguistic gains arising from her interactions with Oliver, Kirsten made the following remarks:

Interviewer: What else beside the tu/vous stuff did he help you with?

Kirsten: Usage of "au" versus "en" versus "dans" versus "à" versus, you know, that kinda stuff. A more in-depth vocabulary, for sure. … it's kind of nice to have a human dictionary on the other end too … I was like "how am I supposed to say?" like for example. … So the "de" and "à" thing, "de la campagne," "à le cité," whatever, stuff like that. I was like "wow," you know, eeeeee [vocalization of glee; laughs]. Because I couldn't get that from a dictionary.

Interviewer: That's something you have to have a little help with, yeah?

Kirsten: Yeah, yeah, and how am I supposed to learn it? That's not in the grammar books, you know [laughing], expressions like that, and other things. It was fun. (Thorne 2003b, p. 50–51)

In these excerpts, Kirsten describes the interaction that allowed her access to the French prepositional system that she allegedly "couldn't get . . . from a dictionary" and that is "not in the grammar books." Many French language students have successfully developed the ability to use French prepositions of location from grammar texts or instructor-provided grammar explanations. Kirsten, however, seemingly required interpersonal mediation, specifically from a desirable age-peer who was willing to provide immediate corrective feedback as part of an ongoing social relationship. Her reflections and IM transcript data suggest the following developmental sequence. In the initial IM conversation with Oliver, she crossed a threshold that marked the first time she was consciously aware of her capacity to communicate meaningfully in French. Kirsten realized this increasing capacity when she states, in reference to this first IM conversation, "that was the first time that I was like, 'I made a connection in French.' I was so proud. It was like, 'wow, that's me, in French, and he understood me!'" (Thorne 2003b, p. 53) After this point, she was able to benefit from Oliver's explicit linguistic assistance and to participate in extended and unrehearsed dialogues in French, largely through his confidence-building enthusiasm for the content of her ideas (this is clearly expressed in the IM transcript data). This brief case study suggests that interpersonal dynamics construct differing capacities to act, which in turn are associated with a range of possible developmental trajectories.

The power of social relationships also has a hand to play in one of the strongest examples of pragmalinguistic learning outcomes reported in ICFLE research. In a series of studies on telecollaboration, Belz and Kinginger (2002, 2003) and Kinginger and Belz (to appear) described the development of address forms used in French and German (T/V).[17] Current sociolinguistic research indicates that T/V usage has become destabilized in the French and German languages (Morford 1997; Wylie and Brière as cited in Belz and Kinginger 2003). Additionally, there is considerable, if also understandable, simplification of the sociopragmatic ambiguity around T/V usage in the restricted contexts of textbooks and classroom discourse. In this sense, T/V use is not simply rule-governed but is instead embedded in a system of meaning potentials that are realized in particular social interactions. Nearly all of the American participants in these interactions exhibited free variation of T/V at the start of the intercultural communication process. Belz and Kinginger tracked usage over time in both e-mail and synchronous CMC sessions and found that after critical moments within exchanges with expert speaker age-peers, the American participants began to systemically modify their usage. These critical moments included explicit feedback and rationales for T-form usage from German and French peers. Additionally, the American students had myriad opportunities to observe appropriate pronoun use by native speakers across synchronous and asynchronous CMC modalities. In this way, pragmatic awareness of T/V as an issue (i.e., "noticing," see Schmidt 1993) led to the approximation of expert speaker norms in most cases. Belz and Kinginger argued that the American students' desire to maintain positive face (in essence, wanting to be liked) with age-peers helped to focus their attention on the role of linguistic form in the performance of pragmatically appropriate communication. In further research, the importance of the social relationships built in these transatlantic partnerships have been linked to positive development of other grammatical and morphological features, namely *da*-compounds in German (Belz 2004, this volume), modal particles in German (Belz and Vyatkina 2005a, 2005b), and lexical and morphological development in Spanish (Dussias, this volume).

This section concludes with a discussion of a different sort of ICFLE project. Hanna and de Nooy (2003) report on four students studying French who participated in public Internet discussion forums associated with the Parisian newspaper *Le Monde* (see also Tudini 2003). The authors present a strong rationale for opting to use public discussion forums rather than more conventional telecollaboration partnerships.[18] While it is a debatable point, Hanna and de Nooy argue that while telecollaboration has many virtues, students are still "safely within the classroom, virtual though it might be" (2003, p. 73) and limited by the fact that they occupy, and predominantly speak from, the institutionally bounded subject position of student or learner. *Le Monde* discussion forums, by contrast, exist to support argumentation and debate about mostly contemporary political and cultural issues. One forum in particular, labeled *Autre sujets* (other topics), included a wide range of participants and topics and was selected as the venue for the study.

The French language learners in Hanna and de Nooy's study were David and Laura, both American, and Eleanor and Fleurie, who were English. Hanna and de Nooy examined their opening posts to the *Autre sujets* forum and then tracked the number and content of the responses they received. Each of the four students opened with a gambit that positioned them as learners of French, but they differed in their tone and effect. Eleanor and Fleurie opted to create new, standalone messages on the forum, with the respective subject lines *Les Anglais* ("The English") and *Une fille anglaise* ("An English girl"). In the content of their posts, Eleanor and Fleurie each made explicit requests for conversational partners to help them improve their French. They received a few cordial as well as abrupt replies, each of which suggested that they actually say something or take a position in the ongoing discussion. Neither did and both disappeared from the forum.

David and Laura, in contrast, both opened with a response to another message, *de facto* entering into a turn exchange system as their messages were marked by the subject line header of the message they had responded to (e.g., *Réf: Combattre le modèle américain*—"Fight the American model"). They also each began by apologizing for the limitations of their French language ability. Hanna and de Nooy interpret this as a sagacious strategy that "reinstates certain cultural borders" and that provided them with "a particular speaking position" (2003, p. 78) that may have yielded advantages in the debate culture of the forum. It is also salient that, immediately following their language apology gambits, they each contributed position statements on the themes of racism and cultural imperialism.

David, in fact, primarily used English in his posts, but with coaching and support from forum participants, he maintained an accepted and significant presence on the forum. Hanna and de Nooy interpret this as an indication that "neither politeness nor linguistic accuracy is the measure of intercultural competence here" (2003, p. 78). Rather, in the circumstances of *Le Monde* discussion forums, participation in the genre of debate is the minimum threshold for membership. The primary take-home message from this delightful study is clear. Framed in vernacular language, it goes something like this: If you want to communicate with real people, you need to self-present as a real person yourself. This suggests an ICFLE agenda that would orient students toward how to recognize genres, and subsequently, how to engage in discussion that does not ultimately revolve around "the self . . . as the exotic little foreigner/the other" (Hanna and de Nooy 2003, p. 73).

Recognizing Technologies as Cultural Artifacts

By definition, ICFLE is made possible through technological mediation. However, in the arena of Internet-mediated language education, the cultural dimensions of the technologies themselves are generally neglected, and neglected at a cost to the quality of ICFLE interaction (Thorne 2003b). To begin, a larger frame of reference is described to help contextualize the critical issue of communication tool choice to mediate ICFLE projects.

The Internet has enabled multiple new opportunities for information gathering, enhanced possibilities for producing and disseminating information to others, and has provoked changes in the granularity of information sharing between spatially dispersed co-workers, friends, and family members. As the research of Jones (2004), Miller and Slater (2000), and Scollon and Scollon (2004) make clear, a dichotomized view of face-to-face and Internet-mediated life, and certainly the distinction between "real" and "virtual," completely dissolves under close examination of lived communicative practice. Especially among the digital native generation (Presky 2001), a descriptor for individuals who quite literally grew up with (and through) the use of Internet information and communication tools, it is apparent that social as well as academic communication is mediated by participation in digital environments such as facebook (www.thefacebook.com), blog networks, instant messaging, and voice and text messaging over cell phones (see Thorne and Payne 2005, pp. 381–386). This increase in mediated communication in the service of community building and maintenance suggests that for many students, performing competent identities in second and additional language(s) may now involve Internet-mediation as often as or more often than face-to-face and non-digital forms of communication.

It is also clear that, unlike CMC L2 use during the 1990s when the Internet was often treated as a proxy or a heuristic environment to assist with the development of face-to-face communication and non-digital epistolary conventions, Internet-mediated communication is now a high-stakes environment that infuses work processes, educational activity, interpersonal communication and, not least, intimate relationship building and maintenance (Castells 1996). However, the Internet does not exist generically as a neutral medium. Rather, Internet communication tools are, like all human creations, cultural tools (Cole 1996) that carry interactional and relational associations, preferred uses (and, correspondingly, inappropriate uses), and expectations of genre-specific communicative activity. Kramsch and Anderson note that information and communication "has become more mediated than ever, with a mediation that ever more diffuses and conceals its authority. The role of education, and FLE in particular, is precisely to make this mediation process visible" (1999, p. 39). Cultures-of-use of Internet communication tools build over time in relationship to use in particular discursive settings and to mediate specific social functions. The suggestion is that technologies, *as culture*, will have variable meanings and uses for different communities. While Internet communication tools carry the historical residua of their use across time, patterns of past use do not determine present and future activity, just as gender, mother tongue, or social class do not determine present and future activity. Rather, the cultures-of-use framework provides another axis along which to perceive and address intercultural variation and similarity (Thorne 2000b, 2003b).

To explicate this point with an example, participants in a recent telecollaborative exchange reported that e-mail was a constraining variable in the intercultural communication process. Not only did many of the e-mail interactions fall flat, in a number of cases they simply did not happen at all. This was due, in part, to the fact that the communication tool decided upon by the project coordinators and instructor, e-mail, was perceived by students as a medium well suited for vertical communication across power and generational lines (professors, parents, employers, and for organization communication), but one that was inappropriate as a tool to mediate interpersonal age-peer relationship building (Thorne 2003b). In an extended ethnographic interview, one student, Grace, reported her conviction that e-mail was such an unsuitable tool for age-peer interaction that it overpowered the coercive force of a graded directive given by the instructor to continue the e-mail exchanges. Although this student liked her keypal and enjoyed the project generally, she chose not to participate because e-mail seemed to be the only modality option.[19] Grace's perspective was not unique—approximately half of the students interviewed (in a class of 24) expressed broadly similar views though usually in less extreme terms (see Thorne 2003b). The fact that other ICFLE research illustrates that e-mail is suitable for all manners of communicative activity (e.g., Fuchs 2004) underscores the point that different populations variably configure Internet communication tools. And these cultural configurations and associations are always transforming as histories of use collide with the exigencies of present needs and contexts. For students like Grace, for example, it is entirely possible that with more explicit or constructive mediation, she might have been able to transform e-mail into a different cultural tool, one that would have better been able to serve her communication needs.

Conclusion

In contrast to approaches to FLE that focus predominantly on language in relative isolation from its use in interpersonal interaction, ICFLE emphasizes participation in intercultural dialogue and development of the linguistic and meta-communicative resources necessary for carrying out such processes. In this essay I have reviewed research that addresses intercultural communication from linguistic, interpersonal, and developmental perspectives, as well as studies describing issues of cultural contestation and the cultures-of-use of Internet communication tools used to mediate ICFLE interaction. This chapter has attempted to describe a variety of practical and theoretical resources relevant to developing interculturally focused pedagogical innovations.

A variety of options exist for incorporating Internet-mediated intercultural communication into curricula. Four models of ICFLE were described, the primary of which was telecollaboration, defined as international class-to-class partnerships within institutional settings. Telecollaboration practitioners tend to formally align their course activities, structure collaborative tasks, and often utilize parallel texts to provide the catalysts for dialogue, cross-cultural analyses, and critical reflection on one's home culture(s). Telecollaboration models are administratively intensive to initiate and maintain due to the high level of coordination between partner classes (e.g., Belz and Müller-Hartmann 2003). However, class-to-class partnerships arguably provide the strongest support for developing sophisticated understandings of intercultural communication through careful design of student-initiated investigations and the explicitly designated role of the instructor as critical mediator and resource. A variant of the telecollaboration model involves connecting FL students with heritage speakers on the same campus, a format that Blake and Zyzik (2002) suggest holds significant promise for language development. Also discussed were open Internet communities such as discussion forums (chat networks and social formations associated with online gaming are other options) that provide the possibility of entering into ongoing, non-educationally oriented discourse communities. The use of interaction in online communities as component parts of instructed FL courses has been shown to provide opportunities for negotiation of meaning (Tudini 2003) and to situate foreign language use in non-educational social contexts (Cononelos and Oliva 1993; Hanna and de Nooy 2003).

Tandem learning has also proven to be a highly productive model that emphasizes dyadic collaborations based on the two principles of reciprocity and learner autonomy. This model illustrates its flexibility by the fact that it is used in formal education settings (e.g., Kötter 2003; O'Rourke 2003) as well as provides thorough and thoughtfully designed infrastructural support for anyone interested in participating in a tandem exchange (Brammerts' *eTandem* project). It was suggested that tandem learning networks could be used to complement FL self-study and distance education formats, or as an accompaniment to conventional FL courses, to provide otherwise limited opportunities for meaningful relationship building through use of the FL. While it is tempting to draw discrete boundaries between tandem learning and telecollaboration, I have made the argument that there is a substantial middle ground shared by both approaches. At the extreme ends of the continuum, the differences are marked, with tandem learning offering support for non-institutional and autonomous dyadic partnerships that may last weeks or years, while telecollaboration is institutionally based, bound to academic calendars, and places emphasis on the teacher's role to facilitate critical reflection (see Müller-Hartmann, this volume; Schneider and von der Emde, this volume) and awareness of the complex relationships uniting linguistic form with intercultural pragmatics, genres, and broader languacultural issues (see Belz, this volume).

At its core, ICFLE approaches are oriented toward two entwined goals. The first is to create conditions to support the development of significant social relationships between persons who have been socialized into varying and varied languacultural viewpoints. The second goal is to make visible and available the conceptual, linguistic, and cultural tools necessary for negotiating what is always and everywhere intercultural communication. A re-orientation of FLE from a focus on communicative competence to a focus on *intercultural* competence (e.g., Sercu 2004) brings with it opportunities to re-assess the processes, objectives, and central value of FLE. It is not an over-bold statement to suggest that the burgeoning research and pedagogical interest in ICFLE approaches are catalyzing a new alchemy within foreign language education, one in which linguistic precision and discourse competence continue to play roles, but in the service of cultivating the capacity to make collectively relevant meanings in the inherently intercultural contexts of everyday life.

Notes

1. I wish to thank an anonymous reviewer for challenging the need for (yet) another acronym and for requesting a rationale for the use of ICFLE.

2. For information on the still vibrant Freinet movement, see *http://www.freinet.org/ icem/history.htm*

3. "Sentences," in opposition to "utterances," for example, are an epiphenomenon of written literacy and have only variable relevance to verbal communication, and for that matter, to synchronous CMC (see McCarthy 1998).

4. Defined by Belz,"*Telecollaboration* involves the application of global computer networks to foreign (and second) language learning and teaching in institutionalized settings. In telecollaborative partnerships, internationally-dispersed learners in parallel language classes use Internet communication tools such as e-mail, synchronous chat, threaded discussion, and MOOs (as well as other forms of electronically mediated communication), in order to support social interaction, dialogue, debate, and intercultural exchange" (2003a, p. 2).

5. For information on the *eTandem* project, visit *http://www.slf.ruhr-uni-bochum.de/ etandem/*

6. Technologies and online social and cultural formations are constantly evolving. To take one quite speculative example, massive multiplayer online games are immensely popular (see Gee 2003) and are already "educational" in the sense players must learn to negotiate the rules of the game as well as other players. Increasingly, large areas of these online worlds are non-English. For the growing

number of students participating in online gaming cultures, the international, multi-lingual, and imminently task-based qualities of these social spaces, where language use is literally social and material action, may one day make them *de rigueur* sites for language learning (or perhaps, somewhat ironically, students will study FLs to enhance their gaming skills and interactional capacity in these language-driven action-scapes).

7. Beginning in the fall of 1999, a number of Penn State colleagues collaboratively developed a multi-year, grant-funded research and pedagogical innovation project to examine the effects of telecollaboration in university-level foreign language classes. The funded research arm of the project ran from 2000 to 2004, but ICFLE courses continue to be taught.

8. *The Penn State Foreign Language Telecollaboration Project* was funded by a United States Department of Education International Research and Studies Program grant (CFDA No.:84.017A). The author was a co-principal investigator on the grant.

9. In particular, I have consolidated Müller-Hartmann's phases two ("project based exchanges") and three ("intensive reading") into one reading and interaction phase.

10. Müller-Hartmann provides the following example of a telecollaborative task developed by one of his American collaborators: "I had each student highlight a moment from the book that impacted them. In the second paragraph I had them make a parallel with our community. The third paragraph (if they had time) was to personalize the message with a 'social' comment or two" (2000, p. 138).

11. In the telecollaborative exchange reported on in Belz (2002), Müller-Hartmann, her collaborator in Germany, had his students engage in an additional phase that involved discussing the telecollaborative process in theoretical and practical terms.

12. Appraisal focuses on three areas: 1) Attitude, covering affect, judgment, and appreciation; 2) Graduation, the linguistic resources speakers use to intensify or mitigate semantic categories; and 3) Engagement, the interactional and linguistic resources speakers use to align or disalign themselves from "the socio-semiotic realities or positions activated and referenced by every utterance" (White 1998, p. 78, cited in Belz 2003, p. 73).

13. Todoya and Harrison (2002), in a telecollaborative partnership linking advanced proficiency Japanese learners with native speakers, found that having students carefully review synchronous CMC transcripts of their interactions helped them learn to analyze complex syntactic structures, interpolate between word level and discourse properties of the communication, and develop strategies for improving their performance in synchronous CMC dialogue.

14. This and all learner names reported in this chapter are pseudonyms.

15. Students of French at *The Pennsylvania State University* interacted with engineering students at the *Ecole Nationale Supérieure de Télécommunications de Bretagne* during the Spring of 2002.

16. In an e-mail, Oliver ended his message with "Bon je garde le 'vous' mais, de grace, utilize 'tu' avec moi!!" [Okay, I get the 'vous' but please use 'tu' with me!!]. In interview, Kirsten, pointing to her e-mail response to Oliver, said "See, I do learn. I changed it!" In the final line of her e-mail, Kirsten had written, "J'attends impatiemment ton réponse!" [I impatiently await your [informal pronoun] response!"]

17. This research was supported by a United States Department of Education International Research and Studies Program Grant (CFDA No.: 84.017A).

18. See Sawchuk (2003) for a discussion of informal learning in computer environments. Sawchuk's study suggests that informal learning activity, because it hovers at the margins of institutional authority, has the potential to catalyze transformative rather than reproductive developmental processes.

19. The focal student discussed in this example, Grace, described her views on e-mail this way (Thorne 2003, p. 56).

> **Interviewer:** Do you e-mail much?
>
> **Grace:** Not not that much. Just mostly for communicating with professors.
>
> **Interviewer:** And for your key-pal?
>
> **Grace:** I just e-mailed him a couple of things in English ... and then I was like, I'm not talking to him any more except in the NetMeetings. And then [the Instructor] was saying how like we have to do that, but then I didn't [laughs]. I didn't e-mail him any more.... Like I just, it just wasn't very convenient I guess. Like if you had AOL Instant Messenger I would just, you know, type in something every so often or whatever, but it's different than e-mail.... It's like, "Oh God, I have to write an e-mail now." Like it's just like, you don't want to, it's like an effort.
>
> **Interviewer:** So how many times a week do you e-mail friends?
>
> **Grace:** Never.
>
> **Interviewer:** Never?
>
> **Grace:** Never.

References

Agar, Michael. 1994. *Language Shock: Understanding the Culture of Conversation*. New York: William Morrow.

Appel, Marie-Christine. 1999. Tandem Language Learning by E-mail: Some Basic Principles and a Case Study. *Centre for Language and Communication Studies Occasional Paper* 54. Dublin: Trinity College Dublin.

Bauer, Beth, Lynne deBenedette, Gilberte Furstenberg, Sabine Levet, and Shoggy Waryn. 2005. The *Cultura* Project. In *Internet-mediated Intercultural Foreign Language Education*, edited by Julie A. Belz and Steven L. Thorne, 31–62. Boston, MA: Thomson Heinle.

Belz, Julie A. 2001. Institutional and Individual Dimensions of Transatlantic Group Work in Network-based Language Teaching. *ReCALL* 13(2): 213–231.

———. 2002. Social Dimensions of Telecollaborative Foreign Language Study. *Language Learning & Technology* 6(1): 60–81. *http://llt.msu.edu/vol6num1/belz/*

———. 2003a. From the Special Issue Editor. *Language Learning & Technology* 7(2): 2–5. *http://llt.msu.edu/vol7num2/speced.html*

———. 2003b. Linguistic Perspectives on the Development of Intercultural Competence in Telecollaboration. *Language Learning & Technology* 7(2): 68–117. *http://llt.msu.edu/vol7num2/belz/default.html*

———. 2004. Learner Corpus Analysis and the Development of Foreign Language Proficiency. *System: An International Journal of Educational Technology and Applied Linguistics* 32(4): 577–591.

———. 2005. Intercultural Questioning, Discovery, and Tension in Internet-Mediated Language Learning Partnerships. *Language and Intercultural Communication* 5(1): 3–39.

————. 2005. At the Intersection of Telecollaboration, Learner Corpus Analysis, and L2
    Pragmatics: Considerations for Language Program Direction. In *Internet-mediated
    Intercultural Foreign Language Education*, edited by Julie A. Belz and Steven L.
    Thorne, 207–246. Boston, MA: Thomson Heinle.
Belz, Julie A., and Celeste Kinginger. 2002. The Cross-Linguistic Development of Address
    Form Use in Telecollaborative Language Learning: Two Case Studies. *Canadian
    Modern Language Review/Revue canadienne des langues vivantes* 59(2): 189–214.
————. 2003. Discourse Options and the Development of Pragmatic Competence by
    Classroom Learners of German: The Case of Address Forms. *Language Learning*
    53(4): 591–647.
Belz, Julie A., and Andreas Müller-Hartmann. 2003. Teachers as Intercultural Learners:
    Negotiating German-American Telecollaboration along the Institutional Faultline. *The
    Modern Language Journal* 87(1): 71–89.
Belz, Julie A., and Nina Vyatkina. 2005a. Computer-Mediated Learner Corpus Research
    and the Data-Driven Teaching of Pragmatic Competence: The Case of German
    Modal Particles. *CALPER Working Paper Series No. 4*, 1–28. The Pennsylvania State
    University, Center for Advanced Language Proficiency Education and Research.
    http://calper.la.psu.edu/publications.php
————. 2005b. Learner Corpus Analysis and the Development of L2 Pragmatic
    Competence in Networked Intercultural Language Study: The Case of German Modal
    Particles. *Canadian Modern Language Review/Revue canadienne des langues
    vivantes* 62(1): 17–48.
Blake, Robert, and Eve Zystik. 2003. Who's Helping Whom?: Learner/Heritage Speakers'
    Networked Discussions in Spanish. *Applied Linguistics* 24(4): 519–544.
Bernstein, Basil. 1996. *Pedagogy, Symbolic Control and Identity*. London: Taylor &
    Francis.
Brammerts, Helmut. 1996. Language Learning in Tandem Using the Internet. In
    Telecollaboration in Foreign Language Learning, edited by Mark Warschauer,
    121–130. Honolulu: Second Language Teaching and Curriculum Center.
Brammerts, Helmut. 1999. Autonomous Language Learning in Tandem via the Internet. In
    English via Various Media, edited by Hans-Jürgen Diller, Erwin Otto, Gerd Stratmann,
    and Anne-Marie Simon-Vandenbergen, 271–328. Heidelberg: Winter.
Brammerts, Helmut. 2003. Autonomous Language Learning in Tandem: The Development
    of a Concept. In *Autonomous Language Learning in Tandem*, edited by Timothy
    Lewis and Lesley Walker, 27–36. Sheffield: Academy Electronic Publications.
Breen, Michael, and Christopher Candlin. 1980. The Essentials of a Communicative
    Curriculum in Language Teaching. *Applied Linguistics* 1: 89–112.
Byram, Michael. 1997. *Teaching and Assessing Intercultural Communicative
    Competence*. Clevedon, UK: Multilingual Matters.
Byrnes, Heidi. 1986. Interactional Style in German and American Conversations. *Text* 2(1):
    189–206.
Cameron, Deborah, and David Block, eds. 2002. *Globalization and Language Teaching*.
    London: Routledge.
Canagarajah, Suresh. 1999. *Resisting Linguistic Imperialism in English Language
    Teaching*. Oxford: Oxford University Press.
Candlin, Christopher. 1989. Language, Culture and Curriculum. In *Language, Learning
    and Community: Festschrift in Honour of Terry R. Quinn*, edited by Christopher
    Candlin and Timothy McNamara, 1–24. Sydney: Macquarie University.
Castells, Manuel. 1996. *The Rise of the Network Society*. Cambridge, MA: Blackwell.
Cole, Michael. 1996. *Cultural Psychology. A Once and Future Discipline*. Cambridge,
    Mass.: Belknapp Press.
Cononelos, Terri, and Maurizio Oliva. 1993. Using Computer Networks to Enhance
    Foreign Language/Culture Education. *Foreign Language Annals* 26(4): 527–534.
Council of Europe. 2001. *Modern Languages: Learning, Teaching, Assessment. A Common
    European Framework of Reference*. Cambridge: Cambridge University Press.

Crystal, David. 2001. *Language and the Internet*. Cambridge: Cambridge University Press.

Dam, Leni. 1995. *Learner Autonomy: From Theory to Practice*. Dublin: Authentik.

Dussias, Paola E. 2005. Morphological Development in Spanish-American Telecollaboration. In *Internet-mediated Intercultural Foreign Language Education*, edited by Julie A. Belz and Steven L. Thorne, 121-146. Boston: Thomson Heinle.

Engeström, Yrjö. 1987. *Learning by Expanding: An Activity Theoretical Approach to Developmental Research*. Helsinki: Orienta-Konsultit.

Engeström, Yrjö, ed. 1999. *Perspectives on Activity Theory*. Cambridge: Cambridge University Press.

Freinet, Celestin. 1994. *Oeuvres Pédagogiques*. Paris: Editions du Seuil.

Fuchs, Carolin. 2004. (Topic) Negotiation in CMC-Based Language Teacher Education: A Qualitative Analysis of a German-American Collaboration Project. Justus-Liebig-Universitüat, Gießen, Germany, unpublished doctoral dissertation.

Fursternberg, Gilberte. 2003. Reading Between the Cultural Lines. In *Reading Between the Lines: Perspectives on Foreign Language Literacy*, edited by Peter Patrikis, 74-98. New Haven, CT: Yale University Press.

Furstenberg, Gilberte, Sabine Levet, Kathryn English, and Katherine Maillet. 2001. Giving a Voice to the Silent Language of Culture: The *Cultura* Project. *Language Learning & Technology* 5(1): 55-102. *http://llt.msu.edu/vol5num1/furstenberg/default.html*

Gee, James P. 2003. *What Video Games Have to Teach Us About Learning and Literacy*. New York: Palgrave/St. Martin's.

Giddens, Anthony. 2000. *Runaway World: How Globalization is Reshaping Our Lives*. New York: Routledge.

Godwin-Jones, Robert. 2005. Messaging, Gaming, Peer-to-Peer Sharing: Language Learning Strategies & Tools for the Millennial Generation. *Language Learning & Technology* 9(1): 17-22.

Gumperz, John, and Stephen Levinson. 1996. *Rethinking Linguistic Relativity*. Cambridge: Cambridge University Press.

Hanna, Barbara, and Julianna de Nooy. 2003. A Funny Thing Happened on the Way to the Forum: Electronic Discussion and Foreign Language Learning. *Language Learning & Technology* 7(1): 71-85. *http://llt.msu.edu/vol7num1/hanna/default.html*

Harvey, David. 2000. *Spaces of Hope*. Berkeley, CA: University of California Press.

Jones, Rodney. 2004. The Problem of Context in Computer-Mediated Communication. In *Discourse and Technology: Multimodal Discourse Analysis*, edited by Philip Levine and Ronald Scollon, 20-33. Washington D.C.: Georgetown University Press.

Kasper, Gabriele, and Kenneth Rose. 2002. *Pragmatic Development in a Second Language*. Oxford: Blackwell.

Kern, Richard. 1996. Computer-Mediated Communication: Using E-mail Exchanges to Explore Personal Histories in Two Cultures. In *Telecollaboration in Foreign Language Learning*, edited by Mark Warschauer, 105-109. Honolulu: Second Language Teaching and Curriculum Center.

———. 2000. *Literacy and Language Teaching*. Oxford: Oxford University Press.

Kern, Richard, Paige Ware, and Mark Warschauer. 2004. Crossing Frontiers: New Directions in Online Pedagogy and Research. *Annual Review of Applied Linguistics* 24(1): 243-260.

Kinginger, Celeste. 1998. Videoconferencing as Access to Spoken French. *The Modern Language Journal* 82(4): 502-513.

Kinginger, Celeste. 2004. Communicative Foreign Language Teaching through Telecollaboration. In *New Insights into Foreign Language Learning and Teaching*, edited by Oliver St. John, Kees van Esch, and Eus Schalkwijk, 101-113. Frankfurt: Peter Lang.

Kinginger, Celeste, and Julie A. Belz. In press. Sociocultural Perspectives on Pragmatic Development in Foreign Language Learning: Microgenetic Case Studies from Telecollaboration and Residence Abroad. *Intercultural Pragmatics* 2(4): 369-422.

Kinginger, Celeste, Alison Gourvés-Hayward, and Vanessa Simpson. 1999. A Tele-Collaborative Course on French-American Intercultural Communication. *The French Review* 72(5): 853–866.

Kötter, Markus. 2002. *Tandem Learning on the Internet: Learner Interactions in Online Virtual Environments*. Frankfurt: Lang.

Kötter, Markus. 2003. Negotiation of Meaning and Codeswitching in Online Tandems. *Language Learning & Technology* 7(2): 145–172.

Kramsch, Claire J. 1993. *Context and Culture and Language Teaching*. Oxford: Oxford University Press.

———. 1998. *Language and Culture*. Oxford: Oxford University Press.

———. 1999. Thirdness: The Intercultural Stance. In *Language, Culture, and Identity*, edited by Torben Vestergaard, 41–58. Aalborg, Denmark: Aalborg University Press.

———. 2000. Second Language Acquisition, Applied Linguistics, and the Teaching of Foreign Languages. *The Modern Language Journal* 84(3): 311–326.

Kramsch, Claire, and Steven L. Thorne. 2002. Foreign Language Learning as Global Communicative Practice. In *Globalization and Language Teaching*, edited by David Block and Deborah Cameron, 83–100. London: Routledge.

Lakoff, George. 1987. *Women, Fire, and Dangerous Things*. Chicago: University of Chicago Press.

Lantolf, James P., and Aneta Pavlenko. 2001. (S)econd (L)anguage (A)ctivity: Understanding Learners as People. In *Learner Contributions to Language Learning: New Directions in Research*, edited by Michael Breen, 141–158. London: Pearson.

Lantolf, James P., and Steven L. Thorne. 2006. *Sociocultural Theory and the Genesis of Second Language Development*. Oxford: Oxford University Press.

Legutke, Michael K., Andreas Müller-Hartmann, and Marita Schocker-v. Ditfurth. In Press. Preparing Teachers for Technology-Supported English Language Teaching. In *Kluwer Handbook on English Language Teaching*, edited by Jim Cummins and Chris Davison. Dordrecht: Kluwer.

Leont'ev, Alexei N. 1981. *Problems of the Development of the Mind*. Moscow: Progress.

Lomicka, Lara. 2001. *A New Perspective on the World: A Qualitative Study of Learning French in an Accelerated Language Classroom*. Pennsylvania State University, University Park, Pennsylvania, unpublished doctoral dissertation.

Martin, James. 2000. Beyond Exchange: Appraisal Systems in English. In *Evaluation in Text*, edited by S. Hunston and G. Thompson, 142–175. Oxford: Oxford University Press.

McCarthy, Michael. 1998. *Spoken Language and Applied Linguistics*. Cambridge: Cambridge University Press.

McDermott, Ray. 1977. Social Relations as Contexts for Learning in School. *Harvard Educational Review* 47: 198–213.

Miller, Daniel, and Donald Slater. 2000. *The Internet: An Ethnographic Approach*. Oxford: Berg.

Müller-Hartmann, Andreas. 2000. The Role of Tasks in Promoting Intercultural Learning in Electronic Learning Networks. *Language Learning & Technology* 4(2): 129–147. *http://llt.msu.edu/vol4num2/muller/*

O'Dowd, Robert. 2003. Understanding the "Other Side": Intercultural Learning in a Spanish-English E-mail Exchange. *Language Learning & Technology* 7(2): 118–144. *http://llt.msu.edu/vol7num2/odowd/default.html*

———. 2005. Negotiating Sociocultural and Institutional Contexts: The Case of Spanish-American Telecollaboration. *Language and Intercultural Communication* 5(1): 40–56.

O'Dowd, Robert, and Karin Eberbach. 2004. Guides on the Side? Tasks and Challenges for Teachers in Telecollaborative Projects. *ReCALL* 16(1): 129–143.

O'Rourke, Breffni. 2005. Form Focused Interaction in Online Tandem Learning. *CALICO Journal* 22(3): 433–466.

Pennycook, Alistair. 2001. *Critical Applied Linguistics: A Critical Approach*. London: Lawrence Erlbaum.

Presky, Michael. 2001. Digital Natives, Digital Immigrants. *On the Horizon*. NCB University Press, 9(5) (October, 2001).

Rommetveit, Ragner. 1974. *On Message Structure: A Framework for the Study of Language and Communication*. New York: John Wiley & Sons.

Savignon, Sandra. 1983. *Communicative Competence: Theory and Classroom Practice*. Reading, MA: Addison-Wesley.

Sawchuk, Peter. 2003. Informal Learning as a Speech-Exchange System: Implications for Knowledge Production, Power and Social Transformation. *Discourse & Society* 14(3): 291–307.

Schmidt, Richard. 1993. Consciousness, Learning, and Interlanguage Pragmatics. In *Interlanguage Pragmatics*, edited by Gabriele Kasper and Shoshana Blum-Kulka, 21–42. Oxford: Oxford University Press.

Scollon, Ron, and Suzanne Wong Scollon. 2001. *Intercultural Communication: A Discourse Approach*, Second Edition. Oxford: Blackwell.

———. 2004. *Nexus Analysis: Discourse and the Emerging Internet*. New York: Routledge.

Schneider, Jeffrey, and Silke von der Emde. 2000. Brave New (Virtual) World: Transforming Language Learning into Cultural Studies through Online Learning Environments (MOOs). *ADFL Bulletin* 32(1): 18–26.

———. 2005. Conflicts in Cyberspace: From Communication Breakdown to Intercultural Dialogue in Online Collaborations. In *Internet-mediated Intercultural Foreign Language Education*, edited by Julie A. Belz and Steven L. Thorne, 178–206. Boston: Thomson Heinle.

Sercu, Lies. 2004. Intercultural Communicative Competence in Foreign Language Education: Integrating Theory and Practice. In *New Insights into Foreign Language Learning and Teaching*, edited by Oliver St. John, Kees van Esch, and Eus Schalkwijk, 115–130. Frankfurt: Peter Lang.

Swain, Merrill. 1985. Communicative Competence: Some Roles of Comprehensive Input and Comprehensible Output in its Development. In *Input in Second Language Acquisition*, edited by Susan Gass and Carolyn Madden, 235–253. Cambridge, MA: Newbury House Publishers.

Swain, Merrill, and Sharon Lapkin. 1998. Interaction and Second Language Learning: Two Adolescent French Immersion Students Working Together. *The Modern Language Journal* 82(3): 320–337.

Tella, Seppo. 1991. *Introducing International Communications Networks and Electronic Mail into Foreign Language Classrooms: A Case Study in Finnish Senior Secondary Schools*. Helsinki: Yliopistopaino.

Thorne, Steven L. 2000a. Second Language Acquisition Theory and some Truth(s) about Relativity. In *Sociocultural Theory and Second Language Learning*, edited by James Lantolf, 219–243. Oxford: Oxford University Press.

———. 2000b. Beyond Bounded Activity Systems: Heterogeneous Cultures in Instructional Uses of Persistent Conversation. In *The Proceedings of the Thirty-third Hawaii International Conference on Systems Science*. New York: IEEE Press.

———. 2003a. Review of Language and the Internet (David Crystal): The Biggest Language Revolution Ever Meets Applied Linguistics in the 21st Century. *Language Learning & Technology* 7(2): 24–27.

———. 2003b. Artifacts and Cultures-of-Use in Intercultural Communication. *Language Learning & Technology* 7(2): 38–67. *http://llt.msu.edu/vol7num2/thorne/*

———. 2004. Cultural Historical Activity Theory and the Object of Innovation. In *New Insights into Foreign Language Learning and Teaching*, edited by Kees van Esch and Oliver St. John, 51–70. Frankfurt am Main: Peter Lang Verlag.

———. 2005. Epistemology, Politics, and Ethics in Sociocultural Theory. *The Modern Language Journal* 89(3): 393–409.

Thorne, Steven L., and J. Scott Payne. 2005. Evolutionary Trajectories, Internet-Mediated Expression, and Language Education. *CALICO Journal* 22(3): 371–397.

Toyoda, Etsuko, and Richard Harrison. 2002. Categorization of Text Chat Communication Between Learners and Native Speakers of Japanese. *Language Learning & Technology* 6(1): 82–99. *http://llt.msu.edu/vol6num1/TOYODA/*

Train, Robert. 2005. A Critical Look at Technologies and Ideologies in Internet-mediated Intercultural Foreign Language Education. In *Internet-mediated Intercultural Foreign Language Education*, edited by Julie A. Belz and Steven L. Thorne, 245–282. Boston, MA: Thomson Heinle.

Tudini, Enza. 2003. Using Native Speakers in Chat. *Language Learning & Technology* 7(3): 141–159. *http://llt.msu.edu/vol7num3/tudini/*

van Esch, Kees, and Oliver St. John, eds. 2003. *A Framework for Freedom: Learner Autonomy in Foreign Language Teacher Education*. Frankfurt am Main: Peter Lang.

von der Emde, Silke, Jeffrey Schneider, and Markus Kötter. 2001. Technically Speaking: Transforming Language Learning through Virtual Learning Environments (MOOs). *The Modern Language Journal* 85(2): 210–225.

Volosinov, Valentin. 1973. *Marxism and the philosophy of language*. Cambridge: Harvard University Press.

Walther, Joseph. 1992. Interpersonal Effects in Computer-Mediated Interaction: A Relational Perspective. *Communication Research* 19: 52–90.

———. 1996. Computer-Mediated Communication: Impersonal, Interpersonal, and Hyperpersonal Interaction. *Communication Research* 23(1): 3–43.

Ware, Paige. 2005. "Missed" Communication in Online Communication: Tensions in a German-American Telecollaboration. *Language Learning & Technology* 9(2): 64–89. *http://llt.msu.edu/vol9num2/ware/*

Ware, Paige, and Claire Kramsch. 2005. Toward in intercultural stance: Teaching German and English through telecollaboration. *The Modern Language Journal* 89(2): 190–205.

Warschauer, Mark, ed. 1996. *Telecollaboration in Foreign Language Learning*. Honolulu: Second Language Teaching and Curriculum Center.

Acknowledgments

This chapter benefited tremendously from the critiques and comments of colleagues, both known and unknown. In particular, I would like to thank Julie A. Belz and anonymous referees for their extensive feedback, suggestions, and challenges. While any shortcomings are my responsibility alone, many of this chapter's strengths were catalyzed by the perceptive commentaries of others.

Chapter 2
The *Cultura* Project

Beth Bauer
Lynne deBenedette
Gilberte Furstenberg
Sabine Levet
Shoggy Waryn

Abstract

This chapter presents an intercultural project designed at M.I.T. that makes use of Internet communication tools to develop students' understanding of the values and attitudes embedded in a foreign culture. Initially designed for an intermediate French class, Cultura has now been developed in Russian, Spanish, and German and has been used at various levels and institutions across the United States, connecting learners in foreign language classes with students living in France, Germany, Mexico, Russia, and Spain. Written by five faculty members from three different institutions, M.I.T., Brown, and Brandeis, this chapter describes the goals, approach, materials, and methodology of Cultura, and provides a detailed description of the ways in which students construct their understanding of other cultures in electronic interactions. It identifies the challenges of implementing such a project, the roles of learners and teachers, the tools and technologies used, and the issues surrounding assessment. Finally, the chapter presents two detailed case studies, a Russia–U.S. exchange and a Mexico–U.S. exchange, which highlight the challenges of adapting Cultura to new languages, cultures, and institutional settings.

Introduction

Effective curricular innovations never happen simply; they require foreign language (FL) professionals to consider the interaction of course content, theoretical and methodological issues, learning tools (technologies), and institutional realities.[1] In this sense, the challenges—for language program directors as well as for faculty developing projects in the field of computer-mediated intercultural FL education—are considerable. In terms of course content, it is clear that the focus of FL classes, which previously tended to lie on the development of linguistic competence, has expanded to include the study of target cultures in their own right. We see manifestations of this refocusing in the *ACTFL Standards*, which refer specifically to aspects of cultural knowledge, and in textbooks that incorporate more in-depth cultural information. Cultural knowledge and intercultural competence (IC), however, are easier to advocate than define (see Byram 1997). Furthermore, while advances in technology, particularly, web-based tools, seem ideally suited to enhancing international and intercultural dialogue, we must ask how best to use these new resources to ensure deep and sustained exploration of the intricate relationships of language, perspectives, values, and all the many invisible components of culture. The very notion of initiating an online exchange with foreign partners immediately raises a host of questions, ranging from the theoretical (e.g., How does pedagogy interact with technology in such an exchange? How does one teach about culture without reifying it?) to the practical and specific (e.g., How does one find a partner institution and an English language class of an appropriate level for one's own FL students? Can electronic exchanges be implemented in multi-section classes?).

In this chapter, we present *Cultura*, a computer-mediated course that focuses on the promotion of students' understanding of the foreign culture (C2) in an intermediate or advanced (third through sixth semester) university-level FL class. Initially developed for French at M.I.T., *Cultura* has now been used in several languages at Brandeis University, Brown University, Columbia University, Smith College, and the University of California at Berkeley. This chapter deals with *Cultura*'s adoption and use in French, Russian, and Spanish at three institutions (Brandeis, Brown, and M.I.T.) that happen to be fairly exclusive, private universities; yet, as indicated by *Cultura*'s successful implementation in foreign partner institutions of varying types, including technological colleges, Ivy League resources and students are not necessary for this project to be productive. Most important are motivated instructors, institutional support for innovative teaching, and certain technological requirements that will be discussed in this chapter.

As we note at the outset, each of the institutions we discuss uses the components of *Cultura* in different ways and at different levels of instruction. Yet, they all share *Cultura*'s basic configuration: a class of FL students on one of these campuses works with a group of students of English in the target culture (France, Russia, or Mexico), viewing materials in both languages on a shared website and communicating in asynchronous web-based forums in which they analyze and discuss their shared materials. In this chapter we will: (1) explain the project's design and methodology; (2) discuss pedagogical and institutional considerations for the implementation of *Cultura*; and (3) present two case studies involving relatively new versions of the *Cultura* project in Russian and Spanish at Brown University. While language and curricular issues are particularly prominent in the Russian case study, the Spanish language exchange with students in Mexico highlights the radical problematization of the very notion of a single national culture that can take place when students begin to compare their own habits and assumptions with those of foreign partners.

The *Cultura* Project: A Description

Foundation

Cultura was built on the premise that IC needs to become a much larger component of the language curriculum. Considering the globalization of our world, which increasingly leads all students to work and interact with people of many different nationalities and cultures, one of the leading educational priorities at the dawn of this century is indeed to provide our students with the ability to understand the languages, values, and attitudes of other cultures so that they can communicate more effectively across these different cultures, whatever their field or discipline. We, in the FL profession, are in an excellent position to play a very important role in that crucial endeavor because we teach both language and culture.

Too frequently, however, the main focus of language classes is on developing linguistic and communicative competencies. Culture remains at the margins, often reduced to lists of facts or "culture capsules" that give a simplified and stereotyped picture of the other culture. IC is much more than accumulating facts about C2. It is to be found at the intersection of knowledge (of both the home culture [C1] and C2), attitudes, and interpretive or investigative skills. As Byram (1997) notes, attitudes include curiosity and openness, along with a willingness to remain flexible as information accrues and perspectives change; these attitudes go along with the ability to acquire and place in context new information. Interaction with native speakers (NSs) must occur for far deeper reasons than merely "getting information on holidays, celebrations, food, celebrity figures, music and so forth" (Moore, Morales, and Carel 1998, p. 121). To reveal their true value, facts must be examined and interpreted in broader contexts, and this can happen only when students are involved in a dynamic process of inquiry. Therefore, our priority with *Cultura* was to "provide students with the investigatory tools by which they could come to an understanding of the perspectives of speakers of the second language" (Moore, Morales, and Carel 1998, p. 121).

The networking capabilities of the Internet seem ideally suited to an in-depth exploration, as they allow students in C1 and C2 to communicate directly. Computer-mediated communication (CMC) is popularly thought to facilitate immediate and authentic intercultural encounters, which in turn are supposed to make a foreign culture more accessible than ever before (Kramsch and Anderson 1999). Many language classes across the United States currently experiment with student communication (via online forums, chats, or webcams) with their peers in the C2. However, as some studies have shown (e.g., Belz 2003, 2005; Kramsch and Thorne 2002; O'Dowd 2003; Ware 2005), CMC does not necessarily lead to better intercultural understanding. Kern and Warschauer caution that a technological tool "does not in and of itself bring about improvements in learning" (2000, p. 2); success depends on the practices of implementation (Dunkel 1991). Similarly, increased access to C2 text does not necessarily mean students will heed the complex interactions of language and culture that the material contains. It turns out that the productive interactions we wish to foster depend for their success on a complex web of factors.

Approach and Materials

In the following paragraphs, we describe *Cultura* and illustrate how it brings students to understand the cultural attitudes, beliefs, values, and modes of interaction embedded within the other culture and to "look at the universe through the eyes of others," a phrase attributed to Marcel Proust that is quoted on *Cultura*'s main web page. In particular, we describe the approach, the tools, the materials, and the process and then provide a detailed illustration of how students work together in the *Cultura* curriculum.

The Comparative Approach

As the Russian social and cultural theorist Mikhail Bakhtin wrote: "In the realm of culture, outsideness is a most powerful factor in understanding. It is only in the eyes of another culture that a foreign culture reveals itself fully and profoundly. A meaning only reveals its depths once it has encountered and come into contact with another, foreign meaning" (1986, pp. 6–7). The *Cultura* approach is comparative: a closed group made up of two whole classes of language learners in two different countries (e.g., learners of French in the United States and learners of English in France) examine and compare, over a period of four to ten weeks, a variety of visual and textual materials originating from both cultures, presented to them on the Web.

Understanding the inner core of another culture, what Edward Hall calls the "silent language," or the "hidden dimension,"[2] is a long process, akin to a journey on which one amasses pictures, words, impressions, fragments, and ideas, which one then tries to assemble into a coherent whole. In keeping with this notion, the original *Cultura* site has been designed to look like an itinerary with several "stops" that provide different materials for students to explore. *http://web.mit.edu/french/culturaNEH/spring2004_sample_site/index.html*

Recognizing that language is culture, that it "reflects and affects one's world view, serving as a sort of road map to how one perceives, interprets, thinks about, and expresses one's view of the world" (Fantini 2000, p. 27), we decided to have the journey start with students on both sides (anonymously) answering three cross-cultural questionnaires. These include (1) a simple word association that probes such apparently universal notions as freedom, work, family, school, individualism, money; (2) a sentence-completion activity that explores, among other things, relationships and roles (e.g., a good neighbor/parent/teacher is someone who . . .); and (3) a set of situations to which students must respond (e.g., you see a mother in a supermarket slap her child, you see two men holding hands, how do you react?). The last questionnaire is designed to explore different attitudes and interactions with a variety of people (strangers, family members), contexts (private vs. public; personal vs. professional), and situations (school, restaurant, movie theater, supermarket). Questionnaire answers are then collected and posted on the *Cultura* website and become the first set of parallel materials that students analyze as they compare their own answers with those of their C2 partners.

After several weeks, the field of investigation expands to include additional materials[3] such as C1 and C2 national opinion polls on similar topics (data), movies and their American remakes (films), a visual module (images), which is meant to become a bicultural visual dictionary, print media from both cultures (newsstand), and a variety of parallel texts (library). The latter include, in the case of French, foundational texts such as the *Bill of Rights* and the *Déclaration des Droits de l'Homme* "Declaration of the Rights of Man," as well as literary, historical, and anthropological texts in which authors from each culture comment on the other. The last module (Archives) gives access to all questionnaire answers and forums from exchanges occurring as part of the *Cultura* project since 1997 (see section "Archives" for more information).

The Online Forums

The main tools for communication in *Cultura* are the asynchronous online discussion forums that accompany each document and questionnaire answer. The forums serve as the springboard for sharing and debating viewpoints both online and in the classroom. They offer students a critical common space in which to share and verify hypotheses and points of view, to ask for help deciphering meanings of words or concepts, and to constantly negotiate meanings and interpretations.

We made two deliberate decisions with respect to the forums. First, the teacher never interferes and allows students to control the conversations.[4] Second, the students use their native language (L1) (or the language in which their education takes place) for posting messages in the forums. The decision to have all students write in L1 on the forums is an important and frequently misunderstood aspect of *Cultura*. It was based on the following considerations: (1) it eliminates possible dominance by a group or individuals with respect to differing proficiency levels in the foreign language (L2) and puts all students on an equal linguistic footing; (2) it enables students to express their views fully and in detail, formulate questions and hypotheses clearly, and provide complex, nuanced information because they are not bound by limited linguistic abilities; and (3) it enables the creation of student-generated authentic texts, which serve both as L2 input for the foreign partners and new objects of linguistic and cultural analysis. For instance, students on both sides of the Atlantic have discovered that American students tend to take themselves as examples and place themselves in the middle of their discourse when expressing their point of view, whereas the French students tend to make themselves the spokesperson for all French people and set themselves outside their own discourse, through the use of the passive voice, the indefinite third person pronoun, or other impersonal expressions (e.g., such as *il faut savoir que* . . . "it must be known that . . .," *il est important de noter que* . . . "it's important to note that . . ."). As one American student astutely remarked in class one day, the American students will not hesitate to see themselves as the voice of authority, while the French will bring in outside and more objective authoritative voices such as the dictionary or experts' quotes.

Note, however, that students use the L2 exclusively for in-class and writing activities (some exceptions were in Russian). The postings, which are done asynchronously outside of class and on students' own time, do not take anything away from students' "contact time" with the L2; on the contrary, the richness of L2 language input and ideas coming from the foreign partners more than offset what could be first perceived as a disadvantage. In-class work, which is done in L2 only, focuses on the interpretation and discussion of postings (especially if students have had difficulty understanding them). In cases where comprehension of postings is an issue (as it was in Russian), instructors can select particularly difficult or complex postings to be read and clarified in class, in terms of vocabulary, structures, and ideas.

The Process

Students work with the different materials (questionnaires, data, films, newsstand, library) in multiple ways: they first analyze them individually at home, then collectively in class as they share observations with their classmates, using the blackboards as mirrors that reflect their thought processes and discoveries and allow them to see emerging cultural and linguistic patterns. For instance, when looking at the side-by-side definitions of the words individualism/*individualisme*, students will immediately see on their own the differences in the meanings of these two words for the Americans (who associate "individualism" with "freedom" and "independence") and the French (who associate "*individualisme*" with "*égoisme*" or "selfishness"). *http://web.mit.edu/french/culturaNEH/spring2004_sample_site/archives/2000f/answers/individualisme.htm*

  The contrastive analysis of the answers to all the questionnaires generates many observations, allowing both sets of students to discover fundamental cultural differences.[5] Then the students enter the online forums to share perspectives, make hypotheses, and raise questions in the L1. After reading postings, students share insights gained from them in class, and the debate continues both there and in the forums. Re-examination of initial interpretations continues as additional materials from the modules (census data, surveys, news articles, and other texts) are explored and discussed in a reciprocal process of construction. This reflects a decidedly constructivist methodology, in which the emphasis is on student-driven interaction that encourages the development of analytical skills (e.g., classification or hypothesis building). Like cultural archeologists, students dig further, unearth patterns, bring new elements to the surface, and make connections that deepen their understanding of both cultures.

How Students Gradually Construct Understanding of the Other Culture: A Detailed Illustration

The following example illustrates how students in a French-American *Cultura* course (intermediate students at M.I.T. and advanced students at INT) moved from the examination of two words, "freedom" and "*liberté*," to the discovery of related, embedded cultural attitudes. As they examined questionnaire answers, M.I.T. students made several preliminary observations. They noted that both sides tended to associate their own country with the word "freedom" or "*liberté*" and that the associations elicited by "freedom" on the American side tended to highlight unlimited rights and choices, while "*liberté*" was often seen as illusory (*limitée* "limited," *impossible* "impossible," *incertaine* "uncertain"), and seemed to carry with it the idea of limits and boundaries, defined mostly by the presence of others, and as illustrated by words like *autrui* or *les autres* "others."

On the corresponding forum, an M.I.T. student, for whom those differences became obvious, reflected: "For the Americans, liberty is real, for the French it is an ideal, almost too utopian to be achieved. That is interesting. Also the basis of the United States is freedom—individual freedom. Whereas for the French equality and community are also important. . . ." Another M.I.T. student chimed in, wanting to understand more: "Why do you feel that liberty and freedom are such illusions? I believe, in the United States, we definitely have certain very important freedoms and liberties. Is it because you interpret the word liberty differently from us? Does it have a more general and community minded meaning, unlike here, where we think of personal liberties?" Olivier, a French student, provided an explanation (translation):[6]

> I think that many French people, when they hear about freedom in the United States, think, for instance, about the right to bear arms. But one can wonder: is freedom to . . . get killed still freedom? In fact, I think that the French have become (too) cynical and "disillusioned" towards words such as freedom, the meaning of which seems to be more and more empty. On the other hand, Americans stay (too) attached to these values and perhaps do not criticize them enough. Freedom can be seen as a rather utopian idea, but it has indisputable concrete manifestations.

That comment elicited many class discussions at M.I.T. (conducted in simple but functional French). Students discovered how skeptically the French seem to view the all-encompassing American notion of freedom (including, for example, the freedom "to get killed," a swipe at what the French see as lax gun control laws). This led to a group discussion on the American concept of freedom, which encompassed the following questions: Is there such a thing as absolute freedom? What about the apparent contradictions reflected in U.S. practices, such as prohibiting the consumption of alcohol until age 21, but allowing gun purchase at age 18? Students also noticed that Olivier described the French as too "cynical" or "disillusioned" and Americans as "perhaps not critical enough." In their view, this suggested a sense of French pride about their own critical faculties. Students also remarked on Olivier's use of expressions like "I think," "one can wonder," "perhaps," "seem," as well as his enclosure of "too" in parentheses, which appeared remarkably diplomatic when compared to most of his classmates, who did not hesitate to make blunt statements about the United States.

This example illustrates how a single participant's comment can lead students to discover several embedded cultural assumptions and to reflect on the particularities of both cultures. On the U.S. side in particular, self-reflection and discovery are enriched by the presence in the classroom of foreign students who bring new cultural paradigms to the discussion and are sometimes better able to point out what they see as contradictions. But the process does not stop there. As students continue working with other questionnaires, they gradually begin to see confirmation of a tendency by their French counterparts to want to set limits. They found a hidden link, for instance, between the "limits" associated with *"liberté"* and those imposed on a child. In a forum about a mother in a supermarket who slaps her child (where the U.S. students and the French responded in radically different manners—U.S. students blaming the mother, French students assuming the child deserved the slap), one French student wrote (translation) that "one needs limits, otherwise it is anarchy," thus highlighting in this new context the apparent yearning by the French for limits, order, and harmony.

Building on the work done with the questionnaires, the modular materials on the website further enabled students' nuanced consideration of "freedom" and "*liberté*." For example, in a national opinion poll on *Les Français et leur cadre de vie* "The French and their Lifestyle" (*http://www.tns-sofres.com/etudes/pol/151203_qualitevie_r.htm*), the French are asked what determines quality of life. The first item to appear is *argent* or "money" (45% of French people cite it as the main factor), whereas *liberté/indépendance/autonomie* "liberty/independence/autonomy" rally only 2% of French responses. This poll then returned M.I.T. students to observations they had made in analyses of the questionnaire answers and the subsequent forums about "money" and "*argent*," in which they had observed that money did not seem very important to the French and that "*liberté*" (which the French had often equated with their country) now seemed relatively unimportant (or perhaps just taken for granted). Contradictions were then debated in class and re-examined in light of the French students' responses.

The same topic of freedom emerged at the end of the students' journey as they read the *Déclaration des Droits de l'Homme* (comparing it with the *Bill of Rights*), and found, in Article 4, the definition of "*liberté*." That reading prompted an M.I.T. student to remark in a forum:

> In article 4 of the French bill of rights it says that liberty is being able to do all that does not harm others. This is different from America where we are given certain rights whether or not they affect others (free speech, freedom of the press, right to bear arms, freedom of association). This reminds me of when the French government sued yahoo.com for offering Nazi memorabilia on its auctions website. In France I guess it is illegal to sell anything having to do with the Nazis. This law seems ridiculous to most Americans. What are your opinions on those types of laws and that case in particular?

Two French students responded to this question, one saying that, on the contrary, he finds it "completely normal to set limits to this kind of propaganda," which he finds "dangerous," the other adding, in regard to the *Yahoo* site, that "it is inconceivable in France to hear or see such racist or xenophobic comments. People would be immediately shocked by such an attitude. I approve of such laws because they prevent succumbing to a climate of violence and racism." That perspective was supported by yet another French student who wrote (translation):

> I think it is normal for the government to want to ban the selling or purchase of Nazi objects. They carry an anti-democratic ideology which promotes inequality. I am surprised in fact that the concept of freedom in the United States is defined as unalienable rights (freedom of press and of speech) since in the Yahoo case, this encourages Nazi groups to express themselves publicly, but when a group of people declare themselves opposed to human rights and they want to propagate those ideas, it seems normal to me to forbid them from spreading that type of ideology.

In-depth analysis of this last comment in class discussion highlighted French tendencies to (1) accept and even desire the limitation of certain freedoms; (2) emphasize the principle of "equality" (as the foundation of democracy); (3) accept the government's role in limiting rights; and (4) insist on what they consider to be "normal," implying that there are norms or limits to be respected (something M.I.T. students associated with French students' frequent use of such expressions as "it is important that . . ."; "it is necessary . . ."; "one must not . . ."). The apparent French tendency to avoid extremes or excess and accept constraints and limits was revealed to our students in other contexts as well, whenever the French website materials stressed respecting conventions and rules imposed by society (Levet and Furstenberg 2002).

As they work their way through questionnaires and additional materials, students are never asked to draw final conclusions based on any single comment or reading. Instead, they are encouraged to avoid stereotyping and urged to keep questioning their partners about the validity of their findings, to verify their hypotheses, and to make connections between documents, looking for either confirmation or contradiction, as they try to "put the cultural puzzle together" (Furstenberg 2003, p. 118). The very process in which students are involved requires them to keep suspending their judgments and to be ready to revise them, question them, expand them, and refine them in the light of new materials and new perspectives. Our hope is that students' work proceeds along the lines described by Simone de Beauvoir, who wrote the following about her journeys to the United States in the preface of her memoirs: "I want to make it very clear that no isolated piece constitutes a definitive judgment: in fact I often do not end with any final viewpoint (*point de vue arrêté*). It is the sum of my indecisions, my additions and rectifications which constitutes my opinion" (1947, p. 10)

Implementation: Lessons Learned

Cultura has been used for more than nine years in a variety of academic settings in versions that have lasted different numbers of weeks. Faced with diverging academic calendars and multiple technological and pedagogical challenges, we have developed a set of recommended practices and implementation guidelines. In this section, we address some of the most frequently asked questions about practical aspects of implementing *Cultura* and illustrate them with examples whenever applicable.

Working with Partners

The key to successful implementation of *Cultura* in any linguistic environment is identifying effective collaborators. At the local level, it helps to work with language faculty—in the same or different departments—who are already using or considering adopting *Cultura*, or to contact users at other universities to share information. Internationally, it is essential to find the right partner instructor (through study abroad, departmental exchanges, or personal connections) and workable institutional conditions. Partner instructors must be willing to devote time to coping with challenges and be good at planning in advance. It is entirely possible that the partners' courses will have dissimilar goals and structures, and their only point of pedagogical intersection will be *Cultura* itself. It helps if one or both partners can secure some funding that would enable faculty to meet face-to-face. If this cannot occur, constant, detailed electronic communication is essential. Faculty are no more immune than students to cultural misunderstandings (see Belz and Müller-Hartmann 2003); classroom cultures can differ so radically from one country to the next that partner instructors must be clear about how they will handle even putatively simple activities such as the analysis of questionnaire answers. This is not to suggest that the classroom culture of one particular institution must become something it is not, but both instructors must be aware of the realities of each other's environment.

Calendars and Scheduling

As a crucial first step, interested partner faculty should establish a reasonable schedule for implementing different aspects of the exchange. *Cultura*, which can be used over an entire semester as the sole course content, requires anywhere from three to six weeks of in-class time just for analysis of questionnaires and forum discussion. In addition, before the start of actual classroom work on *Cultura*, there must be enough time for students to complete questionnaires outside of class and for instructors to collect, process, and post the answers on the web (this takes approximately two weeks). Filling out a questionnaire takes only 30 minutes at most, but it is best to give students at least a week to complete it, given varying access to computers. Because of differences in academic calendars, the pace of the project deserves careful attention. Yearlong courses (in which students may have a semester break but remain in the same groups with the same instructor for an entire year) are the norm in some countries, with later starting dates than in the United States. Frequently, breaks are organized around different holidays. Partner teachers need to work together on scheduling to minimize long periods of silence in the discussion forums, and need to be sure students know when the other university will be on break, so no one becomes worried or insulted by a lull on the forums.

Culturally contingent aspects of technology use such as student access to and familiarity with computers (see Belz 2001 pp. 225–227) and cultural perceptions of appropriate workload as well as different ideas about the "work week" (weekends) also influence scheduling. At INT in France, students had access to computers everywhere on campus, including in the dorms, but preferred to wait until class time to post or read messages (as shown by computer-generated time stamps). In contrast, U.S. students tended to send messages in the middle of the night or over the weekend, and came to class with hardcopies of relevant postings. These different behaviors need to be taken into account when drawing up the schedule because they affect how students will work with material and how long certain tasks will take.

Teacher and Learner Roles

Cultura's highly interactive environment influences the roles of teachers and learners. From the beginning, students are at the center of the process of inquiry. Their own answers to the online questionnaires are the first documents they analyze;

the online discussions generated by their reactions to them become, in turn, the raw material for class discussions; they choose the forums in which they partici-pate and navigate both discussions and other readings in various ways. Both online and in the classroom, each contribution by any member of the group can refocus the discussion in a collaborative construction between individuals and groups. Learners' analytical skills, notably their ability to summarize, evaluate, and react to others' comments, are honed as they move from classroom to forums and back again. The expectation that students will engage in these activities requires that instructors are capable of facilitating them (O'Dowd and Eberbach 2004). It is no exaggeration to state that the work done by teachers is absolutely crucial to the success of any *Cultura* project for more than mere logistical reasons (important as those are). Teachers encourage students to bring together different interpretations to their work, to reflect on them, and to try to make sense of the often contradictory viewpoints embodied in their partners' comments. Importantly, they must sensitize students to the requirements of intercultural learning (O'Dowd and Eberbach 2004), and be ready to become learners them-selves (Belz and Müller-Hartmann 2003), not only studying the two cultures involved in the exchange, but also re-evaluating their own intercultural awareness and learning as much as possible about telecollaboration and how it can facilitate intercultural learning. This does not mean that a teacher must be or become a computer whiz; rather, she or he must be ready to reconsider assumptions about learning and teaching as work on the exchange progresses.

What do these requirements mean for classroom practice? Teachers must make sure that students are given clear instructions on how to do their research before coming to class. In class, students usually work in small groups to discuss their findings (e.g., people who have all analyzed the same words, or groups where no two people have analyzed the same words). The instructor must ensure that the discussions remain on-topic and should ask students to support their analyses and hypotheses with direct quotes and examples taken from their particular materials. We encourage students to record their observations on the board, look at what others have written, ask one another questions, and find connections or contra-dictions between different items contributed by different groups. The teacher does not provide students with answers, but instead encourages students to investigate and hypothesize. Ideally, students will develop an argument and base it on a con-crete text (from the forums, questionnaires, polls, or readings) or other authentic C1/C2 material (images, advertisements, films).

In this environment, the teacher is no longer the sole purveyor of cultural information. We recognize that for some instructors this prospect can appear to "remove" teachers from the equation, their role as "authority figures" taken over by NS student informants in the partner group. Note, however, that the availabil-ity of these informants is a resource for teachers as much as for students; it frees instructors from the responsibility of having all the answers. In *Cultura*, students, teachers, and NSs from the C2 all help construct meanings. "Constructivism," as Kaufman points out, "is open-ended and allows for ambiguity, flexibility, and inno-vative thinking" (2004, p. 303). Note, however, that if *Cultura* is to create a flexible, open-ended learning environment, it is only through very precise statements of goals and tasks on the part of the instructor that this can occur. Equally important is that students be encouraged to notice both connections and contradictions among topics as individual and group analyses unfold. This process is illustrated by the following posting on the forum about a good neighbor by a U.S. student at Brandeis University during fall 2002. In this example, the student refers to aspects of French and U.S. American culture that he has noted previously in other forums and questionnaire answers:

> I find it interesting that French responses to the word "community" and "a good neighbor" emphasize a sort of respect for individualism. This is especially paradoxical since French typically see themselves as less individualistic and more socialistic than Americans. And Americans, typically considered lovers of individualism, seem to have a stronger predilection for community life. Is part of the explanation that French look to the national level to express their sense of community, while the American view is more local and personal?

Such questions are then posed and debated both in the forums and in the classroom as a means of broadening the cultural dialogue.

Technological Support and Institutional Constraints

Before detailing the technological issues that accompanied our use of *Cultura*, we emphasize that the success or failure of *Cultura* depends much more on effective faculty collaboration and well-planned classroom interaction than on the technology itself. Nevertheless, there are a number of issues relating to technology that potential users should consider before implementing an Internet-mediated exchange.

The current availability of course management software (CMS) like *WebCT* and *Blackboard* for the creation of classroom websites has facilitated the adoption of *Cultura* by other schools because these technologies simplify the creation and navigation of Web pages and obviate the need for external discussion software. Templates of *Cultura*'s modules in CMS-compatible format have been developed in French, Russian, and Spanish. However, it is important to note that *Cultura* is not dependent on a specific technology; the original project was developed in simple HTML as no more than a large stack of web pages. The data from the questionnaires were collected via e-mail and copied into the pages, and discussion forums relied on software available at the time. Although the technology has evolved, the need for technical support has not decreased. One of the partner schools hosts and supports the website with technological help from computing support staff or language laboratory personnel (to date the U.S. institution has always been the host). The host institution sets up the website (e.g., posts answers, updates the pages); participants at the partner institution simply log onto that server from their location. The key is to support both groups and anticipate potential problems via thorough troubleshooting.

The ups and downs of adapting and supporting *Cultura* in different technological environments are illustrated by the Russian-American partnership between Brown University and the University of Petrozavodsk. Nearly all users on both sides had no problem seeing Cyrillic at their individual sites, although U.S. students needed instructions on how to activate the Russian keyboard on their machines, and the one or two students using older Macintoshes reported some trouble. A few students in Russia had not used the Internet much; some had trouble with basics like navigating their way around a website and submitting questionnaires, despite training sessions in the computer lab. One pleasant surprise for the Russians was access to a password-protected site that recognized them. All were delighted that they were not only able to log on, but that they were already "in" the system and thus valid participants. In Petrozavodsk, there was a computer lab to which students were brought once a week. In this way, everyone was guaranteed access to the site at least once before every class. However, they were not permitted to print out questionnaire answers and postings (nor was the instructor allowed to use the departmental printer for this purpose). As a result, the students in Russia had to either to take notes from the forums or work from memory during class discussions. Both instructors were aware of these difficulties in advance because they had met with instructional technology staff at Petrozavodsk, and they therefore planned accordingly to mitigate any potential negative influences on in-class work.

The Russian example demonstrates that the exchange can work even when there is a technological mismatch between partner institutions. However, we must consider whether there are any inherent institutional constraints (other than basic access to technology) that might hinder the implementation of *Cultura* in particular educational settings. In short, does it matter whether students are from an urban Ivy League university or a small college? What about students at a large and rurally situated public university, or students from an urban community college? For us the answer lies in the work that faculty must do with students during and in advance of the exchange, if the project is to proceed successfully. Program directors and teachers considering adopting *Cultura* work within a range of educational environments and with student populations whose sense of their national identity and its culture may vary widely. In particular, many student populations may be less receptive to foreign peers' challenges to their views about the unique value of their own cultures and the actions of their national governments. Even where such resistance may be insignificant, it is important to preface the *Cultura* exchange with classroom discussions and activities designed to encourage awareness of the culturally bound nature of perceptions and values. The teachers' manual on the *Cultura* website (*http://web.mit.edu/french/ culturaNEH/guide/index.html*) offers a variety of suggestions.

Tools

There are currently many tools at our disposal such as e-mail, chats, picture websites, webcams, and videoconferencing for facilitating intercultural exchanges. Although many of these tools are used successfully in other intercultural exchanges (see O'Dowd, this volume, for videoconferencing), we decided very early on to concentrate on the use of asynchronous online discussion forums in *Cultura* because they seemed to be the most apt at allowing students to exchange in-depth reflections and to carefully formulate their thoughts. Over the course of the exchange, we have noted that students begin to see foreign interlocutors as individuals and to address and refer to one another by name (rather than as a group).

The fall 2002 exchange between a seventh-semester French culture class at Brown University and an English language class at INT demonstrates how students use the *Cultura* discussion part of the website. While students were roughly the same age and in the same year at the university, the declared goals of the two classes and their schedules were dissimilar. In the United States, the course lasted 15 weeks and met three times a week with *Cultura* as its core component; in France, *Cultura* was used only once a week for six weeks as part of a larger English writing curriculum. Given this arrangement, one would expect the French students to be less engaged in the project than their U.S. counterparts, yet, as the following table suggests, students' use of discussion forums largely made up for the difference in classroom contact time.

Table 1

Quantitative Overview of Message Postings and Readings in Fall 2002 (Brown/INT)[7]

	Total Messages	Lowest per Student	Highest per Student	Combined Semester Average	French Average/ Student	U.S. Average/ Student
Hits		39	671	303	275	452
Read Messages	538	21	523	251	208	310
Written Messages	538	1	46	18	24	13

From Table 1, we observe that while the French students (who had the tighter schedule) visited the site less often over the course of the semester (275 times versus 452 times on average), they compensated by posting more messages (24 per student) than their American counterparts (18 per student). Exchange conditions account for this variation to some extent because the French students tended to concentrate their web activities in smaller periods of time during the week and read and answered as many messages as possible in one sitting. The U.S. students, who had more class meetings, tended to read postings (old and new) several times and participate in only some of the forums.[8] Students exhibited a range of approaches to using the website. For example, one student read 21 messages following a single discussion thread that she had originated, while another read almost all messages (523 out of a possible 538). Because they are asynchronous, the forums accommodate the often significant differences in educational environment between the two partner schools. Furthermore, they serve as the principal source and catalyst of student investigation.

As fruitful as the forums have proven to be, we felt images would allow students to explain (and visualize) more clearly their respective institutional and cultural realities. In spring 2004, students from M.I.T. and Paris II chose to illustrate their daily lives with images that they uploaded to the website, attaching comments to both their own and others' photos. In those photo albums, just like in the online forums, the students are entirely in charge of the content.

These images have added an important dimension to the students' learning. For example, the juxtaposition of photos of a French *banlieue* and an American suburb immediately illustrate the divergent socio-cultural realities lurking behind those words. They also serve to aptly illuminate the different realities of the students' respective lives. An album titled "The daily life of a student at M.I.T. and Paris II," was very revealing in this regard. To illustrate, an M.I.T. student's photo of a food truck prompted a Paris II student to raise the issue of hygiene (putting on its head the clichéd notion that the French do not care about hygiene) and to send, in return, a picture of the whole French class standing in front of a beautiful *boulanger-pâtissier* "bakery-pastery shop" in which one could see an appetizing display of quiches, sandwiches, and tarts. Such photos not only helped to bring to life specific aspects of the students daily routines, but they also became yet another object of cultural analysis just like the postings in the online discussion forums. While examining the content of the images, the M.I.T. students started to reflect on the overall image that the French were projecting of themselves and came up with very interesting interpretations. They saw, for instance, that French students had chosen to show mostly exterior and formal views of their lives (as opposed to their own photos, which depicted more personal and intimate views such as the interior of a dorm room or a student sleeping in a chair). They then made a link between the images chosen by the French students and their discourse on the discussion forums, which again tended to be more formal and to present a more "objective" point of view. Such comments are proof for us that participation in *Cultura* enabled students to look beyond the surface and to uncover hidden cultural perspectives.

Interacting via images has proved to be very popular. A survey of students at the end of the spring 2004 semester revealed that both the M.I.T. and Paris II students chose the online forum photo projects as their favorite elements of the course. With two exceptions (from 12 responses posted) M.I.T. students said such things as: "it was great to see how different/similar life is in the different countries" and "pictures can illustrate concepts better than words." The French students' reactions echoed those of their M.I.T. counterparts: "we really have the impression (*la sensation*) we've shared something with the American students" and "it was great to see the environment and differences concretely."

Archives

All French–American exchanges since 1997 have been archived at the *Cultura* website (*http://web.mit.edu/french/culturaNEH/spring2004_sample_site/index_arch.htm*). When it is not practical or possible to create a live exchange with a partner school in a foreign country or when multi-section courses make such exchanges difficult to implement, archives of previous exchanges can offer a rich source of cultural and linguistic material for intercultural explorations. In fall 2003, a French class at Brandeis University took advantage of the archived materials and created its own experiment.

As in the live situation, the comparative approach remains central to the process. Therefore, students answer the questionnaires (individually and anonymously) so that they may compare their responses with previously posted responses in the archives. This process gives them a sense of their own collectively held views and decreases the risk that they might dismiss archived C1 responses as the product of a U.S. American subculture other than their own. At this point, the process diverges from what would occur in a live exchange. Instead of engaging in an online discussion with their foreign keypals, students read archived forums and look for answers to their questions. It is possible to create a discussion forum for the entire class where students post their own comments as well as reactions to classmates' comments. In this case, students use the target language because participation in such a forum is seen as an extension of class meetings. Because the French archives now extend over many years (with other languages to be added in 2005), students can track a particular concept (e.g., freedom) over time to see if there has been a change in attitudes toward that concept or, as in the live version of the exchange, use the modules (data, library, newsstand) to examine a concept in different contexts. Finally, an instructor may decide to use some of the archived materials in other classes, for instance, responses to the word *banlieue*/suburbs in a beginning French class.

Assessment

Because *Cultura* can be used in a variety of settings, assessment criteria must be clearly defined for students. While CMS tools allow us to track how students use the website, this information should be used primarily for evaluating the effectiveness and flow of the project rather than grading individual students. Note, however, that because CMS makes tracking easy, students can be reminded individually if they are not spending enough time on the site. Assessment of student work, however, is based not on the quantity of postings (there is no mandated number), but on participation in classroom discussion, individual written analyses, class presentations, longer final essays (or other final projects) in the L2, and on their active participation in the forums. Successful completion of the latter requires that students spend considerable time with website materials.

Because different students read different postings and concentrate on different issues, they often follow very different developmental paths in the course. It is therefore important that students map out for themselves and the instructor the trajectory of their investigation over the course of the semester. For that reason, we ask them to record their itinerary in what the French version refers to as a *carnet de bord*, i.e. a journal of their progress. In it they record interesting points of in-class discussions; list questions they have asked, in class and in the forums; paste in forum answers to their questions; and note important or confusing observations made on the forums, highlighting contradictions. Complete *carnets de bord* reflect both the "itineraries" of individual students and their process of reflection and analysis. Additional assignments include L2 essays, in which students explore connections between different concepts they have studied (e.g., family and home), basing their analyses on specific examples from questionnaires, forums, class discussions, or other modules. At the end of the semester, students can work on a final project for which they compare different sets of corresponding C1/C2 documents such as television newscasts, advertisements, newspapers, or websites of one multinational firm.

Two Case Studies: Russian and Spanish

Russian: Logistics and Language

In adapting *Cultura* for a Russian course at *Brown University*, we faced a number of logistical issues, which included class size, project duration, and instructor workloads. The first issue involved matching class size between Russia and the United States. Because English is a popular FL in Russia, classes tend to be large (20 to 25 students). In contrast, fifth semester Russian classes at Brown typically have no more than 12 students. In 2002, the fifth-semester group was unusually small with only six students. As a result, questionnaires were filled out by students in both the third- and fifth-semester courses. Students in Russia attend classes in more or less the same small group for all five years of their undergraduate experience. Therefore, they did not understand why their exchange would last for only one semester and viewed the prospect of losing it during the second semester as a deprivation. As a result, the Russian–American exchange was spread out over two semesters. Another factor that contributed to this scheduling decision was the fact that it took longer for students of Russian to comprehend forum postings.

There were additional institutional differences that affected both faculty and student work. Most language instructors in Russia have a larger course load than instructors in the United States—20 contact hours per week is common—and thus relatively less time to devote to preparation. Furthermore, Russian university FL instruction splits classes by modality (conversation, reading, writing are all dealt with by separate teachers in independent courses). Cultural differences connected with the use of the Internet affected the online forums as soon as certain topics were raised and discussion became more frank.[10] Soon after forum discussion began, some of the Russians asked if they could post anonymously or take a nickname that would mask their identity. When queried about the reason for this, they indicated discomfort with the fact that "other people" (possibly the instructors) had access to their personal opinions.

One of *Cultura's* central design features, the use of the L1 in the forums, was an obvious plus, since it meant that differences in the relative language proficiency of the two groups would not play a significant (possibly intrusive) role in determining the success of the project. In terms of contact hours needed to reach "professional" or "superior" proficiency, the U.S. *Interagency Linguistic Roundtable* (ILR) and *The American Council on the Teaching of Foreign Languages* (ACTFL) both describe Russian as requiring more than 1000 contact hours to reach that level. The suggested time to equivalent proficiency in French or Spanish is just over half that number of hours. The typical fifth-semester student of Russian has experienced only about 260 classroom contact hours. Students of English at Russian universities usually study English in secondary school for anywhere from three to six years before continuing instruction at the university level. In addition, young people in Russia are exposed to English outside the classroom through texts of popular songs and the Internet. On the contrary, most U.S. students of Russian first come into contact with the language and culture at the university level. Thus, for the U.S. students of Russian the discrepancy in proficiency is effectively larger than in the case of French and Spanish.

Although instructors attempted to equalize the linguistic "power relationship" between the two groups with respect to production through the use of the L1 in the forums, the U.S. students were nevertheless hampered by their reading proficiency in Russian. The biggest challenge for U.S. students of Russian is their inability to read Russian at a rate that facilitates the types of deep intercultural exchanges made possible by *Cultura*. NSs of English reading Russian must cope with a huge amount of unfamiliar vocabulary (because the student typically is not acquainted with Slavic roots), syntax (common use of impersonal expressions with and without dative case subjects, for example), and relatively flexible word order where adjectives can be separated from nouns and verbs can occur before subjects. For these reasons, fifth-semester students of Russian have relatively limited experience with texts of any length (more than one to two pages) or complexity. A look at common Russian language textbooks reveals that students may have read short or condensed newspaper articles, examples of schedules and announcements, poems and songs, short excerpts from longer works of fiction (less than five pages), interviews with or letters from NSs, or short stories.[11] Texts tend to be heavily didacticized, both to facilitate basic comprehension and to provide scaffolding that enables class discussion to occur in the L2. In the case of the questionnaire answers, it was common for both the second- and third-year students to have to look up as much as 50% of the vocabulary in the Russian answers, and students reported that reading even one short forum posting carefully (which occurs outside of class as homework) could take more than an hour. On a course evaluation form, one second-year student reported her enjoyment of the project, but added that reading one of the smaller forum postings (100 words) had taken her 90 minutes. Especially in the second-year class, students admitted they sometimes chose postings because of their length.[12] Moreover, the pedagogy associated with the French version of the project assumes that students are able to express a range of attitudinal responses in the L2 during classroom discussions including surprise, doubt, agreement/disagreement. Even in a program that attends to developing conversation management strategies, a fifth-semester student of Russian lacks control of the syntax required for successful use of some of these expressions as well as the connectors necessary to give detailed and coherent explanations. Finally, the process of checking hypotheses using outside sources or modules requires students to navigate large chunks of L2 text that is frequently written in styles very different from anything seen previously.

Thus, it was clear from the start that some important components of *Cultura*'s methodology (notably the extent to which student choice of topics drives both individual and classroom activities) would take a back seat to language issues, which, in turn, would require substantive curricular changes for the exchange to be productive. U.S. students in the French and Spanish exchanges generally did not have global comprehension problems, whereas this was a constant concern with Russian. Solutions included: (1) reducing the number of items in the questionnaires; (2) assigning students specific questionnaire answers—and, subsequently, forum postings—to read at home in preparation for class discussion of them, rather than allowing every student free choice of what to read and talk about in class; (3) providing glossaries and reading guides for some of the more difficult forum postings; and (4) tailoring weekly logbook (journal) activities to materials discussed.

Why was *Cultura* used in third- and fifth-semester Russian courses rather than seventh- and eighth-semester courses, if there are so many language related issues? The *raison-d'être* for *Cultura* is that it gives those students who have not studied abroad access to a greater range of texts and to the diversity of viewpoints occurring within the target culture than they might otherwise encounter in instructed learning. Not every university has a fourth-year Russian language course. It is those second- and third-year students, many of whom do not ever plan to study in Russia, who can benefit the most from the project, assuming that the linguistic difficulties can be overcome.[13] After two years at Brown, it was felt that the exchange, while workable in the second year in a limited way, is much better suited to fifth- or sixth-semester Russian.

Work on the project caused many students to think critically about how meaning is constructed in both Russian and English. This reflection extended to changing the way they thought about linguistic features that could easily have been just so much grammar. For example, a 2003 discussion of the words "friend" and "*drug*" centered on definitions given by seven U.S. students, which involved "love" or "lover." Petrozavodsk students expressed surprise at the number of U.S. mentions of "love," which they translated as the Russian noun *liubov* rather than the verb *liubit* "to love" because it lacked the infinitive marker "to." The U.S. students, who had not anticipated that this difference in these forms could result in misunderstanding, explained that one loves one's friends: "the type of emotion that is linked to these words is hard to divide." Katya, a student from Russia, responded in the following way (translation): "I can't agree that friendship and love are the same thing . . . love, in my understanding, is something different." Her response caused another U.S. student to remind the forum that

> both terms, at least in English, have huge ranges of meanings. I can befriend someone at first meeting, but I have friends that are closer to me than family. Likewise, love is a flexible word. I love my mom and I love chocolate cake and I love that new song I heard on the radio.

Katya's answer reflected that

> in fact it's all a matter of the words (you choose). The word "love" (ljubov) in Russian is associated more with relations between men and women. ☺ It was nice to find out about your associations with that word. Thanks.

In class discussion, and again in a final paper written in Russian, Brian, an American student of Russian, noticed how pragmatics might figure in the different opinions expressed (translation):

> I was surprised that Russians and Americans could talk so long about the various meanings of words like family, friend, and happiness. I thought those words would mean similar things the world over. In the forums we talked a lot about the association between friendship and love.... In my opinion, Jeremy was correct [about friendship and love being hard to divide], but the Russian students didn't think so. However, then I read the next posting and understood. Russians can say, "I love," [using a verb] but the **noun** "love" can be used only about relations between men and women.... It really is all a matter of the words you choose (my new favorite phrase).

Language issues affected work even on linguistically "simpler" content, as the following example illustrates. It is explained in most first-year Russian textbooks that *shkola* "school" denotes only primary or secondary school, never university. Students on both sides of the exchange noticed huge differences in the answers to questionnaire item school/*shkola*. On the U.S. side, the words "Brown University" figured prominently, along with stress-related concepts like "deadline," "exhaustion," and "lack of sleep." The Russian answers, e.g, "childhood," "friends," "lessons," "dependency," "mischief-making," and "[school]bells," were clearly from a different world, but students on both sides were slow to hit upon the reason. A skeptic could argue that it would have been easy enough for the teacher to "give the answer" by reminding them of the cultural note on this subject from their first year textbook. Doing so, however, would have deprived students of the experience that followed, in which they not only found out "the answer," but also discovered some of its social and linguistic implications. The first forum questions from Julia in Petrozavodsk in 2002 were (translation): "Why do you associate the time you spent in school with hard work every day? Do you really have no bright memories at all? What about your friends?" American Sara answered that "we do have friends and fun in school," and that "we use the word school to describe school work." Several Brown students in 2003 explained that they had written "Brown" thinking school was a demographic question, not a word association (it was the first item on the list); that this response only confirmed the difference in semantic networks escaped them. In both years, several more postings were required for the linguistic and social implications of the "culture capsule" factoid to become clearer. Answering the eventual question from Nina at Brown about why no Russian had written a university name, Julia answered bluntly but in detail (translation):

> because university is university, and school—is school. We start school at the age of seven (at that point we're children). In school we acquire our first skills, the necessary knowledge for continuing our studies at university, it's in fact in school that we make our good friends and learn to understand life. At university we learn how to be specialists in various areas of study, while in school we learn only the basics and don't go deeply into the details. It's in fact after finishing "univer" that you can get a job.

This posting provided material for different kinds of in-class analyses. Linguistically, it illustrated certain kinds of discourse markers typical of comparison such as the fact that the use of the conjunction *a* "whereas" rather than *i* "and" indicates a contrast. The content of the response gave students a linguistic "leg up" in order to compare Julia's experience with their own, both individually and nationally. Neither of these things would have happened if the teacher had cut the exchange off with a quick reminder of the difference between "school" and "university" in Russian. There was disagreement among U.S. students about how Nina's description tallied with their own conceptions; they did not seem to expect their own experience to be universal, but as school/*shkola* was further discussed, they were surprised by specific differences within their own culture. In 2002, a Brown student from Lithuania responded to Julia, asking about school bells and September 1st (the traditional first day of the academic year), which he had experienced in his post-Soviet homeland much as she had: "We were discussing in class whether these have emotional associations?" Nina's detailed answer, which described such rituals of September 1st as the *linjejka* or "line" (the opening school ceremonies) made it plain that *shkola* is more than "not university." Nina related images of first-graders reciting poems dedicated to the school and their teachers and the older children leading the newest arrivals to their first classes, and recalled being in that position herself ten years earlier.

Eventually class discussion brought out that Russian pupils in a grade are divided into groups in which they remain throughout their schooling, taking nearly all subjects for years with the same set of people. Such knowledge of C2 does not necessarily equal tolerance for or sympathy with it, as some U.S. students' horrified reactions to this detail made clear ("six years with the SAME PEOPLE??!!"). However, discussion did not end there; U.S. students from small towns or who attended small private schools commented that the grouping concept was familiar to them. Those who had been schooled outside the United States in similar arrangements pointed out what to them were virtues of the system in Russia (stability, "better" friends). In class, several students recalled hearing Russian acquaintances or teachers say that friendships in Russia were "stronger" than in the United States. Thus, students saw not only the "hidden" implications of cultural facts, but also the complex interaction between individual and group conceptions of common "American" culture.

None of the discussion of Nina's posting could have taken place without significant preparatory work on comprehension. Several students came to class on the day it was assigned irritated that Nina appeared to think them too dumb to understand that people make friends in grade school and that 7-year-olds are children. An analysis of their reading revealed they had not heeded her use of the adverb *imenno* "precisely, in fact," which indicated that her statement was meant to differentiate *shkola* and *universitet*, not simply state that schoolchildren make friends, or that the parenthetical "at that point we're children" was meant to set up an association of *deti* "children" with *shkola* and—by analogy—*vzroslye* "adults" with *universitet*.

The design of some of the *Cultura* tasks facilitates a focus on particular grammatical forms such as the use of the perfective future, e.g., *skazhu* "I'll say," *pozvoniu* "I'll call," *otvechu* "I'll answer," and *dam* "I'll give."[14] Analysis of forum postings also leads to the study of the different ways of expressing opinions, agreement, disagreement, or surprise. Depending on the language, this can involve work on impersonal constructions, preposition/case use with the intransitive verbs used to express emotions, the use of the indicative versus the subjunctive, and frequently used connectors and rhetorical devices. Particularly difficult postings are analyzed in class to elucidate troubling lexicon and grammatical structures. Students are asked to keep a list of difficulties in their logbooks or journals as they encounter them.

Users of *Cultura* have observed that our students begin to imitate the discourse of the C2 in their writing. In their French essays, for example, the U.S. students tend to reproduce the structured discourse of their French-speaking counterparts by using such phrases as *d'une part* "on the one hand," *d'autre part* "on the other hand," *de plus* "moreover," *donc* "therefore," *par conséquent* "consequently," as well as more impersonal expressions.[15]

Students are slower to appropriate L2 forms from the postings of their C2 partners in their spoken discourse and must be constantly and systematically encouraged to do so. Instructors can help them by designing specific oral activities in class where students are asked, for instance, to read aloud some comments of interest in front of the whole class or to circulate in the class sharing with other students the postings they have found particularly interesting. At first the students are allowed to glance at the text, but then they must echo the text orally. U.S. students of Russian were given checklists of phrases taken from Russians' postings dealing with family, childrearing, and education and asked to decide to what extent they described their own reality, and how they would change them if they did not.

Spanish: Problematizing National Cultures from Within and Without

Those considering implementation of *Cultura* in their own language programs sometimes express concern that, despite the flexible, iterative nature of its process, students might still generalize and form rigid judgments about either their own culture or that of their partners. Although bicultural comparisons clearly run the risk of oversimplification and polarization, the Brown University–Universidad de las Américas in Puebla, Mexico (UDLA) exchange described below demonstrates how the cultural self-reflections engendered by *Cultura* can foster an increasingly complex sense of national identities and cultural heterogeneity. This Spanish language version of *Cultura* was initiated by the Brown professor, who took advantage of internal grant monies and an existing study abroad arrangement between the two schools to visit the UDLA and meet with the Chair of Modern Languages to explain the project and ascertain the level of institutional and technological support for the exchange. A key factor for both schools was finding an appropriate level and course in which to pilot *Cultura*. Whereas the UDLA offered a third-year English course called "Intercultural Comparisons" that would serve as an ideal partner course for the exchange, the

Brown instructor was committed to directing and teaching a multi-section writing course and a third-year Spanish course on Hispanic Populations in the United States. After consulting with U.S. colleagues who had used *Cultura*, she decided that a pilot version of the exchange (questionnaires and subsequent forums only) could be best integrated into the single-section format and the content of the latter course. In a subsequent trip to Mexico, she met with her partner teacher to discuss calendars and possible modifications to the French versions of the questionnaires, some of which corresponded to course content (e.g., border/*frontera* and immigration/*inmigración* were added to the word association questionnaire). All subsequent questionnaire revisions and scheduling issues were handled though an extensive (and enjoyable) e-mail exchange that continues to this day.

While both Brown and the UDLA are elite, private institutions whose students generally have greater than average access to economic and educational resources, students need only Internet access, technological support for a course management system, and, most importantly, teacher guidance to navigate a fruitful *Cultura* exchange. In fact, while many of the student participants in the Brown–UDLA exchange had traveled outside their own countries and interacted with people from different cultural backgrounds, *Cultura* can be most useful for those who might not otherwise have access to travel, study abroad, or contact with multicultural communities in their country of origin. In the current, often intensely nationalistic post-9/11 political climate, U.S. students may be unprepared for the vehemence of foreign partners' associations with their country. Nevertheless, they can be prepared to confront and even reflect on opinions different from their own and they can be taught strategies for responding diplomatically even when they disagree.

In the Brown–UDLA exchange, several factors contributed to students' general awareness of ethnic, racial, and socioeconomic subgroups and to their cognizance of the blurring of national borders precipitated by globalization.[16] For the Brown students, course content foregrounded the diversity of Latino groups in the United States as well as issues such as immigration, acculturation, trans-nationalization, race, and bilingualism. For the UDLA students, decades of political and economic history lived in the shadow of the giant to the north, sharpened consciousness of intercultural penetration through economic interdependence, the globalization of production, transnational media, migration, and tourism. For both groups of students, a shared border that the Mexican writer Carlos Fuentes (1992, pp. 371–372) has likened to a scar marking the troubled divide between the First World and the developing world, promoted differing degrees of awareness of the porosity of national, cultural, and linguistic boundaries and of the existence of an international subculture of poverty.

If only a few of the students on each side of the Brown–UDLA exchange had direct experience with the geographical border between their nations, many more of them had confronted the demands placed on the intercultural language learner, who operates "at the border between several languages or language varieties, maneuvering his/her way through the troubled waters of cross-cultural misunderstandings" (Kramsch 1998, p. 27). Fairly well-traveled, even on their home turf, many of these students were accustomed to a world where most people know and use more than one language and where each language varies by group and by context. At the UDLA, a university-wide English language requirement fostered awareness of the use of English as a *lingua franca* that transcends national boundaries. For Brown students, a course requirement of volunteer work in local agencies that serve Latino clients placed them in language contact with Spanish speakers from a variety of countries in the Caribbean and Central and South America. Three UDLA students reported that one or both parents were born in a country other than Mexico (e.g., the United States, Chile, Germany). Seven of the 17 Brown students had at least one parent who was born in a country other than the United States, and at least six grew up in households where they frequently heard and/or spoke a language other than English (five Spanish, one Hindi).

As intercultural speakers testing the ill-defined borders of multicultural and multilingual societies, the UDLA/Brown students were typically reluctant to form generalizations about either Mexicans or Americans. Brown students, in particular, felt compelled to insist frequently that their postings reflected the values of a unique university culture they saw as far more liberal, open, and respectful of religious, racial, sexual, and economic diversity than the country at large. For example, they regularly prefaced their frequently critical responses to direct queries about the war in Iraq or U.S. leadership with provisos about the deep divide in the country's current political map. Likewise, the hypothetical situation "A foreigner criticizes your country," prompted postings like the following:

> It was crazy to me to see that so many of the students from Brown said they would agree with a foreigner who criticized their country . . .

> I want to clarify to UDLA students just in case they are not aware: Brown University is quite a liberal school, meaning that a majority of students here seems to be on the left of the political spectrum.

> If anything, as I am sure you know, American nationalism is higher than usual in the wake of the occurrences of September 11, 2001.

In a Brown–UDLA discussion of views on homosexuality, a dialogue elicited by the questionnaire item "You see two men holding hands," students again underscored the liberal bias of their own university culture, citing the current national debate over gay marriage as additional evidence of widespread U.S. homophobia not evident in the Brown *Cultura* questionnaires. On the basis of information gleaned from a public lecture, the American student Lincoln suggested a similar disjunction between the attitudes of UDLA students and those of Mexicans at large:

> On another note, I attended a lecture last week at Brown by a former advisor to Carlos Salinas and Ernesto Zedillo (two former presidents of Mexico) and she said that approximately 70% of all Mexicans were against homosexuality. I do not in any way intend to be offensive, but I was pleasantly surprised when I read the UDLA students' responses to

this topic. Although I have met a few liberal Mexicans, my impression of the country has always been [that it is] rather conservative concerning social issues. I understand that we as Brown students and you all as UDLA students do not speak for our countries, but rather for ourselves.

To this one of the UDLA students replied (translation):

. . . we don't constitute, even in the slightest degree, a representative sampling of our population so that we could generalize and say that all Mexicans tend toward openness in issues relating to homosexuality. Nonetheless, and without trying to label UDLA students, I think that we DO represent a significant portion of the educated youth of our nation (which is for the most part middle, upper middle, and upper class). . . .

Although allusions to university culture surfaced perhaps most prominently among the subcultures mentioned in the UDLA–Brown exchange, students from both schools regularly nuanced and deconstructed the simple Mexican/American binary (already problematized for the three Brown students officially dubbed Mexican-American). Among the diverse cultural subgroups they identified in their postings, many were geographic: Mexico City vs. the border towns; Mexico City vs. Cholula (the town where the UDLA is located); and East Coast U.S. associations with "immigration" vs. those from Texas and the West Coast.[17] Other subgroups mentioned were ethnic (allusions to the indigenous populations of Mexico; references to U.S. ethnic and racial diversity), religious, and economic. In fact, some of the most salient Mexico-U.S. differences in the UDLA–Brown responses to questionnaires tracked the socioeconomic and psychological divide between a developing nation and its First World neighbor. For example, in the situation "You see someone begging," UDLA students regularly distinguished between adult and child beggars, whereas Brown students never see children begging. Among the UDLA associations with the term "police," the words "corrupt" and "corruption" were predominant because police in Mexico are paid so little that they regularly supplement their income with bribes.[18] When queried about why supposedly family-centered UDLA students rarely mentioned the need to consult with their families before accepting a good job in a foreign country (in contrast to several Brown students who said they would talk with their families), the UDLA students explained that they assumed family support since good jobs are so hard to find in Mexico. Finally, for the situation "A foreigner criticizes your country," UDLA students commonly responded with a sometimes vehemently defensive attitude, which they attributed, in forum discussions, to considerable experience with negative attitudes of "superior" or insensitive European and U.S. tourists.

It was in this latter forum that UDLA students were most openly critical of what they regarded as U.S. abuses of power, its status as the most hated country in the world, the self-serving nature of U.S. foreign aid, and the negative consequences of U.S. intervention in Latin America. That this was done with a considerable amount of agreement and little ruffling of feathers can be attributed in part to generally receptive interlocutors, who regularly distinguished between governments and the many cultures and subgroups they represent. Yet civility was also enhanced by the use of discourse strategies (e.g., "Thanks for your comment, X, I agree"; "I agree, Y, but don't you think . . . ?"; "Thanks for your tolerance"; "I'm telling you this sincerely without meaning to offend you"; "I hope you respond"; and "This is my opinion") that can be modeled for students and even required in order to maintain even-handed dialogue.[19]

It is worthwhile noting that, within all language *Cultura* classes, students in the United States, who belong to a "third" culture, often spontaneously assume the role of a mediator between the two cultures being explored, as exemplified by the following example from an M.I.T.–INT forum in spring 2001 where students discuss formality versus informality in body language, modes of address, and food. In his first posting, Ryan clearly identifies himself as a foreign student:

> Hi, I am from Saudi Arabia, and I have to admit how shocked I was when I came to study at the states. I found that students call teachers by their first names, which is something unheard of back in Saudi Arabia. What shocked me even more is having students raise their feet in the face of professors or teachers!! I still remember the first time this happened in front of me at an American high school and the teacher didn't say anything. I guess it is a cultural thing. Even though I haven't really worked in Saudi Arabia, but I think it is a bit more formal than the business environment here. I see my father's colleagues calling him "Engineer . . ." and similarly with the doctors and other professions. The word Mr. or Mrs. is pronounced naturally when meeting older people. . . .

However, in his next posting, Ryan shifts his position and starts explaining the American point of view to the French students:

> Hi again Sophie, that is an interesting point you made about sharing the food. I never thought of that as a concern here in the states. Generally, people are not obliged to invite their neighbors for the food they have. Actually, from what I have seen is that you are not really expected to invite the people around you for food except if you were generous. I can see how inviting your neighbors can cause problems in lectures, but I guess that problem doesn't exist. I certainly like the system of eating in class. I am always busy during the day and I enjoy it when I bring my sandwich and drink to lecture and eat it without being in a rush like as usual :)

His dual position as both an outsider and insider to American culture gives him a unique vantage point and enables him to play a mediating role between the two cultures examined.

Future Directions and Sustainability

As new exchanges develop and additional modules are added, it will be useful to have all versions of *Cultura* (regardless of language or content) available through a centralized gateway that would allow access by interested faculty to all materials. Creating this resource entails mirroring all documents from the various versions. This will provide a vital repository of materials available to interested parties, including: links to the original *Cultura* web site at M.I.T. (along with discussions archives and content modules developed for French); zipped versions of HTML, *WebCT* or *Blackboard* packages for French, Russian, and Spanish; templates and suggestions for the creation of new language versions; updated pedagogical guides and suggestions for classroom activities and assessment; and a centralized, moderated teachers' forum to facilitate exchange of ideas and classroom materials. All these would help solve technical and pedagogical issues as they arise. Colleagues using *Cultura* would be encouraged to add their own archives at the end of any experiment, and teachers or researchers would be able to access and analyze data from any or all of the versions. The central website could be listed in professional web directories.

From its inception, *Cultura* was conceived as a methodology, not a technological product; therefore, it has evolved to meet changing technological standards. The number of faculty using *Cultura* has grown with the appearance of new discussion software, more sophisticated institutional IT systems, and greater instructor familiarity with technology. These adaptations have taken unexpected forms. Some institutions have been using *Cultura* content modules over several semesters, while others do not have a partner school and use only archived discussions from previous exchanges. In any case, new technology, if it is deemed pedagogically desirable, can be readily integrated into the existing design (with the caveat that introducing more advanced technological components is not always logistically possible in both countries). MP3s or voice discussion boards like *Wimba* would allow students to post voice messages alongside text in the discussion boards, which would give them access to features of postings (pronunciation, intonation) not apparent when they appear in written form only. Similarly, video recording would permit posting video clips to illustrate student comments with originally produced footage, e.g., scenes from daily life, short documentaries, interviews, or family footage that could complement the image database.

Conclusion

Despite the many challenges described here, *Cultura* offers a way for students in a language/culture class to work at becoming what Byram calls "truly intercultural learners" (1998, p. 61). We believe that our approach, coupled with the use of the Internet and its online communication tools, can foster productive collaboration with foreign partners. *Cultura* provides conditions in which students can begin to access the complexities of both C1 and C2 attitudes, values and frames of reference as well as understand more about themselves. Student construction of C2 and L2 is part of a process extending far beyond the bounds of a university semester, year, or degree program. It requires reflection on oneself and others, contact with multiple sources of information and perspectives, and opportunities for interpretation of texts, broadly understood. No one academic experience will "produce" interculturally competent students. However, a project like *Cultura* can affect this process substantively. Carefully implemented, it does not reduce cultural knowledge to capsules of discrete facts; it encourages students to explore both individual and socially constructed understandings of cultural phenomena; most importantly, it ties every insight to the culture that is language.

Notes

1. *Cultura's* developers welcome new research. All French experiments have been archived since 1997, and that material represents a rich source of information for those interested in intercultural collaborations. Other languages' questionnaires and forums will be archived during 2005. We ask interested parties to contact us at: *cultura@mit.edu* or visit our website at *http://web.mit.edu/french/culturaNEH/*

2. These are the titles of two of Edward T. Hall's books.

3. The Spanish and Russian versions, which are in a much earlier stage of development, are currently limited to questionnaires and online forums.

4. Teachers never post on the forums themselves and do not control the content of postings, although, in rare cases, they have contacted students individually off-site about significant breaches of netiquette or posting in the wrong language. Any instructor "regulation" of student online activity occurs at the level of project design (for example, the fact that every word association item has its own forum, which helps ensure that discussions will stay on-topic) or as part of the pedagogy of *Cultura's* implementation (giving clear instructions on how to use the site, budgeting enough time for questions to be asked and answered on the forums, requiring students to demonstrate that they are "digging deeper" by asking more—and more specific—questions).

5. In the case of the M.I.T. French–American exchange, these differences include: (1) the importance of the affective dimension in U.S. American culture (words such as "feelings," "considerate," and "caring" coming up frequently in the context of professional as well as personal relationships, as opposed to the prevalent notions of competence, *savoir* "knowledge" and *savoir-faire* "know-how" for the French); (2) the importance the French seem to attach to social norms, their notion of balance, their desire not to go beyond certain limits (as seen in their definition of "freedom") and their frequent criticism of American reactions, which they often deem excessive (as illustrated by the propensity of Americans to want to call the police if a mother is seen slapping her child); (3) the tendency of Americans to want to avoid confrontation when dealing with someone who makes loud comments in a movie theater or who cuts in the line in front of them, unlike the French who will not hesitate to directly confront the "culprit," an attitude which the American students tend to see as paradoxical because it is viewed by them as being very "rude" and inconsistent with the frequent French emphasis on politeness; and (4) the tendency in U.S. American culture to be much more explicit in most situations (except, students discover, when interpersonal relationships are at stake).

6. All French, Russian, and Spanish postings and other student writing have been translated into English for the purpose of this article and are marked "translation."

7. "Hits" designates the total number of times students linked to the discussion section of the website. It also includes about 102 hits from a guest account set up early during the semester before some students were fully registered. "Averages" are based on 10 French students at the INT and 19 students at Brown. Students who dropped the course after two weeks are not included in any figures, which explains a small discrepancy in numbers.

8. Another possible explanation for the variation could be cultural; the impulse for immediate and frank expression of opinion being more characteristic of the French, versus an unwillingness on the part of the U.S. students to be perceived as too blunt.

9. Opinion polls from the *Public Opinion Foundation* (*http://www.fom.ru/*) have already been used in the Brown Russian class. One idea for parallel films, suggested in *Cinema for Russian Conversation* (Kagan, Kashper, and Morozova 2005) are the annual holiday classics *It's a Wonderful Life* and *The Irony of Fate [Ironiia sud'by (ili c liogkim parom!)]*, both of which invoke cultural assumptions about family, friends, and daily life in the respective countries.

10. This happened as soon as political topics like the war in Chechnya or the Putin presidency were raised in the Russia/*Rossiia* forum. While discussion of current events is not *per se* the purpose of the exchange, U.S.–Russian dialogue inevitably carried as baggage the central fact of the two countries' twentieth century relations: the Cold War and its aftermath. Discussion of Russia, as guided by the U.S. students, was itself a reflection of how reporting on Russia takes place in the United States. In both years, "What do you think of Putin?" quickly appeared in the Russia/*Rossiia* forums and held center stage. In 2002, the exchange coincided with the Moscow hostage crisis at the musical *Nord-Ost*, which generated lengthy discussion of the war in Chechnya.

11. This observation relates to first- and second-year Russian texts in common use at U.S. institutions. First-year texts include *Golosa* (Robin, Evans-Romaine, Shatalina, and Robin 2003), *Nachalo* (Lubensky, Ervin, McLellan, and Jarvis 2002), *Russian Stage One: Live from Moscow* (Davidson, Gor, and Lekich 1997) and *Troika* (Nummikoski 1996). Second year texts include *V puti: Russian Grammar in Context* (Kagan and Miller 1996), and *Russian Stage Two: Welcome Back!* (Martin and Zaitsev 2001).

12. This occurred on both sides of the exchange, but for different reasons. Most of the Russian students chose shorter postings because they could visit the computer lab only once per week. In both years, Russians who had outside access to the Internet contributed the overwhelming majority of postings.

13. Since 1997, the number of Brown students who indicate on start of term surveys an intention to study in Russia has nearly always been less than 50% of the total, and in any given year there are fewer than ten students at all levels who actually do so (total semester enrollment of students in first through fourth year from 1995–2004 has ranged between 38 and 55). Nationally, according to the *Institute of International Education*'s 2004 Open Doors report, the most recent figure for US students enrolled in study abroad programs in Russia was 1521 (*http://opendoors.iienetwork.org/?p=50138*), which is a mere fraction of total undergraduate enrollment in the language; the latest *Modern Language Association* figure (2002) for undergraduate language enrollments in Russian at all levels is 20,208 (Welles 2004, p. 10).

14. English L1 students of Russian find the compound imperfective forms—*byt'* "to be" + infinitive—more familiar and often have a hard time recognizing conjugated perfectives as future at all. Nearly all the Russian answers, contrary to U.S. students' expectations, used perfective future verbs.

15. More detailed examples can be found here: *http://web.mit.edu/french/culturaNEH/ classroom/essai/essai1.html*

16. For the differences between intercultural and more recent transcultural approaches that emphasize the "interwoven character of cultures as a common condition for the whole world" see Risager (1998, p. x).

17. Linguistic differences based on geography, such as the use of "y'all" by Brown students from the South and the comparison to the Spanish (not Mexican) *vosotros* "you" (second person plural, familiar) were also mentioned.

18. This is a very simplified summary of a system that, as the UDLA students elaborated in forum discussions, affects not only the police, but all levels of government and public life in Mexico, including language (e.g. *la mordida* or "the bite," i.e. the money that Mexicans pay police in order to avoid getting tickets).

19. While students were given no instruction in this and there has been no formal statistical analysis, it is fair to say that these kinds of "bridging" strategies were frequently used in the forums: in a random sampling of 112 postings (there were 733 in all), 63 included formulae of greeting, politeness, agreement, from simple expressions of thanks (*gracias* "thanks") to enthusiastic ratification ("Hola, Maria, I think your comment is very wise.").

References

American Council on the Teaching of Foreign Languages. 1996. *Standards for Foreign Language Learning: Preparing for the 21st Century.* Yonkers, NY: ACTFL.

Bakhtin, Michael. 1986. Response to a Question from the Novy Mir Editorial Staff. In *Speech Genres and Other Late Essays,* edited by Caryl Emerson and Michael Holquist, 6–7. Austin, TX: University of Texas Press.

Belz, Julie A. 2001. Institutional and Individual Dimensions of Transatlantic Group Work in Network-Based Language Teaching. *ReCALL* 13(2): 213–231.

———. 2003. Linguistic Perspectives on the Development of Intercultural Competence in Telecollaboration. *Language Learning & Technology* 7(2): 68–99. *http://llt.msu.edu/ vol7num3/belz/*

———. 2005. Intercultural Questioning, Discovery, and Tension in Internet-Mediated Language Learning Partnerships. *Language and Intercultural Communication* 5(1): 3–39.

Belz, Julie A., and Andreas Muller-Hartmann. 2003. Teachers as Intercultural Learners: Negotiating German-American Telecollaboration along the Institutional Fault Line. *The Modern Language Journal* 87(1): 71–89.

de Beauvoir, Simone. 1947. Preface of *L'Amérique au jour le jour.* Paris: Gallimard.

Byram, Michael. 1997. *Teaching and Assessing Intercultural Communicative Competence.* Clevedon, England: Multilingual Matters.

Davidson, Dan E., Kira Gor, and Maria Lekich. 1997. *Russian Stage One: Live from Moscow!* Dubuque, IA: Kendall-Hunt.

Dunkel, Patricia. 1991. The Effectiveness Research on Computer-Assisted Instruction and Computer-Assisted Language Learning. In *Computer Assisted Language Learning and Testing: Research Issues and Practice,* edited by Patricia Dunkel, 5–36. New York: Newbury House.

Fantini, Alvino E. 2000. A Central Concern: Developing Intercultural Competence. *SIT Occasional Papers*, edited by Alvino E. Fantini, 25–42. SIT: Brattleboro, VT. *http://www.sit.edu/publications/docs/competence.pdf*

Fuentes, Carlos. 1992. *El espejo enterrado*. Mexico: Fondo de Cultura Economyica.

Furstenberg, Gilberte, Sabine Levet, Kathryn English, and Katherine Maillet. 2001. Giving a Virtual Voice to the Silent Language of Culture: the *Cultura* Project. *Language Learning and Technology* 5(1): 55–102. *http://llt.msu.edu/vol5num1/furstenberg/default.html*

Furstenberg, Gilberte. 2003. Constructing French-American Understanding: The *Cultura* Project. *Politics, Culture, and Society* 21(2): 111–121.

Hall, Edward T. 1969. *The Hidden Dimension*. Garden City, NY: Anchor Doubleday.

———. 1973. *The Silent Language*. Garden City, NY: Anchor Doubleday.

Irony of Fate. Mosfilm, Goltelradio USSR, 1975.

It's a Wonderful Life. RKO, 1946.

Kagan, Olga, and Frank Miller. 1996. *V puti: Russian Grammar in Context*. Upper Saddle River, NJ: Prentice Hall.

Kagan, Olga, Mara Kashper, and Yuliya Morozova. 2005. *Cinema for Russian Conversation*. Newburyport, MA: Focus Publishing.

Kaufman, Dorit. 2004. Constructivist Issues in Language Learning and Teaching. *Annual Review of Applied Linguistics* 24: 303–319.

Kern, Richard, and Mark Warschauer. 2000. Theory and Practice of Network-Based Language Teaching. In *Network-Based Language Teaching: Concepts and Practice*, edited by Mark Warschauer and Richard Kern, 1–19. New York: Cambridge University Press.

Kern, Richard, Paige Ware, and Mark Warschauer. 2004. Crossing Frontiers: New Directions in Online Pedagogy and Research. *Annual Review of Applied Linguistics* 24: 243–260.

Kinginger, Celeste, Alison Gourves-Hayward, and Vanessa Simpson. 1999. A Tele-Collaborative Course on French-American Intercultural Communication. *The French Review* 72(5): 853–866.

Kramsch, Claire. 1998. *Language and Culture*. Oxford: Oxford University Press.

Kramsch, Claire. 1998. The Privilege of the Intercultural Speaker. In *Language Learning in Intercultural Perspective*, edited by Michael Byram and Michael Fleming, 16–31. Cambridge: Cambridge University Press.

Kramsch, Claire, and Roger Andersen. 1999. Teaching Text and Context Through Multimedia. *Language Learning & Technology* 2(2): 31–42. *http://llt.msu.edu/vol2num2/article1/*

Levet, Sabine, and Gilberte Furstenberg. 2002. Français et Américains en vis-à-vis, dialogues et découvertes. *The Tocqueville Review/La revue Tocqueville* 23(2), 101–122.

Lubensky, Sophia, Gerard L. Ervin, Larry McLellan, and Donald Jarvis. 2002. *Nachalo: When in Russia*. Boston: McGraw-Hill.

Martin, Cynthia, Andrew E. Zaitsev, and Dan E. Davidson. 2001. *Russian Stage Two: Welcome Back!* Dubuque, IA: Kendall-Hunt.

Moore, Zena, Betsy Morales, and Sheila Carel. 1998. Technology and Teaching Culture: Results of a State Survey of Foreign Language Teachers. *The Calico Journal* 15(1–3): 109–128.

Nummikoski, Marita. 1996. *Toika: A Communicative Approach to Russian Language, Life and Culture*. New York: Wiley.

O'Dowd, Robert. 2003. Understanding the "Other Side": Intercultural Learning in a Spanish-English E-mail Exchange. *Language Learning & Technology* 7(2): 118–144. *http://llt.msu.edu/vol7num2/odowd/*

———. 2005. The Use of Videoconferencing and E-mail as Mediators of Intercultural Student Ethnography. In *Internet-mediated Intercultural Foreign Language Education*, edited by Julie A. Belz and Steven L. Thorne, 86–120. Boston, MA: Thomson Heinle.

Open Doors 2004: American Students Studying Abroad. Online report of the *Institute of International Education*. *http://opendoors.iienetwork.org/?p=50138*

Risager, Karen. 1998. Language Teaching and the Process of European Integration. In *Language Learning in Intercultural Perspective*, edited by Michael Byram and Michael Fleming, 242-254. Cambridge: Cambridge University Press.

Robin, Richard, Karen Evans-Romaine, Galina Shatalina and Joanna Robin. 2003 *Golosa. A Basic Course in Russian*. Upper Saddle River, NJ: Prentice Hall.

Sotillo, Susana. 2000. Discourse Functions and Syntactic Complexity in Synchronous and Asynchronous Communication. *Language Learning & Technology* 4(1): 82-119. *http://llt.msu.edu/vol4num1/sotillo/*

Ware, Paige. 2005. "Missed" communication in online communication: Tensions in a German-American Telecollaboration. *Language Learning & Technology* 9(2): 64-89. *http://llt.msu.edu/vol9num2/ware/default.html*

Welles, Elizabeth B. 2004. Foreign Language Enrollments in United States Institutions of Higher Education, Fall 2002. *ADFL Bulletin* 35(2-3): 7-26.

Chapter 3

Learning How to Teach Intercultural Communicative Competence via Telecollaboration: A Model for Language Teacher Education

Andreas Müller-Hartmann

Abstract

Much of the research on Internet-mediated foreign language education to date has focused on how participation in telecollaborative partnerships facilitates the development of intercultural or linguistic competence in the foreign language learner. In contrast, this chapter focuses on the ways in which participation in such a partnership might facilitate the development of both intercultural communicative competence and critical media literacy in the foreign language teacher. Because Internet-mediated intercultural exchange is a highly complex social activity, teachers cannot be adequately prepared for their crucial role in such exchanges by simply reading the relevant academic literature in a typical pre-service teacher education seminar; instead, they must build their knowledge base via experiential learning and model teaching, two practices that will afford them the opportunity to become intercultural speakers themselves before they will be required to facilitate the processes of intercultural learning for their own future students. Within a reflective practice model of teacher education, this chapter explores how preservice teachers of English in Germany as well as in-service teachers of various foreign languages in the United States began to build their knowledge base with respect to Internet-mediated foreign language education, critical media literacy, and intercultural communicative competence via participation in a two-tiered, project-based telecollaborative exchange with international partners during their pre- and in-service education.

Introduction

The *Common European Framework* (Council of Europe 2001), which has become the basic guideline for teaching and assessing foreign languages (FLs) in Europe, describes intercultural communicative competence (ICC) as one of the central goals of FL learning (see Byram 1997). At the same time, the use of the computer in language learning has increased dramatically in the last decade (Liu, Moore, Graham, and Lee 2002; Salaberry 2001). Research has shown that telecollaborative projects between learners from different cultures have a strong potential for supporting FL learning and facilitating the development of ICC (e.g., Kern 1998; Kinginger *et al.* 1999; Warschauer 1996). As a result, teacher education programs need to take into consideration both fields of expertise in the education of future language teachers. To facilitate innovative technology use in schools and other educational contexts, it is essential that prospective teachers learn about effective computer use while still at the university. They need to experience the affordances and constraints of international telecollaborative projects and the processes of intercultural learning that such projects entail. Only then will student-teachers be able to reflect on their experiences, enabling them to build a knowledge base that will eventually allow them to integrate such projects into their future professional field of language teaching.

This chapter presents best practices on how to develop student-teachers' knowledge base for ICC, computer-assisted FL learning, and critical media literacy by using complex, technology-enhanced project formats such as international telecollaboration in FL teacher education programs. In the current study, pre- and in-service student-teachers in two upper-level courses at the *Pädagogische Hochschule Heidelberg* (PHH) in Germany collaborate via e-mail and chat with students in two university-level courses at *The Pennsylvania State University* (PSU) in the United States.[1] Both courses at the PHH are teacher education seminars for pre-service instructors of English in Germany. At PSU, one course is an undergraduate German-language and culture course, while the other is a graduate seminar for pre- and in-service teachers of English as a Second Language (ESL), English as a Foreign Language (EFL), and various other FLs as well as Ph.D. students in applied linguistics. The four courses, which all run in the same semester, form an innovative, two-tiered learning arrangement because the PSU students in the graduate seminar (B1) and the PHH students in one of the courses in Germany (B2) participate in a telecollaborative exchange that centers on their observation of the PSU students in the undergraduate course (A1) and the PHH students in the other course in Germany (A2) as the latter students carry out their own telecollaborative partnership that focuses on language and culture learning (see Table 1). Thus, the two B-level courses use the A-level courses as a field laboratory for the construction of the participants' knowledge base of critical media literacy, ICC, and Internet-mediated FL education, among other things. They gain firsthand experiential knowledge of networked intercultural exchanges by discussing electronically the A-level courses with their own keypals in the corresponding B-level course. The PHH students in A2 also gain firsthand experiential knowledge of Internet-mediated FL education via participation in a project-based telecollaborative exchange with the PSU undergraduate students in A1. Because the student-teachers in B1 teach a variety of languages and all the participants in B2 are preparing for careers as English teachers, this exchange takes place in English only. The A-level exchange, however, is bilingual in nature (English and German) because the PSU undergraduate students are students of German and native speakers (NSs) of English, while the PHH students are NSs of German and students of English.

Because the author functioned as a participant observer on the German side of the exchange, data analysis in this chapter is restricted to the experiences of the pre-service teachers at the PHH. Their experiences, however, will inform FL practitioners and administrators in a variety of contexts, including language program directors at U.S. institutions, with regard to the possibilities of international

Table 1

Collaborating Courses

Courses at PSU	Courses at PHH	Academic Year
A1: Intermediate German Conversation and Composition (undergraduate course)	A2: Encounters with the United States: Intercultural ↔ Learning through E-mail Projects (upper-level course— TEFL teacher education)	2000/1–2004/5
↑	↑	
B1:Telecollaborative Language Study:Theory, Praxis, and Research (graduate course in applied linguistics—M.A. and Ph.D. students)	B2:Telecollaborative Language Study:Theory, Praxis, and ↔ Research (upper-level course— TEFL teacher education and TEFL M.A. program)	2002/3 and 2004/5

telecollaboration as a means of experiential learning and model teaching in FL teacher education. The analysis is based on five years of student-teacher portfolio data in A2 and two years in B2. Analytical categories for the development of ICC are taken from Byram (1997). In the following section, the general concept of teacher knowledge is outlined. In the next sections, ICC and media competence (as it relates to FL learning) are discussed. Next, the syllabi of the four parallel courses (A1, A2, B1, and B2) are presented in more detail. In the subsequent section, portfolio data are examined as a reflection of the participants' development of ICC through experiential learning in the pre-service telecollaborative partnerships. Conclusions are presented in a final section.

Developing Teacher Knowledge

Learning to teach a FL is a complex undertaking because it combines knowledge about language learning, the learners, the school setting, and instructional practices (Larsen-Freeman 1990). Freeman and Johnson re-conceptualize language teachers' knowledge base by focusing on the "teacher-learner" (1998, p. 407). Although student-teachers are usually novices to the teaching profession, they do bring prior knowledge to the enterprise, i.e., their own beliefs about language learning and teaching, which are based on their experiences as language learners. Student-teacher belief systems form "a structured set of principles that are derived from experience, school practice, personality, education theory, reading, and other sources" (Richards 1998, p. 67). Teacher education programs need to develop both the knowledge base and the belief system, facilitating their interaction and integration.

The present study, which includes novices and more experienced teachers, focuses on the specific knowledge areas of the development of ICC *through* language learning and the use of technology *for* language learning. In their argument for the development of a specific body of knowledge for language teachers, Tarone and Allwright (2005, pp. 15–16) point out that the use of technology is one area that requires serious consideration when developing pre- and in-service language teachers' knowledge base. While novice teachers usually have little knowledge about the use of technology, experienced teachers might need to "reexamine their classroom practice . . . in light of new possibilities for the delivery of instruction via technology" (Tarone and Allwright 2005, p. 15). The same is true for the development of ICC, which has become one of the mainstays of language learning in a number of contexts.

In international telecollaborative projects, as in any other dynamic classroom situation, teachers have to deal with complex demands, which have been characterized by uncertainty, complexity, uniqueness, instability, and value conflicts (Schön 1983). As a result, reading relevant academic texts alone is insufficient in order to develop teachers' knowledge base in this area. Tarone and Allwright have called the assumption that academic knowledge would suffice in this case the "academic fallacy" (2005, p. 12). While the expert teacher makes her decisions largely on the basis of routines rooted in her practical knowledge of diverse teaching situations, the novice will not be able to draw on such experiences. She needs to develop experiential knowledge to create routines in her future classrooms. To enable student teachers to develop a knowledge base as well as their belief system, they need to get the chance to develop experiential knowledge through action and reflection. As Frank relates, "This reflection on theories, instructional strategies, and management strategies is vital to the process as students construct their knowledge base, make teaching decisions in clinical settings, and formulate their individual teaching styles" (2003, p. 81). At the same time, in the process of becoming reflective practitioners, learners begin to revise their belief systems. Johnson has stated that if "pre-service teachers' beliefs are to shift at all, they must become cognizant of their own beliefs, have opportunities to resolve conflicting images within their own belief system, have access to develop an understanding of and, more importantly, have successful encounters with alternative instructional practices and alternative images of teachers" (1994, p. 451).

Although it might be possible for student-teachers to draw on prior knowledge of ICC, it is more likely that their knowledge and beliefs about innovative classroom practices (such as the integration of technology into the classroom for telecollaborative exchange) is still rather uneven or even non-existent. To illustrate, Egbert, Paulus, and Nakamichi point out that "even when teachers do believe that technology has empowering potential, they do not always know how to make this happen in the classroom" (2002, p. 3). Participation in international telecollaborative projects at the university level can provide such an experience. Furthermore, face-to-face encounters such as residence abroad are not integrated systematically into teacher trainees' courses of study. Because teachers-to-be are later likely to encounter a multicultural student population in their local school contexts, classroom-based intercultural learning experiences are a prerequisite to help teacher-learners develop the necessary skills of ICC. Here again telecollaborative projects provide a means to experience instructional techniques for developing ICC in classroom-based instruction.

Model teaching, then, provides student teachers with the opportunity to experience instructional practices they can emulate in their future classrooms.

Calderhead stresses the relationship between model teaching and the process of reflection: "Much discussion of reflective teaching tends in fact to devalue the modelling of routines which for student teachers might even be an essential stage in the process of becoming reflective about teaching" (1991, p. 534). Experiential learning and reflection on their experience is therefore necessary to develop the knowledge base that enables teachers to handle complex teaching situations in their future classrooms. The process of articulating their reflections during the learning process may be facilitated through portfolio work (see Johnson 1996; Seldin 1993), the approach chosen for this study.

In summary, student teachers need to integrate relevant perspectives on learning and teaching by reading and discussing public knowledge, by experiencing practice in the form of model teaching, and by reflecting on their experiences via portfolios. By doing so, they may integrate the newly acquired knowledge into their belief system, turning into intercultural speakers and prospective organizers of international telecollaborative projects in the process.

Expanding Teachers' Knowledge Base: Intercultural Learning and Media Competence

Intercultural Learning

As the *Common European Framework* points out, ICC is the basis of FL learning. When someone learns a second or a FL, she is already "competent in . . . her mother tongue and the associated culture" (Council of Europe 2001, p. 43). In the process, the learner does not lose this competence, but "becomes plurilingual and develops interculturality. The linguistic and cultural competences in respect of each language are modified by knowledge of the other and contribute to intercultural awareness, skills and know-how. They enable the individual to develop an enriched, more complex personality and an enhanced capacity for further language learning and greater openness to new cultural experiences" (Council of Europe 2001, p. 43; see also Müller-Hartmann and Schocker-v. Ditfurth 2004, pp. 18–27). Before teachers can teach ICC in their language classes, they need to become "intercultural speaker[s]" themselves, i.e., they need to develop the capacity "of establishing relationships, managing dysfunctions and mediating" (Byram 1997, pp. 31–32) before they will be able to support learners in the same process in their future classrooms. Apart from face-to-face encounters or longer stays in the target culture, telecollaboration is the best way to facilitate the development of ICC. By participating in a university-based telecollaborative project, student-teachers have to negotiate course content, experiencing possible institutional constraints and cultural misunderstandings in the process (see Belz and Müller-Hartmann 2002, p. 77).

Byram's model of ICC grew out of the field of teacher education and provides a clear set of factors for analyzing and facilitating intercultural encounters. In addition to affective factors, his concept covers cognitive factors, the interactional skills of interpreting and relating, and critical cultural awareness, all of which make up the "intercultural speaker" (Byram 1997, pp. 33–38; see also Kramsch 1998). As intercultural speakers, learners "may also be called upon not only to establish a relationship between their own social identities and those of their interlocutor, but also to act as mediator between people of different origins and identities" (Byram 1997, p. 38). Because portions of Byram (1997) comprise the syllabus in some of the courses under study, the four components are briefly explained.

Attitudes

The attitudes of learners (and teachers) participating in intercultural partnerships do not necessarily need to be positive, but they "need to be attitudes of curiosity and openness, of readiness to suspend disbelief and judgment with respect to others' meaning, beliefs and behaviors. There also needs to be a willingness to suspend belief in one's own meanings and behaviors, and to analyse them from the viewpoint of the others with whom one is engaging" (Byram 1997, p. 34). Learners need to be able to decenter from their own position, which might even lead to partial or complete re-socialization in another language and culture.

Knowledge

Byram differentiates between knowledge about "social groups and their products and practices in one's own and in one's interlocutor's country" and the knowledge "of the general processes of societal and individual interaction" (1997, p. 58). This includes knowledge about means of communication such as telecommunication as well as knowledge about the conventions of communication; both of these are necessary to negotiate and capitalize on misunderstandings (see Schneider and von der Emde, this volume). While primary and secondary socialization into a culture often leads to a "national" frame of mind, Byram stresses the fact that there are other social identities as well, such as those based on gender, social class, or race. At the same time, knowledge about other groups is not isolated factual knowledge, but rather "relational, i.e., it is knowledge acquired within socialization in one's own social groups and often presented in contrast to the significant characteristics of one's national group and identity" (Byram 1997, p. 36), a fact that could lead to prejudices and stereotypes. On a higher level, if partners know how members of other social groups have acquired their processes of interaction, they will be more competent in understanding the perceptions that group has of itself and of others, thus supporting interaction with members of that group. In face-to-face-interaction as well as in telecollaboration this declarative knowledge needs to be complemented with procedural knowledge of "how to act in specific circumstances" (Byram 1997, p. 36), which is essential for engaging in successful interaction and establishing a relationship.

Skills of Interpreting and Relating

Based on one's knowledge of one's own and other cultures, the intercultural speaker is able "to interpret a document or event from another culture, to explain it and relate it to documents or events from one's own" culture (Byram 1997, p. 61). Critical in this respect is the often unconsciously acquired knowledge of aspects of one's own culture, which may "obscure from the individual the ethnocentric values" (Byram 1997, p. 37) that sometimes make intercultural communication difficult.

Skills of Discovery and Social Interaction

When confronted with a different culture, learners need to be able to "recognise significant phenomena" in that environment "and to elicit their meanings and connotations" (Byram 1997, p. 38) in that culture. At the same time, they must develop "the ability to operate knowledge, attitudes and skills under the constraints of real-time communication and interaction" (p. 61). While real-time constraints do not play a role in asynchronous e-mail communication, they do play a role in synchronous chat communication when cultural content has to be negotiated on the spot (see O'Dowd, this volume, for the case of videoconferencing).

Critical Cultural Awareness

Byram argues that the aforementioned competencies can be further embedded in a "broader educational philosophy" (1997, p. 33), if the teacher guides the learners in reflecting critically on their respective cultures. By pursuing a strategy of political education, teachers help learners to develop "an ability to evaluate, critically and on the basis of explicit criteria, perspectives, practices and products in one's own and other cultures and countries" (p. 63).

Media Competence in Language Teacher Education

In their overview of literature on information technology and teacher education, Willis and Mehlinger asserted almost ten years ago that "most pre-service teachers know very little about effective use of technology in education and leaders believe there is a pressing need to substantially increase the amount and quality of instruction teachers receive about technology" (1996, p. 978). The authors conclude that pre-service teachers feel insufficiently prepared for the use of computers in school (pp. 980, 984). Furthermore, Dunn and Ridgeway, who collected data during a four-year British teacher education program, found that "students may require 4 years (or more) of experience and training before they are confident that they can use technology efficiently" (cited in Willis and Mehlinger 1996, p. 1012; see also Dawson and Norris 2000, p. 7). This conclusion corroborates the findings of studies of in-service teachers (e.g., Egbert, Paulus, and Nakmichi 2002). Other studies have examined the expertise of university faculty in integrating technology in the classroom and found that they are often unable to adequately model these processes, which then leads to low confidence on the part of their students or to qualitatively inferior use of technology in the classroom (e.g., drill and practice) (Cuban 2001, pp. 99–130; Willis and Mehlinger 1996, p. 1012).

Since the mid-1990s, programs for pre-service teachers have been initiated to develop media competence, e.g., *Preparing Tomorrow's Teachers to Use Technology* (PT3) (2002). Legutke, Müller-Hartmann, and Schocker-v. Ditfurth (in press) make a number of recommendations in this field. First, the traditional stand-alone computer course "does not correlate well with scores on items dealing with technology skills and the ability to integrate IT [information technology] into teaching" (*Milken Exchange* 1999, p. 3). Instead, technology should be integrated into general methods courses and it should form part of the whole teacher education curriculum. At the same time, the quality of technology use must improve for students to profit from the enormous potential of technology integration. Second, apart from the improvement of university courses, many studies see the necessity of providing more field-based courses to promote "the creation of authentic technology-rich field experiences" in primary and secondary classrooms (Dawson and Norris 2000, p. 5). University-school partnerships, such as the professional development schools in the United States (see Book 1996), facilitate these experiences, ensuring at the same time an integrated model of teacher pre- and in-service education. Finally, the (continuing) education of university faculty as well as school mentors to provide adequate models for pre-service teachers is mandatory (Willis and Mehlinger 1996, p. 999; Thomas and Cooper 2000). For example, novice teachers can be paired with more expert practitioners and, in the "cascade" model, new experts can then "cascade what they have learnt to their own designated novices" (Barnes and Murray 1999, p. 174). While in-service education is obviously necessary for both groups, the education of interested teachers can also be enhanced through various field-based course models.

While their findings demonstrate the necessity of integrating such courses into teacher education, most of these studies have not concentrated on telecollaboration in pre-service teacher education. Field experiences in schools connected to university courses are extremely difficult to organize because of their complex logistics. Consequently, student-teachers should be able to experience the complex situation of Internet-mediated FL education themselves as participants in such an exchange, with an expert instructor as a model. Such an arrangement includes the cognitive demands of working with partners from another culture in the FL on a common project as well as learning how to deal emotionally with possible misunderstandings in the partnership.

The university seminar provides a secure space for this type of experiential learning and modeling because students do not have to deal with the institutional constraints that such a project might involve in the school setting. Institutional constraints do have an impact on the project in the seminar as well, but they are mostly navigated by the instructor who can explain problems and help the novices to develop an understanding of why the partners acted in certain ways (see Belz and Müller-Hartmann 2002, 2003). The seminar also provides the necessary space for collaborative learning because "pre-service teachers need opportunities to share reflections with each other in a supportive context " as a "community of emerging professionals" (Doering and Beach 2002, p. 2), thereby gaining confidence in enhancing similar projects in future classroom contexts.

In order to develop their knowledge base, student-teachers also need to experience the different roles teachers have to fill when designing and carrying out an international telecollaborative project. The ubiquitous "facilitator" is perhaps "too facile a term to describe the multifarious skills that are needed by teacher trainees" (Barnes and Murry 1999, p. 176) in such projects. Apart from the most obvious role of the teacher, that of language instructor, Legutke, Müller-Hartmann, and Schocker-v. Ditfurth discuss four other categories that need to be taken into consideration:

> In her/his *pedagogical* role the teacher will, for example, promote
> interest in relevant topics, focus on content, on the processes of

intercultural learning and s/he will promote responsible and critical authorship. In her *social* role she will promote human relationships and collaborate with learners in creating a productive and challenging learning climate and in maintaining group cohesiveness. In his *managerial* role he will be in charge of the overall time-frame, he will make sure that schedules are kept, plans followed, and that both institutional constraints as well as affordances to be utilized are taken into account. In her *technical* responsibility the teacher must make participants comfortable with the system and the software, making the technology as transparent to learners as possible (in press; see also Berge 1995).

Finally, to provide examples of good practice to student-teachers, the instructor needs to ensure that course content and methodological processes of the university-based seminar are transferable to the future professional field of the learners.

Context of the Study

Courses

The telecollaborative project under study involved undergraduate and graduate courses at PSU in the United States and upper-level courses (*Hauptseminare*) at the *Universität Gießen* (year 1) and at the PHH (years 2–5) in Germany. The U.S. students in A1 (the first elective beyond the three-semester language requirement) were enrolled in a number of B.A. and B.S. programs. The graduate students in B1 were pre- and in-service ESL/EFL teachers, in-service graduate student teachers of German, Japanese, Russian, and Spanish, and Ph.D. students in applied linguistics who were interested in the use of technology in FL learning from both methodological and theoretical perspectives. The German students in A2 and B2 were enrolled in a teacher education program for EFL teachers at the primary and secondary levels in Germany. The student-teachers in B2 were slightly more advanced than those in B1; some of them were also pursuing an M.A. in Teaching English as a Foreign Language (TEFL).

Due to different institutional calendars, the courses at PSU lasted from the middle of August until the middle of December, while the courses at the PHH began in mid-October and ended in mid-February of the following calendar year. Consequently, the telecollaborative project took place from mid-October to mid-December, usually involving about twice as many students on the German side as on the U.S. side. This discrepancy led to the formation of dyads on the German side from the very beginning of the exchange. Each dyad was partnered with one or two PSU students. Participants collaborated on a series of teacher-guided tasks (see Table 2) via the computer conferencing system *FirstClass*, which enabled the exchange of e-mails and chats. It also provided folders for every transatlantic team where all their data were collected. The system was open for all participants and everybody had access to all texts.

Table 2

Phases and Tasks of Collaboration

Course Phases	Tasks: A1–A2 Collaboration	Tasks: B1–B2 Collaboration	Participants
End of August– Mid-October	Web Project I: • short biographies • information about studying at PSU	Readings on computer-mediated communication, communicative language teaching, and network-based language teaching	USA
	Young adult (YA) novels and films: • Härtling (1997) • Woodson (1998) • Nach fünf im Urwald (Schmid 1995) • American Beauty (Mendes 1999)		
Mid-October– Mid-November	Introductory phase—getting to know each other (German students also read the YA novels)	Discussion of Byram's (1997) text on ICC and data from telecollaborative (TC) exchange	USA/Germany (e-mail and chat)
	Discussion of parallel texts	Observation of Encounters course and possible interviews	
Mid-November– Mid-December	Web Project II: Bilingual essay about the parallel texts	Discussion of Byram (1997) and data from TC exchange	USA/Germany (e-mail and chat)
		Observation of A1 and A2 and possible interviews	
Mid-December– Mid-February	Reflection on collaborative experience and discussion of transfer to a high school context	Reflection on collaborative experience and discussion of transfer to a high school context Presentation of analysis of one transatlantic group's possible development of ICC	Germany
	(end of term requirement: portfolio)	(end of term requirement: portfolio)	

Course Procedures

The A-Level Courses

The telecollaborative exchange consisted of two phases at the A-level. During the introductory phase, students got to know each other and exchanged information about their two educational contexts. This exchange of information was supported by a website (Web Project I) that the U.S. students had constructed during the first two months of their term when the PHH was not in session. Web Project I included personal sites where the participants introduced themselves, as well as an informative site about PSU. In this phase, the participants also collaborated on a number of tasks based on their common reading of parallel young adult novels and their common viewing of parallel films from both cultures. Parallel texts deal with the same topic, but are in different languages (Kinginger *et al.* 1999). The parallel reading/viewing of texts facilitated the exchange of views and opinions among the transatlantic groups, which provided a basis for possible topics for the second and final phase of the exchange, namely, the transatlantic construction of a website (Web Project II). Here, student teams dealt with a wide variety of issues in both societies, including racism, patriotism, or gender relations, to name only a few. After the close of the fall semester in the United States (A1), the German seminar (A2) continued with a reflective phase about the experience gained during the telecollaborative project.

The B-Level Seminars

The collaboration in B1 and B2 consisted of two parts. Over a period of seven weeks, the transatlantic groups discussed Byram's (1997) text *Teaching and Assessing Intercultural Communicative Competence*. To ground this theoretical discussion in concrete data from a telecollaborative project, students examined the development of a telecollaborative partnership between three students (one American, two Germans) from an A-level exchange in 2000/2001 (see Belz 2003, 2005). At the same time, each B-level transatlantic group selected a transatlantic group from the concurrent A-level exchange, which they were required to observe at least twice in the course of their partnership. To clarify, PSU participants in B1 observed PSU participants in A1 *in vivo* as the latter students corresponded with their keypals in A2. Conversely, PHH participants in B2 observed PHH participants in A2 while the latter corresponded with their U.S. keypals in A1. In addition to observing the A-level students, the B-levels students read all the electronic correspondence that the A-level students produced each week as archived in *FirstClass*. Furthermore, some B-level participants interviewed A-level participants about their experiences in telecollaboration. In their own e-mails and chats, the B-level student-teachers exchanged their findings, discussed possible reasons for intercultural misunderstandings, and attempted to analyze transatlantic communication based on Byram's (1997) model of ICC. Students in B1 were required to write full-length seminar papers as their final assessment in the course. To date, two B1 participants in 2002/2003 are writing doctoral dissertations on A-level telecollaboration; two B1 participants in 2004/2005 have completed M.A. theses on telecollaboration, while two other B1 participants in 2004/2005 have used A-level telecollaborative data in their Ph.D. candidacy examinations. Students in B2 were required to maintain reflective course portfolios as a final seminar assessment (see next section).

The Reflective Phase after the Collaboration in the Teacher Education Seminars

The reflective phase, which was essentially the same in A2 and B2, consisted of three basic tasks. First, the student-teachers were required to engage in a general group discussion of their experiences in the telecollaborative project. To prepare for this discussion and to ensure that all individual experiences were represented, the approach of the "magnifying glass" was used. Each student had to develop a "mind-map" on a large piece of paper that included all aspects of the telecollaborative project that came to her/his mind at that point. One item from the mind-map that was found to be particularly interesting, frustrating, or surprising was then drawn (no text allowed) in a magnifying glass on the other side of the paper, i.e., literally and figuratively putting the critical incident under the "magnifying glass." In the ensuing group discussion, students presented their pictures and engaged in a lively discussion of the potential meanings of the critical incidents. This procedure ensured a discussion of all the salient issues and enabled students to learn about their colleagues' experiences, thus working through their own experiences and putting them into a larger context. It also laid the foundation for a more theoretical discussion of the issues involved in telecollaborative projects.

Second, students were required to compile a list of "dos and don'ts" that they would have to consider when doing an e-mail project with a ninth-grade class in secondary school before they joined A2 or B2. In the reflective phase, groups of students reconsidered their original lists and came up with a new list, framed by their experiences during the exchanges with A1 and B1. While the first lists had been completely open and arbitrary, including each individual student's prior knowledge—if any—and assumptions about telecollaborative projects, the second list had to be structured according to Nunan's (1989) six categories of task-based language learning, i.e., goals, input, activities, teacher and learner roles, and the setting. This activity led to an attempt at restructuring their experience in relation to a prospective classroom, thus engaging students in a negotiation of which issues were important for the design of a telecollaborative project.

The third step involved dealing with published knowledge about the pedagogy of e-mail projects as well as research on telecollaborative projects in school settings, including the issue of ICC (e.g., Byram 1997; Donath 1996; Müller-Hartmann 1999). Instead of just discussing the texts in class, students read them in conjunction with an examination of actual data from various telecollaborative projects in school settings. Personal relationship building between teenagers in e-mail communication was highlighted by using examples of very direct German communication strategies (which were negatively experienced by the U.S. partners) and by using an exchange between a German boy of Turkish descent and an American girl. Thus, students' theoretical reading was grounded in situated local practice with perspectives from teachers and learners involved in that practice. Students in B2, who had already dealt with published knowledge and data from telecollaborative exchanges (see Table 2 on page 72), also presented the findings of their observations of A2 during this phase.

Student-Teacher Portfolios

As mentioned previously, portfolios served as the major reflective instrument in A2 and B2 as well as the primary data source in the current chapter.[2] Students were instructed to include reflections on their learning processes in their portfolios in addition to interesting e-mails or chat transcripts from the telecollaborative exchanges. The reflective aspect was deliberately kept as open as possible in order to allow participants to show how they made sense of their learning process. The portfolios had to be written in English, they were graded, and students received course credits on the basis of the portfolios. Due to accreditation procedures in the German tertiary education system, only a segment of the student-teachers elected to receive credit for their participation in A2. As a result, 53 of the 91 participants submitted a portfolio (five of 21 in 2000/2001; 13 of 14 in 2001/2002; 8 of 14 in 2002/2003; 8 of 15 in 2003/2004; and 19 of 27 in 2004/2005). Data from students in B2 comprised the e-mails and chats for both academic years (see Table 1) as well as the portfolios of the 2004/2005 cohort (10 out of 18). Although portfolios are graded, students still tend to be very open and honest about their learning experiences because they realize that it is the level of reflection, not their positive or negative evaluation of the course, that is decisive for receiving credit in the seminar. The e-mail correspondence produced in these exchanges has been analyzed in detail elsewhere in terms of the institutional affordances and constraints operative in the process of intercultural learning (Belz 2002; Belz and Müller-Hartmann 2002, 2003). In this chapter, the analytical the focus lies on the development of these student-teachers' knowledge base with respect to Internet-mediated intercultural FL education, as captured in the pages of their portfolios in the process of retrospective reflection on their experiential learning.

Voices from the Language Classroom: Developing the Medial and Intercultural Knowledge Base

Discussion of the data begins with the students' expectations for a course in which such a complex learning environment is established and then proceeds according to Byram's (1997) components of ICC. It is important to remember that even though the different components are examined separately, they are nevertheless interrelated, making up each student-teacher's individual ICC. Students' emerging knowledge base upon completion of the project is also examined. Data from students in A2 and B2 are dealt with together because the overall aim was the same in both seminars.

Expectations

"How can you organize such projects not to end in a mess?" (Renate 2003A, p. 2)[3]

Before the courses, students' expectations were quite similar. Except for Margit (2002A), who has grown up bilingually, all students expected improvement in their language proficiency, because they were going to be in touch with NSs of English; they also wanted to learn about U.S. Americans and their culture. Quite a few of them saw the pending exchange as an opportunity not only to learn new facts about the other culture or to find out about "other point of views from people in my age and with a different cultural background" (Hermine 2004B, p. 1), but also "to make new friends" (Konrad 2003A, p. 1; Sabine 2002A, p. 1). At the same time, all students—even those who already had telecollaborative experiences (Gudrun 2002A, p. 1; Karina 2004B, p. 1; Patricia 2000A, p. 1)—wanted to improve their technical media skills. In the initial year, even e-mail was a first for a few students, and they expressed their fears about it: "I have to admit that I was worried about using e-mail to communicate, as I had never worked on an e-mail project before and I was doubting my abilities to do so" (Gesa 2000A, p. 1). For most students throughout the projects, chatting was indeed a first and they commented extensively on this experience (for example Cordula 2004B, p. 2; Dagmar and Norbert 2001A, p. 5; Renate 2003A, p. 4), comparing it to e-mail communication (see below). Many students also expressed their regret that only the American students worked on the technical side of Web Project II.

Moreover, they expressed their premonitions about media usage in relation to the complex classroom situation. Beatrice (2003A, p. 3), for example, writes, "I wanted to learn how to manage and organize a whole class of 28 pupils doing an e-mail project and not losing control of what is going on." Others wondered how the integration of media would change teaching and their role as a teacher: "I wondered before the course how the new media could change lessons in school, how they effect the communication and in what way they finally change our role as a teacher" (Norbert 2001A, p. 7).

Attitudes

"They valued us and our opinion and relativized themselves" (Sabine 2002A, p. 10).

At the beginning of the seminar, all the students expressed curiosity and openness about getting to know U.S. American students, an important requirement for developing ICC. This is probably due to the fact that more than half of them had already spent one year in the United States. Kerstin, for example, wrote that she "was basically a bit doubtful [whether the project would work], but at the same time curious and open" (2002A, p. 2). Even students who had misgivings about the United States voiced their concerns openly: "Up to that point I was not very much interested in the United States, in their culture or their people. . . . This seminar though seemed the most pleasant and easiest way to approach [my prejudices]" (Beate 2001A, p. 2). While Beate "felt slightly offended" that her partner corrected her British choice of vocabulary, she still conceded in the end that even though she had considered all Americans as being patriotic she "had to adjust [her] opinion a little" because her partner did not support Bush as president (2001A, pp. 6, 9). Sabine's quote at the beginning of this sub-section shows that students realized that de-centering was an important aspect of achieving ICC. After feeling frustrated at their partners' choice of topic for the final project, Sabine and her German partners proposed another one instead, and were glad when their U.S. partners did not persist in sticking to their original choice, but "relativised themselves" instead, as she puts it, and agreed to a topic change.

Knowledge

"I would not have thought that such a critical film was possible in America" (Berit 2001A, p. 8).

The fact that more than 50% of the students had spent a year in the United States led them to believe that they were cultural experts. Still, they wanted to learn more about the United States and almost all of them mentioned the fact that they had learned a lot about the education system at the university-level and college life in general (e.g., Jutta 2003A, p. 9). Hanna (2004B, p. 2), for example, relates that she "didn't know or realize the fact that American universities have other term times. I thought they have pretty much the same times than in Germany except maybe some holidays." In some cases, this realization was facilitated by the assignment to exchange information about the educational system at the outset of the exchange. Students evaluated this knowledge also in view of the school situation where they have to work with textbooks containing "typical pictures and stories . . . which, sadly enough, seem to produce a lot of clichés" (Pia 2001A, p. 5). They not only acquired factual knowledge, but also actually experienced institutional constraints. One place this came up was with the different assessment procedures. The assessment of Web Project II on the U.S. side put a lot of stress on the teams to come up with a good product (see also Belz and Müller-Hartmann 2003). This was an aspect on which almost all teams commented. Students in B2 mentioned the stress that some of their partners had to deal with because of other requirements, which often reduced the time they had to chat with each other. Gerd (2004B, p. 2) explains that "another difficulty was that our partner often was away on job interviews."

While they acquired other factual knowledge about religion, family life, sexuality, and patriotism, students also became aware of the different means of telecommunication as well as their interactional conventions (Byram 1997, pp. 58, 60). Dagmar and Norbert (2001A, p. 5), for example, commented on chat conventions in the following way: "At the beginning we wrote long and correct sentences but soon we noticed that there is a certain way to chat." And Franz (2001A, p. 10) reflected that his partner's perceived reluctance in the chat may have had something to do with his own level of inquisitiveness, thus reflecting particular cultures-of-use in chats (see Thorne 2003): "Maybe Veronika and I wrote too much and asked too many questions or did too many proposals for further work." Sabine (2003A, p. 9) finally realized "that capital letters in an e-mail meant shouting." Students thus realized the importance of different forms of communication, attributing different potentials to each form. The majority of them also saw the need to have the ability to create hypertexts in their future classrooms, integrating textual, visual, and audio texts.

Interactional Skills

"I discovered my mediator role (. . .)—a role that can be quite exhausting at times" (Margit 2002A, p. 17).

The choice of texts (young adult novels and films) was unanimously commended by the students because the texts allowed them to relate to the different cultural backgrounds. The texts triggered a discussion of stereotypes and prejudices that led the teams to consider which representations might be stereotypes and which might be individually based, negotiating cultural differences and similarities (e.g., Berit 2001A, p. 7). Ilse (2000A, pp. 7–8) describes the potential: "Of course the Americans also learned a lot of new things about the Germans and I hope that it helped to clear up some stereotypes. We had some attitudes and stereotypes about the Americans as well but I got to know another point of view and now I can understand some of their attitudes much more better. All in all I can say that the materials helped to change some of my attitudes and helped to avoid prejudices." By trying to explain common German cultural artifacts, such as the *Gartenzwerg* (little colorful dwarves that can be found in German gardens and are seen as representing a lower-middle-class, conservative attitude), or culturally specific terms, such as *Umsiedler* (people of German descent who live abroad but who are allowed to immigrate to Germany from the former eastern regions because of their birthright), the students realized how difficult it is to make partners understand a concept that does not exist in the other culture.

Students realized the importance of interpreting texts, of looking below the surface to get to hidden meanings. Ulla provides the following summary after talking about the "invisible facts" one has to find by reading between the lines, i.e., interpreting incoming e-mails: "Despite getting to know the other country and culture, you also learn a lot about yourself and your own cultural background when reflecting on it" (2001A, p. 4). Interaction proved to be another cultural minefield, and helped students to become aware of their potential future roles as "intercultural mediator." Ilse, for example, was worried that her partner would feel offended when she "criticized the way Americans cope with violence on TV" (2000A, p. 3). She did so nevertheless and was relieved when the partners did not comment on it. In other cases, German communicative directness led to conflicts (Beate 2001A; Pia 2001A). One group disagreed about how bluntly to tell their U.S. partners that they were unhappy with their performance. Margit (2002A, p. 15) describes the situation and her developing role as a mediator: "I felt bad, mainly because I did not want to poison the German–American relationship. I also thought about the stress the Americans must have been in with the end of their term approaching. . . . I pointed out my "mediator" role I put myself in. . . . I always try to "build bridges" defending the "other side," explaining points of views and "reactions" and focusing on the SIMILARITIES rather than differences." Communicative styles and the fact that lower FL skills on the American side could pose a problem for negotiation were important topics in some of the chats between B1 and B2. Karina (2004B, p. 10), for example, analyzes one of her chats thus: "In this part of the chat I got the feeling that Esther and Bill wanted to kind of protect the two girls [in A1]. They always tried to find excuses for their unwillingness to answer the Germans' questions. . . . While I was more interested to find out why the two girls *did not want* to answer some questions; especially questions about love or the nude scene in the book, Esther was very anxious to excuse why the girls *were not able to* answer the Germans' questions" (see also Doris 2004B, p. 6). By dealing with stereotypes and prejudices in both cultures and by realizing the historical and cultural grounding of some of them, students developed a critical cultural awareness with regard to both cultures.

Teacher Knowledge Base

"We learned something at the PH with relevance to our teaching profession!" (Pia 2001A, p. 15)

In their final evaluations, students reconsidered their expectations at the outset of the course. When reflecting on telecollaborative projects in general, some were still a bit hesitant about their integration into their future language classrooms. Dagmar and Norbert (2001A, p. 4) are a case in point. At the same time, they also realized that a more comprehensive media competence was necessary: "We were curious whether we could realize a similar e-mail project ourselves in a school context. We noticed that it demands a lot of interest in the subject, enthusiasm, knowledge and not only special technical skills." Jutta (2003A, p. 17) still expresses her fears about media usage and handling a school class, but she draws a positive conclusion: "The computer can shut down before you can save your e-mail, the server won't let you in, etc. It's also hard [to] keep an eye on all the students while they are online. . . . I came to the conclusion that this project is definitely worth facing these 'fears' because the benefits seems to be much higher."

In general, frequent references were made to developing a new knowledge base and a feeling of security as to the tackling of a complex teaching situation. Matthias's final comment reads as follows: "In my opinion [A1] is a great enrichment for future language teachers. We didn't only get good advices how to organize or rather how to realize e-mails projects, we also get an insight how to integrate intercultural aspects . . . or how to initiate discussions. . . . Also the analysis of different chats and mails helped us understand how misunderstandings can be caused and prevented" (2003A, p. 13). And Jutta (2003A, p. 18) even ended on an enthusiastic note when answering her initial question "would I do such a project in my classroom?" She writes, "YES, I would definitely try to arrange such a project. I am very much encouraged by this class. I think it is one of the best ways for authentic intercultural (language) learning!"

Participation in a telecollaborative project proved to be emotionally demanding, especially during the final weeks of the exchange when time pressure led to misunderstandings and conflicts. But even though institutional constraints or personal student behaviour created stress and sometimes frustration, the second part of the seminar helped to put things into perspective. Bettina (2003A, p. 8) comments: "as my expectations [motivation of partner] had not been met really, the whole thing started to get stressful. Today I'm glad to have made this experience because of one major point: I personally experienced how important the motivation factor is, how the success of the project can rise and fall with the motivation of its participant." While all students commented on the experiential approach to teaching, i.e., being able to actually do an e-mail project during their own pre-service education, they also appreciated the approach of model teaching. Students, for example, often worried about technical problems, but, as Jutta (2003E, p. 10) notes, they observed that if there was a problem with *FirstClass*, "there was always a back-up plan." She continues, "I'm sure if I did a project myself in my futures profession it might look different because of varying circumstances, but I will never forget the value of having a 'back-up-plan' and of thinking ahead." Beatrice (2003A, p. 11) and others wrote about transferring the evaluation procedure of the magnifying glass (see above) into their own classroom. Bettina (2003A, p. 12) takes the structure of the seminar, the choice of media, and the choice of texts and reflects on why they would work in a secondary school and what she would need to change.

Even though initially some students had been unsure about the relevance of the second part of the seminar, they eventually all commented positively on that phase and many stressed its importance for developing a teacher's knowledge base. Patricia (2000A, p. 3) put it the following way: "In the evaluation phase we slowly became teachers again." Students stressed its importance for reflecting on their experience: "This to me was basically the most important phase, because I got the chance to recap my feelings and thoughts, visualize problems, and become aware of my personal learning progress" (Margit 2002A, p. 7; see also Cornelia 2001A).

Apart from the reflection on the project, this phase was also seen as preparation for future classroom work: "This was the most important part of the seminar in my opinion. As I had no knowledge how to do such a project in school, I learned a lot about the organization and realization of such a project" (Sabine 2003A, p. 9). Having been insecure about the methodological approach, students now realized the correct choice of texts, i.e., parallel texts that involve both participating cultures, and the importance of tasks (see Müller-Hartmann 1999 on tasks in telecollaborative projects). As Bettina (2003A, p. 9) observes, the discussion of Nunan's (1989) tasks shows the progress students have made: "What I liked very much was the idea of building a bridge back to the pre-semester task [dos and don'ts of e-mail projects] after our project had finished. By looking at the posters the groups had made I was able to see how students' conceptions had been changing or strengthened during the project. Our list of do's and don'ts had grown considerably and I was happy to hear about the other's opinion." This "community of emerging professionals" (Doering and Beach 2002, p. 2) also realizes how important collaborative reflection is when many of them comment on the value of having heard other opinions during the group discussions.

At the same time, students began to realize the complexity of the teacher's role in telecollaborative projects, commenting on the different roles that are involved. Taking a chat excerpt from an eighth-grade class as a basis, Bettina (2003A, p. 11) realized "the important role of coordinators" in such a complex learning environment. She also writes about the teacher's task as monitor to "interfere if they detect misunderstandings or difficulties" and she recommends that teachers "should try to resolve them together with the students" (see also Beatrice 2003A, p. 12; Jutta 2003A, p. 13). From the same chat session Jutta

(2003A, p. 13) gleaned the importance of positive feedback ("All your answers are really great!!!") but also the fact that "the teacher leaves things open for the students to develop their own answers." The realization of the importance of student choice—many students remarked positively on the fact that they had had the choice of topics for the Web Project II—and teacher guidance at the same time was definitely one of the most important outcomes in the seminar.

Conclusion

Telecollaborative projects have enabled participants to develop ICC and thus supported their process of becoming intercultural speakers themselves. Student-teachers have perceived their lack of technical skills and desire to develop this area of their knowledge base because they realize that not only are their future students often well versed in media usage, they also see the potential for highly motivational and authentic language experiences. At the same time, the combination of A- and B-level courses has facilitated a research approach for the more advanced students. While they were able to develop their ICC as well, this specific setup allowed them to gain firsthand experience in the analysis of international telecollaborative encounters on the basis of Byram's (1997) model of ICC.

The combination of experiential learning, model teaching, and intensive reflection facilitates the development the student-teachers' knowledge base. Apart from making the step of initiating telecollaborative projects themselves with less fear and greater ease, they are also able to better deal with the affordances and constraints of telecollaborative projects, thus having laid the first basis for possible routines in their future classroom. They still need to try out such encounters in their future local contexts, but the emotional anchors have been set during the pre-service projects, impacting on their teacher beliefs. Even though students had to deal with quite a bit of emotional turmoil during the exchange as well as problems of misunderstandings and conflict, discussions in class after each chat or e-mail session, reflections during the group discussions, and in the portfolio have hopefully given them the necessary amount of security to venture into the complexity of telecollaboration in their future classrooms.

Notes

1. The PHH courses were taught by the author, while the PSU courses were taught by Julie A. Belz.

2. Students in A1 were also required to keep formative as well as summative language learning portfolios in German.

3. All names are reported as pseudonyms. The pseudonyms used here for the students in the A-level courses are the same as those used in various publications by Belz and colleagues and they therefore index the same language learners and student-teachers. For example, the Norbert referred to in Belz and Kinginger (2003, pp. 617–618) is the same Norbert referenced here. The year indicates the particular year in which the student-teacher in question participated in the exchange. A refers to A2, while B refers to B2. Page numbers refer to pages in the student-teachers' portfolios. In all cases, the authentic texts have been quoted, disregarding language mistakes.

References

Barnes, Ann, and Liam Murray. 1999. Developing the Pedagogical Information and Communications Technology Competence of Modern Foreign Languages Teacher Trainees. Situation: All Change and *plus ça change. Journal of Technology for Teacher Education* 8(2): 165-180. *http://www.triangle.co.uk/jit/*

Belz, Julie A. 2002. Social Dimensions of Telecollaborative Foreign Language Study. *Language Learning & Technology* 6(1): 60-81. *www.llt.msu.edu/vol6num1/BELZ/default.html*

———. 2003. Linguistic Perspectives on the Development of Intercultural Competence in Telecollaboration. *Language Learning & Technology* 7(2): 68-117. *http://llt.msu.edu/vol7num2/belz/default.html*

———. 2005. Intercultural Questioning, Discovery, and Tension in Internet-Mediated Language Learning Partnerships. *Language and Intercultural Communication* 5(1): 3-39.

Belz, Julie A., and Celeste Kinginger. 2003. Discourse Options and the Development of Pragmatic Competence by Classroom Learners of German: The Case of Address Forms. *Language Learning* 53(4): 591-647.

Belz, Julie A., and Andreas Müller-Hartmann. 2002. Deutsch-amerikanische Telekollaboration im Fremdsprachenunterricht - Lernende im Kreuzfeuer der institutionellen Zwänge. *Die Unterrichtspraxis/Teaching German* 35(1): 72-82.

———. 2003. Teachers as Intercultural Learners: Negotiating German-American Telecollaboration along the Institutional Faultline. *The Modern Language Journal* 87(1): 71-89.

Berge, Zane L. 1995. Facilitating Computer Conferencing: Recommendations from the Field. *Educational Technology* 36(1): 22-29.

Book, Cassandra L. 1996. Professional Development Schools. In *Handbook of Research on Teacher Education*, edited by John Sikula, Thomas J. Buttery, and Edith Guyton, 194-210. New York: Simon & Schuster Macmillan.

Byram, Michael. 1997. *Teaching and Assessing Intercultural Communicative Competence*. Clevedon: Multilingual Matters.

Calderhead, James. 1991. The Social Context for Language Learning—A Neglected Situation? *Teaching & Teacher Education* 7(5/6): 532-535.

Council of Europe. 2001. *Modern Languages: Learning, Teaching, Assessment. A Common European Framework of Reference*. Cambridge: Cambridge University Press.

Cuban, Larry. 2001. *Oversold and Underused: Computers in the Classroom*. Cambridge: Harvard University Press.

Dawson, Kara, and Aileen Norris. 2000. Preservice Teachers' Experiences in a K-12/University Technology-Based Field Initiative: Benefits, Facilitators, Constraints, and Implications for Teacher Educators. *Journal of Computing in Teacher Education* 17(1): 4-12. *http://www.iste.org*

Doering, Aaron, and Richard Beach. 2002. Pre-service English Teachers Acquiring Literacy Practices Through Technology Tools. *Language Learning & Technology* 6(3): 127-146. *http://llt.msu.edu/vol6num3/doering/default.html*

Donath, Reinhard. 1996. *E-Mail-Projekte im Englischunterricht*. Stuttgart: Klett.

Egbert, Joy, Trena M. Paulus, and Yoko Nakmichi. 2002. The Impact of CALL Instruction on Classroom Computer Use: A Foundation for Rethinking Technology in Teacher Education. *Language Learning & Technology* 6(3): 108-126. *http://llt.msu.edu/vol6num3/egbert/default.html*

Frank, Anna Marie. 2003. Integrating Computer-Mediated Communication into a Pedagogical Education Course: Increasing Opportunity for Reflection. *Journal of Computing in Teacher Education* 20(2): 81-89.

Freeman, Donald, and Karen E. Johnson. 1998. Reconceptualizing the Knowledge-Base of Language Teacher Education. *TESOL Quarterly* 32(3): 397-417.

Härtling, Peter. 2nd ed. 1997. *Ben liebt Anna*. Weinheim und Basel: Beltz Verlag.

Johnson, Karen E. 1994. The Emerging Beliefs and Instructional Practices of Pre-service English as a Second Language Teachers. *Teaching & Teacher Education* 10(4): 439–452.

———. 1996. Portfolio Assessment in Second Language Teacher Education. *TESOL Journal* 6(2): 11–14.

Kinginger, Celeste, Alison Gourvés-Hayward, and Vanessa Simpson. 1999. A Tele-collaborative Course on French-American Intercultural Communication. *The French Review* 72(5): 853–866.

Kramsch, Claire. 1998. The Privilege of the Intercultural Speaker. In *Language Learning in Intercultural Perspective*, edited by Michael Byram and Michael Fleming, 16–31. Cambridge: Cambridge University Press.

Larsen-Freeman, Diane. 1990. Towards a Theory of Second Language Teaching. In *Georgetown University Round Table on Languages and Linguistics: Linguistics, Language Teaching, and Language Acquisition: The Interdependency of Theory, Practice, and Research*, edited by James E. Alatis, 261–270. Washington D.C.: Georgetown University Press.

Legutke, Michael K., Andreas Müller-Hartmann, and Marita Schocker-v. Ditfurth. In Press. Preaparing Teachers for Technology-Supported English Language Teaching. In *Kluwer Handbook on English Language Teaching*, edited by Jim Cummins and Chris Davison. Dordrecht: Kluwer.

Liu, Min, Zena Moore, Leah Graham, and Shinwoong Lee. 2002. A Look at the Research on Computer-Based Technology Use in Second Language Learning: Review of Literature from 1990–2000. *Journal of Research on Technology in Education* 34: 250–273.

Mendes, Sam (Director). 1999. *American Beauty* [Motion Picture]. USA: DreamWorks.

Milken Exchange on Education Technology. 1999. *Will New Teachers Be Prepared to Teach in a Digital Age. A National Survey on Information Technology in Teacher Education. http://www.mff.org/pubs/ME154.pdf*

Müller-Hartmann, Andreas. 1999. Die Integration der neuen Medien in den schulischen Fremdsprachenunterricht: Interkulturelles Lernen und die Folgen in E-mail-Projekten. *Fremdsprachen Lehren und Lernen* 28: 58–79.

———. 2000. The Role of Tasks in Promoting Intercultural Learning in Electronic Learning Networks. *Language Learning & Technology* 4(2): 129–147. *http://llt.msu.edu/vol4num2/muller/default.html*

Müller-Hartmann, Andreas, and Marita Schocker-v. Ditfurth. 2004. *Introduction to English Language Teaching*. Stuttgart: Klett.

Nunan, David. 1989. *Designing Tasks for the Communicative Classroom*. Cambridge: Cambridge University Press.

Preparing Tomorrow's Teachers to Use Technology (PT3) Program. 2002. *http://www.pt3.org/*

Richards, Jack C. 1998. *Beyond Training. Perspectives on Language Teacher Education.* Cambridge: Cambridge University Press.

Salaberry, Rafael. 2001. The Use of Technology for Second Language Learning and Teaching: A Retrospective. *The Modern Language Journal* 84(4): 537–554.

Schmid, Hans-Christian (Director). 1995. *Nach fünf im Urwald* [It's a Jungle Out There: Motion Picture] Germany: Senator Film.

Schön, Donald A. 1983. *The Reflective Practitioner: How Professionals Think in Action.* New York: Basic Books.

Seldin, Peter. 1993. *Successful Use of Teaching Portfolios.* Bolton, MA: Anker Publishing Co.

Tarone, Elaine, and Dick Allwright. 2005. Second Language Teacher Learning and Student Second Language Learning: Shaping the Knowledge Base. In *Second Language Teacher Education: International Perspectives*, edited by Diane J. Tedick, 5–23. Mahwah, NJ: Erlbaum.

Thomas, Julie A., and Sandra B. Cooper. 2000. Teaching Technology: A New Opportunity for Pioneers in Teacher Education. *Journal of Computing in Teacher Education* 17(1): 13–19. *http://www.iste.org/jcte/PDFs/te17113tho.pdf*

Thorne, Steve. L. 2003. Artifacts and Cultures-of-Use in Intercultural Communication. *Language Learning & Technology* 7 (2): 38–67. *http://www.llt.msu.edu/vol7num2/thorne/default.html*

Warschauer, Mark, ed. 1996. *Telecollaboration in Foreign Language Learning*. Honolulu: Second Language Teaching and Curriculum Center.

Willis, Jerry W., and Howard D. Mehlinger. 1996. Information Technology and Teacher Education. In *Handbook of Research on Teacher Education*, edited by John Sikula, Thomas J. Buttery, and Edith Guyton, 978–1029. New York: Simon & Schuster Macmillan.

Woodson, Jaquelyn. 1998. *If You Come Softly*. New York: Puffin Books.

Part Two

Research on Internet-mediated Intercultural Foreign Language Education

Chapter 4
The Use of Videoconferencing and E-mail as Mediators of Intercultural Student Ethnography

Robert O'Dowd

Abstract

As part of the search for effective methods for developing language learners' intercultural communicative competence, this chapter explores the possibilities of engaging learners in ethnographic research with distant peers through the use of networked communication tools such as videoconferencing and e-mail. The chapter begins by providing a review of the literature on the use of ethnographic techniques in foreign language education and by outlining what videoconferencing has been seen to offer network-based language learning to date. Following this, the outcomes of a semester-long networked exchange between two university classes in Germany and the United States will be presented. In the exchange, the German group of EFL learners and the American students of Communication Studies put into practice the skills of ethnographic interviewing to which they had been introduced earlier in their classes. The classes used both e-mail and videoconferencing technology in their interaction together. The qualitative analysis of transcripts, interviews, and questionnaires collected during this study revealed two central outcomes. First, it was seen how synchronic and asynchronic communication tools can contribute to very distinct aspects of ethnographic interviewing and intercultural learning. Second, the German students were often unwilling to take on the role of ethnographic interviewers during the exchange and regularly choose to reject alternative cultural beliefs and behaviour as being inferior to their own. Reasons for this reaction to the online contact are explored.

Introduction

In recent years, cultural aspects of foreign language (FL) education have gained in importance. The term "intercultural communicative competence" (ICC), the overarching aim of FL curricula in many countries (Byram and Fleming 1998), has been defined as the ability to interact effectively in a FL with members of cultures different from our own (Byram 1997; Guilherme 2000). Apart from knowledge of the target culture and attitudes of openness toward and interest in other cultures, effective intercultural interaction includes the skills of being able to discover and understand the symbolic meaning that is attributed to behaviour in different cultures. It also involves an awareness that one's own way of seeing the world is not *natural* or *normal*, but culturally determined.

A consequent challenge facing FL teachers and language program coordina-tors is how to develop such skills, knowledge, and awareness in learners enrolled in their programs. Many educators have turned to training language learners in the skills of ethnographic fieldwork and research in order to accomplish this. While ethnography for language learners is most commonly employed during residence abroad (e.g., the Socrates–Erasmus exchange program), in today's mul-ticultural societies other FL educators have also engaged their learners in ethno-graphic studies of members of the target culture who are living in the students' home cultures.

However, many language educators and program coordinators may find it difficult to provide their learners with access to members of the target culture with whom they can interact in their ethnographic projects. In these cases, the availability of online communication technologies such as videoconferencing and e-mail can offer learners the cost-effective opportunity to interact with native speakers (NSs) from the target group and to develop the skills of ethnography without having to leave their own classrooms. Because the concept of learner ethnography is still relatively recent in FL education, it is not surprising that its application to online contexts is not yet to be found in the literature. Roberts *et al.* do indeed recognize the potential of videoconferencing and other online technolo-gies for such ethnographic research, but the authors also warn that the "affective engagement with others in such intercultural experience will doubtless be differ-ent from that in the field" (2001, p. 242). These comments are quite vague and therefore reflect the need for further research in this area. This chapter explores the experiences of students carrying out ethnographic research with online con-tacts and the ways in which such research may influence the process of inter-cultural language learning.

The outcomes of a semester-long networked exchange between two university classes, one in Germany and one in the United States, are presented. The German group (advanced students of English as a Foreign Language taught by the author) and the American group (students in a course on Communication Studies) put into practice the skills of ethnographic interviewing to which they had been intro-duced earlier in their classes. The exchange capitalized on both e-mail and video-conferencing technology in order to facilitate intercultural communication in English between the participants. The research methodology was based on the principles of action research because little is known about the outcomes of ethno-graphic research in networked environments or about the particular contribution of videoconferencing technology to telecollaboration. Wallace defines action research for teachers as "collecting data on your everyday practice and analysing it in order to come to some decisions about what your future practice should be" (1998, p. 4). As such, action research reflected my aim of analysing the effective-ness of the online culture learning activities in my own classes and then making proposals about how these activities could be adapted and improved in other con-texts. I was also aware, however, of Stenhouse's warning that action research should contribute to "a theory of education and teaching which is accessible to other teachers" (cited in Cohen and Manion 1994, p. 186). The following overarching questions are addressed in this chapter: (1) What can the particular qualities of videoconferencing technology contribute to networked intercultural exchange and student-led ethnographic research?; (2) What can be gained from combining asynchronous and synchronous tools (in this case e-mail and videoconferencing) in networked ethnographic research?; and (3) Can student-led ethnographic research be successfully carried out through networked technologies?

The questions are deliberately broad because it is not my intention to impose my own "researcher-determined categorisation schemes" (Davis 1995, p. 433), but rather to let the most salient issues emerge from the data. In order to find answers to these questions, I, in my role as action researcher, began by examining both the transcripts of the videoconferences and the content of the students' e-mails during the exchange. I then triangulated my findings with data from student feedback collected throughout the project in order to ensure that my interpretation of the data was in agreement with that of the students. This student feedback data included in-depth interviews (carried out by e-mail and face-to-face), end-of-term essays, and qualitative questionnaires (see Appendix 1). In addition, I showed students extracts from their own online interactions and compared their interpretations of them with my own. There were times, however, when it was necessary to *reverse* this process of data triangulation. In these cases, important outcomes and insights emerged from the student questionnaires and interviews, which I had not already identified in the interaction transcripts. I then searched for evidence of the students' comments in the transcripts or asked them to refer me to examples. Following the model of other reports of qualitative research in networked classrooms (e.g., Fischer 1998; Warschauer 1998), representative examples are used in order to illustrate the relevant issues and themes, which emerged repeatedly from the data.

In the next section, I first review the literature on ethnography and ethnographic interviewing in FL education to date. Then I discuss telecollaborative exchanges as a site for the development of student ethnography. Next, I outline reasons for the combination of both synchronous and asynchronous communication in the exchange under study. Following that, I provide an overview of the experiences of language educators in applying videoconferencing technology in their classrooms. In the next section, I offer background information on the two partner classes and describe how this particular exchange was organised and structured. Next, the key research questions are dealt with in detail and finally conclusions and suggestions for further research are drawn.

Ethnography for Language Learners

Ethnography is a well-known qualitative research method that has become very popular of late in the field of applied linguistics and FL education. Researchers have used ethnographic methods to understand the *emic* perspective or how the students and teachers in question understand and experience what is happening in the classroom. However, recent work has highlighted the possibility of not only using ethnography as a tool for the classroom researcher but also as a source of content in the classroom.

The value of ethnography for language and culture learning was recognised initially by Stern (1983), who suggested that teachers use ethnographies of the target cultures in order to create materials for their language/culture classes. In recent years, ethnography has become popular in FL learning as a means for students to learn about language and culture. Ethnography has been used to engage members of the target culture who live in the home culture (Batemann 2002; Robinson and Nocon 1996), in online language learning environments (Fischer 1997; Fischhaber 2002), and in the target culture during periods of study abroad (Barro et al. 1998; Byram 1999; Roberts et al. 2001).

But in what ways does ethnography contribute to developing ICC? To answer this question it is necessary to look at what ethnography actually is and what the interpretation of culture involves. Roberts describes ethnography as a process of understanding "how things get done, what meanings they have and how there is coherence and indeed patterns of flux . . . in everyday life" (2002, p. 35). Ethnography does not consider culture to be a finite set of facts or behaviour but something that is continuously constructed and altered through interaction and through language. In contrast to a Cultural Studies approach, which has focused mainly on the analysis of texts from the target culture (e.g., Kramer 1997), ethnography provides students with a much more hands-on approach in which they engage with the foreign culture on the microlevel of individual behavior, which is then subsequently linked to the macrolevel of the socio-cultural environment.

This approach to studying culture and language is seen by many to be particularly suited to the development of cultural awareness and ICC for various reasons. First, Fischer points out that an ethnographic approach moves away from a more traditional definition of culture and makes learners aware that culture is not simply a set of facts to be learned, but is rather about understanding how "meanings reside in discourse" (1997, p. 108). As a result, words and utterances cannot have absolute meanings. Second, Jurasek maintains that one outcome of student ethnography is "an ever-increasing ability to recognise at least in a limited way what things might look like from the viewpoint of members of another culture" (1995, p. 228). Finally, Roberts et al. see the value of ethnography for intercultural learning in the fact that it is an interactive activity, which engages learners with the foreign culture on a local level via participant observation. Consequently, learners come to understand culture by taking an active part in it. As Roberts et al. note, learners "develop both linguistic and intercultural competences in the experience of fieldwork interaction as both verbal and non-verbal, as embedded in a 'context of situation'" (2001, p. 242).

Bateman (2002) and Robinson and Nocon (1996) describe the successful use of ethnographic interviewing techniques by language learners in their home culture. Both studies report on university-level learners of Spanish in the United States, who conducted ethnographic interviews with Spanish speakers living in their hometowns. Using ethnographic interviewing techniques such as listening actively and asking questions based on the interviewees' responses, it was hoped that students would become more aware of the *emic* or insider point of view

(Firth and Wagner 1997) and discover "natural categories of meaning in the interviewee's mind" (Bateman 2002, p. 320). In both studies, the ethnographic projects improved students' attitudes toward Spanish speakers and increased their desire to continue learning Spanish. Bateman also reports that her students became more aware of their own culture and had opportunities to see it from an outside perspective. However, Bateman also notes that the project led students to generalize a great deal about members of the target culture even though they had only interviewed a few subjects.

Reports of students using ethnography during periods of residence abroad are also common in the literature. The work of Roberts *et al.* (2001), for example, is based on *The Ealing Ethnography Project* at *Thames Valley University*, which involves a two-stage learning process for students of foreign languages. First, students are trained in the skills of ethnography over a one-year period before residence abroad. Then, they carry out ethnographic research on some aspect of the target culture during residence abroad.

If ethnography can only be used in situations where students have regular face-to-face contact with members of the target culture, however, then its usefulness may be of a limited nature. For example, while program coordinators of Spanish or ESL courses in the United States may have opportunities to bring classes into contact with NSs in their neighbourhoods, courses in other languages are not as likely to be as fortunate. In the following section, one way in which the principles of ethnography can be adapted for use in situations where language learners do not have face-to-face access to members of the target culture is examined.

Ethnographic Interviewing

Robinson-Stuart and Nocon explain why language teachers might train learners in the techniques of ethnographic interviewing: "Unlike forms of ethnography that involve long-term participant observation in specific cultural contexts, ethnographic interviewing techniques are transportable tools for understanding an insider's perspective" (1996, p. 437). Such interviewing essentially involves carrying out, over a number of encounters, a series of in-depth interviews with informants from the target culture in order to explore the *emic* perspective, or their natural categories of meaning (Roberts *et al.* 2001; Spradley 1979). The aim of ethnographic interviewing, and ethnography in general, is to provide what Geertz refers to as a "thick description" (1973, p. 6) that synthesizes different observations and converts them into a representative and partial account of the cultural event *from the native's point of view*. The ethnographer is not expected to support or criticise the cultural event under study.

The main characteristics of ethnographic interviewing can be summarised in the following way. First, unlike other types of interviews, ethnographers do not have a pre-planned outline of set questions which are "imposed" on the informant. Instead, interviewers develop their line of questioning based on the information that their informant supplies to them. Second, ethnographic interviews usually require periods of extended contact with informants. A good deal of time is needed to establish rapport and trust between interviewer and interviewee, to identify their *emic* perspective and then to explore in detail the meanings which they assign to behaviour. Third, ethnographic interviewing requires a great deal of what Nemetz-Robinson describes as "creative listening" (1985, p. 45). This means paying careful attention to what the informant is saying, expressing interest in their answers, and following up on the topics and issues that they bring up. The final key characteristic of ethnographic interviewing involves the types of questions informants are asked to answer. Spradley (1979, p. 60) reports that there are over thirty kinds of ethnographic questions, which fall into three main categories. These are: (1) descriptive questions; (2) structural questions; and (3) contrast questions. The first type is designed to gain an overview of the foreign culture; the second type targets the ways in which informants structure their cultural knowledge; the third type requires that informants contrast terms in their language with other terms to establish the precise meanings of particular concepts.

Ethnographic interviewing is of great use as a method of culture investigation within the context of an asynchronous text-based telecollaborative project (Belz 2003; Warschauer 1996a) for the following reasons. First, interviewers have ample time in the asynchronous medium to reflect on what their informants tell them and to decide what line of questioning will best lead to further exploration of this information. Second, learners can receive support and advice from their teachers and classmates on the execution of the interview and the analysis of the data if the ethnographic project is adequately integrated into the course. Learners who are engaged in traditional ethnographic fieldwork during their period of study abroad are unlikely to have access to such support. Finally, text-based electronic interaction may provide support for learners who are shy or not confident about interacting with speakers of the foreign language. This means that learners who would normally be unwilling to carry out face-to-face ethnographic interviews in their local area or in the foreign culture may be happier about using this investigative technique in a virtual environment (see Warschauer 1996b for a discussion of students' increased participation in online interaction).

Nevertheless, there are certain practical problems that might hinder the application of ethnographic interviewing to text-based exchanges. First, e-mail exchanges usually have as their goal a balanced intercultural relationship, which requires both partners to contribute more or less equal amounts of information about themselves and their cultures (O'Dowd 2003). Ethnography, on the other hand, usually involves a less balanced turn-taking relationship. Spradley explains: "The relationship is asymmetrical: the ethnographer asks almost all the questions, the informant talks about her experience" (1979, p. 67). In the case of telecollaborative ethnography it will be necessary for learners to take turns acting as both ethnographers and informants. This reduces the asymmetry of the relationship, but need not necessarily impede the learners from developing a more in-depth picture of the target culture as well as a more critical understanding of their own.

A second drawback in applying ethnography to telecollaboration is related to the non-visual (or text-based) nature of common telecollaborative media such as e-mail and message boards. The informants can more easily avoid or ignore any difficult or probing questions that they do not wish to answer because they are not communicating face-to-face. Furthermore, the time delay in asynchronous communication may mean that the process of receiving content from an informant and then sending back further questions that are based on that content becomes slow and tedious such that students never really get a sufficiently rich picture of the world of their partners. A possible remedy to this problem is the introduction of synchronous communication tools such as chats or videoconferencing. A combination of asynchronous and synchronous tools may provide learners initially with rich, in-depth descriptions (via e-mail or message boards) and then allow them to make follow-up questions via the synchronous medium.

Videoconferencing in Foreign Language Education

Videoconferencing is a point-to-point closed communications system connecting computers that are equipped with video (Roblyer 1997, p. 58). In order to take part in a videoconference, users require a camera, a screen, a microphone, loudspeakers, and the necessary software. Communication usually takes place via Integrated Services Digital Network (ISDN) lines or over the Internet, using Internet Protocol (IP) addresses. Both systems can suffer from low-quality visual images and sound; however, ISDN is considered more reliable due to its greater bandwidth. Low cost tends to make IP the more popular option with educational institutions.

Desktop videoconferencing, which is well suited for one-to-one communication, involves carrying out a videoconference using a web-camera and microphones that are connected to a personal computer. Videoconferencing software applications such as *NetMeeting* allow users to combine the videoconference with a shared whiteboard on their screens where each participant can write, draw diagrams, and make changes to what the other has written. Room-based videoconferencing, on the other hand, emphasizes group-to-group communication. In general, a class sits in front of a large screen where they can view the participants at the other site as well as a smaller image of themselves. This form of videoconferencing is typical in distance-learning programmes because it allows distally located students or teachers to take part in classes.

Wilcox explains that "[t]he stigma of videoconferencing is that, throughout its history, next year has always been the year it was going to 'really take off'" (2000, p. 17) in distance education in general. This would also appear to be the case for FL education. For some time now, much of the CALL literature has spoken about the imminent arrival of videoconferencing in the language classroom and about the benefits that this will have for both teachers and learners (Egbert and Hanson-Smith 1999; Furstenberg *et al.* 2001; Moore 2002). For many, the technology has come to be seen as the next logical addition to the wide range of text- and audio-based communication tools that are currently available to educators. The contribution of visual images to online communication and the immediacy of "live" face-to-face interaction seem to offer a much more authentic and personal side to long-distance telecollaboration. While reports on the use of videoconferencing in FL education are still scarce, a review of how videoconferencing has been used to date may offer some insight into how the technology could contribute to online ethnographic interviewing.

First, there does not appear to be a consensus as to whether the visual aspect of videoconferencing enables learners to see and interpret the body language and other non-verbal cues used by their distant partners. For example, Buckett and Stringer found that the visual aspect "provides a way of gauging reactions (e.g., frowning, smiling, puzzlement), of clarifying meaning (e.g., by mime), and as a way of learning some of the non-verbal gestures relevant to the language being taught" (1997). However, Goodfellow *et al.* (1996) found that the technology did not facilitate natural group discussion and that body language such as gestures and facial expressions were distorted and difficult to interpret. Similarly, Zähner, Fauverge, and Wong (2000) found that transmission delays in desktop videoconferencing interfered with the unmediated turn-taking process between learners of French and learners of English in *The Leverage Project*. Furthermore, students reported receiving limited visual feedback from partners. The authors explain that "participants have a range of signals, eye contact, facial expressions, body language, and so on, to indicate their intention [in face-to-face communication]. Over the network, most of these clues are not available. The visual channel is quite restricted by the nature of desktop videoconferencing" (2000, p. 197). My own previous research into group-to-group room-based videoconferencing between American and Spanish students (O'Dowd 2000) showed that students were able to use the large visual representation of the partner group on the big screen to become aware of cultural differences in appropriate classroom behaviour as well as in posture and appearance. The Spanish students, for example, reported that they were shocked that their American counterparts found it acceptable to sit in a slouched manner and to drink and eat during the conferences.

A reported advantage of videoconferencing is that students often find electronically mediated interaction with distant peers less stressful and intimidating than engaging in traditional oral practice with their teachers. However, this was only the case in desktop videoconferencing set-ups. Butler and Fawkes (1999), for example, relate how students of French at *Monkeaton High School* in England conversed in both French and English every week in a one-on-one format with students of EFL in a partner school in Lille, France. The students were given access to desktop computers with videoconferencing capabilities and interacted with an assigned partner. One of the main findings of the project was that students found it less intimidating to be corrected by their foreign peers than by their teachers. Zähner, Fauverge, and Wong (2000) reported similar outcomes for desktop exchanges; however, the group-to-group format did not always yield the same results. In fact, Kinginger warns of "the new forms of language classroom anxiety induced by the stress of public speaking in a networked or linked environment" (1998, p. 510).

A further finding common to most of the studies reviewed here is the necessity to locate videoconference sessions within a pedagogic structure and to carefully plan the content and development of the sessions in advance. Zähner, Fauverge, and Wong (2000), for example, warn that the success of videoconferencing as a tool for language learning depends on three important aspects. First, students should be given appropriate, engaging tasks. Second, a writing tool (such as a shared whiteboard) should be available to support the oral interaction. Finally, tutors should be on hand in order to step in when problems emerge. In their work on French–American telecollaboration, Kinginger, Gourvés-Hayward, and Simpson point out that teachers have to ensure that "technology is in the service of a coherent teaching approach, and not an end to itself" (1999, p. 861). They offer some examples of tasks which are suited to intercultural videoconferencing exchanges, including comparative discussions of parallel films, children's fairy tales, and other texts that had been written for one of the culture's involved and then adapted for publication in the other. The authors found that the interaction with individual NSs via videoconferencing allowed learners to check their developing theories about the target culture and also reminded them not to make overgeneralisations. In my own research (O'Dowd 2000), I found that videoconferencing sessions were most effective when they formed part of a task-based framework, which involved engaging students in pre-videoconference preparation and post-session analysis of the videoconference. This post-videoconference session usually involved watching a recording of the session and discussing aspects of the session related to language and cultural content.

The findings reported here have various important consequences for program coordinators who are considering integrating videoconferencing technology into their language programs. First, it will be necessary to carefully consider whether room-based or desktop videoconferencing is the most suitable set-up for the learning context. While desktop videoconferencing is more suited for student-to-student tandem learning, room-based videoconferencing is more accommodating to class-based and teacher-guided contexts. Second, videoconferencing should not be seen as an activity which merely involves the actual *contact* time. Instead, students who are going to take part in videoconferencing activities will require class time both before and after the conferences in order to sufficiently benefit from the experience. It remains unclear, however, if videoconferencing can make a particular contribution to intercultural telecollaboration that other communication tools such as e-mail or chat can not. It is also unclear how ethnographic interviewing can be adapted to this networked format.

The Partnership

The Participants

A class of 25 German-speaking learners of English in the fifth or sixth semester of University study in Essen, Germany, was paired with class of 21 American students in a Communication Studies course at the Zanesville campus of the *University of Columbus* in Ohio taught by Sheida Shirvani. Sheida was interested in engaging her class in a project which would give learners hands-on experience in intercultural communication. She explained her interest in the exchange in the following way: "It is not an easy task for me to provide experiences of exposing my students to a new culture so, when I came across this project, I thought my students would benefit from the new first-hand experience rather than reading between the lines of books and articles" (personal communication).

Due to differing semester dates, the partnership lasted for eight weeks in Spring 2003. Students were required to write a minimum of one e-mail per week; a videoconferencing session took place once every two weeks for a total of four sessions. The exchange took place entirely in English because the American group was not studying German and was therefore not interested in interacting in German. As a result, the German students were exposed to a greater amount of interaction in English than would have been the case in an exchange which involved German and English.[1]

Sheida and I exchanged over twenty e-mails during the five weeks prior to the beginning of our exchange in which we told each other about aspects of our private and professional backgrounds, the social and cultural contexts in which our students were studying, as well as how we envisaged carrying out the exchange. These lengthy e-mails served two functions. Obviously, they allowed us to plan our exchange in some detail. However, they also helped to establish a relationship of trust between us and enabled us to demonstrate our commitment to the exchange. Developing a successful telecollaborative exchange requires a great deal of extra work on the behalf of the teachers; those who do not have enough time to establish a working relationship with their partner teacher in the weeks before the exchange are unlikely to be able to invest sufficient time when the exchange begins in earnest. Furthermore, the socio-cultural contexts and the working conditions of teachers and students in both countries may differ radically. This does not mean that the exchanges will inevitably become unworkable because of these differences, but if the teachers are *unaware* of them they may lead to misunderstandings and communication breakdown. Exchanging in-depth e-mails helps teachers to find out more about the socio-cultural and educational contexts within which their partners are operating (Belz and Müller-Hartmann 2003).

During the first days of their classes, both groups of students filled out a short questionnaire to establish their attitudes to the idea of the exchange and working with network-based technologies. In general, the learners were very much at home working and communicating online. A large majority of their friends and family were reported to be online and almost all students in both classes had access to the Internet in their homes. However, the American group appeared to spend more time each day online. Furthermore, only half of the Germans had used technology in other University courses. The American students were more familiar with aspects of network-based learning (see also Belz 2001).

In general, the Germans reported a desire to find out more about the American way of life and culture and to improve their English writing skills. The American group also mentioned an interest in finding out about the target culture, but many of them suggested that they were hoping to "gain a friend" as a result of participation in the project. This possibility was not mentioned at all by the German group. Perhaps this finding echoes Kramsch and Thorne's (2002) suggestion that Internet communication in the United States is considered to be a very human activity which involves establishing close personal relationships and taking a personal interest in the solution of problems. This interpretation appeared to be confirmed in the final feedback of some of the American students. For instance, one student commented that "after a few e-mails she didn't seem like a foreign student but more like a friend," while another American complained that "even when [she] tried to joke with [her German partner] he would respond seriously." These comments also reflect the notion that "in German conversations . . . the topic was more important than the human beings discussing it" (House 2000a, p. 155).

When the students were asked what cultural differences they expected to encounter during the exchange, the American responses appeared to show that they had an image of Germany as a rural, family-oriented society. One American student mentioned, for example, that she imagined the United States to be "a more fast-paced and technology-oriented country than Germany." Such comments seemed to demonstrate the influence of common American stereotypical images of Germany (Kramsch 1993, pp. 208–209); in point of fact, many of the American participants reported living and studying in quite a poor rural environment.

The Germans also seemed to have been influenced by stereotypical portraits of the United States. Their pre-telecollaboration comments often reflected the common portrayal of America in the European media when they suggested that they expected to find differences in issues such as patriotism, national pride, and religion. The exchange took place just weeks after the United States and Britain had invaded Iraq in the second Iraq war and the question of whether the war had been justified or not was frequently at issue. Whereas the vast majority of Essen students were against the U.S.-led invasion, many of the American students clearly supported their government's actions. A military base was located near their hometown and some students had family members in the armed forces. In addition, three of the American participants had been members of the armed forces before taking up their studies.

The Exchange

The partnership was divided into four key stages (see Table 1). In stage one, the U.S. students explored some background information on Essen and Germany, read the relevant literature on ethnographic interviewing, and sent an introductory e-mail to me in Essen. At the outset of stage two, these e-mails were distributed to the students and they chose partners according to the topics which the Americans had suggested. During the initial weeks in the German class, students were introduced to text extracts and videos on the topic of ethnographic interviewing (Agar 1980; Nemetz-Robinson 1985; Roberts *et al.* 2001; Spradley 1979) in order to prepare them for the use of typical ethnographic techniques such as descriptive or grand tour questions and creative listening in their videoconferences and e-mails. International exchange students from France, Poland, and Italy were also invited to the classes to participate in "practice" interviews so the German group could gain first-hand experience in trying out the techniques. As the students read extracts from other ethnographic interviews and studies, they were told that their exchange did not require a critical approach to American culture, but rather an identification of the socio-cultural contexts which shaped the meanings of the behavior and beliefs of their partners.

Table 1
Overview of the Partnership

	German Class	U.S. Class
Stage 1	German university not in session	Introductory mails sent to Essen
Stage 2	Intercultural e-mail correspondence; four videoconferences	Intercultural e-mail correspondence; four videoconferences
Stage 3	Production of essays based on exchange	Production of essays based on exchange
Stage 4	Outcomes of exchange explored in class	U.S. university not in session

Students also began exchanging e-mails with their partners in stage two and they took part in four class-to-class videoconference sessions. The sessions lasted between 45 and 60 minutes each (see Figure 1).

Figure 1
Videoconferencing Between Essen (Inset) and Zanesville (Main Screen)

At the end of this eight-week period (stage three), students from both groups wrote essays reporting on the outcomes of their ethnographic research. As each pair of students had interviewed each other on a wide variety of topics, they were given a certain degree of choice for the topic of their essays. Some of the German students wrote comparative essays on themes, which they had explored with their partner and submitted work with titles such as "Discrimination Against Minorities in Germany and the USA" or "Religion in the USA and Germany." However, others chose to reflect on what they had learned from the intercultural experience itself and produced work on "The Challenge of Interaction between Cultures" and "E-mails: A Good Technique to do Ethnographic Research?" At this point, the American course came to an end. In stage four, the German class read additional texts on intercultural communication (e.g., House 2000b) and discussed their own experiences in the light of these texts.

Research Findings

The Contribution of Videoconferencing to the Intercultural Exchange

In general, videoconferencing interaction can be characterized as a fast and efficient form of long-distance interaction which allows students to quickly respond to and follow up on the comments and explanations of their partners in a way which other text-based telecollaborative tools may not be able to do. This type of interaction is illustrated in the videoconference transcript example 1:

(1)

Mary (USA) (1): We're considered non-traditional. Well, I'm 40 and Randi is about my age (laughter from Americans) and there is a lot of us who have already had our children or are changing job positions. I think a lot of it has to do with the economy because a lot of people are happy to switch jobs because of the downsizing and stuff.

Randi (USA): I've just made a mid-life carrier change myself. I went to a higher university back in the seventies so I'm old. It puts a whole new perspective on everything as an older adult, as an older than average college student I should say.

Mary: Older than dirt

Latasha (USA): This is Latasha. I am also a non-traditional student because after high school I also didn't have the desire to go to college and I became a soldier and that's why I lived in Germany for two years of my life. Once I got out I decided that to me, in our society to get ahead you do need a college degree so I decided to come back to school.

Britta (Germany): um, why did you want to become a soldier? I mean, that is quite unusual for a German woman. So is it unusual for you too?

Latasha: In my family, it was very unusual. In my family, we had a lot of men who were soldiers but I was the first female. I felt it was giving something to my country. I do love being a citizen of the United States and I felt like showing that love to serve. Because a lot of people don't understand what people go through and it's not even because I believe in war or I condone war but I believe I was doing my part because if there was a war situation I would support it but the likelihood that I would have to hurt anyone is extremely slim. I don't condone the war that we have now but I believe it was a chance for me to give something to my society.

Sylvia (Germany): Ok, Hi Latasha, it's Sylvia again. I would like to know if women are treated the same as men in the military? Because I know they have just changed the law in Germany about that and now women can join the military.

Latasha: For me personally I think that women are pretty much equal to men . . .

After asking a question on the subject of non-traditional students, the German group can quickly receive a variety of responses on the topic and then can immediately focus in on one of the comments from the American group which has caught their interest: "Why did you want to become a soldier? I mean, that is quite unusual for a German woman. So is it unusual for you too?" The language of the interaction is of an informal, oral nature (e.g., the use of fillers such as "well" and "um" and the colloquial expression "older than dirt") and the content is made up of personal accounts of social developments (e.g., the rising number of non-traditional students in U.S. universities and the existence of female soldiers in the U.S. military). The extract represents a question-and-answer format, which was common in the videoconferences.

Based on questionnaire data, many German students experienced the video-conferencing interaction as similar to "normal" face-to-face communication; they appreciated the opportunity to engage with their American partners in this way. They also found that turn-taking in this form of communication was more efficient than via e-mail and, consequently, they were able to collect more information about their partners and their culture than they were in their e-mail correspondence. The question-and-answer cycles shown above between Britta and Latasha and then between Sylvia and Latasha illustrate this efficient form of inter-cultural exchange.

A further advantage was that the videoconferencing enabled students to get to know their partners better and, as a result, made them more relaxed in their relationships via e-mail. Evidence for this can be found in Sylvia's e-mail to Latasha immediately after the videoconferencing session referred to above:

(2)

Hi Latasha,

I've just come home from the videoconference and I'm still excited although it was a bit hard to communicate because it was so unusual for us. I was glad I was able to spot you. Now I know what you are like and that helps me to write to you. That's great. On my way home many questions came into my head that I decided to sit down straight away and write to you. . . .

Further evidence appears in various students' comments in their end-of-course online interviews. Ana's (a Polish woman in the course in Essen) comments, for example, are particularly representative of this point of view: "The conference helped me realised whom I write to. Our contact got more personal after that and I think we can understand each other better."

The student feedback also reveals that the students often appreciated the opportunity to find out the points of view of other Americans besides that of their e-mail partners. Hans explained this in the following way in an e-mail interview:

(3)

It was fascinating to see their reaction to certain topics face to face and to discuss the themes you have already talked about with a single person with other people whose attitudes are different to the attitudes of the special e-mail partner. The most important thing was to hear and see them talk and speak freely about their culture and their way of life.

While text-based reactions from partners can also be easily shared with other students (by photocopying correspondence or by forwarding e-mails), the opportunity to actually "see" other reactions in real time seems to be particularly valued by learners. This contribution is also quite significant to the intercultural learning process. By being exposed to the different personal experiences and points of view of the American group in the videoconference, the German group was able to put the information they were receiving from their e-mail partner into a wider context and decide to what extent they could generalize from this information. The following example from one of the German student's end-of-term essays shows how the different views expressed by the Americans during the videoconferences were noted and used by the Germans to write up their conclusions of the exchange:

(4)

One of the most controversial topics during our exchange was the discussion concerning gun control. In one of our video-conferences the opposite opinions Germans and Americans have towards this topic have become quite clear. The most common pro-arguments mentioned by some advocates have been that tens of thousands of guns are used only for competitive target shooting, competitions or for protection and that criminals are the source of crime, no matter how they are armed. One girl of the American group said in the second video-conference that target shooting is one thing that is "bonding" her with her father.

Of course, the teacher needs to provide learners with other materials and content about the target culture which, in turn, will help learners to put this information from the whole class into a more representative context. Learners need to be aware of the extent to which they can generalize about the target culture based on the information provided by one informant, or, in the case of videoconferencing, one class. However, these limitations should not take away from the value of the information that they receive from their partners. The individual stories and opinions of the exchange partners help students put the "factual" and statistical data from their textbooks into perspective and remind them of the dangers of over-generalizing about the target culture. Kern addresses overgeneralization in the following way:

> By comparing what they learn through their e-mail exchanges with what they learn through teachers, textbooks, and other media, learners can evaluate information in a framework of multiple perspectives. For example, when American learners receive detailed personal accounts of life in twenty different French families, they can suddenly see the limitations of global generalizations in textbook portrayals of 'the French family'" (2000, p. 258).

A further contribution of videoconferencing to intercultural learning is that students used the opportunity of face-to-face contact to clarify doubts and explore theories about the target culture which had emerged in their e-mail correspondence. A short extract from the class which took place in Essen just before the second videoconferencing session illustrates this quite clearly:

(5)

Teacher: Have you all thought about what you would like to find out during the conference?

Jutta: I would like to know whether they think there is racism in Germany. Because I got a question from my partner last week, she wanted to know how black people are treated here and if it is ok with me because she would understand if I don't want to talk about that. So I get the impression that maybe they think that all of the German people are racist.

Teacher: But how do you ask that question in a way which doesn't come across as "Do you think we are all Nazis?"

Teacher: That's the problem, because if you ask direct questions like that you will get the answer "of course not," so how do you find out how they really believe?

Jutta: I would ask them about general opinions about Germans I suppose.

Teacher: Remember, when you ask a question you have to hold a microphone. So when you ask a question and they answer, don't just say "thank you" and pass on the microphone. Quiz them about their response. Remember ethnographic interviewing? From their answer, you try to develop it more.

In this extract, Jutta first mentions how she wants to explore in greater detail impressions which she felt their American partners have of Germany. She felt she had identified certain stereotypes about Germany written "between the lines" in their partners' e-mails and she saw the videoconferencing session as an opportunity to find out if these stereotypical images really existed or not. The videoconferencing medium was considered a quicker, more direct way than e-mail to clear up their doubts and to clearly establish how the Americans saw their German counterparts. Müller-Hartmann (2000) similarly found that synchronous communication tools (e.g., text-based chat programs) served this purpose of clarifying aspects of intercultural dialogue which were proving difficult to deal with in the asynchronous mode.

Finally, videoconferencing provided learners with authentic practice in developing the skills of discovery and interaction, i.e., being able to interact successfully with members of other cultures and illicit information about their world view *in real time,* as well as critical cultural awareness (Byram 1997, pp. 52–53). In asynchronous communication, students have ample time to reflect on how to interact appropriately with their partners, but in the videoconferences students are required to elicit knowledge about the American culture and to negotiate meaning between the two groups then and there. This obviously made the task of intercultural communication much more challenging for the students but their feedback would suggest that the occasions when there were misunderstandings or disagreement in the videoconferences proved to be the most insightful and rich with respect to cultural learning for the German group. The following event in the third videoconferencing session, for example, made a particularly strong impression on the German students:

(6)

Mary (USA): This is Mary. I know where I'm from everyone was in support of the war because we all have a military unit in our home town. We are just very supportive of the soldiers. The whole country in general, we don't, this is a real emotional topic for me.

Robert (teacher in Germany): Ok, thank you Mary.

Sylvia (Germany): This is Sylvia again. Would you relate this decision pro-war to what happened Sept 11. That is something I would understand. That happened in your country and this was a war of revenge which made you feel better. Would you agree with that?

Teresa (USA): I'll answer that. I don't think that it was so much revenge but everything changed on September 11th. This is the first time in a long time that the USA was an aggressor in a war and that's an example of how things have changed in this country since that day.

Robert: We have a Polish lady here too.

Ana (Germany): My name is Ana and maybe you know that Poland was the first country to be attacked by Germany and very many people died. For me war is the worst thing and there can be no reason to explain it.

Mary: This is Mary again. I know that this is not a popular opinion. I think the other day I said that war is necessary sometimes. I guess where I'm coming from is if we didn't step in during the civil war we would still have slavery. If we didn't step in during the Nazi time-frame,

Hitler would have killed many more people. I feel like we get blamed a lot of times for stepping in, but a lot of times we are asked to step in and then we get blamed for it. That's where I'm coming from with my feelings, my emotion, my anger 'cos a lot of boys have died (Mary begins to cry) for a cause we had no business being there but we were asked to be there and we were blamed for it later (Mary continues to cry and then the session is disconnected).

In this extract, the American student Mary becomes emotional as she expresses her feelings about the war in Iraq and begins to cry as she explains her ideas. She states at the beginning of this extract that "this is a real emotional topic for me" and it appears that she interprets Ana's comment ("For me war is the worst thing and there can be no reason to explain it") as a direct challenge to her beliefs. In order to defend her beliefs, she then tries to link America's involvement in Iraq to her country's actions against slavery and Nazi Germany. At the end of this excerpt, the IP connection was lost between the two sites and it took the technicians approximately five minutes to restore the connection. In the interim, the German students confessed that they felt very awkward in this situation. When the session restarted, one of the German students immediately suggested changing the subject and the conversation turned to the topic of religion in Germany and the United States.

This emotionally charged event clearly illustrated to the German students how cultural beliefs and values can differ greatly between two supposedly "similar" western societies. An extract from German Katya's final essay demonstrates this point:

(7)

We were discussing the European attitude towards the war in Iraq when suddenly Mary, one of the American students, started crying and began to defend the American point of view very strongly and emotionally. The reason for her strong reaction can be found in her personal background. She comes from a military family which was deeply involved in the war business. She even might have lost some loved ones. Her personal experience didn't allow her to discuss the topic objectively. In my eyes it is almost impossible to exclude a person's individual background from cultural exchange. It is a real challenge to cope with situations like this where a lot of intuition and sensitivity is needed. We felt overwhelmed by Mary's reaction and it would have been easier if we had been prepared for a situation like this. So how can we prevent misunderstanding each other and overcome the fact that we have been trained our whole lives to react to things in a certain way? What are the skills that we need to communicate more effectively?

In this extract, Katya reveals how she and her classmates have become more aware of how social, historical, and personal issues can influence cultural perspectives during the videoconferences. Katya's reflections on Mary's emotional reaction to the question of the Iraq war led her to take into account how the social and political contexts within which a person is living can influence their political views: "The reason for her strong reaction can be found in her personal background. She comes from a military family which was deeply involved in the war business." It appears that the "first-hand" experience of an intercultural difference of opinion and the intense, personal nature of the videoconference interaction meant that the German students were not able to ignore the American perspective; instead, they had to look for the socio-cultural contexts which had shaped the development of their American partners' perspectives. Being able to identify the values which underlie the behaviour of members of the foreign culture is a vital part of Byram's critical cultural awareness or the ability to "identify and interpret explicit or implicit values in documents and events in one's own and other cultures" (1997, p. 53).

Intercultural exchange by e-mail alone might have reduced the possibility of these students looking for the historical and social reasons behind the Americans' perspectives. With one or two exceptions, the e-mail exchanges between the two classes did not involve any misunderstandings or arguments about cultural issues. Students tended to present their perspective on the issues at hand and then wait to receive their partners' point of view. If these opinions differed in any way, this was simply accepted as a difference in opinion but it was rarely followed by any attempt to find out more about the foreign perspective. The "face-to-face" nature of video-conferencing, on the other hand, meant that learners could not simply present opposing perspectives on issues and move on. They were, in a way, obliged by the nature of the medium to delve further into the topics in question in order to find out why the other group felt the way they did. It was when they did this that the link between their partners' behavior and beliefs and the personal, social, and historical factors began to emerge.

Combining Videoconferencing and E-mail

While videoconferencing may allow for a quicker rate of turn-taking and may facilitate discussions on students' doubts and theories about each others' cultures, the e-mail exchange permitted students on both sides to write in great detail about their home culture and to develop their ideas and arguments in a much more fluent and insightful manner. The following extracts taken from the first videoconferencing session and one of the students' e-mails are based on the same subject, multiculturalism in Germany, and are quite representative of the two types of communication in this exchange. Example 8 is taken from the videoconferencing discussion:

(8)

Hans (Germany): We had this thing coming up in our discussion—multiculturalism. How do you feel about multiculturalism in the States?

Janet (USA): This is Janet. And we have many many co-cultures in the United States. How I feel about it personally is that I think it's a plus that we have as many co-cultures as we do. I think it's a good learning experience to experience someone else's culture and try to understand how someone else lives their life and to communicate better with them and I think we would get awfully bored if we were the same.

Hans: You spoke about co-cultures. Are they integrated in your society or are they just this co-cultures living side by side?

Janet: We have a kind of salad bar arrangement. We have many cultures that live side by side and are mixed together in every day settings

Hans: I think that's the same in Germany. Living side by side but I have no example for this.

Eva (Germany): As a French, I have the feeling that it is not the same as in Germany. Here there is a big Turkish community but I never saw a German student speaking to a Turkish student. It is very rare and I am just wondering why there are such differences between the two communities.

Robert (teacher in Germany): Is it different in France than in Germany?

Eva: I think we have a big Arabic community and they are much more integrated, much more adapted than the Turkish community here. I was wondering maybe it is because the African community already speaks French.

Although the conversation is quite animated, it is clear that the cultural content is, at times, superficial. Janet recognizes the value of living in a multi-cultural society and describes multiculturalism in the United States as "a kind of salad bar arrangement," but the German group never gets to hear in detail what this actually means. There is no attempt by the American group to offer concrete examples of what this metaphor means and the German students do not ask. The learners do not progress to a higher level of analysis where they might compare the term "salad bar" with the contrasting notion of the "melting pot." The German response is equally vague. Things are "the same in Germany" but on the spur of the moment Hans cannot offer any practical example of multi-culturalism in Germany. While videoconferencing may be suited to interaction based on students' own experiences or their personal opinions on specific topics (as was the case in their discussions on the Iraq war and gun control), it may not be suitable when they are "put on the spot" and asked to report factual information about general issues in their society with which they may be unfamiliar or have not thought about to any great extent. It could be argued that this is a disadvantage related to other synchronous telecollaborative tools as well (e.g., text-based chats and audio-conferencing); however, the fact that videoconferencing involves face-to-face contact may serve to increase the sensation of awkwardness produced by silences as students search for appropriate examples and explanations.

The opportunity for reflection and perhaps research on discussions topics afforded by the asynchronous medium of e-mail may produce rather different results as the following extract from a German student's e-mail on the same subject illustrates:

(9)

> As a future teacher I know that it's a fact that Turkish children have language problems and that they are mainly caused by cultural differences. There are prejudices on both sides and it's extremely hard to overcome the problems as long as nobody tries to make a step in the other one's direction. Some German parents don't send their children into schools with a high percentage of Turkish children because they fear that their lack of language knowledge could affect their own children's language acquisition process. That sounds hard but it's a reality in our schools. But on the other hand there are schools which especially train and try to integrate foreign pupils. Teachers are specially qualified and try to fill the language gap. In most secondary schools Muslim children have their own lessons in Islam. They don't have to attend classes where the Protestant or Catholic religions are taught. I went to a Catholic school for girls. Even there Muslim girls had their own lessons. You see the situation is not hopeless but it could be better. And of course September 11th didn't help to understand Muslims better . . .

In this extract, the student provides her partner with detailed examples from her own experiences as well as factual information about what she understands to be multiculturalism in German society. Expecting students to supply such detailed information in a videoconference (especially when operating in a foreign language) is probably quite unrealistic. Furthermore, if students were to speak in such detail in the videoconferencing sessions, they would quickly take on a "lecture" format and few students would have the opportunity to speak or ask questions. Writing by e-mail gives students the opportunity to reflect carefully on what they want to explain, to search for factual and statistical information to support their ideas, and to phrase what they mean more carefully. Rich descriptions of the home culture such as this are therefore best suited to the asynchronous written mode, while discussion and clarification of meaning based on this content can later be handled via videoconference.

In reference to the videoconferences, the German students had obviously recognized the intense, emotional nature of face-to-face exchange. On an end-of-term feedback form, Jessica suggested that "even if it became sometimes a bit too emotional you learned much more by this way. It was easier to understand what is important to them and what differs from us." Lucie, referring to Mary's defence of American involvement in Iraq in example 6, suggested that "writing was definitely much easier—if I think to the third videoconference and Mary when she began to cry about the war, phuuuu. Things like that don't happen while writing (or we just don't see it then)." In contrast to their experiences with videoconferences, the German students found that writing e-mails with their distant partners allowed "time to think about answers and questions," topics could be "discussed in a more extensive and detailed way," and the writer could "get more time to collect [his or her] thoughts and formulate them, and it is easier to stay objective."

Feedback from the American group on the same question revealed similar views. Teresa suggested that in the videoconferences "it is difficult to express or ask a question that entails an in-depth answer because of the time limit," whereas Tammy reported that "the e-mails were more personal and allowed the person to write longer and expand more and was not on a time restraint." Finally, Latasha explained her experiences of the two media in the following way: "I enjoyed the videoconference very much, but in the e-mails it's easier to open up, and get time for your thoughts before you write anything. With the videoconference you have to have a quick response, or question. Videoconference doesn't allow for much time."

It appears that teachers can use videoconferencing to develop students' ability to interact with members of the target culture under the constraints of real-time communication and also to elicit, through a face-to-face dialogue, the concepts and values which underlie their behaviour and their opinions. These skills are at the heart of ethnographic fieldwork and are essentially what Byram (1997, p. 52) refers to as the skills of discovery and interaction in his model of ICC. E-mail, on the other hand, can be employed to both send and receive detailed information on the two cultures' products and practices as seen from the insider perspective. In other words, e-mail may be better suited to foster the "knowledge" component of ICC in Byram's (1997, p. 51) model. Learners can take as much time as they wish to describe in detail aspects of their own culture without feeling that they are encroaching on the other students' opportunities to participate. E-mail texts also give learners the opportunity to develop their skills of interpreting and relating at a slower, less stressful pace. Both modes of communication together can contribute to the development of students' attitudes of openness and curiosity as they both involve contact with "real people" from the target culture. If the interaction is sufficiently analyzed and discussed in class under the guidance of a teacher, both tools may also facilitate learners' reflection on their own perspectives, products, and practices and thereby develop their critical cultural awareness.

Online Ethnographic Interviewing

In his work on German–American online exchanges, Fischer reports on an argument which develops between a German and an American student about their respective educational systems and which one was "better" than the other:

> Being right or wrong is not the issue here. This issue is: Has Joern listened to what Sherri is saying? If she thinks school provides challenges for students, that is her perception. And this perception is her interpretation of a social reality. Of course, Joern can say at a later stage that he thinks he is smarter than Sherri. But that attitude has nothing to do with what his task in the learning experience could have been: the research of Sheri's interpretation of a social reality (1998, p. 64).

Like Fischer, I suggest that engaging in research on how members of the target culture interpret their social reality should be considered one of the central aims of telecollaboration, along with becoming more aware of one's own social reality. Because the goal of ethnographic interviewing is understanding "the meaning of actions and events to the people we seek to understand" (Spradley 1979, p. 5), it is ideally suited for developing such awareness in networked partnerships. However, it appears to be difficult to achieve this goal in the short time-span of the current online exchange. While many students did become aware of how their partners' perspectives were shaped by historical, social, and political factors (see the essay extracts by Katya presented previously), other data suggest that students were often unwilling to take on the stance of a researcher or ethnographer whose only aim was to explore and describe their partners' perceptions. Instead, like the German student in Fischer's (1998) example above, many students found themselves drawn into discussions on which culture was "better." In their final essays and on the feedback forms, they often judge or criticize the target culture instead of trying to understand and describe it *from the native's point of view*. While the students have the right to respond in this way, such a response is nevertheless not the aim of ethnographic research. In the following paragraphs, I explore the German students' inability to maintain an ethnographic stance in the course of the exchange.

The e-mail and videoconferencing data show ample examples of the German students using the techniques of ethnographic interviewing in their online interaction. Sylvia, for example, showed an ability to "listen" carefully to what she was being told by her partner and then to ask for more detail when she wrote: "I liked the description you made of Newark and there are some things we would like to talk more about. For example: what are Longburger baskets or what do you mean by Indian Burial Mounds? We are curious to know more about that." Feedback from the German group also showed that the interviewing techniques provided them with a certain amount of guidance in how to engage their partners. Jutta, for example, mentioned she used "open questions" at the beginning of her correspondence to avoid imposing an agenda on her partner and to allow her to speak about what was important to her. Finally, Nadine suggested that being introduced to the technique in general helped students to become aware of the fact that there are good and bad ways of taking part in an online exchange.

However, despite the generally positive reaction of the students to ethnographic interviewing techniques, the German group was often unwilling to retain their stance as observers and "cultural investigators." Like the German student in Fischer's example at the start of this section, some German students tried to establish which of the two cultures is "right" in the interpretation of issues and events. Inevitably, the majority concluded that their own culture held the moral high ground (see also O'Dowd 2003).

The students' unwillingness to consider how their own worldview influenced their exploration of the Americans' perspectives first became clear in the second videoconference during the discussion of gun control in the United States. Although this session began as an attempt by the Germans to find out more about the American perspective on this topic, it quickly turned into a debate as the following extract illustrates:

(10)

Monica (Germany): I want to ask you a question which might be a bit tough and it came up to my mind when Tony asked about the shootings. One thing I could never understand about America was the right for U.S. citizens to possess guns. I thought this would stop after all the shootings you had in schools and so many innocent children died. This never happened and I would like to know what is the attitude of the society in general? Do you consider it as one of your natural laws to possess a gun? (Silence from Americans for 30 seconds as they discuss among themselves.)

Alice (USA): In our constitution we have the right to bear arms. I personally believe this. Guns don't kill people, people kill people. It is the responsibility of that person if they take that gun and use it for violence. A lot of people use guns for sports such as hunting, competitions for shooting. I personally believe that people should be allowed to have guns as long as they are responsible. There are laws that protect the citizens. (She looks at Tony.)

Tony (USA): This is Tony and I'm going to give two viewpoints. The first one, I do believe we should have the right to bear arms for personal safety and for sport. But I'm a police officer also. And it's hard as a police officer, everyone you pull over you wonder if they have a gun. So I can see both viewpoints. As a police officer, I don't think they should be allowed to carry guns. As a regular citizen, I think we should have guns for sport.

Alice: There is an intense debate in this country whether people should have the right to bear guns. A lot of people would like stricter laws and a lot of people would like to just throw them out.

Teresa (USA): What is the law over there? Are civilians allowed to own arms or not?

Hans (Germany): This is Hans. Civilians are currently not allowed to carry guns or weapons. Only people who have a hunting license and who have to be educated to be allowed to do this and it's very formal to get such licenses. You have to give certain reasons to carry them and handle them. That's how it is in Germany.

Lucie (Germany): You said people do sports with guns. But they carry them home again afterwards. I mean you could just leave them there at the sports center. You can't do sports at home.

Alice: Where I live out in the country, I have a shooting range out the back of my house. My father and I both own guns and pistols and we do it to bond together. It's like a father-daughter activity. We take targets out there and we practice shooting. We keep our guns locked in a safe with a combination lock as well. He gets the guns out and I do not have the combination lock. But we do keep our guns locked as well.

Tony: This is Tony again. For me having guns is a skill. It allows you to bond, like she says. But not only that, it gives protection. In the United States we have a lot of crime and we want to protect ourselves.

Hans: I would like to know how can you determine who has the right to have a gun and who is able to bear a gun. I don't know how you determine this right. How do you know if in his mental state a person can show responsibility?

Alice: There is a law, in fact, called the Brady law. The police do a three-day background check. They check for crimes. This helps curb it but unfortunately some people do get guns who should not be allowed to. But at least there are laws which try to stop this problem.

Sandra (Germany): Hi, this is Sandra. And Tony you have just said people need guns to protect themselves because there are so many crimes. But this is somehow like a vicious circle. Because these people who do crime, commit crimes, they get guns easier, too. So this is somehow a paradox, I think.

Tony: It's a paradox in a way but it's the American view that they should be able to protect themselves.

Markus (Germany): This seems to be a topic which everyone is interested in. I watched a movie called "Bowling for Columbine." It won an Oscar for best documentary this year. And he made comments similar to Alice saying people, not guns are killing each other. What do you think can help to prevent people from becoming violent, especially in the suburban areas of the United States?

Alice: We definitely need more community support. We have a lot of social problems over here. Fatherless children. Poverty. A lot of people need help. And this desperation leads them to drugs, gangs to find support.

Although the atmosphere of this exchange was not one of heated debate, it is clear that the German students were engaged in doing more than trying to establish the Americans' *emic* perspective. From the very beginning, when Monica prefaces her question to the Americans with the statement "one thing I could never understand about America was the right for U.S. citizens to possess guns," it is clear to the American group that one of their cultural practices is being called into question and they are expected to either defend it or accept that they were wrong. Similarly, the comments which come later from the German group all carry with them challenges to the Americans' explanations. Lucie suggests that people could leave their guns at the sports center, while Sandra points out that Tony's comment entails a "vicious circle." It seems that instead of trying to understand the American perspective, the Germans want to show them the error of their ways.

When I checked my interpretation of this encounter with Sandra in an e-mail interview, she sent me the following answer:

(11)

You are right saying that we were trying to prove the Americans wrong most of the time. The questions we ask are often meant to be rhetorical like when Hans says "How do you know if in his mental state a person can show responsibility?" The answer here of course can only be "We don't know." So we are trying to put the Americans into a position where they have to admit being wrong. During the videoconferences I sometimes felt like in court. Nevertheless, I do not regret having talked about even the heavy stuff. I think that it is something natural trying to persuade each other that one's own viewpoint is right.

It is interesting that Sandra reports the videoconferences "felt like a court" and that it is "natural" to engage in this type of debate with people from different cultures. This attitude was confirmed in the students' final essays. In reference to this videoconference exchange, Stefanie revealed her critical approach to the foreign culture when she wrote that "*our criticism* about [the American's explanation that gun ownership is a constitutional right], was that, according to statistics, most murderers in the USA are committed by the use of guns" (italics added). In reference to Alice's comment that shooting was a bonding activity for her and her father, Stefanie later wrote: "While others play tennis with their parents, she fires guns in order to bond with her Dad." The ironic tone of this sentence seems to convey Stefanie's opinion of this cultural practice.

After reading her essay and studying the videoconferences, I asked Stefanie why she had "abandoned" the ethnographic approach to her exchange and had instead adopted a more confrontational and critical approach. In her e-mailed reply, she began by explaining how she started out the exchange:

(12)

I had expected my partner and me to exchange information and tell each other about our culture and our way of life. Of course I was aware of the fact that differences would occur (because of the stereotypes and the prejudices we have about the United States of America and its citizens). So I decided to just accept a different viewpoint and not to try to persuade him/her that the way the Germans, especially myself, think about certain issues is the better one. All this was before the first e-mails and videoconferences. When talking about different attitudes towards religion, role of women or education, I still felt relaxed. I always just answered saying things like "That's rather interesting. Well, in Germany we do it a different way. We. ..." I did not mean to prove her wrong, but to make her understand that in another part of the world, things are being treated differently. We were trying to understand each other and find out about what makes us think the way we think.

Stefanie's approach, however, changed for a particular reason:

(13)

But when it came to the questions of whether the war against Iraq was good or whether every citizen should be allowed to possess guns, I changed my mind. I just could not understand the Americans, especially my partner, anymore. The reason for that may be the fact that back then, the war was something that had been in the media for almost a year, I guess and which everyone was into. (I remember that the discussion about Saddam Hussein possessing weapons of mass destruction had begun even before the elections on September 22nd here in Germany.) The war had just been over and I think that everyone of us still had the pictures in mind showing children with terribly burnt bodies, people who had lost their homes and families with all their children having died when the house was bombed. I think that there was and still is a lot of hatred against president Bush here in Germany, and I think that people over here wonder why the U.S. citizens have elected him for president. To put it briefly, my personal viewpoint is that all the incidents were still too recent to talk about them more objectively. Maybe it was just not the right time for an exchange with American students. Maybe a discussion with people from Australia would have been more peaceful.

The same may be true about the discussion about gun control. If you had asked me a year ago, I would not have had such a "strong" opinion as I do now. The explanation for that is quite simple. It is the documentary which I also quote in my essay, "Bowling for Columbine" by Michael Moore. I first saw it in March this year and it impressed me very deeply.

Her comments show that she was unable to stand back and take a scientific approach to the exchange due to the emotional nature of the topics. Her experiences of the recent war in Iraq and her viewing of a film on gun control in the United States meant that she could not "talk about them more objectively." The principles and values of the American group seem to have collided completely with her own and she felt obliged to reject them instead of trying to find out where they come from.

This is probably a justifiable reaction among language learners when they encounter cultural perspectives different to their own. However, this does not necessarily mean it is a desirable outcome of ethnographic research or intercultural learning. A further example may illustrate the point more clearly. Hans concludes his essay in the following way:

(14)

This was the point [after discussing our differing opinions on the Iraq war] I realized that her argumentation is totally opposed to everything I believe in. . . . the differences in our attitudes towards this topic made a discussion about it impossible. The only motivation was at this point to gather enough information to write our essays.

Despite our work on the principles and techniques of ethnography in our classes, Hans does not appear to be aware that the object of the exchange was not to reach agreement on the topics under discussion, but to become more aware of the social, historical, and political factors which had shaped his partners' opinions and beliefs.

According to Byram, the intercultural speaker, that is, the person who is interculturally competent, "can use a range of analytical approaches to place a document or event in context (of origins/sources, time, place, other documents or events) and to demonstrate the ideology involved" (1997, p. 63). In essence, ICC involves the ability to identify the cultural context which gives meaning to people's beliefs and actions. In this case, the "document or event" which needs to be analyzed is the Americans' perspectives on, for example, gun control. The context in which they need to be interpreted probably involves historical reasons (the role of guns in self-defence when Ohio was still part of the American frontier), political factors (the importance students attribute to their rights as American citizens), and modern-day social issues (the need to have guns in order to hunt, take part in competitions in the local community, and, it would seem, to bond with members of your family). The German group was actually given a lot of this contextual information, both directly and indirectly, in the videoconference and in their e-mails, but many of them would appear to have chosen to on concentrate on their own beliefs (themselves products of a cultural context) that the Americans' reasons did not justify their liberal gun laws.

Based on the data examined here, I suggest two main reasons why students were unable to limit their research to an investigation of aspects of the target culture. First, this project was not a typical ethnographic situation in which there was one group of informants and one group of ethnographers. Instead, the exchange required both groups to provide questions and answers with respect to topics at hand. As a result, comparison and debate were perhaps inevitable. This was especially true when students began to exchange their perceptions of emotional topics such as war, multicultural societies, and gun control. It proved too difficult to simply accept and try to understand perceptions and values which appeared to be completely incompatible with their own. The feedback from Sandra and Stefanie appears to confirm this hypothesis.

The second reason for their unwillingness to act as ethnographers is related to the strategies which NSs of German use to interact and to gain insights from their partners. House explains that, in comparison to English speakers, speakers of German "tend to interact in many different situations in ways that can be described as more direct, more explicit, more self-referenced and more content-oriented" (2000a, p. 162). Furthermore, Byrnes comments that German speakers are known for their "inflexibility, at times combative directness, and domineering way of always appearing certain they are right in a discussion" (1986, p. 190). It is possible that this communicative style, as legitimate as any other, may have clashed with the requirements of ethnographic research. Some examples may serve to illustrate this point.

Regularly throughout the exchange, students made statements to their partners about how they interpreted the target culture. They then waited for their partner to either agree with this statement or correct it. One example taken from a videoconference is given in excerpt 15:

(15)

Nadine (Germany): This is Nadine again. Would you relate this decision pro-war to what happened September 11. That is something I would understand. That happened in your country and this was a war of revenge which made you feel better. Would you agree with that?

Teresa (USA): I'll answer that. I don't think that it was so much revenge but everything changed on September 11th. This is the first time in a long time that the USA was an aggressor in a war and that's an example how things have changed in this country since that day.

Here Nadine presents her theory as to why the United States has adapted what she perceives to be an aggressive foreign policy and then checks with the American group to see if they agree with this. In the same way, Günther, writing in an e-mail, puts the following belief about his own culture to his partner and waits for her reaction:

(16)

I know how Germans are seen in many other countries and I am really sorry that many people treat Germans with prejudices because I know that we have one of the best and most democratic governments around the world. The German society is a multi-cultural one and especially in our region people from all around the world live door to door. How do you think about that?

Describing his own government as "one of the best and most democratic governments around the world" and then asking his partner what she thinks about that might appear to be almost a provocation on the part of the German student in order to find out her true opinion of Germany. In his final feedback, Günther seemed to confirm that this had been his strategy for finding out more about the foreign culture and adapting his opinions: "I hoped to find some of my clichés about American society refuted, but either they are rooted too solid, or my partner didn't come up with convincing arguments." Instead of trying to find out more about the context in which the American behavior was located, Günther (and many others) appeared to be looking to their partners for an intensive exchange in which theories and stereotypes about both cultures were put forward and debated before being confirmed or rejected. Sandra makes a similar comment with respect to the videoconferences: "I think that it is something natural trying to persuade each other that one's own viewpoint is right." What Sandra might not realize is that trying to persuade someone else that their opinions and beliefs are wrong may be more "natural" for speakers of German as a conversational style than it is for speaker of U.S. English. However, in intercultural exchanges such an approach may be less appropriate and it is not the goal of ethnographic research. Nevertheless, this "technique" would appear to be very common among learners in intercultural exchanges—even among speakers of other languages. In O'Dowd (2003, p. 234), a Spanish student, Manuel, also used this approach in order to engage his e-mail partner in dialogue.

What then can be done to avoid students drawing rather critical conclusions from their intercultural contact? First, teachers might establish more asymmetrical projects with contacts in the target culture which would more closely resemble the relationship between ethnographer and informant. Such projects are already quite well known and are described by Eck, Legenhausen, and Wolff as "open projects"

(1995, pp. 99–101). Nevertheless, it may be difficult to find members of the target culture (especially classes of students) who are willing to supply information about their culture and lives and yet not receive similar information from their partners.

A second, perhaps more realistic option (and one which may be more relevant to program coordinators) is to offer learners more extensive training in ethnographic techniques and to make them more aware of the ideal outcomes of intercultural contact. Roberts *et al.* (2002) provide a useful description of an introductory course in ethnographic research methods which is offered to language students at some English universities. Language program directors might offer separate courses in the techniques of cultural investigation in order to enhance the cultural components of their language programs. Such courses could be offered in English to students of a variety of foreign languages; the principles could later be applied to the students' specific context within their usual language classes.

When learners become more conscious that their aim is not to debate with their partners but rather to understand how they experience their worlds and why this is so, then they may become more objective in their approaches and less willing to expect their partner to change all the stereotypes which they have of the target culture. As was pointed out earlier in this chapter, the German class had had relatively little time to become acquainted with the principles and techniques of ethnography and this may have been the reason why they were unable to maintain their stance as ethnographers. Further work on this method may have led them to focus less on a "right and wrong" attitude to cultural difference. It is interesting to note that *The Ealing Ethnography Project* for language learning has also encountered the tendency among learners to judge the behavior of their informants according to their own frames of reference. Jordan reports that students often find themselves "slipping into inappropriate value judgements" (2002, p. 344) when they are writing up their ethnographic studies after they have finished their fieldwork.

Conclusion

This chapter set out to explore whether or not language learners could successfully engage in ethnographic research within their own classroom through the use of networked communication tools for the purposed of developing what Byram (1997) refers to as intercultural communicative competence (ICC). Particular attention was paid to the role of videoconferencing technology and its combination with e-mail in order to facilitate this learning goal. Two significant findings emerged. First, videoconferencing and e-mail each supported different aspects of ethnographic interviewing and ICC. Second, it can be quite difficult for teachers to develop in learners a critical cultural awareness during the necessarily short duration of a telecollaborative exchange.

Students found that class-to-class videoconferencing allowed them to bond and to get to know each other better; it allowed for quick and honest exchanges of questions and answers as well as the clarification of meaning; and it enabled them to receive multiple answers to their questions about the target culture. However, the immediacy of the medium in conjunction with the visual cues meant that students were often unable to avoid or ignore awkward subjects and this, in turn, gave rise to misunderstandings and moments of tension between the two groups. Nevertheless, the medium proved to be suitable for the development of learners' skills of discovery and interaction in real time. E-mail, in contrast, was more suitable for sending and receiving more in-depth and extensive descriptions of the two cultures. It also allowed learners more time to reflect on what they were sending and receiving. The e-mail content provided learners with more detailed and well-explained information about the foreign culture which they could analyze and use as a starting point for further investigation. As a result, e-mail may be better suited for developing knowledge of the target culture as well as the skills of interpreting and relating. A combination of both communication tools is ideal for the comprehensive development of ICC and program coordinators may need to consider how to provide students and teachers with opportunities to use both in their telecollaborative projects.

The second main finding of this chapter is related to why the German group was relatively unsuccessful in carrying out their role as ethnographic interviewers. Bredella describes intercultural understanding as the ability to "reconstruct the context of the foreign, take the others' perspective and see things through their eyes" (2002, p. 39). While students in the current study were able to identify the context in which the American behavior and beliefs were located, they were often unwilling to stand back from their own culture and accept this behavior and beliefs as the product of another cultural context. Instead, they often choose to compare it to their own and then reject the alternative as "wrong" or "unconvincing." This was especially the case for issues about which the learners felt particularly strongly.

Teachers need to emphasize to learners that it is necessary for them to abstract themselves from debates in which the cultural values and beliefs of a certain group are determined to be "right" or "wrong" because this is a futile activity and one that is inevitably doomed to failure. Instead, learners need to see themselves more as young social scientists or ethnographers who are objectively researching the cultural context which influences and shapes the way their partners see the world. Their task is not to agree or disagree with their partners, but rather to learn more about their partners' world—and their own. It becomes evident that intercultural exchanges do not involve a "natural" approach to seeing foreign behavior. Therefore, students involved in telecollaborative projects need to receive explicit guidance in developing cultural awareness. Further training in ethnography and in other intercultural learning activities are likely to help develop this attitude of openness to alternative perspectives on one's own and the target culture.

Notes

1. The names of students mentioned in the text are pseudonyms.
2. For a more in-depth discussion of the pros and cons of the different systems of language use in telecollaborative exchanges, see O'Dowd (2005). See Bauer *et al.* (this

volume) for exchanges in L1; see Belz (this volume) for the advantages of bilingual exchanges in the construction of contrastive learner corpora.

References

Agar, Michael. 1980. *The Professional Stranger.* New York: Academic Press.

Barro, Ana, Shirley Jordan, and Celia Roberts. 1998. Cultural Practice in Everyday Life: The Language Learner as Ethnographer. In *Language Learning in Intercultural Perspective,* edited by Michael Byram and Mike Fleming, 76-97. Cambridge: Cambridge University Press.

Bateman, Blair. 2002. Promoting Openness Toward Culture Learning: Ethnographic Interviews for Students of Spanish. *The Modern Language Journal* 86(3): 318-330.

Bauer, Beth, Lynne deBenedette, Gilberte Furstenberg, Sabine Levet, and Shoggy Waryn. 2005. The *Cultura* Project. In *Internet-mediated Intercultural Foreign Language Education,* edited by Julie A. Belz and Steven L. Thorne, 31-62. Boston, MA: Thomson Heinle.

Beers, Maggie. 2001. A Media-Based Approach to Developing Ethnographic Skills for Second Language Teaching and Learning. *Zeitschrift für Interkulturellen Fremdsprachenunterricht* 6(2): 1-26. *http://www.spz.tu-darmstadt.de/projekt_ejournal/jg_06_2/beitrag/beers2.htm*

Belz, Julie A. 2001. Institutional and Individual Dimensions of Transatlantic Group Work in Network-Based Language Teaching. *ReCALL* 13(2): 213-231.

———. 2003. From the Special Issue Editor. *Language Learning & Technology* 7(2): 2-5. *http://llt.msu.edu/vol7num2/speced.html*

———. 2005. At the Intersection of Telecollaboration, Learner Corpus Analysis, and L2 Pragmatics: Considerations for Language Program Direction. In *Internet-mediated Intercultural Foreign Language Education,* edited by Julie A. Belz and Steven L. Thorne 207-246. Boston, MA: Thomson Heinle.

Belz, Julie A., and Andreas Müller-Hartmann. 2003. Teachers as Intercultural Learners: Negotiating German-American Telecollaboration Along the Institutional Fault Line. *The Modern Language Journal* 87(1): 71-89.

Bredella, Lothar. 2002. For a Flexible Model of Intercultural Understanding. In *Intercultural Experience and Education,* edited by Geof Alred, Michael Byram, and Mike Fleming, 31-49. Clevedon: Multilingual Matters.

Buckett, John, and Gary Stringer. 1997. ReLaTe: A Case Study in Language Teaching using the Mbone. Paper presented at Desktop Videoconferencing: Tomorrow's World Today. *UKERNA / JTAP Workshop. http://piglet.ex.ac.uk/pallas/relate/papers/ukerna97.html*

Butler, Mike, and Steevn Fawkes. 1999. Videoconferencing for Language Learners. *Journal of the Association for Language Learning* 19: 46-49.

Byram, Michael. 1997. *Teaching and Assessing Intercultural Communicative Competence.* Clevedon, UK: Multilingual Matters.

———. 1999. Acquiring Intercultural Communicative Competence: Fieldwork and Experiential Learning. In *Interkultureller Fremdsprachenunterricht,* edited by Lothar Bredella and Werner Delanoy, 358-380. Tübingen: Gunter Narr Verlag.

Byram, Michael, and Mike Fleming, eds. 1998. *Language Learning in Intercultural Perspective.* Cambridge: Cambridge University Press.

Byrnes, Heidi. 1986. Interactional Style in German and American Conversations. *Text* 2(1): 189-206.

Cohen, Louis, and Lawrence Manion. 1994. *Research Methods in Education.* London: Routledge.

Davis, Kathryn. 1995. Qualitative Theory and Methods in Applied Linguistics Research. *TESOL Quarterly* 29(3), 427-453.

Eck, Andreas, Lienhard Legenhausen, and Dieter Wolff. 1995. *Telekommunikation und Fremdsprachenunterricht: Informationen, Projekte, Ergebnisse*. Bochum: AKS-Verlag.

Firth, Alan, and Johannes Wagner. 1997. On Discourse, Communication, and (Some) Fundamental Concepts in SLA Research. *The Modern Language Journal* 81: 285–300.

Fischer, Gerd. 1998. *E-mail in Foreign Language Teaching. Towards the Creation of Virtual Classrooms.* Tuebingen: Stauffenburg Medien.

Fischhaber, Katrin. 2002. Digitale Ethnographie: Eine Methode zum Erlernen interkultureller Kompetenz im Fremdsprachenunterricht. *Zeitschrift für interkulturellen Fremdsprachenunterricht* 7(1): 23 pp. *http://www.spz.tu-darmstadt.de/projekt_ejournal/jg_07_1/beitrag/fischhaber1.htm*

Furstenberg, Gilberte, Sabine Levet, Kathryn English, and Katherine Maillet. 2001. Giving a Virtual Voice to the Silent Language of Culture: The Culture Project. *Language Learning & Technology* 5(1): 55–102. *http://llt.msu.edu/vol5num1/furstenberg/default.html*

Geertz, Clifford. (1973). *The Interpretation of Cultures: Selected Essays*. New York: Basic Books.

Goodfellow, Robin, Ingrid Jeffreys, Terry Miles, and Tim Shirra. 1996. Face-To-Face Language Learning at a Distance? A Study of a Videoconferencing Try-Out. *ReCALL* 8(2): 5–16.

Guilherme, Manuela. 2000. Intercultural Competence. In *Routledge Encylopaedia of Language Teaching and Learning*, edited by Michael Byram, 296–299. London: Routledge.

Hanson-Smith, Elizabeth. 1999. Classroom Practice: Using Multimedia for Input and Interaction in CALL Environments. In *CALL Environments: Research, Practice and Critical Issues,* edited by Joy Egbert and Elizabeth Hanson-Smith, 189–215. Virginia: TESOL.

House, Julianne. 2000a. How to Remain a Non-Native Speaker. In *Cognitive Aspects of Foreign Language Learning and Teaching*, edited by Claudia Riemer, 101–118. Tübingen: Gunter Narr Verlag.

———. 2000b. Understanding Misunderstanding: A Pragmatic-Discourse Approach to Analyzing Mismanaged Rapport in Talk Across Cultures. In *Culturally Speaking: Managing Rapport Through Talk Across Cultures*, edited by Helen Spencer-Oatey, 145–165. London: Continuum.

Kern, Richard. 2000. *Literacy and Language Teaching*. Oxford: Oxford University Press.

Kinginger, Celeste, Alison Gourvés-Hayward, and Vanessa Simpson. 1999. A Tele-Collaborative Course on French-American Intercultural Communication. *French Review* 72(5): 853–866.

Kramer, Jürgen. 1997. *British Cultural Studies*. München: W. Fink Verlag.

Kramsch, Claire. 1993. *Context and Culture in Language Teaching*. Oxford: Oxford University Press.

Kramsch, Claire, and Steven L. Thorne. 2002. Foreign Language Learning as Global Communicative Practice. In *Language Learning and Teaching in the Age of Globalization*, edited by David Block and Deborah Cameron, 83–100. London: Routledge.

Moore, Nick. 2002. Review of E-Moderating: The key to teaching and learning online. Language Learning and Technology, 6(3): 21–24. *http://llt.msu.edu/vol6num3/review1/default.html*

Müller-Hartmann, Andreas. 2000. Wenn sich die Lehrenden nicht verstehen, wie sollen sich dann die Lernenden verstehen? Fragen nach der Rolle der Lehrenden in global vernetzten Klassenräumen. In *Fremdverstehen zwischen Theorie und Praxis*, edited by Lothar Bredella, Herbert Christ and Mikael Legutke, 275–301. Narr: Tübingen.

Nemetz-Robinson, Gail. 1985. *Crosscultural Understanding*. New York: Pergamon Press.

O'Dowd, Robert. 2000. Intercultural Learning via Videoconferencing: A Pilot Exchange Project. *ReCALL* 12(1): 49–63.

————. 2003. Understanding "The Other Side": Intercultural Learning in a Spanish-English E-Mail Exchange. *Language Learning & Technology* 7(2): 118-144. *http://llt.msu.edu/ vol7num2/odowd/default.html*

————. 2005. Negotiating Socio-cultural and Institutional Contexts: The case of Spanish-American Telecollaboration. *Language and Intercultural Communication* 5(1): 40-56.

Roberts, Celia. 2002. Ethnography and Cultural Practice: Ways of Learning During Residence. In *Revolutions in Consciousness: Local Identities, Global Concerns in Languages and Intercultural Communication*, edited by Sylvette Cormeraie, David Killick, and Margaret Parry, 36-42. Leeds: International Association for Language and Intercultural Communication.

Roberts, Celia, Michael Byram, Ana Barro, Shirley Jordan, and Brian Street. 2001. *Language Learners as Ethnographers*. Clevedon: Multilingual Matters.

Robinson-Stuart, Gail, and Honorine Nocon. 1996. Second Culture Acquisition: Ethnography in the Foreign Language Classroom. *The Modern Language Journal* 80(4): 431-449.

Roblyer, Michael. 1997. Videoconferencing. *Learning and Teaching with Technology* 24(5): 58-61.

Spradley, James. 1979. *The Ethnographic Interview*. New York: Holt, Rinehart, and Winston.

Stern, H. H. David. 1983. *Fundamental Concepts of Language Teaching*. Oxford: Oxford University Press.

Wallace, Michael. 1998. *Action Research for Language Teachers*. Cambridge: Cambridge University Press.

Warschauer, Mark, ed. 1996a. *Telecollaboration in Foreign Language Learning*. Honolulu: Second Language Teaching and Curriculum Center.

————. 1996b. Comparing Face-To-Face and Electronic Discussion in the Second Language Classroom. *CALICO Journal* 13(2): 7-26.

————. 1998. *Electronic Literacies*. New Jersey: Lawrence Erlbaum Associates.

Wilcox, James. 2000. *Videoconferencing and Interactive Multimedia: The Whole Picture*. New York: Telecom Books.

Zähner, Christoph, Agnés Fauverge, and Jan Wong. 2000. Task-Based Language Learning Via Audiovisual Networks? In *Network-Based Language Teaching: Concepts and Practice*, edited by Mark Warschauer and Richard Kern, 186-203. Cambridge: Cambridge University Press.

Appendix 1
End-of-Term Questionnaire

Name (optional):

Your Home Culture:

This term you have taken part in an online exchange project involving students at the Universities of Zanesville, in the USA and Essen in Germany. This exchange involved interaction via both e-mail and videoconferencing. This questionnaire has been designed to find out your opinion and feelings about these online learning activities. Please take a minute or two to think about the questions before writing down your answers. In all cases be honest with your answers, and where possible, give examples to explain what you mean.

All your identities will remain *anonymous* in my research reports.

Thanks for your help, Robert

1. Generally speaking, what would you say you have learned from this intercultural exchange?
2. How did you find the task of analyzing the e-mails you received from your partner and writing an essay about it? Did you find anything difficult about this task?
3. Did you find it difficult to describe and talk about your home culture to your partner? What strategies or techniques did you use to get across your cultural perspective?
4. How did you find the experience of videoconferencing with the target group? Was it "different" from the e-mail exchange?
5. Do you think that each medium has advantages over the other one for these intercultural exchanges? If so, name them:
   Advantages of e-mail over videoconferencing:
   Advantages of videoconferencing over e-mail:
6. Did you find the ethnographic techniques we learned in the course useful in the exchange? Why? Why not?

Chapter 5
Morphological Development in Spanish-American Telecollaboration

Paola E. Dussias

Abstract

The present study examines the linguistic consequences of computer-mediated communication between foreign language (L2) learners of Spanish and native Spanish speakers. In particular, it investigates whether the benefits attributed to intercultural computer-mediated interactions are transferable to face-to-face communication by examining whether e-mail and chat-room interactions that took place over a period of three months resulted in increased linguistic gains. L2 learners of Spanish were assigned to either an experimental group or a control group. Participants in the experimental group engaged in computer-mediated interactions with native speakers of Spanish residing in Almería, Spain. The learners in the control group interacted electronically with other learners of Spanish of similar proficiency. Linguistic gains were assessed by examining the transcriptions of OPI interviews that were conducted immediately before the learners began the computer-mediated communication sessions and after the last session ended three months later. The results reveal that learners in the experimental group showed increased linguistic control in the use of overt-null subjects in Spanish as well as greater communicative fluency, relative to learners in the control group. These findings suggest the beneficial role of telecollaborative interactions between native speakers and nonnative speakers with respect to linguistic competence.

Introduction

It has been suggested (e.g., Kern and Warschauer 2000; Kern, Ware, and Warschauer 2004) that computer-mediated communication (CMC) provides an ideal forum for language learners to benefit from interaction with native speakers (NS) to enhance foreign language (L2) development. This is because the written nature of the discourse may provide a private, stress-free environment with access to input, self-paced practice, feedback, and opportunities for negotiation of meaning (e.g., Blake 2000; Nagata 1993; Nagata and Swisher 1995; Neri, Cucchiarini, Strik, and Boves 2002; Pellettieri 2000; Rosa and Leow 2004; Smith 2003), while it, at the same time, affords learners with greater opportunities to notice and to reflect on the form and content of the input.[1]

Despite the appeal of CMC as a potential tool to enhance L2 learning, research studies assessing the effects of online interaction on language development and language use are only recently beginning to emerge. The findings reported under this rubric have produced conflicting results, with some studies suggesting that computer-mediated interaction does not result in the development of greater syntactic complexity and lexical richness in the L2 (e.g., Abrams 2003; Blake 2000) and other studies reporting a positive relationship between synchronous and asynchronous interactions and L2 language development (e.g., Belz and Kinginger 2003, Pellettieri 2000; Sotillo 2000). To shed light on the potential benefits of computer-mediated interactions, the present study investigates the role of telecollaboration, defined as the use of Internet-based communication for *intercultural* interactions, on the development of *oral* proficiency in L2 learners of Spanish. The participants were part of a larger group of L2 language learners who were enrolled in fourth-semester college-level foreign language courses. Participants were assigned to either an experimental group (i.e., telecollaboration group) or a control group (i.e., non-telecollaboration group). Learners in the experimental group participated in e-mail and chat-room interactions with NSs of Spanish (i.e., *inter*cultural CMC), whereas learners in the control group interacted electronically with other learners of Spanish of similar proficiency (i.e., *intra*cultural CMC). Linguistic gains were assessed by examining the language samples obtained from *transcriptions* (not the ultimate ratings) of Oral Proficiency Interviews (OPI). These were conducted immediately before the learners began CMC sessions and immediately after the last session ended three months later. To anticipate the outcomes, the findings of four participants reveal that learners in the experimental group showed increased linguistic control in the use of overt-null subjects in Spanish, as well as greater communicative fluency, relative to learners in the control group.

In what follows, an overview of the most recent findings on the relationship between native speaker-nonnative speaker (NS-NNS) interactions and the role of CMC on language outcomes is provided. Next, the present study is discussed, the goal of which was to assess the potential benefits of NS-NNS interactions carried out through synchronous and asynchronous online tools. Finally, we provide a discussion of the potential implications of the role of CMC in L2 development.

NS-NSS Interactions and Language Outcomes

According to the *Interactionist Hypothesis* for second language acquisition (SLA), two aspects of L2 learner interaction have been identified as fostering grammatical development. One is form-focused negotiation. For instance, Swain (1985, 1995) has argued that negotiation of meaning "pushes" learners from the kind of semantic processing characteristic of language comprehension to a more syntactic sort of processing, because the interlocutors work cooperatively to determine the source of the communicative problem, which often arises as a result of the nontargetlike use of lexical, syntactic, or semantic features by L2 learners (see also Swain and Lapkin 1995; Varonis and Gass 1985). The cognitive processes (e.g.,

their development in L1 and L2 Spanish acquisition studies (e.g., Andersen 1990; Guntermann 1992; Lafford and Ryan 1995; López-Ornat, Fernández, Gallo, Mariscal 1994; Montrul and Salaberry 2003; Morales 1986; Ryan and Lafford 1992; Salaberry 2002, 2003; Silva-Corvalán 1982; VanPatten 1987) and because learners demonstrate difficulty with these features at this stage in their L2 development.

In order to determine the occurrence of language gains in oral production, it was first necessary to match learners from the control group with learners from the experimental group on linguistic ability prior to the treatment. To do this, an examination of the pre-treatment speech samples for each of the seven language features listed previously was conducted. The findings revealed that the eight learners were at disparate levels of grammatical development for each of these seven features. In this respect, some learners produced over 60% subject-verb agreement errors, *por/para* errors and *ser/estar* errors in their pre-treatment sample, whereas other learners exhibited over 85% accuracy on the same linguistic features. Additionally, the pre-treatment and post-treatment samples were characterized by inconsistencies and mismatches in the type of grammatical features elicited by the OPI interviewers. For example, whereas a learner may have discussed a particular past event with relatively high linguistic accuracy during the pre-treatment interview, the same linguistic feature was not elicited by the interviewer conducting the post-treatment interview for that same learner. Therefore, for some learners, the data in the pre- and post-treatment samples did not uniformly contain the same type of linguistic features. Given these limitations, only one learner from the control group (Michelle) and one learner from the experimental group (Nick) could be matched on the basis of similar pre-treatment performance (between 35% and 70% accuracy) on two of the seven features investigated (i.e., agreement processes and communicative fluency), and two other learners (Erica from the control group and Susan from the experimental) could be matched at 70% or more accuracy on the use of null-overt subject pronouns and agreement processes in Spanish (Table 1). Therefore, these language features constitute the core of the analysis presented below.

Table 1

Pre- and Post-Treatment Results Provided in Percentage of Incorrect Responses for the Four Focal Learners

	Pre-treatment Scores				Post-treatment Scores			
	Nick	**Michelle**	**Susan**	**Erica**	**Nick**	**Michelle**	**Susan**	**Erica**
Subject-verb agreement errors	64%	40%	9%	8%	63%	38%	8%	11%
Gender Agreement errors	32%	32%	7%	10%	29%	33%	8%	9%
Null/overt subject use	N/A	N/A	30%	35%	N/A	N/A	9%	30%

Results

Overall, there was much variability in the incidence of linguistic inaccuracies in the learners' language, and some students struggled more than others to answer the questions addressed during the interview. Below, the findings for each participant are presented, beginning with the learners in the experimental group.

Nick

In his pre-telecollaboration OPI interview, Nick spent a significant amount of time formulating his responses and exhibited disfluent speech, as evidenced by the occurrence of lexical gaps, lexical innovations, and lexical retrieval difficulties caused by the inaccessibility of lexical information, which required additional time for the planning of the spoken utterances in the second language. Suggestive evidence for this comes from the frequent use of statements such as *¿cómo se dice?* "how do you say . . .?," *¿qué (sic) es la palabra?* "what is the word for," and *no sabe (sic) la palabra* "I don't know the word" preceding the syntactic position where a noun is required. Additional evidence also comes from the occasional use of English nouns and verbs in the course of the interview, the use of lexical innovations (i.e., words composed of English stems and Spanish inflections) and of repetitions of articles and prepositions before the production of Spanish nouns. Examples 1 through 3 below illustrate lexical gaps; 4 through 6 exemplify lexical innovations[4]; and 7 to 9 demonstrate repetition of articles and prepositions befote nouns.[5]

(1)

Si, estoy en estudiante de um, de uh, de, hmm, uh, estoy estudiante de *accounting*; no, no sabe la palabra.

"Yes, I am a student of um, of uh, of, hmm, uh, I am a student of *accounting*; I, don't, don't know the word."

(2)

. . . y después de esto voy a la, a trabajar, uh, (incomprehensible) de, uh, de, uh,

no, no, no conoso (sic) la, uh, la palabra para *insurance*.

". . . and after this I go to the, to work, uh, (incomprehensible) of, uh, of, uh, I don't, I don't, I don't know the, uh, the word for insurance."

(3)

Pero yo tengo un cosa con mi, uh, con me, uh; no sabe la palabra para *legs*.

"But I have a thing with my, uh, with my, uh; I don't know the word for legs."

(4)

Me gusta estudio en la universidad de Alicante en uh, cuatro más *monthos*.

"I would like to study at the University of Alicante in, uh, four more months."

(5)

Si, eh, uh, no lo *understande*.

"Yes, eh, uh, I don't understand you."

(6)

No, es, es más de otras cosas, cosas de porque me quiero hablar con *costumumbres, costum* ...

"No, it is, it is more about other things; reasons why I need to talk to customers ..."

(7)

Somos, uh, cerca de Philadelphia, so, pues, es dos horas en, en, en la dirección de East.

"We are, uh, near Philadelphia, so, well, it is two hours, in, in, in the direction toward East."

(8)

Estoy haciendo la estudiante que estudiando aquí en un, en, en, en poco semanas.

"I am a student who will be studying here in, a, in, in, in a few weeks."

(9)

¿Cómo es la, la, um, como es la, la día allí?

"How is the, the, um, how is the, the day there?"

Nick's pre-telecollaborative speech was also characterized by a lack of control of agreement processes, both within noun phrases (e.g., determiner-noun and adjective-noun agreement), and between grammatical subjects and their corresponding verbs. Adjectives and determiners in Spanish must agree in gender (masculine or feminine) and number (singular or plural) with the noun they modify. Grammatical and semantic gender in Spanish is normally marked with -o at the end of masculine nouns, and -a at the end of feminine nouns. In addition, nouns that end with a consonant can be masculine or feminine. Plural forms are marked by adding -s to singular nouns that end in -o and -a, and -es to those that end in consonant.

Of the 81 nouns preceded by a determiner in Nick's pre-telecollaborative sample, 32% contain gender agreement errors, although only 1% shows mistakes in number agreement. The difference in error rates between the two agreement types may be a consequence of positive transfer of number marking processes between English and Spanish. Both languages use a consonant to mark plurality and in both cases the consonant is orthographically represented with the letters {-s} or {-es}; this overlap may confer an advantage to the learner when computing number agreement during real-time language production in the L2.

Most determiner-noun agreement errors occurred when the noun endings did not provide a cue to its grammatical gender. For instance, the italicized nouns in examples 10 through 15 are masculine; however, in such cases, Nick used the feminine article.

(10)

Durante *la día* cuando, cuando estoy estudiando . . .

"During the day, when I am studying . . ."

(11)

Voy a la, vamos a *la parque*

"I go to the, we go to the park"

(12)

Cuando voy a este restaurante y, uh, a *la menú*

"When I go to this restaurant and, uh, to the menu"

(13)

No sabe la nombre

"I don't know the name"

(14)

No estoy bien a *la golf*

"I am not good at golf"

(15)

Es *nombre vieja*

"It's an old name"

Gender agreement errors also occurred when the gender of the noun was morphologically transparent. That is, nouns such as *baño* "bathroom," *semana* "week," and *familia* "family," which are unambiguously marked for masculine or feminine gender, surfaced with determiners whose gender marking was morphologically incongruent (i.e., *la baño* instead of *el baño*; *el semana* instead of *la semana*; *los familias* instead of *las familias*). Finally, only a negligible amount of agreement errors occurred with nouns that were semantically marked for gender. For example, Nick used the phrase *la estudiante* ("the student, feminine") instead of *el estudiante* ("the student, masculine") to refer to himself.

Lack of agreement between grammatical subjects and verbs was also evident in Nick's pre-telecollaborative speech. Of the 108 verb tokens that appeared in the data set, 48% were correct forms of the Spanish copula *ser/estar*. The vast majority of these, however, were instances of the present singular first person form or of formulaic expressions (i.e., *estoy (sic) estudiante* "I am a student," *¿qué (sic) es la palabra?* "what is the word," *es buena cosa (sic)* "it's a good thing"). If one excludes these cases, 64% of the remaining verbs appeared with incorrect verbal affixes or as entirely uninflected. In examples (16) and (17) below, Nick uses *me levanta* "she/he wakes me up" and *se levántame* (an illicit phrase in Spanish) instead of *me levanto* "I wake up," *báñame* "bathe me" instead of *me baño*, *vas* "you go" instead of *voy* "I go," and *trabajar* "to work" instead of *trabajo* "I work."

(16)

Interviewer: ¿Cuál es, em, cuál es su rutina diaria en estos días? ¿Qué hace usted en estos días?

"What's, em, what's your daily routine these days? What are you doing these days?"

Nick: Uh, cuando *me levanta* de la mañana, tomo un ban, ban, voy a la baño y, y, *báñame*, uh. ¿Qué es la palabra? Uh, se *levántame*, y uh, tomo la ropa y, *vas* a las clases por la mañana (unintelligible), nueve o ocho por la mañana, y tengo clases a la cuatro, y después de esto voy a la, a trabajar, uh, (incomprehensible) de, uh, de, uh, no, no, no conozo la, uh, la palabra para insurance.

"Uh, when I wake up in the morning, I take a ba, ba, I go to the bathroom, and, and, I take a bath, uh. What's the word? Uh, I wake up, and uh, I get dressed and, I go to my classes in the morning (unintelligible), nine or eight in the morning, and I have classes at four, and after this I go to the, to work, uh (incomprehensible) for, uh, for, uh, I don't, I don't, I don't the, uh, the word for insurance."

(17)

Interviewer: . . . pero ¿qué pasa entonces los fines de semana?

". . . but what goes on then on weekends?"

Nick: Trabajar por el fin de semana.

"I work on the weekends."

To determine the impact of the telecollaborative experience on Nick's oral production and linguistic development, an analysis of the OPI transcripts obtained from the post-telecollaboration interview was performed to establish the existence, if any, of gains in the lexical or morphosyntactic domains discussed above. Perhaps the most perceptible improvement in Nick's speech was a decline in disfluency. This is evidenced by the disappearance of lexical innovations from Nick's speech, as well an increased control of vocabulary previously absent from his repertoire. In 18 and 19, for example, Nick uses words (e.g., accountant and insurance company) that were unfamiliar to him at the time of his pre-telecollaboration experience.

(18)

Ah!, Estoy en la, uh, en State College, que es a la universidad de Penn State, uh, dónde me estudiendo, uh, soy estudiendo negocios internacionales y uh, cuent, uh (tisk) contable.

"Ah! I am at the, uh, in State College, which is at Penn State University, uh, where I study, uh, I am studying international business and, uh, account, uh, (tisk) accounting."

(19)

Sí, uh, trabajo en una, una compañía de seguros, para cinco, diez años, uh, horas.

"Yes, uh, I work in an, an insurance company, for five, ten years (self-corrects), uh, hours."

Additionally, Nick's speech exhibits signs of the emergence of manipulations of the linguistic form of his utterances to more precisely convey meaning. In the examples below, the learner is indeed attending to the form of his output and corrects himself as he "pushes" to produce semantically (20) and morpho-syntactically (21–22) accurate utterances. In 20, Nick self-corrects by substituting *años* "years" for *horas* "hours." In 21, he corrects a tense/aspect error, by replacing *preguntaré* "I will ask" for *preguntaba* "I was asking." Finally, in 22 he changes the incorrect person/number marker in *quiero* "I want" for the correct *quieres* "you want" and, at the same time, relocates the pronoun (*me*).

(20)

Sí, uh, trabajo en una, una compañía de seguros, para cinco, diez años, uh, horas.

"Yes, uh, I work in an, an insurance company, for five, ten years (self-corrects), uh, hours."

(21)

Sí, preguntaré, preguntaba sí tendrían algunas um peticiones para empleo.

"Yes, I will ask, (self-corrects), I asked if they had some um employment forms."

(22)

Está bien. ¿Dónde me quiero a pongo? um ¿dónde quieres me pongo?

"That will be fine. Where do I want myself to put (corrects himself)? Um, where do you want me to put myself?"

Not all characteristics of Nick's speech show signs of improvement, however. Agreement is one of them. Sixty-three percent of the verbs that appeared in Nick's post-telecollaborative interview surfaced with subject-verb agreement errors. In addition, of the 93 nouns in the post-telecollaborative sample, 29% contained determiner-noun or adjective-noun agreement errors, as compared to 32% in his pre-telecollaborative sample. As with the pre-telecollaboration sample, these errors occurred with nouns that were transparent for gender (e.g., *la mercado* "the market," *la teatro* "the theater," *la gimnasio* "the gym," *la teléfono* "the telephone," and *la trabajo* "work") as well as with nontransparent nouns (e.g., *la cine* "the movies," *la avión* "the airplane," and *la nombre* "the name").

Susan

In her pre-telecollaborative sample, Susan displays the type of linguistic control characteristic of learners with a higher level of proficiency in Spanish as a second language. For example, Susan is able to narrate events in some detail and discuss topics dealing with personal interests using general vocabulary. In grammatical terms, she shows competency in subject-verb agreement processes, employs clitics in syntactically and discursively appropriate environments, links sentences together smoothly, uses complex structures (e.g., embedding), and shows some command of tense/aspects distinctions as seen in examples 23 and 24.

(23)

Um, hmm, no sé (risa). Pienso que lo que, ah, pasó es que los padres de las chicas pagaban un poco más para las chicas que no podían pagar, um, porque eramos todos una familia grande, y todos saben todos y todos ayudan todos.

"Um, hmm, I don't know (laughs). I think that what happened is that the girls' parents paid a little more for the girls that could not pay, um, because we were all a big family, and everyone knew everyone, and everyone helped everyone."

(24)

Ahm, es un grupo de servicio para los estudiantes que viven en los dormitorios; sí, so, pues organizamos uh actividades para ellos y uh. . . .

"Ahm, it is a service group for students that live in the dorms; yes, so we organize uh activities for them, and uh . . ."

Nonetheless, one type of sentence-level error in Susan's speech is in the domain of agreement. Of the total number of determiner-noun combinations used in her 1586-word sample, 9% contained subject-verb agreement errors, and 7% exhibited gender agreement errors between the determiner and the noun. Approximately 60% of the gender-agreement errors involved nouns whose gender was non-transparent, such as *fin* "end," *clase* "class," *actividad* "activity," *calle* "street," and *coche* "car." The remaining 40% of the errors occurred with nouns whose inflection provided the incorrect cue to gender (i.e., nouns are masculine that despite ending in -*a* such as *problema* "problem") or with feminine nouns that surfaced with masculine determiners (*los cosas* "the things," *el cama* "the bed," and *los ruedas* "the wheels").

At the discourse level, there is evidence that null subjects are part of Susan's interlanguage competence, although overt subjects continue to appear in environments where null subjects are required.[6] One hundred sixty-three tensed verbs appeared in Susan's pre-telecollaboration sample. Following Cameron (1992; see also, Flores-Ferrán 2004; Silva-Corvalán 1994), verbs that required the obligatory omission of subjects were excluded from the analysis conducted in order to determine the pattern of null/overt subject use by Susan. These cases, 42% in the data, included instances in which the learner used verbs with non-personal pronouns (*eso es por qué quieran, um, implementar los uniformes* "that is why they want to, um, implement uniforms"), existential verbs (*había como diesiseis chicas en el equipo* "there were about sixteen girls on the team"), verbs with subjects referring to time expressions (*hace mucho tiempo* "a long time ago"), and verbs referring to atmospheric conditions (*hacía calor* "it was hot"). Environments in which the grammatical subject needed to be obligatorily expressed for semantic reasons were omitted from the analysis. Subjects accompanying verbs in constructions of contrast with *pero*, as shown in 25, were also excluded because the learner's use of the overt pronoun is mandatory to preserve the meaning of the utterance. In other words, by overtly using the pronoun *él* in the phrase *él estaba allí*, the speaker makes it clear that the subjects of *quería* and *estaba* refer to different entities.

(25)

Quería hacer, uh, la derecha, pero él estaba allí, entonces nos chocamos.

"(I) wanted to turn, uh, right but he was there so (we) crashed."

In addition, cases in which the grammatical subject was expressed to avoid ambiguity created by the underspecificity of verbal morphology or to indicate switch reference[7] (Ávila-Jiménez 1995, 1996; Bayley and Pease Álvarez 1997; Cameron 1992; Flores-Ferrán 2002; Morales 1986; Silva-Corvalán 1982, 1994) were also excluded from the analysis. In example (26), for instance, a null subject in place of the pronoun *yo* would signal to the hearer that the first noun phrase functions as the subject of both verbs. In 27, when one compares the target noun phrase of the verb *organiza* "to organize" to the noun phrase of the trigger *no permiten* "they do not allow," one finds that there has been a switch in reference from *él* to *los adultos*. Therefore, the noun phrase accompanying *organiza* was coded as a switch in reference, and was excluded from the analysis.

(26)

Mi familia fue cuando yo tenía como tres años.

"My family went when I was about three years."

(27)

Es muy similar a, a la película de Footloose, sobre un chico que vivía en Chicago y . . . se movía a Tejas, a una ciudad muy muy pequeño, y los adultos no permiten bailar, y él organiza ahm a los estudiantes . . .

"It is very similar to, to the movie Footloose, about a boy who lived in Chicago, and ... moved to Texas, to a very very small city, and the adults do not allow dancing, and he organizes ahm the students ..."

Subjects that required obligatory expression for the reasons explained above accounted for 12% of the data. The remaining 73 verbs (44% of the total number of verbs) were analyzed to calculate the incidence of subjectless sentences in Susan's speech. Of these, 51 verbs (70%) were correctly produced with a null subject, and the remaining 22 verbs (30%) incorrectly surfaced with overt subjects.

Susan's post-telecollaborative sample, however, showed a marked decrease in the use of overt subjects where null subjects were required. A total of 180 tensed verbs appeared in Susan's 1690-word sample. As in the previous case, verbs that obligatorily required null subjects (16% in the data) and overt subjects (14% in the data) were excluded from the analysis. Of the remaining 127 verbs, only 12 verbs (approximately 9% of the data) were incorrectly used with an overt subject, thus signaling an increase in accuracy for this particular feature at 28.5%. Despite Susan's linguistic progress in the use of subject expressions in Spanish, determiner-noun and subject-verb agreement errors continued to be areas that resisted improvement. Eight percent of the nouns used by Susan during the interview contained errors in which there was a mismatch between the gender of the determiner and that of the noun, compared to 7% in the pre-telecollaboration sample.

Overall, the evidence discussed above suggests that increasing learner opportunity for engaging in interactions with NSs via network-based tools may enhance second language acquisition processes with regard to particular linguistic features. To shed further light on this finding, the next section presents the results of the two participants in the control group, who engaged in a similar telecollaborative experience, but with native English-speaking peers learning Spanish.

Michelle

In her pre-collaborative interview, Michelle struggled to communicate in Spanish with the interviewer. Her speech was disfluent and characterized by long and frequent signs of hesitation scattered throughout in her 458-word sample. She exhibited difficulty producing simple utterances, and the construction of basic conversational sentence units was hindered as she strived to create appropriate language forms. This is exemplified below, where Michelle repeats strings of words to produce the correct verbal form, although she is sometimes not successful in her attempts, as shown in example 28.

(28)

El día, um, uh, *hace* um, *hazo* edificios y uh, muy uh, comprar con mis amigas.

"During the day, um, uh, he does um, I do buildings and, uh, very, uh, to buy with my friends."

(29)

OK, sí. Uh, *limpi*, uh, *limpial*, uh, *limpio* el, uh, el pool?

"OK, yes. Uh. I clean, uh, I clean, I clean the, uh, the pool?"

Michelle was able to respond to simple statements but in a highly restricted manner and with much linguistic inaccuracy. For example, approximately 40% of the verbs used in her pre-telecollaborative interview contained errors in subject-verb agreement (30–31), surfaced in their infinitival form (32–33), and appeared in the incorrect tense or with missing auxiliaries (34–35).

(30)

Tiene una amiga que *viva* con mi.

"I have a friend who lives with me."

(31)

Yo *tienen*, uh, las fiesta, fiestes grandes, um . . .

"I have, uh, parties, big parties, um . . ."

(32)

OK, uh, *levantar* mi cama, uh, a las siete y uh, voy, uh, uh, a mi, um, casa a las, um, ocho para clase español.

"OK, uh, to wake my bed up, uh, at seven and uh, I go, uh, uh, to my, um, house at, um, eight for my Spanish class."

(33)

¿Me quiera, um, tú, um, *caminar* a, um, *y dar*, dar las cartas del día?

"Do you want, um, you, um, to walk to, um, and to give, the letters of the day?"

(34)

Uh, um mi otro hermana uh, uh, tiene um, 28 años y um, um, *casada* en noviembre.

"Uh, um, my other sister uh, uh, is um, 28 years old and um, um will be married in November."

(35)

Uh, *estudiando* español y uh, business, uh, como, accounting, uh . . .

"Uh, I am studying Spanish and uh, business, uh, like, accounting, uh . . ."

Michelle's speech was also characterized by a lack of control of gender agreement processes (32% error rate in her pre-treatment sample). In addition, she demonstrated strong interference from English both at the level of sentence structure and at the lexical level. For example, in 36 she incorrectly ends the sentence with a preposition, and in 37 she uses English nouns while attempting to communicate in Spanish.

(36)

El um, que, um, el, um, que tu nadas en?

"The um, that, um, the, um, that you swim in?"

(37)

Y mi final hermano Kevin es un artist.

"And my last brother Kevin is an artist."

After the computer-mediated interactions with her native English peer learning Spanish, Michelle exhibited many of the same linguistic and lexical difficulties. Thirty-three percent of the determiner-noun combinations that occurred in her post-treatment sample appeared with gender agreement errors, and 38% percent of subject-verb combinations contained agreement errors (e.g., *Tiene tres hermanos y una hermana* "I have three bothers and a sister," *viajará a España* "I will travel to Spain"), in infinitival forms (*asistir la universidad de Salamanca* "I will attend the university of Salamanca"), with tense errors (*en el verano [pasado]* . . . *tiene una programa pequeño* "Last summer . . . it has a small program"), or without auxiliaries (*um, fui um, a la universidad en el verano y um, tenido, um, que asiste* . . ."um, I went um, to the university last summer and um, I had, um, to attend . . ."), compared to 40% in her pre-telecollaborative speech.

As in the pre-telecollaboration interview, Michelle continued to experience difficulties accessing lexical information and necessitated hesitation to create appropriate language forms in her post-CMC sample:

(38)

Uh, me gusta, um, (pause) me gusta, um, ir de compras, uh, ir al cine, um, visitar mis amigas, um, viajar a otros ciudades, um, uh, *jug, juga, jugar, jugo* al volleyball.

"Uh, I like to, um, (pause) I like to, um, go shopping, uh, go to the movies, um, visit my friends, um, travel to other cities, um, uh, play, play, play, I play volleyball."

(39)

Y uh, mi hermano Kevin um, es un *artist*.

"And uh, my bother Kevin um, is an artist."

(40)

Él tiene un, um, (pause) una *wife*.

"He has a, um, (pause) a wife."

In 38, she launches several attempts to produce the correct form of *jugar* "to play" before failing; 39 and 40 are instances of the use of English words during the interview, which suggest a limited command of more basic vocabulary. Particularly revealing is that fact that in 39 Michelle experiences the very same lexical gap as in her pre-telecollaborative interview shown in example 37.

Erica

Erica's pre-telecollaborative sample shows that she is able to handle most uncomplicated communicative tasks and successfully sustain the conversations initiated by the interviewer. She is able to narrate complicated events, and makes effective use of familiar vocabulary with sufficient lexical and grammatical accuracy to participate effectively in informal conversations with her interlocutor. For example, Erica used 70 different nouns to describe and narrate events in a number of content areas; of these, the vast majority (90%) exhibited correct gender agreement between the determiner and the noun. This was true even for cases where the noun endings did not provide an obvious cue to gender (*una población* "a town," *una conección* "a connection," *una ciudad* "a city," *una region* "a region," *un día* "a day," and *un lugar* "a place") or where the nouns employed by the learner were low in frequency (e.g., not commonly needed to complete communicative tasks that appear in fourth-semester Spanish textbooks) and therefore not normally encountered by fourth-semester language learners (*el castillo* "a castle," *el mar* "the sea," and *la costa* "the coast"). By and large, Erica was also able to supply the correct subject-verb agreement throughout her pre-telecollaboration interview. Of the 103 verbs present in her sample, only 8% contained subject-verb agreement errors. To illustrate, Erica uses the first person form *llamaré* "I will call" instead of the third person plural form *llamaron* "they called" in example 41; in 42 *estudia* "she studies" is used instead of *estudio* "I study"; finally, in 43, Erica uses *contesta* "she answers" in place of *contesto* "I answer."

(41)

Muchas personas llamaré.

"Many people called."

(42)

Estudia español.

"I studied Spanish."

(43)

Yo contesta.

"I answer."

Tense/aspect distinctions and the use of overt/null subjects are among the linguistic characteristics that appear to occur with some vacillation in Erica's pre-CMC sample. For example, of the 69 verbs that Erica produced while narrating past events, 39% displayed tense/aspect errors, as illustrated in examples 44 and 45.

(44)

Uh, yo tenía cerca de 6 años y una amiga mía era, uh, su padre, um, era un instructor de básquetbol y, uh, por eso yo aprendía uh, baloncesto ....

"Uh, I was about 6 years old and a friend of mine was, uh, her father, um was a basketball instructor and, uh, that's why I was learning, uh, basketball ..."

(45)

Um, un amiga mio, um, ella trabajaba allí, y um, ella tenía, um, más años que yo y, um, ella estoy, *está estudiando* a Penn State también, y, um, y ella me dijo de este trabajo y, um, cuando, um, *iba* allí, um, una, un mujer, um, me preguntó si um, *quiero* trabajar como recepcionista, y por eso yo *encuentro* el trabajo.

"Um, a friend of mine, um, she was working there, and um, she was, um, older than I was and, um, she was, was studying at Penn State as well, and, um, and she told me about this job and, um, when, um, I went there, um, a, a woman, um, asked me if um, I wanted to work as a receptionist, and that's how I found the job."

Erica also shows an emergent grasp of the environment that license null and overt subjects in Spanish. Seventy-six of the 103 verbs in Erica's pre-CMC sample were analyzed for the presence or absence of grammatical subjects. Twenty-five verbs were omitted because they required the obligatory presence or absence of an overt subject. Of the remaining 78 verbs, approximately 35% surfaced with overt subjects, although by target language standards, their environment licenses null subjects. Three of the four instantiations of the pronoun *ella* in 45 represent a case in point. An additional example is provided in 46:

(46)

Había una conección entre el castillo y mi mente porque, um, cuando tenía pocos años y era una niña, um, tenía sueños con el príncipe en el caballo blanco, y, um, *yo* imaginaba un castillo y cuando, uh, *yo* entré en el castillo, um, *yo* pensaba um, ... como el castillo era mi hogar.

"There was a connection between the castle and my mind because, um, when I was younger and I was a girl, um, I used to dream of a prince on a white horse, and, um, I used to imagine a castle and when, uh, I entered the castle, um, I thought um, ... that the castle was my home."

Given the developing nature of the tense/aspect distinctions and overt-null subjects in Erica's interlanguage, these two linguistic aspects will become the main focus of the post-telecollaboration analysis.

First, there is no improvement after the semester-long synchronous or asynchronous interactions with her NNS peer in the accuracy with which Erica marks tense/aspect distinctions. Of the 140 verbs that appear in her post-CMC sample, 51 verbs occur while narrating and describing past events. Of these, 43% appeared with the incorrect marker for tense or aspect, compared to 39% in her pre-CMC sample. An example is provided below:

(47)

Um, sí, um, tenía, cuantos años, 8 años quizás, y um, estaba cantando para, um, mi coro y, *escoge* um, Noche de Paz, y um, la primera vez *yo cantaba* la canción en ingles y entonces en español y la tercera um, tiempo, *canto, cantaba* en alemán, y um, cuando estaba cantando en alemán, no recordaba las palabras, pues, uh, (risa), yo *canto* en palabras que *tienen* sonido en alemán, pero no *sé* que cantaba en eso momento, pero nadie, um, nadie *daba cuento* a eso, pero a mi *tiene*, uh, muy nerviosa y, pero no nadie, nadie conto.

"Um, yes, um, I was, how old, maybe 8 years old, and um, I was singing for, um, my choir and, I chose um, Holy Night, and um, the first time, I sang the song in English, and then in Spanish, and the third um, time, I sang in German, and um when I was signing in German, I could not remember the words, so, uh (laughs), I sang words that sound like German, but I didn't know what I was singing at that moment, but nobody, um, nobody realized it, but I was, uh, very nervous, and, but, nobody realized it."

The use of overt-null subjects seems to have remained roughly the same as well. That is, in 30% of the cases in which a null subject would have been appropriate, Erica employed an overt subject, in comparison to 35% in her pre-CMC sample as seen in example 48:

(48)

Muchas tardes *yo*, uh, trato hacer mi tarea para mis clases, pero, uh, no paso todavía, um, pero um, en las noches tengo muchas actividades; um, *yo* canto en un coro de a capella.

"Many afternoons I, uh, try to do my homework for my classes, but, uh, I don't still don't pass, um, but, um, in the evenings I have many activities; um, I sing in a choir of a cappella."

Accuracy in subject-verb agreement and gender-agreement processes remained largely unchanged. Eleven percent of the 140 verbs in the post-CMC sample appeared with errors in subject-verb agreement in comparison to 8% in the pre-CMC sample; also, 9% of the determiner-noun combinations surfaced with gender-agreement errors. Finally, the use of lexical innovations, which was absent from Erica's first interview, is now present in her speech. In 49, Erika uses the word *instructó* instead of enseñó, and in 50, she uses *arribe* (from the English word *arrive*) in place of its Spanish equivalent *llegar*:

(49)

Era muy diverte cuando, um, ella *instructó*, um, la clase.

"It was a lot of fun when she taught the class."

(50)

Sí, sí, había mucho tráfico y no podía um, *arribe*.

"Yes, yes, there is a lot of traffic and I could not arrive."

Overall, the experience of ongoing e-mail and chat communications in Spanish with English-speaking peers does not seem to have provided learners in the control group with the benefits that were observable during spontaneous oral production for the experimental group.

Discussion and Conclusion

The present study aimed at investigating whether synchronous and asynchronous intercultural interactions foster the development of grammatical competency in learners of Spanish as a second language. In past research, evidence for effectiveness of network-based communications on the development of second language competency has been mixed. Contrary to some past research (Abrams, 2003; Blake, 2000), in the present study, the learners in the experimental group showed improvement in some areas of syntactic development, whereas the learners in the control group did not. Perhaps the most significant gains were obtained by Nick, whose post-telecollaboration speech sample showed an emergent ability to attend to the form of his utterances, and a decrease in the number of pauses, hesitations, and lexical interference from English, which signaled shortcomings in his L2 language abilities. Interactions with NSs of the target language also enhanced Erica's grammatical competence. In particular, her increased use of null-overt subjects in Spanish subsequent to her telecollaborative experience indicates an understanding of native-like discourse strategies.

It is important to note, however, that these findings cannot be taken as an indication that the learners in the control group did not experience improvement in their language abilities or that there is a direct causal relationship between participation in telecollaboration and linguistic gains in the experimental group. In fact, there is ample evidence to support the claim that the types of pedagogical intervention and classroom instruction which allow learners to maintain the overall goal of language for communication while at the same time helping learners to notice structural regularities and to create hypotheses about the target language, are able to assist learners in the attainment of grammatical accuracy (e.g., Doughty and Varela 1998). In short, the language classroom can provide learners with input-rich environments that draw attention to form without compromising processing for meaning. What these findings suggest, however, is that the gains obtained from NS-NNS interactions via the use synchronous and asynchronous tools seem to readily transfer to spontaneous language production. Hence, our finding lends support to the claim made in Sotillo (2000, p. 102) that the type of language elicited in synchronous and asynchronous discussions between NS and NSS reflects the complexity and characteristics of face-to-face interactions. In addition, the results of the present study provide further suggestive evidence that chat interactions and chat logs can be valuable linguistic material for helping students to reflect on their interlanguage (Belz, this volume; Toyoda and Harrison 2002; Tudini 2003).

Naturally, the descriptive nature of the present study warrants caution when generalizing the results presented here to other populations of learners. Further research needs to explore the advantages conferred by network-based communication to larger populations of learners, and should examine the types of input, feedback, and self-repair that may lead to the development of grammatical competence. Future research should also include additional posttests to determine whether the gains observed in this study are sustained long after the telecollaborative interactions have ended. Future studies should also examine how computer-mediated interactions fair with different types of grammatical structures and with learners at different stages of developmental readiness.[8] This is particularly important because not all grammatical forms may be equally amenable to improvement[9] (see, for example, Doughty and Williams 1998 and the articles therein) nor are all learners similarly ready in developmental terms to acquire particular structures (Mackey and Philp 1998). These and other studies should lead to a better understanding of the short- and long-term effects of network-based intercultural interactions in the development of second language competencies.

Notes

1. Recent research indicates, however, that CMC is not as stress-free as has been suggested, and that learners in such interactions may actually experience considerable intercultural tensions (see Belz, 2001, 2003, 2005a; Schneider and von der Emde, this volume)

2. For work on German investigating grammatical development in a telecollaborative environment, the reader is referred to Belz 2004; Belz and Kinginger, 2003; Belz and Vyatkina (in press).

3. This project was funded by a United States Department of Education International Research and Studies Program Grant (CFDA No.: 84.017A) to the *Center for Language Acquisition*, Pennsylvania State University.

4. In examples 4 through 6, Nick uses the word *monthos* in place of the Spanish *meses, understande* in place of *entiendo,* and *costumumbre* instead of *clientes.*

5. Examples presented throughout are given exactly as they were produced by the learners. No errors are corrected. Translations are provided for the intended meaning rather than the literal meaning. Non-targetlike forms in the examples are italicized throughout.

6. Spanish is a null-subject language; that is, a language whose grammar licenses sentences with non-overt subjects.

7. Silva-Corvalán (1982, 1994; see also Flores-Ferrán, 2002; Morales, 1986) has shown that there is a higher frequency for the use of overt subjects in a switch reference environment.

8. Belz and Vyatkina (in press) have suggested that pronouns of address seem more amenable to unassisted development in telecollaboration than do modal discourse markers which require considerable pedagogical intervention.

References

Abrams, Zsuzsanna. 2003. The Effect of Synchronous and Asynchronous CMC on Oral Performance in German. *Modern Language Journal* 87(2): 157-167.

Andersen, Roger. 1990. Models, Processes, Principles, and Strategies: Second Language Acquisition Inside and Outside the Classroom. In *Second Language Acquisition-Foreign Language Learning*, edited by Bill VanPatten and James F. Lee, 45-68. Clevedon, Avon: Multilingual Matters.

Ávila-Jiménez, Bárbara. 1996. Subject Pronoun Expression in Puerto Rican Spanish: A Sociolinguistic, Morphological, and Discourse Analysis. Doctoral dissertation, Cornell University.

———. 1995. The Scope and Limits of Switch Reference as a Constraint on Pronominal Subject Expression. *Hispanic Linguistics* 60(7): 1-27.

Bayley, Robert, and Lucinda Pease-Álvarez. 1997. Null Pronoun Variation in Mexican-Descent Children's Narrative Discourse. *Language Variation and Change* 9: 349-371.

Belz, Julie A. 2001. Institutional and Individual Dimensions of Transatlantic Group Work in Network-Based Language Teaching. *ReCALL* 13(2): 129-147.

———. 2003. Linguistic Perspectives on the Development of Intercultural Competence in Telecollaboration. *Language Learning & Technology* 7(2): 68-117. *http://llt.msu.edu/vol7num2/belz/default.html*

———. 2004. Learner Corpus Analysis and the Development of Foreign Language Proficiency. *System: An International Journal of Educational Technology and Applied Linguistics* 32(4): 577-591.

———. 2005a. Intercultural Questioning, Discovery, and Tension in Internet-Mediated Language Learning Partnerships. *Language and Intercultural Communication* 5(1): 3-39.

———. 2005b. At the Intersection of Telecollaboration, Learner Corpus Analysis, and L2 Pragmatics: Considerations for Language Program Direction. In *Internet-mediated Intercultural Foreign Language Education*, edited by Julie A. Belz and Steven L. Thorne, 207-246. Boston, MA: Thomson Heinle.

Belz, Julie A., and Celeste Kinginger. 2003. Discourse Options and the Development of Pragmatic Competence by Classroom Learners of German: The Case of Address Forms. *Language Learning* 53(4): 591-647.

Belz, Julie A., and Nina Vyatkina. In press. Learner Corpus Analysis and the Development of L2 Pragmatic Competence in Networked Intercultural Language Study: The Case of German Modal Particles. *Canadian Modern Language Review/Revue canadienne des langues vivantes* 62(1).

Blake, Robert. 2000. Computer Mediated Communication: A Window on L2 Spanish Interlanguage. *Language Learning & Technology* 4(1): 120-136.

Cameron, Richard. 1992. Pronominal and Null Subject Variation in Spanish: Constraints, Dialects, and Functional Compensation. Doctoral dissertation, University of Pennsylvania.

Doughty, Catherine, and Elizabeth Varela. 1998. Communicative Focus on Form. In *Focus on Form in Classroom Second Language Acquisition*, edited by Catherine Doughty and Jessica Williams, 114-138. Cambridge, UK: Cambridge University Press.

Echeverría, Sergio. 1978. *Desarrollo de la comprensión infantil de la sintaxis Española*. Concepción, Chile: Universidad de Concepción.

Flores-Ferrán, Nydia. 2002. A Sociolinguistic Perspective on the Use of Subject Personal Pronouns in Spanish Narratives of Puerto Ricans in New York City. Munich, Germany: Lincom-Europa.

———. 2004. Spanish Subject Personal Pronoun Use in New York City Puerto Ricans: Can We Rest the Case of English Contact? *Language Variation and Change* 16: 49-73.

Foster, Pauline, and Peter Skehan. 1996. The influence of planning and task type on second language performance. *Studies in Second Language Acquisition* 18: 229-323.

Gass, Susan. 1997. *Input, Interaction and the Second Language Learner*. Mahwah, NJ: Lawrence Erlbaum Associates.

Gass, Susan, and Evangeline Varonis. 1994. Input, Interaction, and Second Language Production. *Studies in Second Language Acquisition* 16: 283-302.

Guntermann, Gail. 1992. An Analysis of Interlanguage Development Over Time: Part II, *ser* and *estar*. *Hispania* 75: 1294-1303.

Kern, Richard, Paige Ware, and Mark Warschauer. 2004. Crossing Frontiers: New Directions in Online Pedagogy and Research. *Annual Review of Applied Linguistics* 24(1): 243-260.

Kern, Richard, and Mark Warschauer. 2000. Theory and Practice of Network-Based Language Teaching. In *Network-Based Language Teaching: Concepts and Practice*, edited by Mark Warschauer and Richard Kern, 1-19. Cambridge: Cambridge University Press.

Kitade, Keiko. 2000. L2 Learners' Discourse and SLA Theories in CMC: Collaborative Interaction in Internet Chat. *Computer Assisted Language Learning* 13(2): 143-166.

Lafford, Barbara A., and John M. Ryan. 1995. The Acquisition of Lexical Meaning in a Study Abroad Context: The Spanish Prepositions *por* and *para*. *Hispania* 78: 522-547.

Lee, Lina. 2001. Online Interaction: Negotiation of meaning and strategies used among learners of Spanish. *ReCall* 13: 232-244.

———. 2002a. Enhancing Learners' Communication Skills Through Synchronous Electronic Interaction and Task-Based Instruction. *Foreign Language Annals* 35: 16-23.

———. 2002b. Synchronous Online Exchanges: A Study of Modification Devices on Nonnative Discourse Interaction. System: *An International Journal of Educational Technology and Applied Linguistics* 30: 275-288.

———. 2004. Learners' Perspectives on Networked Collaborative Interaction with Native Speakers of Spanish in the US. *Learning Language & Technology* 8 (1): 83-100. *http://llt.msu.edu/vol8num1/lee/default.html*

Long, Michael. 1981. Input, Interaction, and Second Language Acquisition. In *Native Language and Foreign Language Acquisition* edited by Harris Winitz, 259-278. New York: Annuls of the New York Academy of Science.

———. 1983. Native Speaker/Nonnative Speaker Conversation and the Negotiation of Comprehensible Input. *Applied Linguistics* 4(2): 126-141.

———. 1996. The Role of the Linguistic Environment in Second Language Acquisition. In *Handbook of Research on Second Language Acquisition,* edited by William Ritchie and Tej Bhatia, 413-468. New York: Academic.

López-Ornat, Susana, Almudena Fernández, Pilar Gallo, and Sonia Mariscal. 1994. *La Adquisición de la Lengua Española*. Madrid: Siglo XXI.

Mackey, Alison. 1999. Input, Interaction, and Second Language Development: An Empirical Study of Question Formation in ESL. *Studies in Second Language Acquisition* 21(4): 557-587.

Mackey, Alison, Rhonda Oliver, and Jennifer Leeman. 2003. Interactional Input and the Incorporation of Feedback: An Exploration of NS-NNS and NNS-NNS Adult and Child Dyads. *Language Learning* 53(1): 35-66.

Mackey, Alison, and Jenefer Philp. 1998. Conservational Interaction and Second Language Development: Recasts, Responses, and Red Herrings? *Modern Language Journal* 82: 338-356.

Montrul, Silvina, and Rafael Salaberry. 2003. The Development of Tense/Aspect Morphology in Spanish as a Second Language. In *Spanish Second Language Acquisition: State of the Science*, edited by Barbara Lafford and Rafael Salaberry, 47–73. Washington, DC: Georgetown University Press.

Morales, Amparo. 1986. *Gramáticas en contacto: Análisis sintácticos sobre el Español de Puerto Rico*. Puerto Rico/Madrid: Editorial Playor.

Nagata, Noriko. 1993. Intelligent Computer Feedback for Second Language Instruction. *The Modern Language Journal* 77(3): 330–339.

Nagata, Noriko, and Virginia Swisher. 1995. A Study of Consciousness-Raising by Computer: The Effect of Meta-linguistic Feedback on SLA. *Foreign Language Annals* 28: 336–347.

Neri, Ambra, Catia Cucchiarini, Helmer Strik, and Lou Boves. 2002. The Pedagogy-Technology Interface in Computer Assisted Pronunciation Training. *Computer Assisted Language Learning* 15(5): 441–467.

Pellettieri, Jill. 2000. Negotiation in Cyberspace: The Role of Chatting in the Development of Grammatical Competence. In *Network-based Language Teaching: Concepts and Practice*, edited by Mark Warschauer and Richard Kern, 59–86. Cambridge: Cambridge University Press.

Pica, Teresa. 1994. Research on Negotiation: What Does it Reveal about Second-Language Learning Conditions, Processes, and Outcomes. *Language Learning* 44: 493–527.

Rosa, Elena, and Ron Leow. 2004. Computerized Task-Based Instruction in the L2 Classroom: The Effects of Explicitness and Type of Feedback on L2 Development. *Modern Language Journal* 88: 192–217.

Ryan, John M., and Barbara A. Lafford. 1992. Acquisition of Lexical Meaning in a Study Abroad Environment: *Ser* and *estar* and the Granada Experience. *Hispania* 75: 714–722.

Salaberry, Rafael. 2000a. L2 morphosyntactic Development in Text-Based Computer-Mediated Communication. *Computer Assisted Language Learning* 13(1): 5–27.

———. 2000b. Revising the Revised Format of the ACTFL Oral Proficiency Interview. *Language Testing* 17(3): 289–310

———. 2002. L2 Acquisition of Tense-Aspect Morphology. *Tense-Aspect Morphology in L2 Acquisition*, edited by Rafael Salaberry and Yasuhiro Shirai, 1–20. Amsterdam and Philadelphia: John Benjamins.

———. 2003. Tense-Aspect in Verbal Morphology. *Hispania* 86(3): 559–573.

Schmidt, Richard. 1990. The Role of Consciousness in Second Language Acquisition. *Applied Linguistics* 11: 219–258.

Schneider, Jeffrey and Silke von der Emde. 2005. Conflicts in Cyberspace: From Communication Breakdown to Intercultural Dialogue in Online Collaborations. In *Internet-mediated Intercultural Foreign Language Education*, edited by Julie A. Belz and Steven L. Thorne, 178–206. Boston, MA: Thomson Heinle.

Shehadeh, Ali. 1999. Non-Native Speakers Production of Modified Comprehensible Output and Second Language Learning. *Language Learning* 49(4): 627–675

Silva-Corvalán, Carmen. 1982. Subject Expression and Placement in Mexican-American Spanish. In *Spanish in the United States: Sociolinguistic Aspects*, edited by Jon Amaste and Lucía Elías-Olivares, 93–120. New York: Cambridge University Press.

———. 1994. *Language Contact and Change: Spanish in Los Angeles*. New York: Oxford University Press.

Smith, Bryan. 2003. Computer-Mediated Negotiated Interaction: An Expanded Model. *The Modern Language Journal* 87(1): 38–57.

Sotillo, Susana. 2000. Discourse Functions and Syntactic Complexity in Synchronous and Asynchronous Communication. *Language Learning & Technology* 4(1): 82–119. *http://llt.msu.edu/vol4num1/sotillo/default.html*

Swain, Merrill. 1985. Communicative Competence: Some Roles of Comprehensible Input and Comprehensible Output in Its Development. In *Input in Second Language Acquisition*, edited by Susan Gass and Carolyn Madden, 235–245. Rowley, MA: Newbury House.

————. 1995. Three Functions of Output in Second Language Learning. In *Principles and Practice in Applied Linguistics: Studies in Honor of H. G. Widdowson*, edited by Guy Cook and Barbara Seidlhofer, 125–144. Oxford, UK: Oxford University Press.

Swain, Merrill, and Sharon Lapkin. 1995. Problems in Output and the Cognitive Processes They Generate—A Step Towards Second Language Learning. *Applied Linguistics* 16(3): 371–391.

Toyoda, Etsuko, and Richard Harrison. 2002. Categorization of Text Chat Communication Between Learners and Native Speakers of Japanese. *Language Learning & Technology* 6(1): 82–99.

Tudini, Vincenza. 2003. Using Native Speakers in Chat. *Language Learning & Technology* 7(3): 141–159. *http://llt.msu.edu/vol7num3/tudini/default.html*

Varonis, Evangeline, and Susan Gass. 1985. Non-Native/ Non-Native Conversations: A Model for Negotiation of Meaning. *Applied Linguistics* 4: 71–90.

VanPatten, Bill. 1987. Classroom Learners' Acquisition of *ser* and *estar*. In *Foreign Language Learning: A Research Perspective*, edited by Bill VanPatten, Thalia Dvorak, and Jim F. Lee, 19–32. Cambridge: Newbury House.

Acknowledgments

The writing of this paper was supported in part by research assistance from the *Center of Language Acquisition* at The Pennsylvania State University. I would like to thank Jim Lantolf for his generous support. I am indebted to Julie A. Belz and an anonymous reviewer for their insightful suggestions and careful reading of the paper. All remaining errors are my sole responsibility.

Chapter 6
A Study of Native and Nonnative Speakers' Feedback and Responses in Spanish-American Networked Collaborative Interaction

Lina Lee

Abstract

Networked collaborative interaction (NCI) promotes the negotiation for meaning and form that plays a crucial role in the development of language competence. This chapter reports and discusses a study that focused on the examination of relationships among error type, feedback types, and responses in synchronous communication between native teachers and non-native speakers (N = 26) working on two tasks—an open-ended question and a goal-oriented activity. The results revealed that differences were found not in the various types of negotiation moves but in the proportional use of particular moves. The native speakers had an overwhelming tendency to use recasts to provide corrective feedback. This feedback also had the positive effect of drawing learners' attention to form, which led to the repair of errors. Successful uptake, however, does not guarantee second language acquisition. In addition, lexical rather than syntactical errors were the main triggers for negotiation moves generated by both groups of interlocutors. NCI as a form of written visual communication facilitated the response to corrective feedback. Learners generated high rates of repairs for both lexical and syntactical errors. Overall, this study demonstrates that NCI is a powerful communication tool for the enrichment of language learning.

Introduction

In recent years, many foreign language (L2) programs have moved their curriculum toward a communicative-based approach that emphasizes the importance of genuine human interaction in L2 development. Central to such interaction is negotiation of meaning that elicits negative feedback using various types of negotiation moves (e.g., recasts, confirmation checks, and clarification requests) to facilitate comprehension (Long 1996). Crucial to the feedback is a focus-on-form procedure that brings learners' attention to linguistic problems for output modification (Long 1996; Long and Robinson 1998). Modified output, therefore, promotes learners' language accuracy and fluency through increased control over L2 forms (Swain 1995). Feedback through negotiation of meaning and form plays a beneficial role in language acquisition and should be encouraged in language classrooms. Given the limited time that many students spend in the regular classroom and the lack of opportunities that they have to use the target language to interact with others outside the classroom, how can we find an effective means of providing them with acquisition-rich interaction through out-of-class communicative activities? Schmidt (1995) claims that conscious "noticing" of linguistic forms is necessary in order for learning to take place. Through the use of networked collaborative interaction (NCI), how can we make feedback available to L2 classroom learners, engage them in attention to form, and encourage uptake?

NCI has been increasingly implemented in L2 instruction to extend learners' communicative experience beyond the spatial and temporal limitations of the classroom. NCI takes place in real time during which learners are exposed to input, feedback, and output in a way similar to that which they would experience through face-to-face communication. NCI, however, is different from spoken discourse in its textual representation, which relies heavily on writing and readings skills; thus, learners may need more time to process input and output (Abrams 2003). Learners may also pay attention to certain aspects of written discourse on the screen that facilitate input comprehension (Warschauer 1997) or edit the initial response using self-corrections (Blake and Zyzik 2003). This activity, in turn, may lead them to provide and attend to feedback more frequently than during face-to-face oral exchanges. To date, the studies of the potential role of feedback and its effects on L2 development have been conducted mainly in the oral mode (e.g., Ellis, Basturkmen, and Loewen 2001; Iwashita 2003; Leeman 2003; Lyster and Ranta 1997; Mackey 1999; Morris 2002; Oliver 2002). In order to gain a better understanding of the impact of interactive negotiation and feedback in L2, studies must be conducted in different instructional contexts including NCI using both native (NS) and nonnative speakers (NNS).

Only a limited number of research studies have examined the effect of computer-mediated communication (CMC) on learners' interaction (e.g., Blake 2000; Chun 1994; Darhower 2002; Lee 2001, 2002b; Pellettieri 2000; Smith 2003; Tudini 2003). Although these studies are valuable, to the best of my knowledge, no research within the interactionist tradition has explored closely the relationship among error types, feedback types, and uptake moves that learners generate during NCI. The current study is the first NCI research to include NS secondary teachers and NNS learners of Spanish from two U.S. institutions. The distinct roles of the interlocutors in the exchange (e.g., teacher-like vs. learner-like) compound the proficiency differential (e.g., proficient vs. less proficient) and these two interlocutor features together rather than one alone may affect the preference for type of feedback, the nature of the negotiation move, and the amount and types of responses. This paper examines such NS-NNS interaction by addressing three major questions: (1) What types of feedback[1] do NSs and NNSs provide to each other during NCI?; (2) What types of linguistic triggers on the part of the NNSs lead to what types of corrective feedback by the NSs?; and (3) Upon receiving feedback, do NSs and NNSs respond to each other? What types of NNS linguistic problems lead to what types of immediate uptake moves? The analysis of these issues provides language professionals with important pedagogical information for technology-based teaching. Furthermore, language educators will gain insight into a reactive approach to focus-on-form involving the provision and use of feedback during teacher-learner interaction.

Interaction, Negotiation of Meaning, and L2 Development

The early work of Evelyn Hatch in the 1970s led L2 researchers to develop and explore the relationship between interaction and second language acquisition (SLA). Hatch (1978) claims that learners acquire an L2 through interacting with others rather than learning grammatical structures in order to interact. For years, SLA researchers have developed theoretical arguments in support of oral interaction and its effects on the development of learners' interlanguage (e.g., Gass, Mackey, and Pica 1998; Long 1996; Pica 1994; Swain and Lapkin 1998). One of the most compelling theories is the Interaction Hypothesis (IH). The IH suggests that learners not only need to have the opportunity to receive comprehensible input (Krashen 1985) but also to negotiate for meaning to solve communication problems and further achieve mutual understanding (Long 1996). Crucial to the input is how it is made comprehensible through interactive negotiation. Long (1996) points out:

> . . . negotiation of meaning and especially negotiation work that triggers interactional adjustments by the NS or more competent interlocutor, facilitates acquisition because it connects input, internal learner capacities, particularly selective attention, and output in productive ways (pp. 451–452).

Similarly, Pica (1994) stresses the potential role of negotiated interaction in allowing learners to attend to both meaning and form as they engage in trying to understand and be understood. Learners' attention to problematic discourse can arise either from their own production or from what is produced by their interlocutors; the noticing of a mismatch may lead to linguistic modifications (Gass and Varonis 1994). In contrast to semantically processed input, modified output resulting from meaning negotiation fosters L2 development because it pushes learners to reflect consciously on linguistic forms as they engage in syntactic processing (Swain 1995).

Existing SLA research suggests that oral interactive negotiation improves comprehension and L2 development (e.g., Gass and Varonis 1994; Mackey 1999; Pica 1994), draws learners' attention to notice differences between their L1 and L2 (e.g., Gass 1997; Long 1996; Long and Robinson 1998; Schmidt 1995), and pushes learners to produce modified output (Swain and Lapkin 1998). Similar results regarding CMC have been found by L2 researchers as well (e.g., Blake 2000; Kern 1995; Lee 2001, 2002b; Pellettieri 2000; Smith 2003; Tudini 2003). In their studies, Chun (1994) and Kern (1995) found that learners produce a wide range of discourse structures in CMC and that it further fostered their sociolinguistic and interactive competence. A study conducted by Fernández-García and Martínez-Arbelaiz (2003) compared the negotiation generated by three different groups— NNS-NNS, NS-NS, and NS-NNS in the oral and CMC modes. The findings revealed that the NS-NNS group negotiated in the oral mode significantly more than in the CMC mode and learners tended to employ L1-based strategies to solve the communication problems. The burden of negotiation of meaning through written discourse without non-verbal cues pushed learners to employ a wide range of negotiation moves to solve communication breakdowns in learner-learner synchronous online exchanges (Lee 2001, 2002b). Both Pellettieri's (2000) and Smith's (2003) studies of negotiation routines in CMC yielded similar results. Their findings showed that approximately one-third of all turns were negotiated by the learners. More importantly, learners produced lexical and syntactic output modifications in response to learners' feedback during CMC.

Feedback, Negotiation Moves, Uptake and Second Language Acquisition

The potential role of feedback through negotiation of meaning has been explored extensively by L2 researchers (e.g., Iwashita 2003; Long 1996; Long, Inagaki, and Ortega 1998; Mackey 2000; Mackey, Gass, and McDonough 2000; Oliver 2000). Corrective feedback supplied by teachers or NSs is a response to learners' problematic utterances. It is often considered a focus-on-form procedure that overtly draws learners' attention to L2 forms (Long 1996; Long and Robinson 1998), a process hypothesized to be necessary for SLA (Mackey 2000; Schmidt 1995; Williams 1999). Although learners cannot provide corrective feedback to NSs, they often negotiate meaning or form using negotiation moves (e.g., confirmation checks or clarification requests) to overcome comprehension difficulties that arise due to their own insufficient L2 knowledge or underdeveloped interlanguage structures. NS corrective feedback on learners' linguistic errors and NNS negotiation of meaning to comprehend NS discourse, therefore, play a fundamentally distinct role during NS-NNS interactions.

Corrective feedback viewed as negative evidence provides direct or indirect evidence to learners about what is not possible in the L2 (e.g., Long 1996; White 1990). Oliver labels this "negative feedback" to indicate "differences between the target language and a learner's output" (2000, p. 120). Explicit negative feedback indicates clearly that what the learner has said is incorrect (e.g., "You should say Y but not X." "X is incorrect. The correct form is Y."). It is unlikely that direct correction is made during naturalistic conversations because it is viewed as impolite. In contrast to explicit feedback, implicit feedback contains various types of negotiation moves[2] (e.g., confirmation checks or requests for help) that are a reaction to non-target forms. Recent studies have focused on the role of implicit negative feedback and its effect on language learning (e.g., Ayoun 2001; Iwashita 2003; Mackey 2000; Mackey, Oliver, and Leeman 2003; Morris 2002, 2005). The findings of these studies in different contexts have shown that implicit feedback is often available and used by L2 learners. Importantly, both explicit and implicit corrective feedback fosters learners' increased awareness of forms and pushes them to produce modified output that may lead to the development of learners' interlanguage (Swain and Lapkin 1995).

One of the most common ways of providing corrective feedback is the use of recasts, especially within teacher-learner and NS-NNS interactional contexts. Recasts are frequently available for learners in language classrooms but less often through conversational interaction (Mackey and Philp 1998). Recasts are reactive rather than preemptive because they are given in response to the learner's initial non-target-like utterance. Recasts can involve a partial or full reformulation of an utterance (see Long 1996; Oliver 1995, for a comprehensive discussion of recasts). Long (1996) argued that confirmation checks can function as recasts using additional cues, such as rising or falling intonation. In CMC, recasts and confirmation checks are distinguished by the written question mark (e.g., "on the right" vs. "on the right?"). The written discourse displayed on the screen and self-paced setting of CMC may help learners to notice these two distinct interactional features and further respond to them.

Research studies of the role of recasts have shown conflicting findings, with some studies suggesting that some recasts are available and beneficial to L2 learners (e.g., Doughty and Williams 1998; Iwashita 2003; Leeman 2003), whereas others are not (e.g., Izumi 1998; Lyster 2002, 2004). In a study of university-level beginning French classes, Doughty (1993) argued that NS teachers tended to use recasts when there was only a single error. Oliver (1995) found that in interaction involving NS-NNS children, recasts were more likely to occur after subject-verb agreement errors. Izumi (1998) followed Oliver's (1995) work on the provision of corrective feedback in task-based conversation between NS-NNS pairs. Her findings revealed that learners did not use negative feedback, including recasts, nor did they respond to feedback frequently. In a similar vein, Lyster and Ranta (1997) found that recasts were not as effective as other types of feedback, such as clarification requests, repetitions, or elicitations. In their study of the use of question forms using two groups of adult learners, Mackey and Philp (1998) found that recasts proved to be beneficial for advanced learners and facilitative of learners' short-term L2 development. They argue, however, that learners need to have adequate language proficiency to process the implicit feedback and they also need to be oriented toward form in order for uptake to occur.

The above research shows considerable variability and suggests that learners may or may not respond to corrective feedback from interlocutors. Uptake as the learner's response to corrective feedback includes the use of self-repair or repetition of the correct form provided by the interlocutor. Topic continuation and acknowledgment of recasts are viewed as "no response" to corrective feedback because learners did not make the attempt to correct linguistic errors (Mackey and Philp 1998). Noticing the linguistic gap between L1 and L2 during the interaction is essential for uptake to occur. It is difficult for learners to pay attention simultaneously to meaning and form due to limited information processing capacity (VanPatten 1990) unless they "are able to draw on automatized knowledge of the L2" (Ellis 1999, p. 8). In other words, learners need to have sufficient linguistic skills to repair errors. Additionally, it has been argued that learners may not have a chance to respond to corrective feedback or may not repair errors because they do not necessarily notice corrective feedback as deliberate (e.g., Ellis, Basturkmen, and Loewen 2001; Lyster 1998a, 1998b, 2004; Oliver 2000). It is claimed that the learner's response to corrective feedback is facilitative of acquisition (Ellis, Basturkmen, and Loewen 2001). Other L2 researchers, however, argue that uptake does not guarantee acquisition because learning may take place without uptake (e.g., Mackey and Philp 1998; Morris 2002).

Studies to date show inconsistent findings with respect to the role of uptake in SLA. Some previous research suggests that learners' uptake rate is generally low (Izumi 1998; Lyster and Ranta 1997; Mackey and Philp 1998; Morris 2002; Oliver 1995, 1998). In contrast, an ESL study conducted by Ellis, Basturkmen, and Loewen (2001) found that uptake was largely successful (74.1%) and the majority of instances involved the negotiation of form as opposed to meaning. They suggest that uptake is an optional move and learners may not have a chance to or may choose not to respond to feedback. They further point out that uptake is considered successful when the learner demonstrates the understanding of a linguistic element or uses it correctly. In a study of relationships among error types, feedback types, and learner repairs, both Lyster (1998b) and Morris (2002) concluded that learners tended to use negotiation moves for lexical errors and recasts for syntactic errors during the interactive negotiation. Morris (2002) and Pica (1994) found that lexical items were negotiated and repaired more frequently than syntactic elements.

The relatively few existing studies on CMC in the interactionist tradition including both NSs and NNSs (e.g., Blake and Zyzik 2003; Toyoda and Harrison 2002; Tudini 2003) showed that corrective feedback provided by the NSs triggered negotiation and output modification. González-Lloret (2003) found that clarification requests were the preferred way to provide feedback among NNSs. In their recent study of heritage speakers and NNSs of Spanish in online interactions, Blake and Zyzik (2003) revealed that lexical negotiations through the use of recasts, clarification requests, and expansions had a positive effect on vocabulary use. Learners did not seem to notice or pay attention to morphological errors. As a result, the rate of grammatical negotiations was low (four out of thirty instances) in comparison to the rate of lexical negotiations (twenty-four times). Because lexical elements are meaning-oriented and have more communicative value than syntactic forms (VanPatten 1996), it is logical that learners solve semantic problems before they attend to syntactic errors. These findings are consistent with those reported in Tudini's (2003) and Smith's (2003) studies of synchronous CMC.

In summary, research has shown that the role of feedback including recasts, negotiation moves, and uptake in both oral and CMC contexts is controversial, mixed, and inconclusive. The current study, motivated by the ongoing discussions and debates on the potential impact of feedback on L2 learning, explores closely the relationship among error types, feedback types, and immediate responses involving NS teachers and NNS learners of Spanish engaged in NCI. The main goal of this study is to examine how both NSs and NNSs generate feedback and to what extent feedback is used to solve both linguistic and comprehension problems during NCI. (Refer to "Introduction" at the beginning of this chapter for specific research questions.)

Method

Participants

The participants for this study were thirteen NS teachers and thirteen NNS learners of Spanish from two U.S. institutions. All participants completed a questionnaire concerning their personal, educational, and linguistic backgrounds. The

NNSs were enrolled in a third-year advanced Spanish course at a northeast U.S. university. They were required to use the Blackboard as part of their course requirement. Most of these students had three years of Spanish in high school and two or three semesters of Spanish in college prior to the study. They did not have opportunities to use Spanish outside the classroom. The NSs were secondary teachers of Spanish who were enrolled in the course "Integrating Technology into Language Teaching" at an eastern seaboard university. One of the course requirement for the NS teachers was to interact with the NNS students selected for this study using one of the Blackboard communication tools—"Virtual Classroom." Thirteen groups were paired up with one NS and one NNS in each group. The participants' profiles are summarized in Table 1.

Table 1
Participant Profiles

	Nonnative Speakers (N = 13)	Native Speakers (N = 13)
Gender	Female = 12 Male = 1	Female = 13
Age	19 to 20 (Mean = 19.2)	28 to 45 (Mean = 34.7)
Nationality	Americans	Hispanics living in U.S.
Education	Undergraduate students	Graduate students
Language Proficiency	Intermediate level[3]	Native fluency

Tasks/Procedure

As has been described in the literature, tasks should be designed in ways that ensure a primary focus on meaning but also allow for incidental attention to form (Ellis 2003; Long 1985; Swain and Lakpin 1998). Crucially, task-based activities should provide conditions that allow learners to maintain the balance of fluency, accuracy, and complexity of language development (Skehan 1998).[4] Two types of two-way tasks were chosen for the current study: a goal-oriented activity and an open-ended question. Closed tasks with one possible outcome, a type of goal-oriented activity, have been suggested to promote more interaction because learners need to exchange information in order to complete the task (Long 1989; Skehan 1998). Open-ended questions are viewed as two-way information exchange activities that focus on meaning and turn-taking using a variety of negotiation moves, such as confirmation checks and clarification requests (Duff 1999).

Within this study, a goal-oriented activity called "spot-the-differences" was used as the first two-way exchange. Participants were expected to work collaboratively to identify fifteen differences between two drawings of Santa Claus. The open-ended question involved the role of advanced technology in society. The specific sub-questions were as follows: (1) Do the new information technologies contribute to the creation of the so-called global village? (2) In what ways do the new technologies influence your professional life, your personal life, and the lives of your classmates and family members? and (3) Do the new information technologies allow the exchange of ideas in a more democratic way? Give examples for and/or against.

NCI was carried out in Spanish using the "Virtual Classroom," one of the communication tools supported by *Blackboard*.[5] Twenty-six participants formed thirteen NS-NNS pairs for two 50-minute chat sessions. Both sessions took place at mid-semester after participants were familiar and comfortable with *Blackboard*. No particular instructions were given to the two groups. However, they were encouraged to focus on the topic at hand. The NS and NNS groups did not have the opportunity to interact with one other prior to the study and participants were not given time for pre-task planning. Discussions were automatically saved in *Blackboard*'s archives and were retrieved later for data analysis.

Data Analysis

Transcripts were coded for error types, feedback types, and modification devices using Varonis and Gass' (1985) coding scheme. The researcher and a trained instructor coded the data to ensure consistency. Each coder first worked individually and then both coders compared and discussed the discrepancies until they reached the final agreement.[6] Example (1), taken from the current study,[7] illustrates the scheme during lexical negotiation:

(1)

1. **NS:** Es la próxima etapa, no? **[trigger]**

   (It is the next stage. no?)

2. **NNS:** Que es "etapa"? **[indicator]**

   (What is "etapa"?)

3. **NS:** "stage" **[response]**

   ("stage")

4. **NNS:** O.K. Gracias! **[reaction]**

   (O.K. Thanks!)

In the above example, the unfamiliar word *etapa* "stage" serves as the trigger for negotiation. Upon encountering communication difficulty, the NNS expressed the need for clarification of the unknown word by using the Spanish for "what is" (line 2). The NS partner then made an attempt to respond to the incomprehensible message from the NNS using L1 translation (line 3). Finally, the NNS brought closure to the negotiation by acknowledging the response (line 4). In this case, the question "What is x?" was coded as a "clarification request," one of the negotiation moves used to elicit feedback. The answer to this request was coded as a "response" to the clarification request.

Two types of linguistic errors were coded (see Table 2). Inter-rater reliability was high (r = .92).

Table 2
Types, Definitions, and Examples of Error

	Error Type	Definition	Example
1	Lexical	Incorrect, inappropriate choices of lexical items including non-target derivations of nouns, verbs and adjectives	—"abrazo" for "brazo" ("hug" for "arm") or —"realizar" for "darse cuenta de" ("carry out" for "to realize")
2	Syntactic	Incorrect usage of articles, verb section, pronouns, prepositions, gender, subject, verb and adjective agreement, wrong verb conjugations	—"la sistema" instead of "el sistema" —"fue nervioso." (He was nervous.) instead of "estaba nervioso." (He was nervous.)

Table 3 illustrates types of feedback with their definitions and examples. Inter-rater reliability for coding feedback types was high (r = .95).

Table 3
Types, Definitions and Examples of Feedback

	Feedback Type	Definition	Example
1	Explicit	To directly correct non-target form to target form	—El subjuntivo de "sufrir" es "sufra" no "sufre." (The subjunctive of "sufrir" is "sufra" not "sufre.")
2	Implicit	To provide a clue to non-target form or incomprehensible message using modification devices or recasts.	—Quieres decir "cuento" no "cuenta? (Do you mean "cuento" [story] not "cuenta" [bill]?)

Five types of modification devices were identified and coded for providing implicit feedback. Table 4 shows each type and a definition of the type of modification device along with an example. Inter-rater reliability for coding was high (r = .90).

Table 4

Categories, Definitions and Examples of Modification Devices
as Implicit Feedback

	Type of Modification Device	Definition	Example
1	Confirmation check	To repeat parts of the statement to ensure understanding	—La gente no tiene derecha. (People don't have right hand side?) —Derecha? (Right hand side?)
2	Clarification check[8]	To express confusion or ask for help due to unfamiliar words or incomprehensibility	—Los precios han aumentado mucho. (Prices have increased a lot.) —Qué es "aumentado"? (What is "aumentado"?)
3	Recast	To reformulate all or part of non-target form	—No lo sabieron. (They did not know it.) —No lo sabían. (They did not know it.)
4	Request for help	To ask for help with non-understood message[9]	—Hmm . . . No entiendo. Puedes explicar mas? (Hmm . . . I don't understand. Can you explain more?
5	Use of keyboard symbol	To signal uncertainty or confusion of a lexical item or an idea	—Las piernas son pequenas. (The legs are small.) —???? or :<

The information in Table 5 describes responses to feedback. The researcher coded responses by either "response" or "no response" to feedback. Any learner's response to feedback was considered uptake, but this may not necessarily involve using the correct form (see Ellis, Basturkmen, and Loewen 2001 for a review). It should also be noted that "response" to the recast refers to "repeat the recast" and "no response" is "continue on task" or "acknowledge the recast." (For more discussion, see Mackey and Philp 1998.) Inter-rater reliability for coding was high ($r = .94$). Within the category of "response," five types[10] were identified and coded (see Table 5), with high inter-rater reliability ($r = .90$).

Table 5

Categories, Definitions and Examples of Responses to Feedback

	Type of Responses	Definition	Example
1	Repair[11]	To correct errors made on lexical items or grammatical structure	—**NNS**: No pago el cuento. (She did not pay the story.) —**NS**: El cuento? (The story?) —**NNS**: Es la cuenta. Lo siento. (It is the bill. I'm sorry.)
2	Elaboration	To elaborate the original idea or concept in Spanish	—**NNS**: Los picos? Que son? (The points? What are they?) —**NS**: Son los puntos en el sombrero. Es como el punto del lápiz. (They are points on the hat. It is like the point of the pencil.)
3	Use of L1	To use English to substitute words or ideas in Spanish	—**NNS**: No entiendo la palabra "chistoso" (I don't understand the word "chistoso") —**NS**: "chistoso" es funny. ("chistoso" is funny.)
4	Repetition	To repeat and confirm the reformulated target form	—**NNS**: Las mujeres no tienen mucho libre. (Women don't have much free.) —**NS**: Quieres decir la libertad? (Do you mean the freedom?) —**NNS**: Si, si. la libertad. (Yes, yes the freedom.)
5	Use of keyboard symbol	To signal agreement, certainty or uncertainty on the request	—**NS**: Quieres decir la pantalla no la ventana? —**NNS**: si :-)

Results and Discussion

Research Question 1

The first research question addresses the types of feedback both NSs and NNSs provided for negotiation of meaning and form during NCI. The results shown in Table 6 support those reported in previous synchronous CMC studies (Blake and Zyzik 2003; Fernández-García and Arbelaiz 2002; Lee 2002b; Tudini 2003) revealing that both explicit and implicit feedback were provided by the NSs and NNSs.

Table 6
Number and Percentage of Feedback Type Used by NSs and NNSs

Feedback Type	NSs (N = 13)	NNSs (N = 13)
Explicit	2 (2.5%)	0 (0%)
Implicit	79 (97.5%)	53 (100%)
Total	81 (100%)	53 (100%)

However, there was a difference in the degree to which each type of feedback was employed by the NSs and NNSs. Both NSs and NNSs gave very little or no explicit feedback. It is logical to assume that they would not need to provide any explicit feedback to their partners since the latter are NSs who would not make errors in Spanish. One NS made the attempt to explicitly correct her partner's errors twice; once for a lexical error involving *realizar* "to carry out" instead of *darse cuenta* "to realize" and once for a morpho-syntactic error involving the present subjunctive form of *sufrir* "to suffer." Within a social context, it is unlikely that a partner would directly correct the other's mistakes, especially when they are not well acquainted with each other. Therefore, the majority of interactional moves involved implicit feedback.

The NSs used implicit feedback 79 times while the NNSs used implicit feedback 23 times. Recasts resulted in the highest rate of corrective feedback (53.1%) initiated by the NSs, whereas the clarification check (49%) was the most frequent modification device used by the NNSs. Both groups used other types of modification devices as well (see Table 7).

Table 7
Number and Percentage of Modification Devices Used as Implicit Feedback

Type of Modification Device	NSs (N = 13)	NNSs (N = 13)
Confirmation check	11 (13.9%)	9 (17%)
Clarification check	12 (15.3%)	26 (49%)
Recast	42 (53.1%)	2 (3.8%)
Request for help	10 (12.6%)	8 (15.1%)
Use of keyboard symbol	4 (5.1%)	8 (15.1%)
Total	79 (100%)	53 (100%)

Similar to the results reported in González-Lloret (2003), the NNSs tended to use clarification checks to provide implicit feedback. The majority of the feedback initiated by the NNSs was triggered by unknown lexical items (50 times at 94.3%). In many cases, when the input was incomprehensible to the NNSs, they asked for clarification, such as "What is x?" "What do you mean by y?" or "I don't understand what you said." The results are consistent with Lee (2002b) who found that clarification checks prompt the NS to provide additional information to make the input understandable as shown in example 2:

(2)

1. **NS:** La computadora es azul y la pantalla amarilla.

   (Is the computer blue and the screen yellow?)

2. **NNS:** que es la pantalla? **[Clarification check]**

   (what is pantalla?)

3. **NS:** Pantalla es el vidrio de la computadora. Es la ventana.

   (Screen is the glass of the computer. It is the window.)

4. **NNS:** screen? (screen?) **[Use of L1]**

5. **NS:** correcto. (correct.)

6. **NNS:** La pantalla mia es roja.

   (My screen is red.)

The unknown lexical item *pantalla* (line 2) was not understood by the NNS. The NNS then negotiated the meaning of the unknown lexical item using a clarification check. In the response to the NNS, the NS explained what *pantalla* is in Spanish (line 3) and the NNS responded to the feedback by using the L1 to confirm the meaning of the new word (line 4). The evidence from the current study also suggests that, similar to the claim made by Lyster (1998a), the clarification check is effective as it requires the partner to make input adjustments and more importantly, provides the learner with elaborated and modified input in the L2. In this study, the clarification check appears to have a positive short-term effect on comprehension and acquisition of vocabulary as the NNSs often incorporated new words into later interaction (see examples 2, 3, 5, 6). Although these findings corroborate those found in Blake's (2000) and Smith's (2003) studies of learners' negotiation in CMC, further research is needed in order to confirm the long-term effect of clarification checks on the acquisition of L2 vocabulary.

Unlike face-to-face interaction, in text-based NCI learners cannot use nonverbal cues such as gestures or facial expressions. However, emoticons and repeated question marks are used as nonverbal negotiation devices to facilitate the negotiation of meaning. For instance, the NNSs used the sad face "☹" to show the incomprehensibility, confusion, or dislike of an idea and multiple questions marks "???" to signal uncertainly or to ask for help from their NS partners. In this sense, emoticons function as clarification checks, requests for help, or confirmation checks. As can be seen in example 3, the use of keyboard symbols clarified the meaning of the word *involucrada* (involved, in line 1), changing what initially appeared to be incomprehensible into comprehensible input.

(3)

1. **NS:** Estas involucrada? (Are you involved?)

2. **NNS:** ??? **[Keyboard symbol]**

3. **NS:** Es como ayudar a la comunidad o participar en algunas actividades.

   (It is like to help the community or to participate in some activities.)

4. **NNS:** Ahora entiendo. No, no estoy involucrada porque no tengo tiempo.

   (Now I understand. No, I'm not involved because I don't have time.)

In this example, multiple question marks functioned as a clarification check that asked the NS to provide input modification. It is evident that this particular negotiation improved mutual comprehension. However, it remains difficult to ascertain whether emoticons and creative uses of punctuation marks make for a more salient trigger of input modifications than text-based clarification requests as the proportional use of such keyboard symbols is small (15.1%). It is possible that the keyboard symbol was the quick and easy way to provide feedback as the learners were engaged in synchronous exchanges. Lee (2001), in her study of online interaction among the NNSs, has also confirmed that learners used symbols to compensate for the lack of face-to-face interaction and to clarify meaning. The use of keyboard symbols may be affected by learners' preference and style of negotiation strategies.

To summarize, lexical items rather than syntactical elements were the main trigger for negotiation moves generated by both NSs and NNSs. Almost half of negotiation moves following unknown lexical items involved clarification checks (49%) initiated by the NNSs. In contrast, a great majority of feedback moves provided by the NSs were triggered by learners' linguistic errors (both lexical and syntactic items). The use of recast (53.1%) was the most salient modification device as corrective feedback provided by the NSs to respond to learners' non-target-like forms. The following discussion seeks to find out what types of NNSs' linguistic errors lead to what types of implicit feedback provided by the NSs.

Research Question 2

The analysis yielded a total of 97 linguistic errors made by the NNSs, 66% were syntactic errors and 34% were lexical errors (see Table 8).

Each error was made by a NNS student, which may or may not result in the provision of feedback by a NS teacher. Table 9 shows that 71 out of 97 linguistic errors received implicit feedback from the NSs. The findings reveal that in some cases there was no need for negotiation when errors did not cause communication problems.

Table 8
Number and Percentage of Error Type

Lexical	33 (34%)
Syntactic	64 (66%)
Total	97 (100%)

Table 9
Number and Percentage of Implicit Feedback per Error Type

Lexical	29 (40.8%)
Syntactic	42 (59.2%)
Total	71 (100%)

It is important to note that there was a difference found in the distribution of feedback provided by the NSs shown in Table 7 (79 times) and in Table 9 (71 times). Of the 79 feedback moves, 8 were used for unclear messages which focused on the meaning (content) rather than the form (linguistic error). In other words, sometimes the NNS's utterance was grammatically correct but the NS did not understand the intended meaning. Requests for help, confirmation checks, and keyboard symbols, therefore, were used for meaning clarifications rather than linguistic modifications.

Table 10 shows that 73.2% of NNS linguistic errors received implicit feedback from their NS teachers during the NCI. In contrast to previous findings that showed that NSs were disinclined to point out learners' linguistic errors (Iwashita 2003), both lexical (87.9%) and syntactic errors (65.6%) received a high rate of feedback moves in the present study. It is possible that as teachers themselves, the NSs may have less tolerance for the NNSs' non-target-like utterances. Additionally, from the pedagogical point of view, grammatical accuracy and lexical growth should be equally important for developing learners' L2 language competence. It may be difficult for the NS teachers to ignore errors and they may have felt obligated to implicitly correct learners' imperfect utterances. It is also possible that the text-based communication via a computer screen would draw interlocutors' attention to focus on form more easily than through the oral modality. The NSs, therefore, generated a high frequency of corrective feedback to push learners to modify output.

Table 10
Rate of Implicit Feedback per Error Type

Lexical	29/33 (87.9%)
Syntactic	42/64 (65.6%)
Total	71/97 (73.2%)

A comparison of the distribution of the feedback types provided by the NSs across the error types produced by the NNSs appears in Table 11.

Table 11
Number and Percentage of Errors Receiving Implicit Feedback across Feedback Types and Error Types

Type of Modification Device	Lexical	Syntactic	Total
Confirmation Check	6 (20.7%)	3 (7.1%)	9 (12.7%)
Clarification Check	11 (38%)	1 (2.4%)	12 (16.8%)
Recast	6 (20.7%)	36 (85.7%)	42 (59.2%)
Request for help	5 (17.2%)	1 (2.4%)	6 (8.5%)
Use of keyboard symbol	1 (3.4%)	1 (2.4%)	2 (2.8%)
Total	29 (100%)	42 (100%)	71 (100%)

The most striking type of implicit feedback was the recast (59.2%) used by the NSs. During the negotiation routines, the NSs showed a strong tendency to use recasts to provide corrective feedback about non-target-like forms (see example 4). This study supports the findings by Lyster and Ranta (1997) that teachers have an overwhelming tendency to use recasts. By resorting to the use of recasts, the NS avoided embarrassing the learner. Directness of explicit feedback may result in a partner who is too demoralized to participate in discussions.

As mentioned, Doughty (1993) argues that the NS teachers in her study tend to use recasts when there is only one error. In this study, the recast in response to a single error appeared in several occasions, such as *Mi computadora [*esta] grande y hay dos lapices en la mesa* "My computer is big and there are two pencils on the table" and *Tengo ropa [*amarillo] y zapatos negros* "I have yellow clothes and black shoes."[12] The NS immediately reformulated the wrong choice of the verb *está* to *es* and the wrong gender of the adjective *amarillo* to *amarilla*. In these cases, the recast was provided as an attempt to highlight the error to draw the learner's attention to focus on form. The learner was able to incorporate the correct form into the follow-up turn, such as *Tienes ropa amarilla?* "Do you have yellow clothes?" The evidence appears to support the claim made by Lyster (2004) that learners benefit from less salient recasts which have been shortened to high-light one particular error. By contrast, the NS did not use full or partial recasts when multiple errors were present in sentences, such as *Mi abuelo murió [*cinco años pasados] pero mi abuela todavía [*es] viva* "My grandfather died five years ago but my grandmother is still alive" or *Es posible que [*muchos tiempos] los estudiantes no [*pueden] usar la computadora en [*algunas] lugares* "It is possi-ble that many times students cannot use the computer in some places." In these cases, the NSs continued the discussion as the errors did not cause comprehen-sion problems and they may have felt reluctant to interrupt the flow of communi-cation. Pedagogically, students need to write correctly to maintain a balance between function, content, and accuracy. One of the corrective techniques is to make students re-examine and revise the exchanges with guided instruction.

In addition, Table 11 shows that the majority of implicit feedback moves following syntactic errors were recasts (85.7%), whereas 79.3% of lexical errors incited other types of modification devices, in particular, the use of clarification checks (38%) and confirmation checks (20.7%). Lyster (1998b) and Morris (2002) also found that syntactic errors favored recasts and lexical problems invited negotiation moves. Example 4 illustrates how a NS utilized the recast to correct a syntactic error made by an NNS:

(4)

1. **NS:** La pantalla en mi dibujo es amarilla. (The screen of my picture is yellow.)

2. **NNS:** ¿Qué color son los zapatos? (What color are the shoes?)

3. **NS:** ¿De qué colores son los zapatos? (What color are the shoes?)

4. NNS: Si. Los mios son rojos. (Yes. Mine are red.)

5. **NS:** Ahora el gorro. El mío tiene tres colores, rojo, verde y amarillo.

   (Now the cap. Mine has three colors, red, green and yellow.)

6. **NNS:** ¿Es gorro como sombrero? (Is "gorro" like hat?)

7. **NS:** Correcto. (Correct.)

8. **NNS:** Tengo gorro azul y blanco. ¿De qué color es la bufanda?

   (I have blue and black cap. What color is the scarf?)

In this particular case, the recast drew the learner's attention to the form. After reading the message corrected by the partner, the NNS noticed the mismatch between input and output and repeated the same structure in line 3 (¿De qué color? = "what color?") several turns later (line 8). The recast is more salient in CMC than in face-to-face interaction as the learner reads the correct written text on the screen. Moreover, written discourse can easily be retrieved by the use of the vertical scroll bar. While this study makes no claim on the positive effect of recasts for L2 development, the data seems to suggest that the recast did reorient the learner's attention toward the accurate form.

Although only 20.7% of lexical errors received recasts as implicit feedback (see Table 11), the majority were triggered by the misuse of the definite article or gender as is illustrated in example 5:

(5)

1. **NNS:** Los dos tienen las vestidas verdes. (Two have green dresses.)

2. **NS:** Llevan vestidos verdes. (They wear green dresses.)

3. **NNS:** si, los vestidos son verdes ☺!! (Yes, the dresses are green ☺!!)

In this case, the NNS did not know the word "dress" in Spanish is masculine. Instead, she wrote both the article *la* and the noun *vesitda* in the feminine form (line 1). To avoid confusion, the NS teacher immediately used the recast to highlight the syntactic problems that caused the lexical error[13] (line 2). As learners at the intermediate proficiency level have great need for interlanguage restructuring, it is crucial for them to receive models of the target language that may draw their attention to target-like-forms and further that encourage them to use correct forms (as demonstrated in example 5). Lyster (1994) points out that it is likely that learners benefit from focus on form to overcome incorrect target language features. The long-term effect of recasts on the developmental levels of the learner is a worthwhile issue for further research.

This study found evidence that lexical errors tended to invite the use of modification devices (79.3%) rather than recasts. Example 6 illustrates how the NS negotiated inappropriate lexical items using both clarification checks (line 2) and confirmation checks (line 6).

(6)

1. **NNS:** Son hombres pequenos. (They are small men.)

2. **NS:** ¿Quienes son hombres pequenos? **[Clarification request]**

   (Who are the small men?)

3. **NNS:** Son las personas que ayudan Santa Claus. Personas pequenas, si?

   (They are people who help Santa Claus. Small people, yes?)

4. **NS:** Oh si éntiendo. Son duendes. (Oh yes I understand. They are elves.)

5. **NNS:** Mis duendes no tienen piernas pequenas. (My elves don´t have small legs.)

6. **NS:** No son estrechas? **[Confirmation check]**

   (They are not skinny?)

7. **NNS:** si, tienen piernas estrechas. (yes, they have skinny legs.)

The example above demonstrates that approximation and circumlocution are typical communication strategies that the NNSs used for negotiation of meaning due to the lack of vocabulary knowledge, as Lee (2001) reported in a previous study. The NNS used approximations twice to substitute the correct and appropriate Spanish words, such as *hombres pequeños* "small men" for *duendes* "elves," and *piernas pequeñas* "small legs" for *piernas estrechas* "skinny legs." As a result of interactive negotiations, not only did both interlocutors achieve mutual comprehension, but they reinforced the appropriate usage of L2 lexical items.

In conclusion, in spite of the distinctly different language proficiency levels of the two groups (NSs vs. NNSs), clarification and confirmation checks appeared to be the two most frequent modification devices used for lexical negotiations. Recasts were primarily triggered by morpho-syntactic errors made by the NNSs.

The question remains as to whether these feedback moves resulted in responses. If so, what types of NNSs' linguistic problems led to what types of immediate uptake moves? The following discussion attempts to answer these questions.

Research Question 3

As can be seen from Table 12, the NSs responded to more than 90% of their partners' feedback. The NSs were foreign language teachers and hence accustomed to dealing with NNS discourse. Therefore, the tendency to respond to learners' feedback was likely more probable when confusion arose. In contrast, the NNSs only responded to 58.2% of the NS teachers' feedback. This aligns with the findings reported by Lyster and Ranta (1997) that 55% of teachers' feedback moves resulted in uptake moves.

Table 12
Number and Percentage of Responses to Implicit Feedback

Implicit Feedback	NSs (N = 13)	NNSs (N = 13)
Responses	48 (90.6%)	46 (58.2%)
No responses	5 (9.4%)	33 (41.8%)
Total	53 (100%)	79 (100%)

A high percentage of implicit feedback provided by the NSs (41.8%) was not responded to by the NNSs. The following example demonstrates how a NNS did not seem to know how to respond to the NS's request for help (line 5) regarding a problematic message (line 4).

(7)

1. **NS:** Que sabes de la famosa aldea global? Tu crees que la tecnologia esta contribuyendo a la creacion de esta aldea global?

   (What do you know about the famous global village? Do you believe technology is contributing to the creation of this global village?)

2. **NNS:** que es la aldea global? es una idea del mundo a ser uno?

   (what is the global village? Is it an idea of the world to be one?)

3. **NS:** Bueno me imagino que por medio de la tecnologia de la informacion podemos estar en contacto con todo el mundo y de esa forma volvernos una aldea global. Si, creo que la idea principal es que el mundo este unido por medio de la red. Me comprendes?

   (Well I can image that through information technology we can be in contact with everyone and by this way we become a global village. Yes, I believe the principal idea is that the world is united by the web. Do you understand me?)

4. **NNS:** No se. Si, pienso que la nueva technologia esta ayudando este causa pero no me gusta todo el mundo usa mucho computadora. No es personal y no conoces bien la gente.

(I don't know. Yes, I believe the new technology is helping this cause but I don't like everyone to use a lot computer. It is not personal and you don't know people well.)

5. **NS:** Hmm... ¿Me puedes explicar un poco más? **[Request for help]**

(Hmm... Can you explain a little bit more to me?)

6. **NNS:** Tienes un Palm Pilot? No puedo hacer nada sin eso.

(Do you have a Palm Pilot? I cannot do anything without that.)

Multiple errors found in line 4 prevented the NS from understanding the NNS's intended message. The NS provided feedback using a "request for help" (line 5) that challenged the student to elaborate and articulate her thoughts, a step crucial to building learners' language proficiency at the advanced level (Lee 2002a). The learner, however, failed to respond to the NS's feedback. Rather, the student initiated a new topic (line 6).

Table 13 presents the distribution of responses used by the NSs and the NNSs to respond to their partners' feedback.

Table 13
Number and Percentage of Responses to Feedback

Type of Responses	NSs (N = 13)	NNSs (N = 13)
Repair	0 (0%)	20 (43.5%)
Elaboration	33 (68.7%)	6 (13.1%)
Use of L1	10 (20.8%)	10 (21.7%)
Repetition	3 (6.3 %)	8 (17.4%)
Use of keyboard symbol	2 (4.2%)	2 (4.3%)
Total	48 (100%)	46 (100%)

Two salient responses shown in Table 13 were NS elaborations (68.7%) and NNS repairs (43.5%). Interestingly, L1 was used in similar proportion by the NSs (20.8%) and NNSs (21.7%) respectively, whereas the lowest rate of response was in the use of keyboard symbols by both groups (4.2% by the NSs and 4.3% by the NNSs).

As mentioned previously, 94.3% of feedback moves initiated by NNSs were triggered by unknown lexical items. Upon receiving the clarification requests, such as "I don't understand. What is . . .?" from the NNSs, the NSs tended to elaborate the new word to explain the meaning. Of the 33 instances of elaboration, the majority were used for clarifying the meaning of the word. Elaboration often occurred when the NNS made the clarification request, such as "I don't understand. What is . . .?" In most cases, elaboration was provided to clarify the meaning of a particular lexical item as shown in example 8:

(8)

1. **NS:** Si. En el pico del zapato o en el borde?

   (Yes.At the tip of the shoe or at the edge?)

2. **NNS:** que es un pico en tus palabras? **[Clarification check]**

   (what is un pico in your words?)

3. **NS:** La punta (The tip)

4. **NS:** Perdón, el pico es la punta. El zapato termina en pico (>) y el borde del sombrero y los zapatos también terminan en pico (>). Me comprendes? **[Elaboration]**

   (Sorry, the pico is a tip. The shoe ends in a point (>) and the edge of hats and the shoes also end in a point (>). Do you understand me?)

5. **NNS:** Si, ahora comprendo. En la punta de su zapato.

   (Yes, Now I understand. At the tip of his shoe.)

The illustration above shows that the NNS struggled to understand the unknown word *pico* (tip in line 2). The NS twice elaborated on the meaning of *pico*, and also produced a keyboard marker, to enhance comprehension (line 4). It is logical to assume that NSs usually would not use Spanish to clarify input knowing their interlocutors were at the intermediate level of proficiency. In addition, the use of Spanish language elaboration demands both learners' linguistic and cognitive skills to process modified input. In some cases, the negotiation occurred over several turns in an attempt to achieve mutual comprehension.

With regard to the use of English, the findings show that use of English was the second preferred response move used by the NSs when Spanish elaboration as the first attempt to try to solve a lexical and grammatical problem was unsuccessful. Of the ten uses of English, five of them were used for grammar explanations. It is possible that learners' linguistic limitations forced the NSs to use English to clarify unclear messages. For instance, as shown in example 9, after several negotiated turns (line, 3, 4, 5, 6 and 7), the NS finally gave up and used L1 (line 8) to explain the use of the aspectual problem, which the NNS understood and accepted:

(9)

1. **NNS:** Antes muchas personas no sabieron usar la computadora.

   (Before many people did not know how to use the computer.)

2. **NS:** Si, como mis abuelos no sabían nada de la computadora.

   (Yes, like my grandparents did not know anything about the computer.)

3. **NNS:** Por que es "sabian" no "sabieron?" (Why is it "sabian" not "sabieron"?)

4. **NS:** Es la descripción del pasado. (It is the description of the past.)

5. **NNS:** Pero ya termino la accion. Sabieron si?

   (But the action is complete. Sabieron yes?)

6. **NS:** "Supieron" quiere decir "enterarse de algo"

   ("Supieron" means "enterarse de algo")

7. **NNS:** Que es enterarse? No se la palabra.

   (What is enterarse? I don't know the word.)

8. **NS:** to find out or to discover. So in this case, you wanted to say "they did not know" not "they did not find out" Me comprendes? (Do you understand me?)

9. **NNS:** Si, no sabian. (Yes, they did not know.)

One possible explanation for resorting to English may be because it is fairly difficult to explain an advanced grammatical concept in the target language. In order to avoid confusion, English seems to be a good option after several turns of negotiation. In certain circumstances, English may be necessary to support the comprehension of Spanish. Until learners gain more knowledge and understanding of Spanish, English is a good choice to solve linguistic or communication problems and to keep the flow of the conversation going.

Regarding the NNSs' uptake, Table 14 displays the distribution of error types across uptake types used by the NNSs. 43.5% of uptakes were repairs, whereas 21.7% involved the use of L1 and 17.4% were repetitions.

Table 14
Distribution of Error Types across Types of Uptake Moves Used by NNSs

Type of Uptake Moves	Lexical	Syntactic	Total
Repair	14 (46.7%)	6 (37.5%)	20 (43.5%)
Elaboration	4 (13.3%)	2 (12.5%)	6 (13.1%)
Use of L1	6 (20%)	4 (25%)	10 (21.7%)
Repetition	5 (16.7%)	3 (18.8%)	8 (17.4%)
Use of keyboard symbol	1 (3.3%)	1 (6.2%)	2 (4.3%)
Total	30 (100%)	16 (100%)	46 (100%)

Of the forty-six uptake moves, thirty (65%) were responses to lexical problems, whereas sixteen (35%) were responses to syntactic errors. These findings are similar to those found in Morris's (2002) and Pica's (1994) studies confirming that lexical items were negotiated and repaired more frequently than syntactic elements. Interestingly, L1 use (21.7%) as uptake was used similarly for lexical problems (20%) and syntactic errors (25%). In response to the implicit feedback from the NS, the NNS tended to use their L1 to confirm the meaning of the unknown lexical item (see example 2). One puzzling result is that L1 was used to respond to the clarification request received from the NSs as shown in example 10:

(10)

1. **NNS:** Nunca ha tomado una clase de Blackboard.

   (He/She has never taken a Blackboard class.)

2. **NS:** ¿Quién? (Who?) **[Clarification request]**

3. **NNS:** I have never taken Blackboard. **[Use of L1]**

4. **NS:** Bien. "he" para yo y "ha" para él o ella. (O.K. "he" for I and "ha" for he or she.)

5. **NNS:** Gracias! No he tomado. (Thanks! I have not taken.)

Negotiation occurred when the NNS misused the verb "to have" *haber* in line 1. Instead of making the attempt to correct the morphological error from *ha* "he or she has" to *he* "I have," the learner used L1 to express the meaning (line 3). It is possible that syntactic problems are more difficult to process than lexical errors as Morris (2002) suggested in his study of negotiation moves, recasts, and learner repair in the foreign language classroom. Another explanation could be that the occurrence of the use of L1 might be related to learners' language proficiency and personal learning style.

In this study, the corrective feedback provided by the NSs had a positive effect on drawing learners' attention to form that led to repairs. The results revealed that 46.7% of lexical errors were repaired after receiving either clarification or confirmation checks. In most cases, uptakes involved the confusion between two lexical forms, such as *cuento* "story" vs. *cuenta* "bill" or *brazo* "arm" vs. *abrazo* "hug." Example 11 illustrates how the learner repaired (line 4) the lexical error from *derecha* "right hand side" to *derecho* "right" immediately after receiving the confirmation check (line 2) provided by the NS:

(11)

1. **NNS:** La gente no tiene derecha para leer los e-mails de otros.

   (People don't have right hand side to read other people' e-mails.)

2. **NS:** Derecha? (Right hand side?) **[Confirmation check]**

3. **NNS:** No tiene derecho, si? (Do not have right, yes?) **[Repair]**

4. **NS:** Si, estoy de acuerdo. Debemos respetar la privacidad de otras personas.

   (Yes, I agree. We should respect other people's privacy.)

Repair as uptake involving negotiation of meaning facilitated the NNS's understanding of L2 vocabulary as the learner noticed the ill-formed lexical item. In addition to lexical repairs, the NNSs self-corrected 37.5% of syntactic errors in the use of temporal and aspectual morphosyntax, such as the use of *fui* "I went" versus *fue* "he went" and *trabajo* "I work" versus *trabajé* "I worked." These findings did not corroborate those found in the studies of CMC conducted by Blake and Zyzik (2003) and Tudini (2003). In their studies, the NNSs tended to ignore the syntactical errors in order to maintain the conversational flow.

Although the rate of the use of repetitions was low (17.4%), the rate at which repetitions were used in the negotiation of lexical problems (16.7%) was very similar to that for syntactic errors (18.8%) shown in Table 14. Anecdotal evidence based on observations made of online exchanges suggests that the use of repetition was often followed by a recast initiated by the NSs, especially with advanced grammatical structures such as is shown in example 12:

(12)

1. **NNS:** Cuando me graduo, voy a hacer mucho dinero usando la computadora.

   (When I graduate, I'm going to make a lot of money using the computer.)

2. **NS:** Cuando te gradues, vas a ganar mucho dinero? **[Recast]**

   (When you graduate, are you going to make a lot of money?)

3. **NNS:** Si, cuando me gradue, gano mucho dinero. **[Repetition]**

   (Yes, when I graduate, I make a lot of money.)

4. **NS:** Que bien. Tambien quiero ganar mucho.

   (Great! I also want to make a lot.)

In this excerpt, the verb *me graduo* "I graduate" in the sentence *Cuando me graduo, voy a hacer mucho dinero* (line 1) was used incorrectly. In this particular case, the NNS did not know that certain adverbial conjunctions, such as *cuando* "when" require the subjunctive when the event "to graduate" has not yet occurred. The subjunctive *me gradúe* should be used instead of the indicative *me graduo*. This type of grammatical concept is too advanced for learners at the intermediate level to figure out on their own without the assistance of an expert. Not only the target form of the verb *graduarse* in the present subjunctive but also the correct lexical item *ganar* "to make money" instead of *hacer* "to do something" were repeated correctly in the immediate follow-up response. It is possible that written discourse, as represented on the screen via CMC, allows learners to notice the difference between target and non-target like forms (Pellettieri 2000; Warschauer 1996). Recasts via CMC seem to have a more positive effect on drawing the learner's attention to linguistic form than do the recasts occurring in the face-to-face interaction. This current study makes no claim on the short-term or long-term effect of immediate uptake on learners' interlanguage systems. However, further studies should address the long-term effect of incorporated recasts on learners' linguistic improvement in NCI environments.

Conclusion

Conversational interaction has become central to communicative language teaching and learning. NCI allows L2 learners to extend communication beyond classroom limits. More importantly, it affords unique opportunities for learners to use the target language to develop their communicative language competence. Like face-to-face interaction, NCI offers a powerful forum for learners to receive input, provide feedback and produce output through interactive negotiation. The current study focused on the examination of types of feedback and responses used by both NSs and NNSs working in dyads to complete two task-based activities. The efficacy of NCI made it possible to capture the commonly used feedback features—recasts by the NSs and clarification checks by the NSs. Feedback, in particular as a source of negative evidence, is essential to bring learners' attention to particular linguistic forms to make output adjustments. The evidence presented in this study showed that the NSs played a teacher-like role that fostered negotiation of meaning and focus-on-form interaction. Additionally, the NSs provided the NNSs with authentic language discourse, new lexical items, and correct grammatical structures through recasts and modification devices. The findings of the current study suggests that a reactive approach to form-focused instruction may induce learners to pay attention to linguistic form, which in turn may restructure their interlanguage and increase language accuracy.

Learner uptake in response to corrective feedback, including successful repairs, is crucial for SLA. The findings demonstrate that the NNSs produced indications of uptake in 50% of their follow-up responses. A high rate of linguistic error was repaired (43.5%) following confirmation and clarification checks. Given that NCI is based on written communication, the availability of written visual display on the screen might have contributed to these high rates of learner uptake. However, lexical errors (30 instances) were repaired at a higher rate than syntactic errors (16 instances). This suggests that L2 vocabulary knowledge plays a crucial role in NCI as it elicits learners' feedback to unfamiliar linguistic input as well as promotes corrective feedback on their developing interlanguage systems. Unlike previous studies which have focused on NNSs' uptake, this study examined NSs' efforts to resolve negotiations of meaning. The results showed that L2 elaboration for unknown lexical items and the use of L1 for syntactic problems had a positive impact on learners' comprehension. Until students at intermediate levels of proficiency gain more control of advanced structures, the L1 is a good option for negotiation of complex grammar.

Although the findings support Long's Interaction Hypothesis (1996), the current study did not address whether responses to implicit feedback led to L2 development but simply identified feedback features used by both NSs and NNSs to negotiate meaning and form in the immediacy of ongoing dialogue. More empirical studies focusing on the relationship between feedback types and imme-diate repairs are needed to determine the effect of uptake moves in NCI environ-ments. Future studies could also address other factors that may affect the negotiation process, such as task types, language proficiency levels, and gender. In this study, two types of tasks were used; an open-ended question and a goal-oriented activity, but the effect of each type of task was not compared. Additional studies could address this issue to determine the relationship between task type and corrective feedback. NCI supports the goal of empowering learners to become active and effective language users, fosters a wide array of interaction, and pro-motes negotiation of meaning. In conclusion, this research suggests that NCI has the potential to extend and enrich students' language learning experience beyond the classroom setting.

Notes

1. Both linguistic errors (e.g., lexical or syntactic items) and unclear or incomprehen-sible written discourse (e.g., the entire message is problematic) are considered in this study. Corrective feedback is provided by the NSs to indicate NNSs' linguistic errors while NNSs negotiate meaning or form when they encounter difficulty understanding NSs' output.

2. The term "negotiation moves" is used wherever previous SLA research is referenced in this paper. Lee (2001, 2002b) uses "modification devices" in the analysis of the data of the current study.

3. The Spanish Oral Proficiency Tests—SOPT (based on the ACTFL Proficiency Guidelines) was administered to the NNSs before the study (for details, see Lee 2000).

4. Task type affects the extent to which the negotiation of meaning takes place. Long (1996) examined the notion of a one-way versus a two-way task. A one-way task only allows one participant to give information. In contrast, a two-way task involves the exchange of information between two interlocutors and focuses on meaning, there-fore, more modified interaction may occur in the process of the two-way exchange.

5. *Blackboard* is a software program that allows teachers to bring courses online using multi-channel web tools (for more information about *Blackboard*, visit *http://www.blackboard.com*).

6. The author is aware of Smith's (2003) modification to the Interactionist coding scheme in application to CMC. However, the current study is building on the author's previous research (see Lee 2001; Lee 2002b) drawing on a similar data set. Thus, the same coding scheme created by Varonis and Gass (1985) is used for this study.

7. All examples presented in this paper were taken from the current study and with-out any correction. While accents, tildes and umlauts are supported in *Blackboard*, students often do not use them.

8. As the current study is building on the author's previous research (see Lee 2001; Lee 2002b), the term "clarification check" is used instead of "clarification request" to indicate unknown lexical items and instances when a NNS asks for an explanation from his or her interlocutor.

9. The category "non-understood message" often implies multiple linguistic errors that indicate the entire discourse is problematic. In this study, requests for help refer to instances when learners asked their interlocutors to elaborate on an earlier utterance.

10. In this study, both the NS and NNS immediate responses to feedback were considered to help identify distinct negotiation strategies used to reach mutual understanding.

11. Repair is defined as the correction made by NNSs immediately after receiving corrective feedback from NSs.

12. Words in square brackets with an asterisk represent linguistic errors.

13. It should be noted that in this study, morphological errors that caused lexical problems were coded as lexical errors.

References

Abrams, Zsuzsanna. 2003. The Effect of Synchronous and Asynchronous CMC on Oral Performance in German. *Modern Language Journal* 87: 157–167.

Ayoun, Dalila. 2001. The Role of Negative and Positive Feedback in the Second Language Acquisition of the Passé Composé and the Imparfait. *Modern Language Journal* 85: 226–243.

Blake, Robert. 2000. Computer Mediated Communication: A Window on L2 Spanish Interlanguage. *Language Learning & Technology* 4: 120–136.

Blake, Robert, and Eve Zyzik. 2003. Who's Helping Whom?: Learner/Heritage-Speakers' Networked Discussions in Spanish. *Applied Linguistics* 24: 519–544.

Chun, Dorothy. 1994. Using Computer Networking to Facilitate the Acquisition of Interactive Competence. *System* 22: 17–31.

Darhower, Mark. 2002. Instructional Features of Synchronous Computer-Mediated Communication in the L2 Class: A Sociocultural Case Study. *CALICO Journal* 19: 249–277.

Doughty, Catherine. 1993. Fine-timing of Feedback by Competent Speakers to Language Learners. *Georgetown University Roundtable on Languages and Linguistics*: 96–108.

Doughty, Catherine, and Jessica Williams. 1998. *Focus on Form in Classroom Second Language Acquisition.* Cambridge, UK: Cambridge University Press.

Duff, Patricia. 1999. Tasks and Interlanguage Performance: An SLA Research Perspective. In *Tasks and Language Learning: Integrating Theory and Practice,* edited by Graham Crookes and Susan Gass, 57–95. Bristol, PA: Multilingual Matters Ltd.

Ellis, Rod. 1999. *Learning a Second Language through Interaction.* Philadelphia, PA: John Benjamins Publishing Company.

——. 2003. *Task-based Language Learning and Teaching.* Oxford, England: Oxford University Press.

Ellis, Rod, Helen Basturkmen, and Shawn Loewen. 2001. Learner Uptake in Communicative ESL Lessons. *Language Learning* 51: 281–318.

Fernández-García, Marisol, and Asunción Martínez-Arbelaiz. 2003. Learners' Interactions: A Comparison of Oral and Computer-Assisted Written Conversations. *ReCALL* 15: 113–136.

Gass, Susan. 1997. *Input, Interaction and Second Language Learners.* Hillsdale, NJ: Lawrence Erlhaum.

Gass, Susan, Alison Mackey, and Teresa Pica. 1998. The Role of Input and Interaction in Second Language Acquisition: An Introduction. *The Modern Language Journal* 82: 299–307.

Gass, Susan, and Evangeline Varonis. 1994. Input, Interaction and Second Language Production. *Studies in Second Language Acquisition* 16: 283–302.

González-Lloret, Marta. 2003. Designing Task-Based CALL to Promote Interaction en Busca de Esmeraldas. *Language Learning & Technology* 7: 86–104.

Hatch, Evelyn, ed. 1978. *Second Language Acquisition*. Rowley, MA: Newbury House.

Iwashita, Noriko. 2003. Negative Feedback and Positive Evidence in Task-Based Interaction. *Studies in Second Language Acquisition* 25: 1–30.

Izumi, Shinichi. 1998. Negative Feedback in Adult NS/NNS Task-Based Conversation. Paper presented at the annual meeting of the *American Association for Applied Linguistics*, Seattle, WA.

Kern, Richard. 1995. Restructuring Classroom Interaction with Networked Computers: Effects on Quantity and Quality of Language Production. *Modern Language Journal* 79: 457–476.

Krashen, Stephen. 1985. *The Input Hypothesis: Issues and Implications*. London: Longman.

Lee, Lina. 2000. Evaluating Intermediate Spanish Students' Speaking Skills through a Taped Test: A Pilot Study. *Hispania* 83: 127–138.

———. 2001. Online Interaction: Negotiation of Meaning and Strategies Used among Learners of Spanish. *ReCALL* 13: 232–244.

———. 2002a. Enhancing Learners' Communication Skills through Synchronous Electronic Interaction and Task-Based Instruction. *Foreign Language Annals* 35: 16–23.

———. 2002b. Synchronous Online Exchanges: A Study of Modification Devices on Nonnative Discourse Interaction. *System* 30: 275–288.

———. 2004. Learners' Perspectives on Networked Collaborative Interaction with Native Speakers in the US. *Learning Language & Technology* 8: 83–100.

Leeman, Jennifer. 2003. Reasts and L2 Development: Beyond Negative Evidence. *Studies in Second Language Acquisition* 25: 37–63.

Long, Michael. 1985. Input and Second Language Acquisition Theory. In *Input in Second Language Acquisition*, edited by Susan Gass and Carolyn Madden, 377–393. Rowley, MA: Newbury House.

———. 1996. The Role of Linguistic Environment in Second Language Acquisition. In *Second Language Acquisition*, edited by William Ritchie and Tej Bhatia, 413–478. Handbook of Research on Language Acquisition: Vol. 2. San Diego: Academic Press.

Long, Michael, Shunji Inagaki, and Lourdes Ortega. 1998. The Role of Implicit Negative Feedback in SLA: Models and Recasts in Japanese and Spanish. *The Modern Language Journal* 82: 357–371.

Long, Michael, and Peter Robinson. 1998. Focus on Form: Theory, Research and Process. In *Focus on Form in Classroom Second Language Acquisition*, edited by Catherine Doughty and Jessica Williams, 15–41. New York: Cambridge University Press.

Lyster, Roy. 1994. Négociation de la Form: Stratégie Analytique en Classe D'immersion. *Canadian Modern Language Review* 50: 447–465.

———. 1998a. Recasts, Repetition, and Ambiguity in L2 Classroom Discourse. *Studies in Second Language Acquisition* 20: 51–81.

———. 1998b. Negotiation of Form, Recasts, and Explicit Correction in Relation to Error Types and Learner Repair in Immersion Classrooms. *Language Learning* 48: 183–218.

———. 2004. Differential Effects of Prompts and Recasts in Form-Focused Instruction. *Studies in Second Language Acquisition* 26: 399–432.

Lyster, Roy, and Leila Ranta. 1997. Corrective Feedback and Learner Uptake. *Studies in Second Language Acquisition* 19: 37–66.

Mackey, Alison. 1999. Input, Interaction and Second Language Development: An Empirical Study of Question Formation in ESL. *Studies in Second Language Acquisition* 21: 557–587.

Mackey, Alison. 2000. Interactional Feedback on the L2 Morpho-Syntax: Learners' Perceptions and Developmental Outcomes. Paper presented at the *American Association of Applied Linguistics*. Vancouver, British Columbia, Canada.

Mackey, Alison, Susan Gass, and Kim McDonough. 2000. Do Learners Recognize Implicit Negative Feedback as Feedback? *Studies in Second Language Acquisition* 22: 471-497.

Mackey, Alison, Rhonda Oliver, and Jennifer Leeman. 2003. International Input Incorporation of Feedback: An Exploration of NS-NNS and NNS-NNS Adult and Child Dyads. *Language Learning* 53: 35-66.

Mackey, Alison, and Jenefer Philp. 1998. Conversational Interaction and Second Language Development. Recasts, Responses, and Red Herrings? *The Modern Language Journal* 82: 338-356.

Morris, Frank. 2002. Negotiation Moves and Recasts in Relation to Error Types and Learner Repair in the Foreign Language Classroom. *Foreign Language Annals* 35: 395-404.

————. 2005. Child-to-Child Interaction and Corrective Feedback in a Computer Mediated L2 Class. *Language Learning & Technology* 9: 29-45.

Oliver, Rhonda. 1995. Negative Feedback in Child NS/NNS Conversation. *Studies in Second Language Acquisition* 17: 459-483.

————. 1998. Negotiation of Meaning in Child Interactions. *The Modern Language Journal* 82: 372-386.

————. 2000. Negotiation of Meaning in Child Interactions. The Relationship between Conversational Interaction and Second Language Acquisition. *The Modern Language Journal* 84: 119-151.

————. 2002. The Patterns of Negotiation for Meaning in Child Interactions. *The Modern Language Journal* 86: 97-111.

Payne, J. Scott, and Paul Whitney. 2003. Developing L2 Oral Proficiency through Synchronous CMC: Output, Working Memory and Interlanguage Development. *CALICO Journal* 20: 7-32.

Pellettieri, Jill. 2000. Negotiation in Cyberspace: The Role of Chatting in the Development of Grammatical Competence. In *Network-Based Language Teaching: Concepts and Practice*, edited by Mark Warschauer and Richard Kern, 59-86. Cambridge, UK: Cambridge University Press.

Pica, Teresa. 1994. Research on Negotiation: What Does it Reveal about Second Language Learning Conditions, Processes and Outcomes? *Language Learning* 44: 493-527.

Schmidt, Richard. 1995. Consciousness and Foreign Language Learning: A Tutorial on the Role Attention and Awareness in Learning. In *Attention and Awareness in Foreign Language Learning*, edited by Richard Schmidt, 1-63. Technical Report No. 9. Honolulu: University of Hawaii, Second Language Teaching and Curriculum Center.

Skehan, Peter. 1998. *A Cognitive Approach to Language Learning*. Oxford: Oxford University Press.

Smith, D. Bryan. 2003. Computer-Mediated Negotiated Interaction: An Expanded Model. *The Modern Language Journal* 87: 38-57.

Swain, Merrill. 1995. Three Functions of Output in Second Language Learning. In *Principle and Practice in Applied Linguistics: Studies in Honour of H. G. Widdowson*, edited by Guy Cook, 125-144. Oxford: Oxford University Press.

Swain, Merrill, and Sharon Lapkin. 1998. Interaction and Second Language Learning: Two Adolescent French Immersion Students Working Together. *The Modern Language Journal* 82: 320-337.

Toyoda, Etsuko, and Richard Harrison. 2002. Categorization of Text Chat Communication Between Learners and Native Speakers of Japanese. *Language Learning & Technology* 6(1): 82-99.

Tudini, Enza. 2003. Using Native Speakers in Chat. *Language Learning & Technology* 7(3): 141-159.

VanPatten, Bill. 1990. Attending to Form and Content in the Input: An Experiment in Consciousness. *Studies in Second Language Acquisition* 12: 287–301.

———. 1996. *Input Processing and Grammar Instruction in Second Language Acquisition.* Westport, CT: Ablex.

Varonis, Evangeline, and Susan Gass. 1985. Non-Native/Non-Native Conversation: A Model for Negotiation. *Applied Linguistics* 6: 71–90.

Warschauer, Mark. 1997. Computer Mediated Collaborative Learning: Theory and Practice. *The Modern Language Journal* 81: 470–481.

White, Lydia. 1990. Second Language Acquisition and Universal Grammar. *Studies in Second Language Acquisition* 12: 121–133.

Williams, Jessica. 1999. Leaner-Generated Attention to Form. *Language Learning* 49: 583–625.

Part Three

New Developments in Internet-mediated Intercultural Foreign Language Education

Chapter 7

Conflicts in Cyberspace: From Communication Breakdown to Intercultural Dialogue in Online Collaborations

Jeffrey Schneider
Silke von der Emde

Abstract

This chapter addresses problems of misunderstanding and conflict that arise in online collaborations between native speakers and language learners. Rather than devising strategies for avoiding conflict, it establishes a dialogic paradigm for making conflict and tension a valuable component of intercultural learning. To demonstrate the practical effects of this theoretical shift to a dialogic model and away from strategies embodied in the communicative competence model, we present a qualitative analysis of online discussion transcripts, face-to-face class discussions, and student postings gathered during a MOO collaboration in fall 2003 between fifth-semester students studying German at Vassar College in New York state and advanced students studying applied linguistics and English at the University of Münster in Germany. As our data suggest, online exchanges are most successful when they include a coherent, intercultural content focus with the potential to raise issues of cultural difference, meaningful project work, and regular opportunities for reflection on the exchange and meta-reflection on intercultural learning.

Introduction

Online collaborations between language learners and native speakers (NSs) represent an exciting and challenging educational opportunity for both students and teachers of foreign languages (FLs). By supplanting textbook exercises with "the real thing," that is, authentic communication with NS peers, such tele-collaborative exchanges have brought a new practical relevance to the study of FLs in U.S. college classrooms. Yet despite the increasing ubiquity of Internet access in schools and universities around the world, network-based collaborations between groups of students from different cultures are not simply a matter of "plug-and-play." Indeed, even after surmounting considerable organizational hurdles (see Belz and Müller-Hartmann 2003), many telecollaborations have disappointed teachers and students alike with some rather unsatisfying outcomes ranging from superficial exchanges of information (O'Dowd 2003) to "chasm[s] of intercultural misunderstanding" in which one set of partners feels frustrated, misunderstood, or even personally attacked (Belz 2003, p. 82).

To a large extent, it has been easier for researchers to recommend steps for moving online exchanges beyond superficial conversations than it has been to address intercultural misunderstandings and conflict.[1] Indeed, too often efforts to teach communicative competence betray a desire to diminish or even eliminate conflict entirely, either in face-to-face situations or in online collaborations. We propose, however, that the value of online exchanges may lie precisely in their potential to allow students to deal with conflicts among the participants because, as Julie A. Belz observes, "it is a mistake to assume that smooth, agreeable, and accommodating interactions are the only kinds of learning events from which students may learn" (2005). Clearly, online exchanges represent an important opportunity for students from two different cultures to gain a much broader understanding of what it means to communicate with NSs of the language they are studying. But to the extent that conflict seems inimical to notions of success-ful communication, telecollaborations also underline the inadequacy of "commu-nication" and "communicative competence" as organizing principles for FL study. While research on intercultural communication has proposed "intercultural com-petence" as an important corrective to the reigning communicative paradigm, we argue for extending intercultural learning itself into a fully dialogic model. As we document here, a dialogic approach to online exchanges offers a conceptual struc-ture for making conflict a central and productive source for learning rather than a debilitative stumbling block to communication.

The call for placing dialogue and conflict at the center of the foreign language enterprise is not entirely new. In fact, Claire Kramsch articulated such a call in her still radical challenge for foreign language education to "embrace conflict" rather than "achieve consensus" (1995). Written at a time when FL programs were just beginning to institute intercultural online exchanges, Kramsch's article focused on differences within FL departments in the United States, especially the different research traditions that inform the study of FL learning in this country: Second Language Acquisition (SLA), which is generally "empirically based" and "valued for the rigor and integrity of its data collection and its readings of the data, the soundness of its measurements, and the well-foundedness of its claims" (p. 8), and the literary and cultural studies scholarship conducted by members of the *Modern Language Association* (MLA), which tends to pride itself on "the richness of its textual interpretations" as well as "its theoretical sophistication" (p. 8). Rather than laying out a course for consensus, Kramsch warned back then that the various practical concerns and theoretical approaches existing in the field of FLs "are irreducible to any common ground," for "the only common ground we have is dialogue itself" (p. 11). At the time of its publication, Kramsch's call for revaluing conflict elicited some rather harsh reactions from SLA scholars (see Bernhardt 1995; Byrnes 1995). Fortunately, there now seems to be a much larger basis for interdisciplinary dialogue because, as Kramsch (2002) has observed recently, cur-rent postmodern and poststructuralist trends in both camps have resulted in many more shared theoretical assumptions across the humanities and social sciences.

As scholars trained in literary and cultural studies, we conceptualize this chapter as an effort to continue this interdisciplinary MLA-SLA dialogue in several ways. First, we point out some of the conceptual differences between dialogic and communicative approaches to online interactions and explain to what extent conflict is not only a possibly inherent feature of intercultural communication, but also a valuable one.[2] Second, we want to expand the conceptual tools that researchers and teachers in the United States have for conducting and assessing intercultural communication by engaging with the important work on intercultural learning being conducted in Europe. Dialogue, rather than wholesale adoption, is required here too because, as Kramsch (2001, p. 202) has observed, the study of intercultural communication has drawn too little on cultural studies and other humanities approaches. Moreover, adapting this model for the American FL classroom requires its own intercultural negotiations. Finally, to illustrate the practical consequences of implementing a dialogic approach to intercultural learning, we offer a qualitative analysis of materials drawn from an online collaboration in fall 2003 between students studying German at *Vassar College* and students studying applied linguistics and English at the *University of Münster*. While we hope that teachers will find in these pages specific tips, strategies, and practices that they can integrate into their own telecollaborative partnerships, our emphasis in this article is on articulating the larger theoretical considerations and curricular structures that should inform any intercultural online exchange.

From Communication to Dialogue

Although the terms "communication" and "dialogue" are often used interchangeably, the call for FL learning to move from a focus on communication to a model based on dialogue encompasses more than a mere semantic shift. To appreciate the distinction and its implications for conducting online collaborations between language learners and NSs, it is important to understand the conceptual blind spots within communicative language teaching (CLT) and their implications for intercultural interactions. Initially, the notion of "communicative competence," which was developed in the work of the linguistic anthropologist Dell Hymes (see Duranti 1997; Hymes 1997), compelled FL researchers to view communicative competence as involving not only an ability to use grammatical structures and vocabulary (linguistic competence) correctly, but also an ability to use language appropriately in a given socio-cultural context. And since its introduction in the 1970s, CLT has evolved to stress the importance of helping students develop a variety of competences, which include not only linguistic or grammatical competence, but also discursive, strategic, and socio-cultural competence (see Savignon 2002).

The conceptual problem of using this approach for intercultural communication becomes apparent in a recent article by Sandra J. Savignon, arguably the founder and leading proponent of CLT, and Pavel V. Sysoyev (2002). For instance, the fourth component in their "taxonomy of socio-cultural strategies" reads as follows: "Using diplomacy for the purpose of maintaining a dialogue of cultures in the spirit of peace and mutual understanding; redirecting a discussion to a more neutral topic; dissimulation of personal views to avoid potential conflict" (p. 513). Yet in their study of thirty Russian high school students studying English at

Tambov Grammar School, this fourth strategy proved to be "the most difficult" one for students to follow, since disguising their own viewpoints represented a significant departure from their strategies for dealing with disagreements in their own culture (p. 517). While it is clear that engaging with interlocutors from another culture will require some modulation of one's own cultural assumptions in order to "maintain a dialogue of cultures," it is questionable whether "mutual understanding" will take place if one of the interlocutors is induced to dissimulate or suppress his or her point of view. Indeed, as the Russian students in their study indicate, disguising their contradictory views to avoid conflict involves an act of self-violence, which would seem to call into question the very notion that such dialogues are taking place in a "spirit of peace."

Instead of offering a generalizable socio-cultural strategy, then, Savignon and Sysoyev would seem to be teaching these future English speakers specific cultural strategies to interact "successfully" with U.S. speakers of English—but on U.S. American rather than mutual terms because U.S. Americans tend to view conflict as undesirable and socially inappropriate. Implicitly, this strategy insists that learners of English adopt questionable NS standards and forego their privileges as non-native speakers (NNSs), to use Kramsch's (1997) eloquent formulation. But the ruse of promoting the strategy as a necessary socio-cultural skill also effectively levels cultural differences. Deborah Cameron, for instance, charges that "a standard for 'effective communication' is always in practice based on habits and values which are not cultural universals, but are specific to a particular cultural milieu" (2002, p. 80). As a result, efforts to identify socio-cultural competence are merely another form of cultural imperialism while still nominally supporting language diversity. Likewise, David Block fears that such encroaching socio-cultural norms, which he labels "McCommunication," will diminish the current diversity in communicative styles as "we all follow the same recommendations on how we should and shouldn't talk" (2002, p. 120). In addition to realizing that there is not one right way to communicate (or disagree), students also need to be aware that cyberspace is not, as Kramsch and Thorne warn, a "utopian middle landscape, where native speakers and non-native speakers can have access to one another as linguistic entities on a screen, unfettered by historical, geographical, national, or institutional identities" (2002, p. 85).

The European model of intercultural competence (see, for example, Byram, Gribkova, and Starkey 2002) offers several important conceptual correctives to CLT approaches like the one represented by Savignon and Sysoyev. First, instead of focusing foremost on skills and strategy development, the intercultural competence model (IC) emphasizes the importance of helping students develop "intercultural attitudes," defined as "curiosity and openness" toward the views of others and an ability to distance oneself from "one's own values, beliefs, and behaviors" (Byram, Nichols, and Stevens 2001, p. 5). Second, rather than emphasizing linguistic skills designed primarily for encoding and decoding messages, IC insists that intercultural speakers need a much broader set of skills, including the ability to obtain knowledge about the other culture as well as the ability to interpret documents, utterances, and events from both cultures. Moreover, in explicit opposition to asking students to adopt the norms and standards of the other culture, IC requires interlocutors to make their own values "explicit and conscious" (Byram, Nichols, and Stevens 2001, p. 7). This insistence on foregrounding and respecting cultural and individual differences among participants—in place of asking one group to dissimulate—has underscored IC's ethical and political commitment to placing intercultural communication on an explicitly egalitarian foundation. It also signals that IC is not primarily driven by a desire for the utilitarian effectiveness of "McCommunication," but rather implicitly prioritizes dialogue in the service of intercultural learning.

Because IC encourages an engagement with cultural difference, it is surprising that the model has little to say about open conflict, except in the terms of helping students "become more aware of their own values and how these influence their views of other people's values" (Byram, Nichols, and Stevens 2001, p. 7). We suspect that this general silence about conflict in IC derives from its articulation within a European context, in which it is politically imperative that people from different linguistic and cultural backgrounds find some common ground. For our purposes, however, we want to build on this European model by drawing out and making more explicit what we see as its dialogic foundation and its ability to enable productive conflicts. Within cultural studies, the notion of dialogue is most closely associated with the Russian literary theorist and philosopher Mikhail Bakhtin and his circle, whose work is multifaceted and extremely pertinent to contemporary philosophical concerns as well as language learning as an intercultural project. Bakhtin's theories focus primarily on the concept of dialogue, and on the notion that language—any form of speech or writing—is not a self-unified system but the result and site of struggle, that is, conflict. Language, and what is conveyed through language—ideas and statements of truth, for example—are always the product of the interactions between (at least) two interlocutors.[3] As a result, his theory insists that all discourses and utterances arise out of a fundamental engagement with an Other, whether that Other is someone from a different culture and with a different language, or someone from within the same culture and language. Thus, rather than supporting a normative model of encoding and decoding utterances, this model insists on the fundamental openness of linguistic utterances to interpretation, which can potentially, if not inherently, lead to conflicts.

Moreover, dialogic conceptions of communication emphasize that utterances are not merely the product of interlocutors, but in fact shape the interlocutors as well. Because neither language nor subjects within language are unitary, conflict and struggle are inevitable features of dialogue: not only because meaningful dialogue with another challenges our worldview and sense of self, but also, as Julia T. Wood points out, because dialogue forces us to "wrestle with the discomfort that comes from lack of closure and lack of unquestionably right answers" (2004, p. xvii). But perhaps the most important difference between notions of "communicative competence" and dialogic engagement is the ideal nature of conflict and its suspicion of common ground. As Wood helpfully summarizes, "dialogue does not necessarily idealize or seek common ground. The search for (and belief in) common ground may thwart, rather than facilitate, genuine dialogue, because almost inevitably the dominant culture defines what ground is common or legitimate. . . . [D]ialogue allows differences to exist without trying to resolve, overcome, synthesize, or otherwise tame them" (2004, pp. xvii–xviii). Thus, in contrast to Savignon and Sysoyev's (2002) socio-cultural strategies, it is more essential to help students to tolerate and feel comfortable with conflict rather than encourage them either to deny their own cultural approaches to disagreements or rush to find common ground. Indeed, the open and egalitarian forms of communication imagined by the model of intercultural competence can only take place when members from different cultures learn to acknowledge and respect differences.

Like the model of intercultural learning, dialogic approaches to interaction call for materials, experiences, and encounters that de-center students from their own culture's worldviews and require them to critically evaluate perspectives, practices, and products in one's own and other cultures through interpretation. These goals are at once practical and political, but also intellectual. As such, they reflect the combination of attitudes, skills development, and knowledge production that are the hallmark of liberal arts education in the United States. Perhaps more than anyone else, Gerald Graff (1992) has advocated for developing a pedagogy and curriculum—a sense of intellectual community—out of the differences that inhere in a diverse world. Because there exists, as he notes, "a deep cognitive connection between controversy and intelligibility" (Graff 2003, p. 12), the presence of conflict is in fact a measure of the university's—or a language course's—"vitality, not its decline" (Graff 1992, p. 4). Obviously, translating these ideas into practice is neither easy nor automatic. But the first step requires a course and curriculum organized around "teaching the conflicts."

Dialogue in Practice: The Vassar–Münster Exchange

Since 1998, faculty members in the German Studies Department at *Vassar College* and in the English Department at the *University of Münster* have been conducting an annual online intercultural exchange. Over the years, the exchange has evolved from an experimental course in which we investigated and documented the language learning benefits of online collaborations (see von der Emde *et al.* 2001) to a standard component of the curriculum in both departments. At Vassar, the exchange is now part of a fifth-semester advanced intermediate language and cultural studies course entitled "Intermediate German III: German Culture and Media." At Münster, the exchange occurred as a component of a didactic *proseminar* on online language learning. Thus, while Vassar students are still reviewing higher-level grammar concepts (passive, relative pronouns, subjunctive) within a content-based format, the students at the University of Münster already have fairly strong language skills in English and are training to be secondary school teachers of English.

In the fall semester of 2003, which served as the basis for this study, there were fourteen students from Vassar (eight women and six men) ranging from freshmen to seniors. Of the fourteen participants, two were German majors and two were foreign students whose native language was not English (four students subsequently declared majors in German, and one declared a minor). At the

University of Münster, eleven students (eight women and three men) were
enrolled in the course, most a couple years older than the Vassar students. The
exchange was conducted in Vassar's bilingual German–English MOO called
MOOssiggang, an open source, web-based learning environment that permits both
chat functions and asynchronous forms of writing in a multimedia setting.[4] As
part of the exchange, students from each university met twice each week for about
an hour in small intercultural working groups composed of two to three students
from each institution. Together they discussed news reports, documentary films,
and the results of their own independent research. The discussions alternated
between the two languages; usually one day was conducted in German, the other
day was conducted in English. Vassar students also met for a third "workshop"
session every Friday in which they reported on their online group discussions to
the others in the class, analyzed the kinds of issues that came up in their groups
(including conflicts), and worked together on grammar. In addition to the transcripts from the online MOO discussions, students at Vassar were asked to post on
the course's *Blackboard* site individual summaries (in either English or German)
of their small group discussions as well as reflection pieces on various assigned
readings ranging from the primary texts related to the exchange to secondary texts
on FL learning and intercultural learning. After four weeks of online discussions,
the five intercultural groups then divided into ten subgroups consisting only of
members from each university for the purposes of completing an online final
project in the MOO. The five intercultural groups formed once again at the end of
the exchange to discuss their projects and assess the intercultural learning that
took place during the telecollaborations.

A Meaningful Academic Content Focus
with High Stakes for the Students

Two specific aspects distinguish the Vassar–Münster exchange from the kinds
of exchanges that have been documented in the literature on networked collaborations. First, the exchange was not the primary focus of the course at either
Vassar or Münster, but rather an integral aspect of two larger but different courses:
developing a critical understanding of technology in FL teaching (at Münster) and
studying media (at Vassar). Students in the Vassar class, for instance, spent the
first seven weeks of the semester studying three paradigmatic "case studies"
related to media in twentieth-century Germany: the role of radio and film as tools
of Nazi propaganda, the discourse and policies on popular music in East Germany
during the youth movement of the 1960s and early 1970s, and the coverage of
domestic terrorism in the capitalistic boulevard press in West Germany during the
1970s. Second, the exchange, which took place during the second half of the
Vassar semester, not only brought these two intercultural groups together
online, but also asked both groups to *study* their own intercultural learning at
the same time.

     The topic of the exchange was a intercultural analysis of two deadly school
shootings: the first at *Columbine High School* in Littleton, Colorado, in April 1999,

and the second at the *Johannes Gutenberg Gymnasium* in Erfurt, Germany, in April 2002. Overall, school violence in Germany and in the United States proved to be an ideal topic for this particular constellation of students, because it allowed for students' different linguistic skill levels in the L2 as well as different cultural knowledge and motivations for participating in an intercultural online exchange to become productive features rather than hindrances in the exchange. Although the students at the University of Münster were not necessarily interested in media studies more generally, the topic of school violence allowed them to combine their focus on language learning with their interest in learning about American high school culture and thinking critically—and proactively—about possible solutions for deadly violence they might encounter in their future careers as English teachers in German *Gymnasien*. Meanwhile, because most of the Vassar students had started studying German fairly recently, they were eager to improve their language skills by interacting with NSs, especially since many were interested in studying abroad in Germany for a semester or a year. But because most of the Vassar students had attended American high schools in a post-Columbine atmosphere, they were also deeply interested in revisiting the issue, especially in light of a seemingly similar school shooting in Germany that most had never heard about. Moreover, because the topic of school violence required students to investigate media representations of the incidents, including the role that media might have played in contributing to these acts of violence, it brought a desirable coherence to the course by implicitly building on the units that the Vassar students had studied in the first half of the semester.[5]

The topic gave the exchange a tight focus on two seemingly similar acts of school violence. But exploring the two incidents also eventually led students to focus on the important differences that marked the two events, including the different kinds of victims (students at Columbine, teachers at Erfurt, for example), the different motivations of the attackers (anger at being taunted by fellow students vs. anger at being expelled), the different forms of press coverage in *Time Magazine* (for example, Gibbs 1999) and *Der Spiegel* (for example, Brinkbäumer *et al.* 2002), and the different visual meditations offered by Michael Moore's documentary *Bowling for Columbine* (2003) and a German television documentary about Erfurt one year later (Bernd and Dickmann 2003). Perhaps most importantly, the choice of materials compelled the students to respond equally strongly to the events in their own culture as much as in the culture they were studying because the aftermath of both the Columbine and Erfurt shootings raised important questions about the culturally specific factors that might have led to the incidents.

As a violent outcome of conflict, both school shootings also offered plenty of impetus for potential conflicts between students on both sides of the Atlantic. For example, in response to Michael Moore's film, which explores the issue of gun control in the United States, heated discussions developed in every group around whether gun laws in the United States cause or contribute to violence. Although this is already an ongoing debate in the United States, here the discussion of gun law differences signified the importance of drawing distinctions between U.S. and

German culture, something on which the German students eagerly insisted. The American students, on the other hand, while initially agreeing with Moore's reading of American culture, seemed eager to deconstruct an all too literal reading of the film on the part of the German students. The following dialogue (reproduced in English with some deletions due to space limitations) took place in German in an intercultural group consisting of two students at the University of Münster, Christine and Ingrid, and two American students from Vassar, Felicity and Nora,[6] and is illustrative of the conflicts that arose in the course of the exchange:

1 **Christine** (to Felicity): It is definitely easier to get a gun permit in the USA ...

2 **Ingrid says:** Here you have to show your gun permit if you want to buy a weapon.

3 **Felicity asks:** How difficult is it to get a gun permit?

4 **Ingrid asks:** Do you believe that most Americans have a gun at home?

5 **Christine says:** Yes, it's pretty difficult. You either have to need a gun permit in your job or you have to be a registered member in a club. . .

6 **Ingrid says:** if someone plans something like this, then he'll get a gun no matter how, I think.

7 **Felicity says:** I am not for weapons but I don't want us to make assumptions [*Annahmen*].

8 **Ingrid** (to Felicity): What do you mean?

9 **Felicity** (to Ingrid): I think we're making assumptions [*Annahmen*] about the gun laws in Germany and in America.

10 **Ingrid says:** Yes but here it is harder to get guns than in America— that's what the film Bowling for Columbine showed.

11 **Christine says:** I only want to say that owning guns is not part of our culture. Except when someone uses guns in their job.

12 **Nora says:** I am getting the impression (from the article) that Germans blame culture (especially American culture) not weapons.

13 **Felicity** (to Ingrid): because we don't really know the laws in either country.

14 **Ingrid says:** but we know that it is definitely easier in the USA

15 **Christine** (to Felicity): You simply have to believe us. I have tried to explain it as best I can. If you don't have a compelling [*triftig*] reason to own a gun, it's impossible to obtain a weapon in Germany.

16 **Ingrid says:** I wouldn't say that people blame the USA for this

17 **Felicity asks:** here you can't buy guns in every supermarket or bank.

18 **Ingrid says:** here weapons are only available in special shops—you don't see them in normal stores.

19 **Christine says:** And even in these special stores you can't buy an automatic. They wouldn't even have something like that.

20   **Ingrid says:** exactly

21   **Felicity says:** I am against weapons and I find it shocking that you can buy weapons in a supermarket but I only want that we don't make assumptions about America.

22   **Christine says:** But one can get illegal weapons here just as easily. O well. Whatever. ;-)[7]

In this exchange, the conversation almost turns hostile at times. The two students from Germany stress the differences in the gun laws in Germany and the United States. Felicity, however, insists that the Germans prove their points and inquires more deeply about whether the differences in laws and gun culture in Germany and the United States are in fact as substantial as Ingrid and Christine insist (turns 7, 9). While Felicity seems upset by the generalizations on the part of her German partners (turn 13), they are frustrated that she won't admit that there are differences in the two countries (turns 14–15).

One of the reasons for conflict lies in Felicity's lower linguistic abilities as indicated by her repeated use of the word "*Annahmen*" for "assumptions" instead of "*Verallgemeinerungen*" or "*Vermutungen*." As a result, it takes quite awhile until the Münster students understand what she is saying. Moreover, as she noted in a *Blackboard* post and in class discussion, her partners used German vocabulary (for example, "*triftig*," turn 15) that is significantly above her comprehension level (at least during the discussion), so that even when they do answer her question, she doesn't realize it right away. Nevertheless, the conflict between Felicity and her partners from Münster is not essentially a linguistic one. Indeed, once they do understand what she is trying to articulate, Christine and Ingrid remain quite insistent on making Felicity admit that she is wrong: "It is DEFINITELY easier in the U.S." (*Es ist definitiv einfacher in den USA*) (turn 14) and "You simply HAVE to believe us" (*Das musst du uns jetzt einfach glauben*) (turn 15). Although Ingrid acknowledges early on that it would be possible for someone in Germany to obtain a weapon illegally if he or she really wanted to carry out a school shooting (turn 6), Christine only does so at the end of the conversation (turn 22). Her "*naja*," whatever," a code-switch from German into English, seems to indicate her exasperation with Felicity's resistance, although her smiley face also seems to signal that she didn't find the heated debate insulting or hurtful.

Nor would it be accurate to conclude that conflict could have been avoided by pointing out to Felicity and Nora that Ingrid and Christine seem to be exhibiting "German conversational styles" in their willingness to make strongly declarative statements of truth (see, for example, Belz 2003). Although this may be the case, we share Kramsch's concerns that any essentialism of "national traits and cultural characteristics . . . seems too reductionist" (2001, p. 205). But acknowledging different conversational styles also does not alter the stand-off between the two groups. Moreover, because the disagreement revolves around perceptions that some members of the group are making stereotypical assumptions about the other members' culture, having students merely return to "the facts" would also be insufficient, although students in this group did go on to research gun laws in both countries as part of their final project. Instead, the deeper roots of the conflict in this exchange lie in the extent to which each side is unwittingly interpolated into representing their own national cultures. For instance, when Ingrid asks whether her Vassar partners "believe that most Americans have a gun at home" (turn 4), Felicity responds by saying, "I am not for weapons but I don't want us to make assumptions" (turn 7). Although Ingrid was following up a line of argument in *Bowling for Columbine* with a question about her partners' beliefs (rather than asking them to produce on the spot any reliable facts), the Vassar students read it as an assumption that most Americans, and perhaps even the students themselves, are weapons-owners or weapons-lovers.[8]

Again, because the Vassar students understand Ingrid's question quite well, the source of the conflict is not a linguistic or discourse pattern problem. While Ingrid probably posed the question genuinely and innocently, it is legitimate, even insightful that the Vassar students interpret her question, as well as this entire debate about gun control, as a much larger gesture designed to insist on fundamental differences about violence in Germany and the United States. Thus, Nora cites the *Spiegel* articles in order to offer what literary critics call a symptomatic reading (turn 12), that is, by suggesting that the content of this discussion ("weapons laws") is merely a symptom for something else, a much deeper belief that the origin of violence in Germany is in fact the prevalence of American culture. Although it elicits a denial from Ingrid, who counters with "I wouldn't say that people blame the USA for this" (*ich würde nicht sagen, dass die USA dafür verantwortlich gemacht werden*) (turn 16), Nora is actually not asking whether Ingrid consciously subscribes to that theory. We understand Nora's decision to place her concern in the form of an impression based on her reading rather than a direct question as an implicit effort to open up space for everyone to take a step back in the heated discussion and consider broader questions. We also see it as a promising entry point for what could be a larger argument about the German reaction to Erfurt, an occurrence which clearly shocked a country whose citizens think of themselves as enlightened about gun laws and violence. Although the group is talking ostensibly about *Bowling for Columbine*, Nora perceives that finding the underlying reasons for the specific focus of their discussion—rather than expecting any conclusions from it—may in fact be more valuable for understanding how Germany understands the Erfurt incident.

After a couple of subsequent and fairly controversial discussions on the issue of gun laws, the group then watched and discussed the German television report about Erfurt. In their discussion, which took place this time in English, Nora and Felicity (along with their partner Michel, a French exchange student studying at Vassar for the year) initiate a different tack by asking their German partners to consider whether the causes for Erfurt lie in the German past:

1 **Nora fragt:** Michael Moore explored the concept of "violent American culture" (cowboys!) as a possible reason for Columbine. Similarly, do you think that "violent German culture" could be a possible reason for Erfurt?

2 **Nora fragt:** do you think that there could be reasons specific and native to Germany that could have led to erfurt?

3   **Christine** (to Nora): I'm not sure. I don't think that Germans are proud of their past. (and there's definitely no reason to be proud of being German ...)

4   **Nora fragt:** I think it was interesting how Moore explored the "nur in Amerika?" concept in his film. I want to do this, even just for the sake of discussion, for Erfurt. So the question becomes: Only in Germany?

5   **Christine** (to Nora): but Americans are proud of their cowboy-past. at least some are.

6   **Ingrid sagt:** and we cannot be proud of our past

7   **Nora fragt:** what do you mean, Ingrid? ...

8   **Nora** (to Ingrid): going back to the question about Germany's violent past and how it affects Germany's relation to violence today ... could you elaborate on that?

9   **Christine sagt:** can we talk about the documentary again? ;-)

10 **Felicity sagt:** I think Nora's question is interesting ...

11 **Felicity fragt:** just curious, do you guys not want to talk about Germany's history?

12 **Ingrid** (to Felicity): no, but I didn't understand your question ...

13 **Christine** (to Felicity): no. I would prefer to talk about German history to talking about the movie. but we have to summarize the results of the discussion ... and I'm not sure if that belongs to the task?!

14 **Felicity** (to Ingrid): Nora asked a interesting question about whether Germany's history could be related to things like Erfurt (like we wonder whether America's violent past is connected to our violent present). I thought it would be an interesting discussion. But no one else seems interested.

15 **Felicity fragt:** was I clear?

16 **Nora ruft:** we can wait until Wednesday ... but I won't forget the question!

17 **Nora sagt:** ok, briefly, back to the film

18 **Christine** (to Felicity): but seriously. I don't think that you can compare a mainly positively presented past (like cowboys) to an absolutely negative past (like the Nazis). I mean, if an American says: I want to carry a gun coz I have a cowboy backgound. A German couldn't say: I want to carry a gun because my ancestors were Nazis?! I don't think that's comparable ...

19 **Ingrid sagt:** ok, lets keep it for next time

20 **Michel** (to Christine): you're right, but that may precisely create another type of relation to violence

21 **Felicity sagt:** In actuality, our cowboy past was not positive, even though people still see it as if it was. We killed a lot of Native Americans. Which was not good.

22 **Nora** (to Christine): we'll talk about this more next time, but I don't agree that Americans are necessarily proud of their "cowboy" past. They certainly don't use it as an excuse to carry guns, at least

23 **Christine** (to Michel): yeah I know but then this wouldn't explain Erfurt.

24 **Michel sagt:** this doesn't I think

25 **Nora sagt:** especially now in our PC world, we don't want to admit "cow-
    boy history" and the decimation of Native Americans[9]

In this discussion, the Vassar students drew on their background in German
(media) history to try to push the discussion beyond differences in gun laws. On
the one hand, the Vassar students try to confront a literal reading of *Bowling for
Columbine* while avoiding any unwitting interpolation into defending American
culture. While their attempt to distance themselves from a positive portrayal of
the American West seems to disavow the positive role that most Americans still
attribute to their mythic "manifest destiny," it does offer important information
to their German partners that there are other, more self-critical discourses circu-
lating in the United States.

On the other hand, they also ask their partners to apply Moore's logic about
historical continuities in Germany. Ingrid and Christine point out that any simple
or literal application of that logic ("a German couldn't say: I want to carry a
gun because my ancestors were Nazis," turn 18) easily leads to absurdities,
although the persistence of their Vassar partners implies that this was probably
not their intention. But rather than engage the question, Ingrid and Christine
seem to try to avoid this uncomfortable topic by making an appeal to the "task,"
that is, discussing the German T.V. documentary (turns 9 and 13). When Nora
and Felicity insist that talking about the German past might precisely be
discussing the Erfurt shooting, we see the Germans' deeper dilemma surfacing:
If Germans have an aversive relationship to violence and guns because of their
Nazi past, as Michel is quick to point out, then it becomes difficult to explain the
growing tendency toward violence in Germany. In this case, Erfurt seems to con-
tradict in ominous ways the implicit claim that the Nazi past has enabled contemporary Germans to escape the kind of violent culture that seems to ensnare the
United States.

Although it bordered on the impolite, we see real value for intercultural learning in Nora and Felicity's insistence on posing the question again and again rather
than politely withdrawing it in response to their partners' obvious discomfort.
After all, in persisting even in the face of silence, Nora and Felicity gain valuable
knowledge about Germany's complex relation to its past in a way that helps them
understand the sense of shock that the Erfurt incident caused among Germans,
who, it would seem, experienced a "loss of innocence" that such deadly rampages
do not only happen in the United States. As Byram *et al.* note, students "need especially to know how to ask people from other cultures about their beliefs, values
and behaviours; these can be difficult to explain because they are often uncon-
scious" (2001, p. 6). Our example illustrates Byram *et al.*'s point that it is not
always possible for interlocutors to articulate what essentially remains uncon-
scious. In this group, we observe how Nora, an English major, and Felicity, an Art
History major, draw on subtle strategies for interpreting their partners' statements and silences—strategies that they practiced in the first half of this course,

in prior German Studies courses they have taken, and in their home departments. But this exchange also demonstrates that persisting in the search for a new understanding is not just a matter of having the right skills or knowledge, but also a matter of tolerating and remaining curious about conflicts, disagreements, and tensions. In this case, all five students demonstrate that they are learning to deal with conflict without risking a total breakdown in communication.[10]

Project Work

After discussing these rich and provocative texts, students were asked to document the results of their dialogues, independent research, and analyses of the two events in a final project. These projects were located spatially off a room in the MOO called the documentation center (*"Doku-Zentrum"*). Unlike earlier exchanges where we insisted on intercultural groups, the project groups in this particular exchange consisted only of members from each university. Our decision to use separate group projects was motivated by a desire to free both sets of students from any obligations to reach a "common ground" or mutual understanding in order to complete their project and thus complete the class. Moreover, it fascinated students to compare what each project revealed about what their partners took to be the most important outcomes of their dialogues. Even more importantly, the projects not only became the means of demonstrating how valuable the dialogue with NSs had been, but also a further document that, as we shall see, enabled the participants of the exchange to take their dialogue to yet a deeper level.

Even though the projects were completed by teams consisting of students from one institution, all proved surprisingly dialogical in nature. Indeed, nearly all the groups built open-ended and interactive rooms, which sought to raise questions rather than give answers. For example, one Vassar group created several linked rooms focusing on different reactions to Erfurt, including *Amtsreaktion* "the government reaction," *Medienreaktion* "the reaction of the press," Erfurt & Paintball, and *Reaktion der Leute* "reaction of the people." Rather than trying to find a common denominator among possible positions and explanations, each of these rooms depict all the conflicting perspectives on the various topics in order to encourage the visitors to the rooms to draw their own conclusions. Although this project space was implicitly interactive, others built an explicitly interactive space. One group from Münster, for instance, built a virtual bowling alley that enables visitors to "bowl" for prizes, which are in fact statements about Columbine and U.S. American culture (see Figure 1).

Many groups used their project spaces to demonstrate what they had learned about the target culture, while still others used their engagement with the target culture to shine a critical light on their own. Thus, one Vassar group, which called its project *Fragebogen Experiment* "Questionnaire Experiment," created a room called the *Media Effekt Raum* "Media Effect Space." It features an image of an enormous crowd in front of the cathedral in Erfurt. The image appeared familiar from the German television documentary, and many students presumed that it was a picture of the memorial service for the slain teachers and student from Erfurt. But

Figure 1
Student Project Room

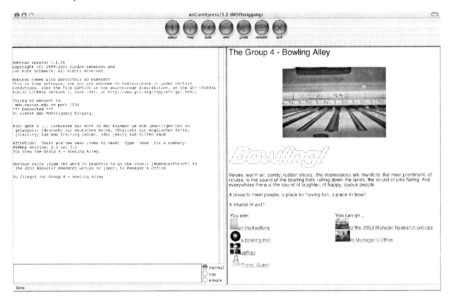

as the builders of the room make clear, the picture was in fact taken during the spontaneous show of support following the terrorist attacks in the United States on September 11, 2001. In their text, the students acknowledge that all the Münster students knew about Columbine, but none of the Americans knew about Erfurt before beginning the exchange. These students go on to provocatively criticize the U.S. media landscape by suggesting that a similar show of solidarity and empathy in response to a tragedy in another country would probably be unimaginable in the United States.

Finally, all the groups sought to make productive the conflicts that had arisen in their conversations with the NSs. One of the Vassar groups, for instance, explicitly embedded the concept of conflict in the structure of their project by calling one of their rooms *Missverständnisse* "Misunderstandings," which contains the following text: "The students in group 1 came up against some misunderstandings. Basically the misunderstandings dealt with history, violence and the law. This room has information about our discussions but it does not have any answers. Why? Because there aren't any concrete answers. . . ."[11] From this first room, visitors can visit three other rooms that deal with the important disagreements and questions that this group encountered in their sessions with their Münster partners: *zum Geschichtsunterricht* "to History Lessons," *zum Waffengesetz* "to Weapons Laws," and *zur Gewalt* "to Violence." Rather than focusing on information or articulating definitive answers, however, all three rooms end with questions.

As this brief overview indicates, all projects offered creative representations of the authentic dialogues that were begun in their conversations with the NSs, and which students seemed to view as ongoing. Indeed, because these project spaces sought to summarize and represent cultural differences in relation to the two incidents of school violence as well as the intercultural dialogues about them, they also became springboards for continuing the dialogues rather than final articulations. Indeed, thinking and talking about their own and their partners' projects became the opportunity for new insights as students were asked to respond to the project spaces of their partners. For instance, in responding to the "bowling project," Tim, one of the Vassar students who had worked with that group, commented on one of the prizes called "the NRA," which the students in that group had represented with an American flag:

> One aspect of their project that I noticed specifically was the NRA room. This room shows liberal feelings. When I read the first sentence, it was clear that Torsten and Katrin weren't neutral about this topic: "Who are these crazy people?" I liked this. But I also noticed something else in this room. The image in this room was a big American flag. I hope Torsten and Katrin don't associate all Americans with the NRA![12]

Tim responded positively to what might otherwise be an incendiary association of the American flag with the NRA. Although he expressed his hope that his Münster partners did not associate all Americans with the NRA (one possible reading of the room), he nevertheless articulated his pleasure at this rhetorical gesture.

Yet when other Vassar students passed on Tim's reaction during his absence from class one day, it facilitated a potent discussion among the entire intercultural group when all groups met for one final discussion, which was conducted in English:

1 **Torsten sagt:** I have one more question, about a specific cultural misunderstanding

2 **Tim fragt:** Yes Torsten?

3 **Torsten sagt:** Last Wednesday, we went to the bowling alley, and Anke said that some poeple were embarassed about my using the Stars and Stripes in the NRA prize

4 **Torsten sagt:** and that they were just too "polite" to tell me

5 **Katrin meint:** That would be a controverse topic for a discussion . . .

6 **Tim sagt:** Interesting. Well I'll say that I reacted strongly to it, but I was not embarassed.

7 **Cathy sagt:** Yeah . . . well . . . The U.S. flag is a very strong symbol

8 **Desmond sagt:** Cathy is right

9 **Torsten sagt:** I changed it in the meantime

10 **Katrin sagt:** I think the problem is that the flag isn't such a strong symbol for us.

11 **Torsten sagt:** I was just wondering why no one would tell me that I might have made a mistake there

12 **Desmond sagt:** to use the flag as a symbol of NRA is saying that Americans are NRA fans, gun fanatics

13 **Tim sagt:** I wrote in my response that I hoped Torsten and Katrin did not equate the NRA with the United States as a whole.

14 **Cathy sagt:** To relate it directly to something assigns a meaning to it.

15 **Katrin ruft:** We don't!

16 **Cathy sagt:** I'm sure that was not your intention though

17 **Torsten sagt:** I know now I did not think about that one enough

18 **Tim sagt:** It felt rather crappy to see my country's symbol on the page of such a insipid organization

19 **Torsten sagt:** I replaced the flag by the NRA symbol

20 **Tim sagt:** However, that's no reason for you to feel you should change it

21 **Katrin sagt:** I think that is a good solution.

22 **Cathy sagt:** Right, I saw it Torsten. It works nicely.

23 **Desmond sagt:** to prevent further misunderstandings yes

24 **Torsten sagt:** I think it is better this way

25 **Cathy sagt:** Assuming that's more what you wanted to express

26 **Torsten sagt:** good

27 **Tim sagt:** Maybe you should have left the flag there though.

28 **Torsten sagt:** thank you

29 **Cathy sagt:** Unless of course you wanted to express a direct correlation

30 **Torsten meint:** I think the reason why I put it there was relating both things somehow . . .

31 **Cathy fragt:** Did you mean to do that?

32 **Torsten** (to Cathy): I did, but I did not think about how others might think about this

33 **Desmond sagt:** I think it came a little strong

34 **Torsten sagt:** so I learnt something there

Torsten smiles.

35 **Desmond sagt:** and a bit shocking to some

36 **Tim sagt:** I guess in order to prevent misunderstanding its smart, but just because its something I cringe at when I see it doesnt mean it should be censored. Bowling for Columbine was terrible to see, but it needed to be seen for positive change

37 **Cathy sagt:** Interesting. Well, I say also, be true to what you want to express, above all

38 **Katrin fragt:** You learned something about the culture, didn't you?

39 **Torsten sagt:** I did

Torsten begins this discussion by expressing some dismay that his American partners had not directly told him that the apparent association of the flag with the NRA had offended them, but was instead passed on by our language fellow Anke, a student from Münster who was studying and working at Vassar that year. Based on this information—or at least his interpretation of this information—Torsten had decided to remove the flag and replace it with the NRA's own symbol. His reference to his partners as "too polite" (turn 4) should remind us that politeness itself can cause confusion and hurt feelings because different cultures code and interpret politeness differently. Nevertheless, because Torsten changed the image to prevent his American partners from feeling offended, it seems that the experience has helped him acquire this socio-cultural strategy. While it is also true that Cathy and Desmond support the assumption of politeness by confirming that using "the flag as a symbol of [the] NRA is saying that Americans are NRA fans, gun fanatics" (turn 12), it is also the case that (American) politeness cuts both ways. Thus when Cathy, a first-semester student, discovers that Torsten really meant to "express a direct correlation" (although without intending to offend his partners), she tells him, perhaps somewhat naively, to "be true to what you want to express" (turn 37). Since her response doesn't actually engage with the statement that Torsten was trying to make, it is ultimately unclear whether she now found as much enjoyment in the rhetorical gesture as Tim did, or whether she is just trying to offer him polite encouragement.

Torsten thinks that the lesson he has learned is that Americans and Germans have a different sensibility for the flag as a symbol (turns 10, 17, 34). While this is no doubt true, Tim actually tries to teach Torsten a different lesson (turns 18, 20, 27, 36). But what Torsten doesn't understand is that Tim—while indeed being shocked at his decision to display the American flag as a symbol for the NRA (turn 18)—would have liked him to have left the image because he thinks that conflict and provocation have an important intellectual and dialogic function. He even considers it "censorship" (turn 36) if his own "crappy" feelings had legitimated Torsten's decision to replace the image. In fact, Tim only reluctantly acknowledges that removing the flag might be valuable for preventing misunderstandings (turn 36). But it is important to recognize that Tim's efforts to encourage Torsten to restore the image are not mere demonstrations of politeness. Instead, Tim indicates that exactly such jarring moments—the moments of conflict—are essential for learning and for enabling positive change to take place.

In his subsequent evaluation of the dialogues with the German partners, Tim makes this point even more clearly:

> The gross generalizations and assumptions that some of the German students made, especially about gun control in the United States were intimidating at first and even offensive but I now realize that these moments of tension were what led to the success of the project. Because we were open to discussing these topics to reveal the realities of our respective countries and citizens, we were able to dissipate such intense stereotypes, which became my definition of success as we moved forward in our discussion. Confronting stereotypes is a first step to understanding a culture other than one's own and being able to influence such ingrained concepts is essential

to improving the relations between individuals and even nations. In my opinion, education with these kinds of goals is working toward an even greater goal making the world more understanding and compassionate.

As Tim acknowledges, it can be very "intimidating" and painful to confront the stereotypes that others have about your own culture. His emphasis on the larger political implications recognizes the paradox inherent in dialogic approaches to interaction and culture: that only by working through conflict rather than avoiding it can there be any hope of a more compassionate world that can embrace—rather than merely tolerate—its own diversity.

Emphasis on Reflection and Meta-Reflection

While Tim may have already entered this course with respect for provocative statements and cultural differences, we also gave students ample opportunities to develop these intercultural attitudes on their own (see Byram 1997). Thus, in addition to arranging for students to engage with others (whether through online interactions or in the form of primary texts), it is equally important to provide learners with activities that ask them to step back from the discussions and reflect on them—especially if the interactions involve conflict. Several kinds of assignments and activities proved particularly helpful in achieving this goal. First, we asked students to summarize their discussions and different phases of the project, often in English, and Tim's two assessments serve as examples of how effective this kind of activity proved. Second, we set aside time in every class and in one session each week for students to report and focus together on the insights they were gaining as well as the problems and conflicts they were encountering in their intercultural groups. Because all the groups were working on one common topic, class discussions that brought all the Vassar students together allowed them to understand that there was not one correct or even "effective" way to address the topic.

Although all of the five groups experienced differences of opinion, communication problems, and even conflict at different times, none of these conflicts was in fact predictable or followed a single pattern. In her final reflection on the online exchange, for example, one Vassar student stated:

> While working on the project with the Münster students, I found the *Sitzungen* [class sessions] to be very important. Without them, I would not know what was happening in the other groups (other than looking at Felicity's computer only to find Nora wwrriittiinngg lliikkee tthhi-iss!). Every group experienced different problems, whether it was the European point of view versus an American point of view (in *Gruppe* [group] five), conservatives versus liberals (in *Gruppe* one), or the NRA and the American flag (in *Gruppe* four). With these conversations at the table, we were like friends, casually chatting about our experiences in other places (in this case the conference rooms [in the MOO]). The professor guided our discussions very well so we could come up with solutions to the problems that we encountered.

While Maggie seems to find differences in attitude between German and American students in one group, there is by no means a clear-cut pattern of behavior across cultures. Because the Vassar contingent also consisted of a French exchange student as well as a student from Bulgaria, her own terminology refers to "Europeans" rather than just "Germans." (Although all the students from Münster who participated in the exchange were Germans, this category would also seem too narrow for students who travel all over Europe and have close contacts with people from other European countries.) Moreover, as Maggie notes, political differences cut across national groups. Indeed, at one point in these discussions "at the table," she herself stated that she sometimes felt intimidated because she held much more conservative opinions than most of the other Vassar students in the class. Thus, cultural conflicts were by no means restricted to differences of perception between Germans and Americans. Indeed, by reporting and analyzing the various situations across the different groups, the Vassar students also noticed differences among themselves, which helped break down monolithic notions of culture that might have formed along a German/American axis.

Third, we assigned several secondary texts on intercultural learning, including *Developing the Intercultural Dimension in Language Teaching* (Byram, Gribkova, and Starkey 2002) at the beginning of the exchange and *Foreign Language Learning as Global Communicative Practice* (Kramsch and Thorne 2002) at the end. These texts, of course, have figured in our own attempts to develop and assess this exchange. But they also gave our students the conceptual tools and vocabulary for analyzing the intricacies of communicating with their partners and thus completing the reflective assignments. Moreover, these readings also enabled them to produce meta-level reflections about the value of this kind of online exchange and even the FL learning enterprise as such. Daphne, for example, noted at the end of the semester:

> My learning goals have been greatly affected by the last half of the semester. I find that my approach to language learning is different because of our discussions, the Byram and Kramsch/Thorne articles. I aim not only at simply acquiring the language to mimic a native speaker, as before. I realize my unique perspective as a non-native speaker and the potential of using this to move the experience away from the more traditional methods of language learning. I of course hope to improve my speaking, writing and comprehension, especially because I plan to study in Germany in just a year. But I feel fortunate to have had such a realization that there is much more to get out of these courses than that, and in fact there are things that I can offer to the process.

All students seem to have welcomed the opportunity to test their own experiences vis-à-vis scholarly debates on the language learning process. They also recognized their need to integrate their study of German into their own larger educational goals as liberal arts students.[13]

Nevertheless, our students, like many researchers, also initially viewed conflict as a potential sign of a communication failure. Even in their discussion of *Foreign Language Learning as Global Communicative Practice*, which describes significant communication breakdowns between French and American students, both the Münster and Vassar students began by insisting that they never had encountered similar problems in their conversations. They all agreed that in each of their conversations there hadn't been any conflicts, everything was fine, they all got along, and they agreed on everything. Only after a while were students willing to admit that conflicts and disagreements had surfaced in their own interactions:

> **Tim sagt:** Agreed. I would say there were small points of tension though due to cultural differences
>
> **Katrin sagt:** that we are talking about academic topics and that we have the same opinions about it.
>
> **Desmond fragt:** suppose it isn't an academic topic, what do you think will happen?
>
> **Katrin meint:** it would have been more difficult in a controverse conversation or in a private talk . . .
>
> **Tim sagt:** I bring it up not as a problem by any means, but rather because it displays the phenomenons described by this article we just read
>
> **Katrin** (to Desmond): I mean that we share the feelings about it . . .
>
> **Katrin** (to Desmond): it might be more problematic if we had different points of view or something.
>
> **Desmond sagt:** definitely
>
> **Cathy sagt:** It's true Tim
>
> **Desmond sagt:** each trying to convince each other
>
> **Katrin** (to Desmond): that's what I mean.
>
> **Desmond sagt:** impose their opinion on the others, chaos

Even in this brief exchange, and perhaps especially with their partners, acknowledging that conflicts had arisen proved a thorny operation. While Tim used the words "intimidating" and "offensive" in his personal reflections, he reduces these incidents here to "small points of tension." Admittedly, it can be difficult and even counterproductive to ask intercultural learners to remain focused on conflicts. But as Katrin and Desmond agree, the academic context of having to learn from the conflicts proved essential to ensuring that disagreements were not taken personally and were made productive.

Conclusion

There can be no doubt that a dialogic approach to online exchanges between language learners and NSs entails hefty risks. For students, online interactions with NSs can increase certain anxieties they already tend to associate with FL learning—the fear of making mistakes and the subsequent embarrassment that might follow—even as mediated communication lowers their inhibitions to produce language. Truly dialogic interactions will probably also provoke situations in which language learners encounter resistance to their interpretations, confront stereotypes about themselves and their culture, and are forced to deal with disagreements they can't really resolve. As Tim already noted, the experience can be "intimidating," "offensive," and, well, "crappy." For teachers, open-ended dialogues make it difficult to feel prepared, not only because class sessions become driven by the kinds of spontaneous interactions that take place between students (rather than objectives spelled out on a syllabus and revolving around a discrete and knowable text), but also because, as Kramsch and Thorne conclude, "what is teachable is far more complex than usually thought" (2002, p. 100). In addition to dealing with vocabulary, grammar, and guidelines for appropriate language use (the basis of cultural competence), teachers must now also help students gain intercultural competence, develop sophisticated interpretative skills, and acquire sensitivity to the heteroglossia of dialogue itself. Moreover, with dialogue—carried out at many levels and with many interlocutors—comes the risk of teachers losing control over students' experiences in the classroom, a risk with additional consequences for junior faculty members who require positive course evaluations from students for tenure and promotion. Finally, for departments struggling with enrollments, as many German Studies departments are, it is important that students find the rewards of learning a FL enough motivation to enroll in more advanced courses. Fortunately, even though many students may initially approach language learning with conventional expectations about linguistic proficiency, intellectually stimulating courses and exchanges can help—as Kramsch (1997) suggests and Daphne's enthusiastic posting above illustrates—students access, explore, and delight in their "privilege" as NNSs.

Thankfully, it is not the case that dialogic learning will always lead to intercultural conflicts. Moreover, it would also be a mistake to assume that conflicts and disagreements always signal successful intercultural learning, either in face-to-face interactions or online. But as Graff also points out, because "culture itself is a debate and not a monologue" (1992, p. 8), cultural conflicts are also not going away any time soon. And neither are intercultural ones. The solution, however, does not lie in imparting socio-cultural strategies for more "effective" communication that would help students avoid conflict altogether, but rather lies in helping them to deal with conflict as a learning opportunity. Since students who engage with interlocutors from other cultures will likely encounter conflicts, there are real practical reasons to give intercultural learners experience and conceptual skills for dealing with unexpected tensions. But "teaching the conflicts" also makes sense as an intellectual enterprise, since conflict can lead to new insights into the foreign as well as into one's own culture. As Nora, one of the Vassar students in this exchange, wrote: "That is the interesting thing for me: The not-in-agreement [Nichtübereinstimmung], not the agreement. . . . that is our goal, to raise questions."[14] For our students, true dialogue means being able to appreciate conflict, or "Nichtübereinstimmung," as Nora says, because they also value the insights and questions that result from the struggle to deal with disagreement and differences.

Researchers of online learning have wondered aloud whether the Internet actually makes those goals more difficult to achieve. Whether in synchronous chat, asynchronous e-mail, or, as in the case of the MOO, programs that offer both kinds of modalities, online communication does lack "paralinguistic meaning signals" (Belz 2003, p. 92), such as body language and facial expression, that often help us understand the tone that the interlocutor was trying to convey. Moreover, as Kramsch and Thorne write, the phatic forms of interaction so common in cyberspace seem to have called forth a situation in which "the modern view of communication as the discourse of truth gives way to a post-modern view of communication as the discourse of trust" (2002, p. 85). Researchers, including ourselves, are only now beginning to pursue the constraints and affordances for intercultural learning that inhere in particular forms of online media. And just as it is true for researchers, it may be that students participating in online exchanges will need to consider directly, through readings, activities, and discussions, how the media they are using both help and hinder their online interactions with NSs. But we have also found that embedding telecollaborative partnerships in an openended and *academic* pursuit of intercultural knowledge is an integral component for ensuring that students continue to learn about the language and culture they are studying, even in the face of conflict.

Ultimately, the risks of conflict in online collaborations are not only worth taking, but are in fact already imperative in the aftermath of September 11, 2001. Even as the *Modern Language Journal* (Byrnes *et al.* 2004) solicited articles reflecting on the importance of language study after 9/11, the *American Council on Education* (ACE) was concluding that "although more colleges are requiring foreign-language courses, most fail to provide their students with a sufficiently internationalized education" (Bollag 2003, p. A33; see also *Facts in Brief: Institutional Commitment to Internationalization is Low at U.S. Campuses* 2003). As the ACE conclusions imply, FL programs need to offer more than language instruction for communicative purposes, and they need to achieve more than helping students become "a sympathetic observer" (Wesche 2004, p. 282). While many recent public discussions of FL instruction have revolved around its "strategic" value, Mary Louise Pratt insists that "the real role language has to play in national security" (and, we might add, global peace), "is that of developing and sustaining the vast spectra of personal, institutional, commercial, diplomatic, and intellectual relations that prevent conflicts from turning into national security crises in the first place" (2004, p. 291). "Teaching the conflicts" as conflicts is certainly an important start. But fostering intercultural "intellectual relations" should also be an important component to any (online) intercultural exchange at the university level. As we see it, a dialogic approach that sets new learning goals and allows students to explore intercultural differences in open-ended ways demonstrates best the inherent value of university-based language learning in a post-9/11 world.

Notes

1. O'Dowd, for instance, stresses the importance of integrating exchanges "fully into the classroom as opposed to treating them as mere pen-pal activities" (2003, p. 121). And rather than letting students merely "chat" or exchange e-mails, Andreas Müller-Hartmann (2000) urges the adoption of specific task-based assignments that lead

students to work together to complete projects. While different authors point to the specific advantages and disadvantages of different activities and different software (see, for example, Thorne 2003), all emphasize a "comparative approach that asks learners to observe, to compare, and to analyze parallel materials from their respective cultures" (Furstenberg *et al.* 2001, p. 58). Comparative cultural approaches that promote intercultural learning clearly raise the stakes for students participating in such exchanges. But as a number of studies points out, they also increase the possibility that serious conflicts might emerge during online contact. In analyzing and responding to conflicts in various telecollaborative partnerships, SLA scholars emphasize the importance of helping students to become aware of different genre conventions (Kramsch and Thorne 2002), to understand their partners' discourse patterns and other linguistic issues (Belz 2003), and to develop socio-cultural strategies for engaging with NSs (Savignon and Sysoyev 2002). But as far as we know, no one has specifically addressed how to anticipate and productively deal with serious conflicts that regularly occur in online exchanges.

2. Carol Morgan and Albane Cain (2000) also offer a theoretically sophisticated dialogic approach to FL learning through intercultural exchange. The evidence that they use for making their case is based on an exchange of materials produced for the most part by students at the junior high and early high school level attending a school in England and a school in France. But because the students themselves never interacted directly with one another, different interpretations of the materials or issues never threatened to erupt into conflicts.

3. For an excellent overview of Bakhtin's work, see Emerson (1997).

4. In an article published in an AAUSC volume edited by Judith A. Muyskens, Richard Kern called them "one of the most novel environments for social interaction and collaborative learning on the Internet" (1998, p. 76). Though MOOs have been used in educational settings for a long time (see Haynes and Holmevik 1998 for a useful overview), they remain robust, extremely flexible, and visually attractive open source software learning environments that offer language learners and teachers a number of advantages, including the ability to create, personalize, and make authentic their own virtual learning spaces. (For a variety of different uses at other intermediate levels in the language learning and cultural studies classroom, see Schneider and von der Emde 2000; von der Emde and Schneider 2003; von der Emde, Schneider, and Kötter 2001). The *enCore* system that we use can be accessed via standard web browsers and enables users to store and share written work, websites, video clips, and audio materials. The *enCore Consortium*, which was recently formed to promote the educational uses and the continuing development of the *enCore Open Source Project*, plans to release version 5.0 later in 2005, which will expand the easy-to-use menu-driven programming features while also supporting non-western character sets as well as languages that read right-to-left, such as Arabic. For more information on the *enCore Consortium*, see the organization's website at: *http://www.encore-consortium.org/*

5. Our decision to build the course around the study of media and to then use the representation of school violence in the media as a topic for the exchange was inspired in part in response to Kramsch and Thorne's (2002) conclusions about an exchange between students studying French at the University of California at Berkeley and students learning English at a French *lycée* in a Paris suburb. According to their analysis, the exchange was hampered from the beginning, not only because the

Berkeley students lacked sufficient information about France, but also because the topics were "of primary interest to Berkeley college students, not necessarily to French *lycéens* from Ivry" (2002, p. 90).

6. Pseudonyms have been used throughout.

7. The German text reads:

Christine (to Felicity): Es ist definitiv einfacher in den USA einen Waffenschein zu bestellen ...

Ingrid sagt: hier muss man aber seinen Waffenschein vorzeigen, wenn man eine Waffe kaufen will

Felicity fragt: wie schwer ist zu eine Waffenschein bekommen?

Ingrid fragt: glaubt ihr denn, dass die meisten Amerikaner zuhause eine Waffe haben?

Christine sagt: ja, ziemlich schwierig. Entweder du musst einen Waffenschein beruflich benötigen oder eingetragenes und aktives Mitglied in einem Verein sein ...

Ingrid sagt: wenn jemand so etwas plant, dann besorgt er sich eine Waffe-egal wie, glaube ich

Felicity sagt: Ich bin nicht vor Waffen, aber iche will dass wir nicht Annahmen machen.

Ingrid (to Felicity): was meinst du?

Felicity (to Ingrid): ich glaube dass wir Annahmen über die waffengesetzen in Deutschland und in Amerika machen.

Ingrid sagt: ja, aber hier ist es schwerer an waffen zu kommen als in america—was auch der Film Bowling for Columbine gezeigt hat

Christine sagt: Ich sage ja auch nur, dass das besitzen von Waffen in Deutschland nicht zu unserer Kultur gehört. Ausser man übt einen bestimmten Beruf aus.

Nora sagt: Ich gewinne den Eindruck (von der Artikel), dass die Deutschen die Kultur (besonders amerikanisch Kultur) beschuldigen. nicht Waffen

Felicity (to Ingrid): weil wir nicht wirklich wissen, was die gesetzen sind in die beide Staaten.

Ingrid sagt: aber wir wissen, dass es in den USA einfacher ist

Christine (to Felicity): Das musst du uns jetzt einfach glauben. Ich habe versucht es so gut es geht zu erklären. Wenn du keinen triftigen Grund hast eine Waffe zu besitzen, ist es dir nicht möglich in Deutschland eine Waffe zu erhalten.

Ingrid sagt: ich würde nicht sagen, dass die USA dafür verantwortlich gemacht werden

Felicity fragt: hier kann man nicht Waffen kaufen in Jede Markt oder bank.

Ingrid sagt: hier gibt es die Waffen nur in speziellen Läden dafür—man sieht sie in keinem normalen Geschäft

Christine sagt: Und selbst in speziellen Läden kann man keine "Automatic" kaufen. Sowas haben die gar nicht da.

Ingrid sagt: genau

Felicity sagt: Ich bin gegan Waffen and ich finde es schockierend das man kann waffen in die Markt kaufen aber ich denke nur dass wir nicht Annahmen über Amerika macht.

Christine sagt: Aber man kann hier genauso leicht illegal an Waffen gelangen. naja, whatever ;-)

8. After the discussion, Felicity worried even more: not only that her insistence on not making assumptions might have annoyed her German partners, but also that her partners interpreted her insistence on that point as a statement of her personal support for weapons: "I thought that they were making assumptions, so I asked the same question again. But they had already answered my question but the answers had gone by too fast and they were too difficult for me to understand. So I talked a lot about how we shouldn't make assumptions and they thought I was pro guns and I am against weapons. Maybe the Germans are now a little angry with me." (Ich dachte, dass sie Vermutungen machen, so ich fragte die selbe fragen wieder. Aber sie haben schon meine Fragen antworten aber die Antworten zu schnell vorbei gegangen und sie waren zu zu schwer für mich zu verstanden. Also ich habe viel gesprochen, über wie wir nicht Vermutungen machen können und sie haben gedacht, dass ich pro-Waffen bin und ich bin gegan Waffen. Velleicht sind jetzt die Deutschen ein bisschen ärgerlich an mich.) Billy, another Vassar student working in a different group, noted in a *Blackboard* posting at the end of the semester: "Because we were clearly analyzing the Germans far more than they were us, I think we Americans were more conscious of the stereotype building/destroying potential of the MOO's context. Rather than letting divisive issues arise organically, we pre-emptively dispelled stereotypes, which we thought they were likely to have. We declared our unfamiliarity with guns and opposition to the *Todesstrafe* [death penalty] unprovoked. Our semester spent close-reading media made us hypersensitive to the impression our words were making."

9. This discussion was in English originally. Within our exchange we usually leave it up to the students how they want to organize the use of German and English in their discussions. We only ask them to give approximately equal time to both languages. Most students switch languages for successive sessions (German on Mondays, English on Wednesdays).

10. Indeed, over the course of the exchange, members from both groups demonstrate a certain amount of pleasure in serious debate. Though these two discussions make it seem that each set of partners alternated in their enjoyment, and often at the expense of the other partners, it is also the case that they could share in that pleasure at the same time, as in this discussion, which took place in between the two presented here:

Felicity sagt: well, Moore says that Americans are paranoid and this paranoia is fed by the media and the government. it makes people frightened. it makes people want to go out and buy guns.

Christine sagt: Felicity, that's the same thing that's happening over here in Germany. The only difference is that we cannot get guns that easily.

Felicity (to Christine): I will concede that it is harder to get guns in Germany than it is in America, but it's still not that hard.

Felicity (to Christine): I was reading a news article which said that anyone over 18 in Germany can get a starter pistol or an air gun. Is this true?

Christine sagt (to Felicity): give it a try ;-) (just kidding) but if you cannot get guns then there is still the possibility to get knives and other weapons.

Ingrid sagt: if you really want one you can probably always get an gun.

Christine sagt: I seriously think that the gun-issue is not the answer to the problem.

11. "Die Studenten in Gruppe 1 haben auf ein paar Missverständnisse gestoßen. Sinngemäß waren die Missverständnisse über Geschichte, Gewalt, und Gesetze. Dieser Raum hat Information über unsere Diskussionen, aber er hat gar keinen Antworten. Warum? Weil es gibt keinen bestimmten Antworten..."

12. "Ein Aspekt ihres Projekts, der mir besonders aufgefangen hat, war das NRA Raum. Dieses Raum zeigt liberalische Gefuhlen. Es war klar, dass Torsten und Katrin nicht neutral über dieses Thema war, wenn ich der erste Satz gelesen habe: 'Wer sind diese verrückte Menschen?'. Das hat mir gefallen. Ich habe aber etwas anderes in diesem Raum beobachtet. Das Bild für dieses Raum war ein großes amerikanisches Flag. Ich hoffe, dass Torsten und Katrin nicht alle Amerikaner mit dem NRA assozieren!"

13. We initially hit upon this idea as we began to become aware that using technology in the classroom—and conducting our own investigations into its effects—were also leading us to transfer to students more responsibility for their own learning. Indeed, a liberal arts education means helping students understand what is at stake in the course they are taking and how activities in class relate to the larger world outside the classroom. As we started engaging with scholarly debates about the goals and methods of FL learning, we wanted our students to engage as well. Other teachers and researchers have found similar value in assigning such texts. See, for example, Celeste Kinginger *et al.* (1999) and Julie A. Belz (2002).

14. "Das ist die interessante Sache für mich: die Nichtübereinstimmung, nicht das Einverständnis.... das ist unser Ziel, die Fragen zu aufbringen."

References

Belz, Julie A. 2002. Social Dimensions of Telecollaborative Foreign Language Study. *Language Learning & Technology* 6(1): 60–81.

———. 2003. Linguistic Perspectives on the Development of Intercultural Competence in Telecollaboration. *Language Learning & Technology* 7(2): 68–99.

———. Forthcoming. Telecollaborative Language Study: A Personal Overview of Praxis and Research. In *Proceedings of the Symposium on Foreign Language Distance Education and Distributed Learning*, edited by David Hiple and Irene Thompson. Honolulu: National Foreign Language Research Center.

Belz, Julie A., and Andreas Müller-Hartmann. 2003. Teachers as Intercultural Learners: Negotiating German-American Telecollaboration along the Institutional Fault Line. *Modern Language Journal* 87(1): 71–89.

Bernd, Hermann, and Barbara Dickmann. 2003. Erfurt: Ein Jahr danach. In *ZDF-Reportage*. Mainz: Zweites Deutsches Fernsehen.

Bernhardt, Elizabeth B. 1995. Response to Claire Kramsch. *ADFL Bulletin* 26(3): 15–17.

Block, David. 2002. "McCommunication": A Problem in the Frame for SLA. In *Globalization and Language teaching*, edited by David Block and Deborah Cameron, 117–133. London/New York: Routledge.

Bollag, Burton. 2003. Report Urges Federal Effort to Triple Number of Students Studying Abroad. *The Chronicle of Higher Education*, 21 November 2003, A33.

Brinkbäumer, Klaus, Annette Bruhns, Uwe Buse, Jürgen Dahlkamp, Carsten Holm, Ulrich Jaeger, Felix Kneip, Beate Lakota, Jürgen Leinemann, Udo Ludwig, Cordula Meyer, Sven Roebel, Andrea Stuppe, Barbara Supp, Andreas Wassermann, and Steffen Winter. 2002. Moerderischer Abgang. *Der Spiegel*, 29 April 2002, Available: *http://www.spiegel.de/spiegel/0,1518,193959,00.html*.

Byram, Michael. 1997. *Teaching and Assessing Intercultural Communicative Competence*. Clevedon: Multilingual Matters.

Byram, Michael, Bella Gribkova, and Hugh Starkey. 2002. *Developing the Intercultural Dimension in Language Teaching*. Strasbourg: Council of Europe.

Byram, Michael, Adam Nichols, and David Stevens, eds. 2001. Introduction. In *Developing Intercultural Competence in Practice*, 1–8. Clevedon: Multilingual Matters.

Byrnes, Heidi. 1995. Response to Claire Kramsch. *ADFL Bulletin* 26(3): 13–15.

Byrnes, Heidi, J. David Edwards, Ron Scollon, Roger Allen, Mari Wesche, Wendy W. Allen, and Mary Louise Pratt. 2004. Teaching Languages and Cultures in a Post-9/11 World: North American Perspectives. *Modern Language Journal* 88(2): 268–291.

Cameron, Deborah. 2002. Globalization and the Teaching of "Communication Skills." In *Globalization and Language Teaching*, edited by David Block and Deborah Cameron, 67–82. London/New York: Routledge.

Duranti, Alessandro. 1997. Linguistic Anthropology: History, Ideas, and Issues. In *Linguistic Anthropology*, edited by A. Duranti, 1–38. Malden, MA: Blackwell.

Emerson, Caryl. 1997. *The First Hundred Years of Mikhail Bakhtin*. Princeton: Princeton University Press.

Facts in Brief: Institutional Commitment to Internationalization is Low at U.S. Campuses. (3 November 2003). American Council on Education 2003 [cited 15 November 2004]. Available from *http://www.acenet.edu/hena/readArticle.cfm?articleID=192*.

Furstenberg, Gilberte, Sabine Levet, Kathryn English, and Katherine Maillet. 2001. Giving a Virtual Voice to the Silent Language of Culture: The *Cultura* Project. *Language Learning & Technology* 5(1): 55–102.

Gibbs, Nancy. 1999. On March 4, Eric Harris and Dylan Klebold Sat for this Class Picture. On April 17, They Both Went to the Prom. What They Did Next Left Their School . . . in Sorrow and Disbelief. *Time*, 3 May 1999, 20–35.

Graff, Gerald. 1992. *Beyond the Culture Wars: How Teaching the Conflicts Can Revitalize American Education*. New York: W.W. Norton.

———. 2003. *Clueless in Academe: How Schooling Obscures the Life of the Mind*. New Haven: Yale University Press.

Haynes, Cynthia, and Jan Rune Holmevik, eds. 1998. *High Wired: On the Design, Use, and Theory of Educational MOOs*. Ann Arbor, MI: University of Michigan Press.

Hymes, Dell. 1997. On Communicative Competence. In *Linguistic Anthropology*, edited by A. Duranti, 53–73. Malden, MA: Blackwell.

Kern, Richard G. 1998. Technology, Social Interaction, and FL Literacy. In *New Ways of Learning and Teaching: Focus on Technology and Foreign Language Education*, edited by Judith A. Muyskens, 57–92. Boston: Thomson Heinle.

Kinginger, Celeste, Alison Gourvès-Hayward, and Vanessa Simpson. 1999. A Tele-Collaborative Course on French-American Intercultural Communication. *The French Review* 72(5): 853–866.

Kramsch, Claire. 1995. Embracing Conflict versus Achieving Consensus in Foreign Language Education. *ADFL Bulletin* 26(3): 6-12.

———. 1997. The Privilege of the Nonnative Speaker. *PMLA* 112: 359-369.

———. 2001. Intercultural Communication. In *The Cambridge Guide to Teaching English to Speakers of Other Languages*, edited by Ronald Carter and David Nunan, 201-206. Cambridge: Cambridge University Press.

———. 2002. Language and Culture: A Social Semiotic Perspective. *ADFL Bulletin* 33(2): 8-15.

Kramsch, Claire, and Steven L. Thorne. 2002. Foreign Language Learning as Global Communicative Practice. In *Language Learning and Teaching in the Age of Globalization*, edited by David Block and Deborah Cameron, 83-100. London/New York: Routledge.

Moore, Michael. 2003. *Bowling for Columbine*. Santa Monica, Calif: MGM Home Entertainment.

Morgan, Carol, and Albane Cain. 2000. *Foreign Language and Culture Learning from a Dialogic Perspective*. Clevedon: Multilingual Matters.

Müller-Hartmann, Andreas. 2000. The Role of Tasks in Promoting Intercultural Learning in Electronic Learning Networks. *Language Learning & Technology* 4(2): 129-147.

O'Dowd, Robert. 2003. Understanding the 'Other Side': Intercultural Learning in a Spanish-English E-mail Exchange. *Language Learning & Technology* 7(2): 118-144.

Pratt, Mary Louise. 2004. Language and National Security: Making a New Public Commitment. *Modern Language Journal* 88(2): 289-291.

Savignon, Sandra J. 2002. Communicative Language Teaching: Linguistic Theory and Classroom Practice. In *Interpreting Communicative Language Teaching: Contexts and Concerns in Teacher Education*, edited by Sandra J. Savignon, 1-27. New Haven: Yale University Press.

Savignon, Sandra J., and Pavel V. Sysoyev. 2002. Sociocultural Strategies for a Dialogue of Cultures. *Modern Language Journal* 86(4): 508-524.

Schneider, Jeffrey, and Silke von der Emde. 2000. Brave New (Virtual) World: Transforming Language Learning into Cultural Studies through Online Learning Environments (MOOs). *ADFL Bulletin* 32(1): 18-26.

Thorne, Steven L. 2003. Artifacts and Cultures-of-Use in Intercultural Communication. *Language Learning & Technology* 7(2): 38-67.

von der Emde, Silke, and Jeffrey Schneider. 2003. Experiential Learning and Collaborative Reading: Literacy in the Space of Virtual Encounters. In *Between the Lines: Perspectives on Foreign Language Literacy*, edited by Peter Patrikis, 118-143. New Haven: Yale University Press.

von der Emde, Silke, Jeffrey Schneider, and Markus Kötter. 2001. Technically Speaking: Transforming Language Learning through Virtual Learning Environments (MOOs). *Modern Language Journal* 85(2): 210-225.

Wesche, Mari. 2004. Teaching Languages and Cultures in a Post-9/11 World. *Modern Language Journal* 88(2): 278-289.

Wood, Julia T. 2004. Foreword: Entering Into Dialogue. In *Dialogue: Theorizing Difference in Communication Studies*, edited by Roger Anderson, L. A. Baxter, and K. N. Cissna, xv-xxiii. Thousand Oaks, CA: SAGE.

Chapter 8

At the Intersection of Telecollaboration, Learner Corpus Analysis, and L2 Pragmatics: Considerations for Language Program Direction

Julie A. Belz

Abstract

The research on Internet-mediated intercultural foreign language education to date has examined a variety of topics ranging from the development of L2 grammatical competence to intercultural tension to networked models for language teacher education. The theoretical frameworks and methodological approaches applied in such examinations have been equally wide-ranging, including socio-cultural theory, interactionist approaches to language learning, intercultural communicative competence, appraisal theory, cultural studies, action research, and grounded theory. Very few studies, however, have explored the application of the burgeoning field of contrastive learner corpus analysis to networked intercultural foreign language instruction. The aim of this essay is to encourage language program directors and foreign language teachers to consider the inherent synergy between telecollaborative pedagogy and learner corpus analysis as well as the ways in which their inter-illumination may influence the development of L2 competence in general and L2 pragmatic competence in particular.

Introduction

The most salient aspect of telecollaborative foreign language (FL) study, Kinginger notes, is "the inclusion of other people" (2004, p. 103). The "other people" to whom Kinginger refers are the native-speaking netpals with whom FL learners interact via Internet communication tools in the context of telecollaborative partnerships.[1] To date, research on telecollaborative instruction generally has fallen into two categories: (1) descriptive reports in which the administrative, logistical, pedagogical, social, and technological aspects of such programmatic innovations are addressed (e.g., Bauer *et al.* 2005; Belz 2005a; Fischer 1998; Furstenberg *et al.* 2001; Kinginger *et al.* 1999); and (2) empirical studies designed to explore the relationship between telecollaborative instruction and the most widely recognized outcomes of FL education, namely, intercultural and linguistic competence.[2] Researchers have examined the development of intercultural competence (Byram 1997) from a number of theoretical and methodological perspectives, including appraisal theory, grounded theory, ethnography, cultural studies, and action research (e.g., Belz 2003b; O'Dowd 2003; Warschauer 1996). The majority of the work on the influence of technology-mediated interaction on the development of L2 linguistic competence has occurred within the interactionist approach to Second Language Acquisition (SLA). Scholars have elucidated in aggregation the number and types of negotiation sequences occurring within various kinds of mediated interaction including telecollaboration (e.g., Blake and Zystik 2003; Lee 2004, 2005; Pellettieri 2000; Smith 2003, 2005; Sotillo 2000). Others have provided aggregational reports on different linguistic features in mediated FL interactions such as lexical density and syntactic complexity (Abrams 2003; Chun 1994; Dussias 2005; Kern 1995).

The purpose of the current chapter is to engage language program directors and FL teachers in a consideration of the synergy between particular aspects of telecollaborative pedagogy—beyond the inclusion of other people—and the emerging field of learner corpus analysis (Granger 1998a; Granger, Hung, and Petch-Tyson 2002; Granger and Petch-Tyson 2003). These aspects include the electronic nature of the "process data" (Chapelle 2003, p. 98) or learner production, its developmental scope (i.e., telecollaborative partnerships typically span several weeks or months), the authenticity of telecollaborative interactions (see Kasper 2001, p. 34), their bilingual format (cf. Bauer *et al.* 2005; Furstenberg *et al.* 2001), and the blended nature of telecollaborative courses. According to *Wikipedia*, blended learning denotes the "integration (or the so-called blending) of e-learning tools and techniques with traditional methods." In the current chapter, "blending" is used to refer to the alternation of Internet-mediated *inter*cultural sessions with face-to-face *intra*cultural sessions. The first four above-mentioned dimensions of telecollaborative pedagogy facilitate the establishment of unique learner corpora (Granger, to appear; Nesselhauf, to appear) within the burgeoning field of learner corpus analysis because such corpora contain *Internet-mediated, longitudinal, bilingual* data as well as *integrated* native speaker (NS) control corpora. The importance of meticulously documented longitudinal data has been the topic of much discussion in SLA circles as of late (Ortega and Iberri-Shea 2005). The final aspect affords classroom-based, *developmental pedagogical intervention* in the form of corpus-enabled, *data-driven learning*. The general argument advanced here is that the utilization of telecollaborative process data for the compilation of an integrated contrastive learner corpus and the subsequent introduction of corpus-enabled results into the telecollaborative classroom in the form of data-driven learning may contribute to L2 development in general and to L2 pragmatic competence in particular. Competence is not restricted to the accuracy of particular forms but also encompasses frequency and distribution of use.

In this chapter, this argument is developed on the basis of data drawn from *The Telecollaborative Learner Corpus of English and German* or *Telekorp*, a new learner corpus of over one million tokens, which is composed of bilingual, Internet-mediated interactions among more than 200 learners of German and English recorded during six years of telecollaborative partnerships (Belz, Reinhardt, and Rine 2005). The bilingual nature of the interactions under study means that *Telekorp* is composed of four sub-corpora: L1 German, L1 English, L2 German, and L2 English. In *Telekorp*, every single utterance that each participant produced over the course of eight- to ten-week telecollaborative partnerships has been archived in a series of relational tables in association with approximately 30 task and learner variables (cf. Granger 2003, p. 538). In addition, numerous types of ethnographic data were collected for each learner, including retrospective interviews (Barron 2003, p. 107), written portfolios, instructor field notes, and videotaping of classroom sessions. As a result, *Telekorp* is also of import for the production of ethnographically thick and ecologically valid microgenetic analyses of the development of L2 competence (see Kinginger and Belz 2005), an issue at the core of SLA research.

In the first of the following sections, the concepts of data-driven learning and learner corpus analysis are illustrated on the basis of NS and learner concordance lines taken from the L1 and L2 German sub-corpora of *Telekorp* for the German word *Meinung* "opinion." This analysis demonstrates how contrastive learner corpus analysis allows the teacher-researcher to address learner proficiency not only at the global and prescriptive level of grammatical accuracy but also at the local and thus descriptive level of frequency of occurrence and distribution (across speakers, genres, and media). Further, the bilingual nature of the data enables the immediate comparison of learner production to a baseline NS corpus thereby obviating the time-consuming need to seek out or perhaps even construct (see Cobb 2003; Granger and Tribble 1998) an external NS control corpus, which may be only tenuously comparable to the learner corpus in question (see Granger 1998b, p. 13).

In the next section, the ways in which the blended nature of telecollaborative pedagogy—in conjunction with learner corpus analysis—may contribute to L2 pragmatic learning with respect to the performance of apologies is demonstrated. In the context of a synchronous chat in a telecollaborative session, NSs of German commented on the perceived frequency with which their American keypals "apologize." In a subsequent non-telecollaborative session, NS and learner patterns of use of the tokens *sorry*, *Entschuldigung/entschuldigen* "excuse me; sorry," and *es tut mir leid* "I'm sorry" are examined in the form of a corpus-enabled, quantitative overview as well as at the local level of group-specific concordance lines.

Finally, the relationship of telecollaborative pedagogy and learner corpus analysis to the implementation of (developmental) pedagogical interventions is illustrated. Corpus-driven pedagogical interventions based on telecollaborative data can be "developmental" in two senses. First, such interventions are developmental because they are based on the entirety of L2 production for each individual learner over the duration of the networked exchange, i.e., they are based on the documentation of L2 change over time. Second, they may be termed "developmental" because the administration of the intervention itself occurs in successive stages in the course of the ongoing telecollaborative correspondence and is sensitive to evolving L2 use. The second type of developmental intervention is only possible if the telecollaborative data are entered into the corpus on a daily basis as they are produced (see Belz and Vyatkina 2005, p. 24). Such a compilation procedure is a powerful pedagogical tool for both instruction and dynamic forms of L2 assessment (Poehner and Lantolf 2003) because it affords the corpus retrievable concretization of the learner's emerging L2 competence on a day-by-day basis. In order to illustrate the concept of corpus-based, developmental pedagogical intervention in the first sense, a case study of a low-intermediate learner of German is presented. The potential influence of corpus-based intervention on this learner's misuse of formal pronouns of address as well as her under-use of particular cohesive ties is examined.

Learner Corpus Analysis and Data-Driven Learning

The term *data-driven learning* originally referred to the use of information from NS corpora in the FL classroom (Johns 2002; Johns and King 1991, p. iii). For example, a FL teacher may use a NS corpus (e.g., *The British National Corpus*) in order to produce a computer-generated concordance of a particular FL feature. A concordance is "a screen display or printout of a chosen word or phrase in its different contexts, along with the text that comes before and after it" (McCarthy 2004, p. 5). In a classroom activity, learners examine the concordance in order to discover authentic patterns of L2 use for particular lexical items or grammatical features (e.g., Conrad 1999). NS concordances lines from *Telekorp* for the German word *Meinung* "opinion" illustrate this concept in Figure 1 (see also Möllering 2001 for the use of NS corpora in the teaching of L2 German).[3] This word was chosen for analysis because it occurs in expressions of opinion, the mastery of which is necessary in an exchange designed to facilitate bilingual, intercultural dialogue. Nevertheless, learners of German consistently have demonstrated difficulty with the appropriate use of such phrases. The concordance lines in Figure 1 (and all others in this chapter) were produced by exporting relevant text files from *Telekorp* into *Wordsmith Tools* (Scott 2001), a well-known software package for corpus analysis.

Despite the efficacy of NS concordance lines, corpus linguist Sylviane Granger maintains that "one should not exaggerate the impact of NS corpora on foreign language teaching" (1994, p. 25) because such corpora do not necessarily provide access to the actual problems of learners. Instead, Granger suggests that teacher-researchers must focus on learner productions in order to ensure that learners' grammatical needs are met. In order to do so in an empirically grounded and systematic fashion, Granger recommends the construction of computerized learner corpora such as the *International Corpus of Learner English* (Granger, Dagneaux, and Meunier 2002). *Learner corpora* are defined as "electronic collections of authentic FL/SL textual data assembled according to explicit design criteria for a particular SLA/FLT purpose. They are encoded in a standardized and homogenous way and documented as to their origin and provenance" (Granger 2002, p. 7). With the help of a learner corpus, FL teachers can quickly examine large amounts of learner productions in order to ascertain where learners may be having difficulties with L2 grammar. Using a method known as *contrastive learner corpus analysis*, learner language behavior, as represented in a learner corpus, can be compared to the language behavior of NSs, as represented in a NS corpus, in order to establish how the linguistic performance of these two groups may differ from each other (see Biber and Reppen 1998; Granger and Tribble 1998; Nesselhauf 2004). To illustrate this point, representative learner productions for *Meinung* are drawn from the L2 German sub-corpus of *Telekorp* and presented in Figure 2.

Figure 1
NS Concordance Lines for *Meinung*

1 should differentiate. Ich bin der **Meinung**, dass man sich immer nur über einzelne Menschen, die man auch

2 Liebe der Erwachsenen. Ich bin der **Meinung**, dass Kinder denken können, sie seien in einander verliebt, aber

3 schreckliches mit ihnen. Ich bin der **Meinung**, dass der Unterschied zwischen Amerika und Deutschland in de

4 harmful influences. Wir sind der **Meinung**, dass Zensur nicht der richtige Weg ist. Die häufigsten Gründe fü

5 möchte den Film nicht, weil er der **Meinung** war, dass er ziemlich langweilig war. Das liegt vielleicht auch da

6 sie geschrieben hat, bin ich derselben **Meinung**. Sie ist nur auf Karriere und Erfolg (materielle Dinge) aus und ve

7 und das hat viel mit der deutschen **Meinung** zu tun, dass Amerikaner viele Probleme mit der Wirklichkeit hab

8 USA. Wir haben uns unsere eigene **Meinung** über Bush gebildet und würden gerne wissen, wie ihr darüber de

9 bin ich eigentlich fast der gleichen **Meinung** wie du. Bein uns gibt es auch viele Vorurteile gegenüber Auslan

10 ch die Amerikaner sehe. Also, meine **Meinung** scheint sehr negativ zu sein, aber ich finde die meisten Amerikan

11 das aber heute noch machen. Meiner **Meinung** nach gibt es in Deutschland normalerweise kaum öffentliche Au

12 ist ganz eindeutig und klar. Meiner **Meinung** nach gab es relativ früh Hinweise im Film, die auf die Homosex

13 a most difficult question . . . ? Meiner **Meinung** nach können die jungere Generation die Stereotype der alte über

14 gibt so viele Sendungen, die meiner **Meinung** nach nicht für Kinder geeignet sind. Aber wie du schon gesagt h

15 in Amerika sehr aktuell ist. Unserer **Meinung** nach ist es sehr traurig, dass diese Thema auch heute immer noc

The most immediately salient information in such a comparison relates to frequency of use. The contrastive learner corpus analysis reveals that the learners use *Meinung* 30 times per 100,000 tokens of e-mail interaction, while the NSs use the same term 23 times. Thus, the learners overuse this term in comparison to NSs, which may indicate that the NSs use a broader range of lexical resources for

Figure 2
Learner Concordance Lines for *Meinung*

1	Mans Fleischeslust. Wir sind auf der **Meinung** dass unsere Land so konservative ist im bezug zu nacktheit weil w
2	Heidelinde, In meine **Meinung**, du hast nicht ein Gelegenheit verpassen. Ich finde Baseball sehr la
3	multi-dimensional issue. In meiner **Meinung**, diesen sind einige die Grunde warum wir wissen nicht immer was
4	majority of the people. Es ist meine **Meinung**, dass dieser Rassist und Homosexualitätsfeindlich Ansichten sind
5	wie sie sind in Deutschland? Meiner **Meinung** nach dass diese Problem mit viele Filme passiert. Dass ist alles für
6	ie schen von der Erwachsen. Meiner **Meinung** nach die Liebe des Ben und Anna ist daß es war nicht total echt. S
7	hoenheit nicht verherrlichen. Meiner **Meinung** nach der Schoneheit in der Gesellschaft ist, dass es nicht so wichti
8	haetten wir eines guttes Chat. Meiner **Meinung** nach "American Beauty" ist dass die Problemen in das Film etwa
9	filme gestohlen hat. Meiner **Meinung** nach diese Überlegung ist es ist ok. In unsere Welt Leute sollen n

the expression of opinions in German. A cursory analysis of chat interaction in *Telekorp* indicates that NSs tend to use *Meinung* more frequently in asynchronous communication, while they chose other forms such as *glauben* "to believe" and *denken* "to think" in synchronous expression. This brief discussion illustrates how corpus analysis speaks to aspects of proficiency, i.e., frequency and distribution of use, that are not typically addressed in traditional forms of instruction based on deterministic rather than probabilistic grammars.

A comparison of Figures 1 and 2 also reveals a wealth of information with regard to differences in syntactic structure, lexical collocation, phraseology, and grammatical accuracy for the two populations under study. First, the NSs use the idiomatic phrases *der Meinung sein* "to be of the opinion" (lines 1–6) and *meiner Meinung nach* "in my opinion" (lines 11–15) with roughly equal frequency, whereas the learners tend to use only the second phrase (lines 5–9). Alphabetical sorting on the first word to the left of the searched item reveals that the NSs use more lexical variation within the two above mentioned idiomatic phrases than the learners do, e.g., "I am of the opinion" (lines 1–3) but also "we are of the opinion" (line 4) and "I am of the same opinion" (line 6); "in my opinion" (lines 11–14) but also "in our opinion" (line 15). Such detailed examples provide learners with authentic data that keypals have actually used for both the expansion of their lexical resources and the fine-tuning of their understanding of the idiomatic phrases. Second, the learner concordance lines reveal typical transfer errors that never occur in the NS data, e.g., "in meiner Meinung" (lines 2–3; a transfer from the English "in my opinion") and "wir sind auf der Meinung" (line 1; a transfer from the English "we are of the opinion"). Finally, the concordance lines highlight important syntactic differences in the use of the given idiomatic phrases. For example, the phrase *meiner Meinung nach* makes use of a rare post-position in German. This is one reason why this phrase presents English-speaking learners of German with difficulties. Because of the verb-second constraint in the main clause in German, this phrase must be followed by the conjugated verb when it is used in sentence initial position. Thus, what the learners characteristically recognize as a "preposition" (*nach* "after, according to") appears to be uncharacteristically (but accurately) followed by a verb, if they do not parse *meiner Meinung nach* as a unit. This structure is illustrated in the last five concordance lines of Figure 1. Learners consistently place a different element (typically a noun) in this slot—even after repeated, explicit instruction—as is seen in the last five lines of Figure 2.

One of the advantages of data-driven learning based on contrastive learner corpus analysis is that learners can examine authentic examples of differences in NS and learner use. The added instructional value of *Telekorp* is twofold. First, the NS and learner comparisons are not drawn from a learner corpus and an *external* NS corpus. Instead, they are based on learner and NS productions *in the very same interactions*—thus ensuring a high degree of comparability of the results of contrastive learner corpus analysis. Second, the learners are examining data that they have produced (Seidlhofer 2002), if the data are entered into the corpus while the partnership is in progress. Thus, their overuse of *Meinung* is not with respect to some unknown set of NSs at another time in another context, but with respect to their own keypals in interactions in which they themselves have participated. Belz and Kinginger (2003) have argued that learners' desire to maintain positive face in front of their NS keypals in telecollaborative partnerships has contributed to their increasing approximation of NS norms with respect address form choice. Thus, if learners can be shown aggregate patterns of learner use with respect to patterns of use of their NS keypals for the same items this may increase their awareness of localized norms of use.

Learner Corpus Analysis, L2 Pragmatics, and Blended Learning

In the following representative excerpt from a synchronous chat between the Americans Kate and Angela and the Germans Karsten and Jette in 2004, the issue of "apologizing" takes center stage. In the course of this episode, the learners use three relevant lexical items: *sorry, Entschuldigung/entschuldigen* "excuse me; I'm sorry," and *es tut mir Leid* "I'm sorry."

(1)

1   **Kate:** lol

2   **Karsten:** what does lol mean?

3   **Kate:** laughing out loud—it is an American term

4   **Kate:** Natalia hat gesagt, dass ihr in Deutschland das auch screiben *(Natalia said that you write that in Germany, too)*

5   **Karsten:** sorry, nee!! *(sorry, no!!)*

6   **Kate:** Nein, es tut mir leid. *(no, I am sorry)*

7   **Kate:** We are supposed to tell you that the project is in the "tasks" folder

8   **Angela:** ok so how old were you when you were Aufklaehert *(learned about sex and birth control)*?

9   **Kate:** You can read it and then e-mail us the topic you chose

10 **Jette:** At the age of 12.

11 **Kate:** Entschuldigung *(excuse me)* Angela—I didn't mean to interrupt

12 **Karsten:** We do know that it's in the folder. but we try to make sure that we are talking about the same, at least nearly

13 **Kate:** okay—we just wanted to check

14 **Kate:** Entschuldigung *(excuse me)*

15 **Karsten:** Sorry, but why do you "entschuldigt euch" *(excuse yourselves)* that often, and what for?

16 **Kate:** in Amerika wir sagen „excuse me" zu sagen "sorry" *(In America we say "excuse me" to say "sorry")*

17 **Kate:** I guess that Germans don't do that

18 **Karsten:** Please try to ask us something, 'cause I don't have a clue what to talk about!!!!!! sorry!

19 **Jette:** There must be a reason to say sorry

20 **Angela:** ok—es tut mir leid *(ok—I am sorry)*

In turn 4, Kate relates that another German keypal, Natalia, told her that Germans use the abbreviation *lol* in German-language chat. Karsten denies this in turn 5 by using the English word "sorry" in conjunction with an emphatic form (*nee*) of the word *nein* "no" in German. Kate responds to his denial by apologizing for her original assertion with the German phrase *es tut mir Leid*. In turn 7, Kate relays to her German partners a piece of organizational information from her instructor on the U.S. side. In turn 8, Angela picks up the assigned topic of discussion, which relates to a German-language novel that both groups had read. In turn 9, Angela continues with more details about the organizational information. Jette responds to Angela's on-task question in turn 10, which is followed by Kate's apology for interrupting their discussion with the organizational information. Here she uses the German word *Entschuldigung* to perform her apology. In turn 12, Karsten tells her that they already have this information and then states that they would like to stay on the same topic in their chat. In turn 14, Kate again apologizes to Karsten, this time for interrupting the discussion with the organizational information. In the following turn, Karsten asks Kate why they apologize ("excuse themselves") so often and for what reasons, indicating that he has not understood her motivations for apologizing in turns 6, 11, and 14. His question, perhaps, is prefaced ironically with the English word "sorry." In turn 16, Kate explains that Americans use the phrase "excuse me" as an apology token[4] and follows this with the insightful comment that this may not be the case in German conversation (see Byrnes 1986). In his rejoinder, Karsten directs Kate to ask a question because he doesn't know what to talk about. He follows this with another apology token in the form of "sorry!" In turn 18, Jette informs Kate that Germans only say they are sorry when there is a reason to do so, indicating that, from her German perspective, there was no cause for the three apologies that Kate has uttered up to that point in the chat. In turn 20, Kate seems to acknowledge this reasoning and subsequently apologizes for apologizing.

The alternation of telecollaborative and non-telecollaborative sessions in conjunction with contrastive learner corpus analysis affords the classroom-based exploitation of this learning opportunity *par excellence* (see Allwright 2005). In a subsequent non-telecollaborative session, the instructor can draw the learners' attention to this authentic excerpt in plenary (see Kasper 1985, for referential and meta-lingual teaching phases in L2 pragmatic instruction). Schmidt (1993, p. 35) has argued that *noticing* is particularly important for the development of L2 pragmatic competence. Participants Kate and Angela can share their insider perspectives on this interaction, while other learners weigh in on whether or not they feel that Americans or Germans apologize more, what constitutes a legitimate reason for an apology, and what lexical resources are used in order to perform an apology in each language under study. Because learners have access to all previously conducted telecollaborative interactions, they can support their assertions with textual data and share this evidence with their classmates.

Learners can then be presented with the comprehensive results of contrastive learner corpus analysis for the focal items as seen in Table 1. These data reveal that despite Karsten's assertion that Kate apologizes too much, Germans actually use the word *sorry* nearly twice as frequently as the Americans do in the very same interactions. In contrast, however, the Americans use *Leid* in the phrase *es tut mir Leid*

Table 1
Lexical Comparisons

| | All E-mails (2000–2004) | | | |
| | Germans | | Americans | |
Search Item	Raw	Per 10^5	Raw	Per 10^5
sorry	207	62.8	91	36.5
Leid	32	9.7	98	39.3
entschuldig*	8/5	2.43/1.52	9	3.61

four times as often as the Germans do. Thus, each language group appears to over-use the targeted apology tokens in their L2 in comparison to NS uses of those same tokens. Both groups exhibit a low frequency of use for *Entschuldigung/entschuldigen*—only eight uses for the NSs and nine for the learners—indicating that Kate's two uses of it in example 1 were indeed uncommonly frequent. However, when one examines the content of the German concordance lines for *entschuldig* in Figure 3, one sees that there are actually only *five* referential uses of *entschuldig* (lines 1–3, 7–8). The NSs excuse themselves for not corresponding frequently enough (lines 1–3) or for not providing the Americans with corrections of their L2 German (line 7), both explicit stipulations of the telecollaborative partnership. In one case, a NS excuses himself because he called his American keypal by the wrong name (line 8). In three additional cases (lines 4–6), the NSs use this form meta-lingually in order to tell their American keypals not to apologize, thus lending some support to Karsten's assertion that Kate apologizes too often.

Learner concordance lines are given for *entschuldig* in Figure 4. Like their NS keypals, the learners excuse themselves for not corresponding frequently enough (lines 4, 6–7); however, unlike the Germans, the Americans also excuse themselves for their "poor German," for making mistakes in German, and for other language-related errors (lines 3, 8–9). In contrast, the Germans never excuse themselves for infelicities in their L2 English. Thus, it would appear, linguistic errors are not a reason to apologize in German, at least in the context of the interactions under study.

An examination of NS and learner concordance lines for *Leid* in Figures 5 and 6 reveal further differences with respect to the group-specific use of this item. For example, the NSs sometimes modify the phrase *es tut mir Leid* with adverbials such as *echt* "real" or *wirklich* "really" (lines 1–2, 5–7, 9 in Figure 5), while the learners use the unmodified phrase almost without exception (lines 1–16 in Figure 6). With respect to the distribution of the phrase within an e-mail, both NSs and learners use it directly after openings and before closings as well as within the middle of a message; however, learners tend to use it more frequently in the first two positions, which raises the issue of the appropriate timing of an apology in this context. Syntactically, NSs use the phrase most frequently immediately prior to a subordinate clause introduced with the conjunction *dass* "that." Learners also use it in this configuration but they often omit the necessary punctuation (lines 5, 7, 9, 13, 15, 17 in Figure 6)—

Figure 3
NS Concordance Lines for *entschuldig**

1 zunächst möchte ich mich bei dir **entschuldigen**, weil du sehr lange auf meine Antwort warten mußtest. Ich war

2 Hallo Cheryl, **entschuldige**, dass ich so lange nicht zurückgeschrieben habe, aber über das

3 mich bei euch beiden erst einmal **entschuldigen**!!! Es tut mir wirklich ganz arg leid, dass ich mich bei euch bis j

4 du brauchst dich nicht dafür zu **entschuldigen**; schliesslich ist ja diese project unter anderem dazu da, dass m

5 hler, du brauchst dich auch nicht **entschuldigen**, dass dein Deutsch schlecht sei, es ist wirklich gut. Ich bin fro

6 war aber dafür musst du dich nicht **entschuldigen** !—"Ich glaube, dass es war nicht Kinderpornographie, wann sc

7 be ich keine Korrekturen für dich. **Entschuldigung**. But that really is a very difficult sentence. You did a

8 "Linda" heisst und nicht "Linde". **Entschuldigung**, wenn ich einen Fehler gemacht habe.

Figure 4
Learner Concordance Lines for *entschuldig**

1	Group. **Entschuldigung** mir, aber ich bin heute nicht zu unterricht gegangen. Habe ich
2	ch weiss nicht mehr wie ich meine **Entschuldigung** ausdruecken koennte!! Ich habe dir eine E-mail am Donnersta
3	ail dich nicht erwaehnt. Auch bitte **entschuldig** meines schlechtes Deutsch. Fuer 1,5 Jahren hab' ich das nicht stu
4	ben. See ya! Russell Hallo alle! **Entschuldigung** dass ich habe letzte ein Email nicht geschrieben. Ich bin kür
5	th a situation like this before? Ich **entschuldige** mich weil ich nicht hier gestern war. Ich wohne weit von Schule,
6	rrow. C U Emmi. Hallo Damen, **Entschuldigung**, dass ich letztens kein Email geschrieben habe. Ich weiß das
7	hrieben, und ich muss micht dafür **Entschuldigungen**. Es ist bei mir ein Fehler, weil ich habe zu viel hier zu tun.
8	nicht jezt besucht. Auch **entschuldigung**, wenn ich ein Fehler gemacht habe. Ich fühle mich wie ein K
9	allgemeinen angesehen wird. **Entschuldigung**, wenn mein Satz sich beleidigend anhört. I think you may ha

Figure 5
NS Concordance Lines for *Leid*

1	Es tut mir wirklich ganz arg **leid**, dass ich mich bei euch bis jetzt nur einmal gemeldet habe. Das wird si
2	lege mich mal ins bett. Tut mir echt **leid**. Ich hoffe ich kann morgen zur uni gehen, dann können wir ja noch ein
3	watch „Sex and the City"? Es tut mir **leid**, dass ich schon gehen muss, aber ich habe noch einiges zu tun. Wir we
4	wir den Pflichtteil erledigt :-) Tut mir **leid**, dass dein Semester so schlecht läuft. Du kannst gar nichts dafür. Und j
5	sein und er tut uns schrecklich **leid**, trotz seiner Dummheit. Es ist leider ein immer noch verbreiteter Geda
6	alleingelassen, es tut mir wirklich sehr **leid**! Bis Morgen, Carola
7	Liebe Beth! Hallo, es tut mit soooo **leid**, dass Du die ganze Zeit nichts von mit gehört hast … Ich bin auch ganz
8	Hallo Kate und Angela! Es tut uns **leid**, wir haben es so verstanden, dass nur wir den rough draft machen solle
9	gegenseitig hilft. Es tut mir wirklich **Leid**, dass du Lärm in deiner Wohung hast, aber du musst Geduld haben. B

Figure 6
Learner Concordance Lines for *Leid*

1   deine E-mails gelesen, und es tut mir **Leid**, ob ich leicht zu verwirren ins Chat waren. The quote you selected

2   text was in exaggeration? Es tut mir **Leid**, weil ich verwirrt bin. : (Either way . . . I don't find it insulting at all.

3   ending. Was denkst du? Es tut mir **leid**. Ich dachte dass ich war nicht zu schwer, aber ich denke auch dass dies

4   It gets pretty complicated. Es tut mir **leid**, dass ich so viel English spreche, aber es ist schneller für mich als Deu

5   sind Sie ganz behilflich! Das tut mir **leid** das du so viele Fehler Korrigieren müssen. Deutsches Radio hören wir

6   Squash oder was es ist. Es tut mir **leid**, aber die Seit fuer unsere Klasse ist um. So muss ich jetzt gehen. Spate

7   Hallo Christa! Es tut mir **leid** dass du krank war, ich war auch krank seit ein Woche und so weiss ich

8   von ihnen sehr viel lernen. Es tut mir **leid** ob mein Deutsch nicht richtig ist, weil ich ein bisschen vergessen habe

9   Hallo Berit, Wie geht's? Es tut mir **leid** das die leste e-mail war so klein, aber unsere Sitzung war fertig fuer den

10 Samira, Leila, und Käthe! Es tut mir **leid**. Jetzt haben wir technische Probleme mit First Class. Es ist ein Proble

11 d to get to another class. Es tut mir **leid**! I hope you're not mad at me! Habt ihr die Website gesehen? Wir hof

12 muss schnell schreiben! (es tut mir **leid**) Danke schön für meinen Fehler korrigieren. Meine grammatik sind se

13   Hallo! Es tut mir **leid** dass ich nicht so lange mit dir gesprochen habe. Ich hatte auch First Cl

14 atmosphere.) Und ich tut mir **leid** aber heute finde ich keine Fehler von dich! Bis bald und fröhliches We

15   Hello, Es tut mir **leid** dass mein Subjekt immer so langweilig ist . . . Hallo oder Hallo Manfre

16 ld mit euch sprechen, und es tut uns **Leid**, dass wir nicht eine langere e-mail geschrieben haben. Liebe, Alison u

17   Hi Silja Es tut mir wirklich **leid** das du krank bist. Ich hoffe das du schnell besser wird! Your explanati

something that NSs never do—or they confuse the conjunction *dass* with the article *das* "the" (lines 5, 9, and 17). Furthermore, the learners inappropriately begin the subsequent subordinate clause with *ob* "whether, if" or *weil* "because"—also something that the NSs never do in these data. Learners may notice variations with respect to NS observation of the German spelling reform. According to the new usage rules, *Leid* should be capitalized; however, only one NS does so (line 9 in Figure 5). In contrast, several learners adopt the new spelling rules (lines 1–2, 16 in Figure 6). Learners' attention my be directed to this difference and they may be encouraged to consider why they spell "correctly" in German more frequently than Germans do in this case. This topic can be pursued in subsequent intercultural interactions, which may reveal the numerous passions surrounding the German spelling reform.

From the semantic perspective, the differences between NS and learner uses of *es tut mir Leid* seem to mirror those for *entschuldig**. On the whole, Germans use this phrase with their American keypals in order to apologize for breaking the rules of the partnership with respect to frequency and length of correspondence, class attendance, or other task assignments (lines 1–3, 7–8 in Figure 5). In addition, they use this phrase to express regret about or empathy for a certain situation in their keypals' lives (lines 4, 9 in Figure 5). In contrast, as with *entschuldig**, the learners often use this phrase to apologize for their own linguistic shortcomings in their L2. For example, they apologize for comprehension difficulties (lines 1–2 in Figure 6); for using too much English (line 4); and for the perceived deficiency of their German (lines 5, 8). They also use this phrase to apologize for transgressions against the rules of the partnerships (lines 9, 13, 16); for writing about "boring" topics (line 15); for cutting their correspondence short (lines 6, 11–12); for technical difficulties (line 10); and to express empathy for aspects of their partners' life situations (lines 7, 17).

Based on the authentic, project-based interaction between learners and NSs in example 1, a potential "languacultural rich point" (Agar 1994) between the particular interlocutors in question was exposed. This rich point concerns the lexical resources used to apologize in the respective L2s, the scope of legitimate reasons for doing so, and the frequency with which one typically employs the resources that one chooses. Corpus analysis is particularly beneficial with respect to the later point because frequency of use is generally not amenable to introspection (by neither learners nor NSs). With recourse to a contrastive learner corpus such as *Telekorp,* one can answer these questions not for an abstract set of NSs with whom the learners are not familiar but with respect to the interactions that the learners themselves have engaged in up to that point and in comparison to other learners in previous telecollaborative partnerships. As the partnership progresses, one can ascertain how the learners developed with respect to these lexical, grammatical, and pragmatic points by continuing to track their L2 productions using *Telekorp.* In addition, learners can document their own development with respect to certain lexical, grammatical, and pragmatic features by engaging in meta-lingual reflection on their progress—as documented quantitatively in the corpus—in the form of portfolio entries which they could then discuss with their instructors (Belz and Vyatkina 2005, pp. 36–39).

Learner Corpus Analysis and Developmental Pedagogical Intervention

In this section, two corpus-based developmental pedagogical interventions on a single learner's use of address forms and cohesive ties are presented. This learner was chosen for analysis because she participated with the author in two consecutive telecollaborative German-language courses (fall 2002 and fall 2003) and one non-telecollaborative language course (spring 2004). According to Kern, Ware, and Warschauer (2004, p. 248), researchers have not yet provided longitudinal accounts of learners in technology-mediated environments nor have they thoroughly addressed the issue of developmental transfer between telecollaborative and non-telecollaborative courses (e.g., Abrams 2003). Scholars working in non-educational contexts have also begun to stress the importance of longitudinal analyses of mediated interpersonal communication (Kutz and Herring 2005). The case study format is chosen because it illustrates well the ways in which contrastive learner corpus analysis with *Telekorp* facilitates the production of individualized learner profiles and thus individualized assessment and instruction.

The Focal Learner

Lori (a pseudonym), a NS of English, is a white American woman from a working-class background (Fussell 1983; Lubrano 2004). In fall 2002, when the author first came to know her as a student in a university-level language course at a large public institution on the East Coast of the United States, she was a 20-year-old undergraduate student in her fourth semester of study. In an interview, Lori reported that she was born and grew up in a "very rural" area of the eastern United States. She further explained that her home was so isolated that she had to take "half an hour trip to get to a grocery store." During her childhood and adolescence, Lori had little or no contact with people from other cultures. She stated that there were "not even any black people" in her high school. Prior to fall 2002, Lori had never traveled outside the United States and she had only once left her home state. As a result, her weekly electronic exchanges with her German keypals in 2002 represented both the first and most extensive contact that she had ever had with a person from another culture (see also Kinginger *et al.* 1999, p. 855).

In high school, Lori excelled academically and participated in a number of honors courses, including German. On a biographical survey, she stated that it was a source of "pride" for her that she was able to read a novel in German. Nevertheless, she had not contemplated a college career. Instead, she had planned to get a job after graduation at the nearby factory where her mother worked; she also considered joining the military. However, a high school teacher suggested to her that she "had what it takes to succeed in college" and, as a result, Lori enrolled in the local branch campus of the major public institution in her state where she studied for three semesters prior to transferring to the main campus in fall 2002.

When the author first met her in that same semester, she was majoring in physics, but her interest in German as an academic course of study was already quite high as evidenced by a number of questions concerning course requirements for a minor in German.

In terms of written performance, Lori displayed the characteristics of a low-intermediate learner of German on the ACTFL proficiency scale, although her self-perception was that she rated as "advanced" in each of the traditional language skills, as she indicated on a pre-semester biographical survey. Her oral performance was somewhat less proficient. By spring 2004, Lori had switched her major to German because she had "always loved the language" and was receiving high grades in all her courses. Her written German had developed noticeably, particularly with respect to vocabulary, her use of idiomatic phrases, and the placement of the conjugated verb in the main and dependent clauses. Her oral performance was still somewhat hesitant, although this may be associated in some way with her rather reticent personality. At the time of this writing (spring 2005), the author learned via e-mail correspondence with Lori that she had dropped out of college for personal reasons and was once again considering a career in the military, although she hoped to return to the university in the following semester in order to graduate as a German major.

Pedagogical Intervention: Interpersonal Relationships

Second-Person Pronouns

In German, there are three basic ways to say "you": (1) *du* (informal singular); (2) *ihr* (informal plural); and (3) *Sie* (formal singular and plural). As a result of the German case system, ten different "you"-forms exist. Informal forms are referred to as T pronouns, while formal forms are referred to as V pronouns (Brown and Gilman 1960, p. 254). These pronouns are of enormous social relevance because they not only index the word "you," but also a wealth of additional information, including social status, political orientation, occupation, age, and interpersonal familiarity (Delilse 1986). As a result, their appropriate use is of vital importance in the building and maintenance of interpersonal relationships such as the ones negotiated in telecollaborative partnerships. Kasper and Rose (2001, p. 4) note that "[a]dult learners get a considerable amount of L2 pragmatic knowledge for free. This is because some . . . aspects [of pragmatic knowledge] may be successfully transferred from the learners' L1." Transfer is not likely to be possible, however, in the case of second-person pronouns for English-speaking learners of German because there is no corresponding form–function mapping between L1 and L2.

Lori's Classroom-Based Instruction in Second-Person Pronoun Use

To date, Lori has taken a total of nine university-level German courses as outlined in Table 2.

Table 2

Lori's College-level German Courses and Explicit *da*-compound Instruction

Semester	Course	Instructor	*da*-compound Instruction	Grade
Sp 2001	1: Intermediate German	A	"brief introduction"	A
Fall 2001	None	None	None	N/A
Sp 2002	None	None	None	N/A
Fall 2002	2: Telecollaboration	Author	None	A
Sp 2003	3: Famous Figures in German History	B	Turneaure (1987)	A–
Fall 2003	4: German Novelle	C	None	A
Fall 2003	5: Advanced Grammar	D	Dippmann and Watzinger-Tharp (2000)	A–
Fall 2003	6: Telecollaboration	Author	Intervention	A
Sp 2004	7: Holocaust Literature	Author	None	A
Sp 2004	8: Culture, Language, and Literature	D	None	A
Sp 2004	9: Schiller	E	None	A

Lori relates that she received no explicit instruction in the grammar and use of address forms in any of these courses other than the brief (and inadequate) explanations common in introductory textbooks (see Belz and Kinginger 2003, pp. 599–600). Prior to the onset of telecollaboration in 2002, Lori's U.S. cohort was instructed to use T with their NS keypals. In all cases, the Germans initiated correspondence with their U.S. partners using T; no German ever used V to address an American keypal in any year.

Procedure

At the close of the 2002 course, it was established via corpus analysis that Lori inappropriately used V forms over the course of the partnership almost without exception. Her inappropriate uses occurred in the face of explicit direction on the part of her instructor to use T, explicit peer assistance on the part of her keypals, and roughly two months of correspondence from her NS keypals that contained only T forms. In December 2002, Lori participated in a post-telecollaboration retrospective interview during which she was shown excerpts of her 2002 discourse containing second-person pronouns and asked to comment on specific uses. In the course of this interview, it became clear that Lori was unaware of particular pragmalinguistic and grammatical aspects of address form competence in German (Belz 2005b), e.g., she did not know that *ihr* and *euer* are T forms; she thought that *sie* with a lower case "s" was an informal second-person pronoun when it is actually a third-person singular and plural pronoun. Her use of "sie" caused intercultural misunderstandings because her NS interlocutors interpreted it as an inappropriate V form. At the end of the interview, Lori was shown concrete examples of her T/V use for the semester in comparison to that of her NS keypals. In the fall 2003 semester, Lori once again participated in a telecollaborative course with the author. As a result, two ten-week L2 production cycles, roughly one year apart, are archived in *Telekorp* for Lori.

The Data

Lori's aggregate T/V use for 2002 and 2003 is compared in Table 3. In 2002, Lori uses 55 V forms and only 3 T forms, all in the singular. She has no uses of any T forms in the plural, although she corresponded with more than one person. The better part of her V uses occur in the nominative case in the form of *Sie*. Following Lori's exposure to her aggregate T/V use in the 2002 partnership, her use of T/V in 2003 changes drastically. She has only one occurrence of a V form in the nominative case and 4 occurrences as a possessive adjective; in contrast, she uses T forms a total of 59 times. Her uses span both singular and plural forms as well as all the cases. These data seem to indicate that Lori's development of appropriate T use in telecollaboration was not particularly sensitive to rule-based explicit instruction in the form of textbook examples nor was it amenable to explicit peer assistance in the course of the 2002 partnership (cf. Belz and Kinginger 2003, pp. 631–638); instead, Lori's use of T begins to approximate NS norms following exposure to and teacher-guided examination of corpus-enabled comparisons of her overall T/V use with that of her keypals.

Table 3
Overall Comparison Lori's T/V Use in 2002 and 2003

Form	Lori (2002) Raw	Lori (2003) Raw
du (T)	1	26
dich (T)	2	2
dir (T)	0	2
dein* (T)	0	9
ihr (T)	0	12
euch (T)	0	4
eu(e)r* (T)	4	4
Sie (V)[5]	46 + 2	1 + 1
Ihnen (V)	1	0
Ihr* (V)	7	4

Corpus analysis is also of potential use in the disambiguation of polysemous forms. For example, learners may be uncertain of the referential value of *I/ihr** in particular contexts as illustrated in Lori's interview data (see also Kinginger and Belz 2005 for the case of Grace). An examination of concordance lines such as those given in Figure 7 may facilitate this disambiguation through awareness raising activities.

In lines 1–3, *ihr* is used as the second-person plural pronoun ("you all") in the nominative case, a form that Lori did not use at all in 2002, but which the NSs used consistently and frequently. In contrast, this same form occurs as a third-person singular feminine possessive adjective ("her") in lines 4–5. In line 6, the same form functions as a third-person plural possessive adjective ("their"). It is noteworthy that this form never occurs in its function as a second-person singular/plural formal possessive adjective ("your") in the NS data. A similar exercise may be designed for *S/sie*. In general, both learners and NSs will use "sie"-forms; however, they will differ dramatically with respect to the function of the forms used. Constrastive learner corpus analysis with *Telekorp* draws attention to the precise nature of these form-meaning pairings in contexts with which the learners are familiar.

Although Lori's 2002 problems with a word as seemingly simple as "you" may possess a certain "shock value" (Bardovi-Harlig 1999, p. 680) with regard to the state of her L2 pragmatic competence, much research indicates that learners of European languages do have considerable difficulty with the appropriate use of second-person address forms at the intermediate or even advanced levels (e.g., Dewaele 2004; Kinginger 2000; Kinginger and Belz 2005; Norris 2001; Thorne 2003) based, in part, on the fact that "rules" of use are typically negotiated in context (e.g., Brown and Gilman 1960; Mühlhäuser and Harré 1990). Corpus-enabled data-driven learning and developmental intervention of the type examined here may facilitate the development of appropriate use of this important carrier of interpersonal meaning.

Pedagogical Interventions: Cohesive Ties

The Cohesive Function of the *da*-Compounds

One of the ways in which textual cohesion is achieved in texts is through the use of pronominal reference (Halliday and Hasan 1976; Kallmeyer 1972; Stemmer 1981). German possesses a set of pronominal adverbs that allows speakers to create textual coherence by indexing nominal phrases as well as larger syntactic units and concepts (Donceva 1982; Meraner 1988; Starke 1982). For instance, the compound *darüber* "there-about" in example 2 anaphorically refers to the noun *das Projekt* "the project":

(2)

Wir sollen **das Projekt** am Dienstag im Entwurf präsentieren und wir haben uns noch nicht einen gemeinsamen Gedanken **darüber** gemacht....

Figure 7
NS Use of *ihr**

1   ganz super interessant zu hören, dass **Ihr** in der High School IMMER das Thema "racism" habt, und die Leute

2   Hi Eric, wir fanden es sehr schön, dass **ihr** eine Gliederung mit einer Arbeitsaufteilung ins Netz gegeben haben.

3   chat and the others culdn't. Bekommt **ihr** auch immer ein Thema, welches ihr dann mit uns besprechen sollt? I t

4   sondere Beziehung, die Cinderella zu **ihrem** Vater hat, dadurch sehr gut zu Ausdruck kam. Als sie als Engel vor

5   denn sie wirkt sehr selbstbewusst **ihre** Stiefschwestern und ihrer Stiefmutter gegenüber. Besonders die Szen

6   ob es normal ist, dass deutsche Eltern **ihre** Kinder ab einem bestimmten Alter allein lassen. Da ich den Film nic

7   wobei ich eine Familie kenne, die **ihr** Kind mit fünf Jahren (!) an Silvester allein gelassen haben. Das ist jedo

Ich weiß, dass ihr Noten für das Projekt bekommt, deshalb verstehe ich nicht ganz wieso es euch so unwichtig ist. (20 November 2004; NS in e-mail)

'On Tuesday we are supposed to present the project in draft form and we have not yet even talked about it ... I know that you are getting grades for the project, therefore I don't really understand why it is so unimportant to you.'

In example 3, in contrast, the compound *dazu* "there-to" refers to the entire preceding passage:

(3)

Ich war mal auf einem Nachthemdenball, da hatte jeder Pyjamas und Nachthemden an, das war an sich schon lustig, aber es waren alle betrunken, und das finde ich dann schon traurig. Warum kann man nicht auch ohne Alkohol Spass haben? Ich kann das schon!! Soweit **dazu**. (22 November 2004; NS in e-mail)

'Once I went to a pyjama party and everybody was wearing pyjamas and nightgowns, that was fun just by itself, but everybody was drunk and I find that to be really sad. Why can't one have fun without alcohol? That's enough about that.'

In addition to the two types of anaphoric reference shown above, *da*-compounds also cataphorically refer to elements that have not yet been introduced into the discourse as seen in example 4 where the compound *davor* "there-for" refers ahead to the entire subsequent infinitive phrase.

(4)

Die Frage ist nur, ob Sex zu einem absoluten Tabuthema zu machen präventiv gegen diesen Trend wirkt und wenn wir Kinder nicht aufklären, und nackte Körper als etwas anstössiges suggerieren, dies Kinder **davor** schützt, früh an Sex zu denken. (6 November 2004; NS in e-mail)

'The question is whether or not making sex into an absolute taboo topic works against this trend in a preventative fashion and if we don't educate children about sex and suggest that naked bodies are something distasteful, does this protect children from thinking about sex at an early age?'

Speakers of English tend to have particular problems with the detection, comprehension, and use of cataphoric *da*-compounds.

Lori's Classroom-Based Instruction in *da*-Compound Use

Lori reports that she received explicit instruction in the grammar and use of the *da*-compounds in three of the German courses listed in Table 2. During her first semester of college, she states that she received a "brief introduction" to the *da*-compounds in course 1, an intermediate-level language course at a branch campus of her current institution. She did not receive explicit instruction on the *da*-compounds in course 2, the first telecollaborative course in which she participated.

In course 3, Lori received instruction on the *da*-compounds in the form of Turneaure, a textbook for "students in composition and conversation classes who have completed a second-year review of German grammar" (1987, p. xiii). The entire treatment of the compounds in this text consists of a half-page explication entitled "da-compounds preceding infinitive and dependent clauses" (p. 127). This minimalist treatment of the *da*-compounds is characteristic of those materials commonly in use in the North American context (Belz 2005c, pp. 45–46), despite the importance of the compounds as cohesive ties. In fact, the compounds are not mentioned at all in a number of popular textbooks (e.g., Donahue and Watzinger-Tharp 2000; see, however, Byrnes and Fink 1987); in most other cases, essential linguistic aspects of the compounds are omitted such as the full range of syntactic configurations in which they occur (e.g., cataphoric constructions), the multiplicity of functions which they serve, and their frequency of occurrence in actual usage in any one function or construction (e.g., DiDonato, Clyde, and Vansant 2004; Moeller, Adolph, Mabee, and Berger 2002; Terrell, Tschirner, and Nikolai 2002).

In fall 2003, Lori was concurrently enrolled in three German courses. In course 4, Lori received no instruction concerning the *da*-compounds. In course 5, Lori enjoyed explicit instruction in the grammar and meaning of the compounds in the form of Dippmann and Watzinger-Tharp, a "practical review" of German grammar that is intended to provide second-year college students with a "solid grammar foundation" that is "need[ed]" for continued language learning (1987, p. v). In this common reference work, the *da*-compounds are introduced in the space of five pages (pp. 145–150). In a first section, learners are informed that *da*-compounds function as a "pronoun substitute" (p. 145). In a second section, learners are provided with a list of prepositions that do not form compounds (e.g., *ohne, seit, außer*). In a third section that occupies approximately one-third of a page, learners are told that some *da*-compounds "anticipate[. . .] what is expressed in the following clause" (p. 149). This information is followed by an eight-item exercise in which learners are directed to express the given German sentences in acceptable English. This cursory introduction to "anticipatory *da*-compounds" (p. 149) constitutes one of the few references to cataphoric uses of the *da*-compounds in common textbook materials (see Belz 2005c, p. 52; Folsom 1979, p. 46, for the frequency of cataphoric constructions in use). In a final segment of Dippman and Watzinger-Tharp (1987), learners are instructed that most prepositional phrases, including the *da*-compounds, typically occur at the end of the German sentence.

Procedure

At the end of fall 2003, Lori received individualized, focused instruction on the meaning, syntax, and frequency of use of the *da*-compounds based on her own discourse from the 2002 telecollaborative partnership. The *da*-compounds were chosen for intervention for this particular learner[6] because contrastive learner corpus analysis revealed that: (1) Lori significantly under-used this feature in comparison to both her NS keypals and her U.S. classmates; (2) traditional, classroom-based instruction did not appear to facilitate her development of their use; (3) no NSs offered peer assistance in the use of the *da*-compounds in two years of tele-collaborative interaction (see Belz and Kinginger 2003, pp. 620–631 for unsolicited peer assistance in the use of other L2 features); and (4) unassisted exposure to the compounds in the course of telecollaboration similarly did not appear to facilitate their development.

Using *Telekorp*, a contrastive learner corpus analysis was conducted for Lori's use of the *da*-compounds on the basis of the 2002 e-mail data. E-mail correspondence was selected for study because very few *da*-compounds occurred in chat discourse. The results of this analysis were conveyed to Lori in the form of a written response to her penultimate course portfolio, the primary method of assessment in the telecollaborative courses. The intervention was not conducted earlier because available resources in 2002 and 2003 did not allow for exhaustive data entry into the corpus until the end of the semester.

After providing Lori with a corpus-based exposition of the syntax and functions of the compounds (using examples that her keypals had produced), the author related to Lori that she had uncovered a major difference in the way that Americans and Germans in the 2002 partnership had used the compounds. First, Lori was presented with Appendix 1 and told that the Germans used approximately twice as many compounds as the learners had used. Second, Lori's attention was drawn to the fact that 21% of the Germans' uses of the compounds occurred in cataphoric constructions, whereas only 8% of the learners' uses of the compounds occurred in such constructions. This information was conveyed to her in the form of Appendix 2. Third, Lori was shown her own personal use of the compounds in comparison to that of classmates by means of Appendix 3. She was informed that "[t]he most relevant part of all of this for [her]…is that [she] produced almost no *da*-compounds in [her] correspondence over the entire course of the semester." Finally, the author wrote to Lori that she "would like [her] to begin to pay attention to the use of *da*-compounds in [her] texts!" and suggested that she "go over the e-mails of [her] partners from [fall 2003] and list their use of *da*-compounds" for an entry in her final course portfolio. In her final course portfolio, dated December 19, 2003, Lori did include an entry in which she circled all the *da*-compounds in the e-mails of her keypals and labeled them as either cataphoric or anaphoric.

In spring 2004, Lori participated with the author in an advanced intermediate German composition and conversation course that centered on the classic 1961 juvenile novel, *Damals war es Friedrich,* by Hans Peter Richter. Richter's *Friedrich*, which traces the histories of two childhood friends, one Christian and one Jew, from 1925 to 1942, was one of the first German novels to explore National Socialism and its effects from the perspective of young adults. One of the primary assignments in this course was the maintenance of a reading log in which students were required to reflect on their reactions to and classroom discussions of the novel. The first entry in Lori's 63-page, handwritten reading log occurred on January 19, 2004, which was 32 days after the author's receipt of her final course portfolio in the 2003 telecollaborative course and 43 days after Lori's receipt of the corpus-based pedagogical intervention on the *da*-compounds.

The Data

In fall 2002, Lori used a total of five *da*-compounds in 6001 words of e-mail correspondence. Her rate of *da*-compound use in these data was 0.83 occurrences per 1000 words. The average rate of *da*-compound use for all learners in the 2002 partnership was 1.32 per 1000 words, while the average rate of NS *da*-compound use was 1.91 occurrences per 1000 words. Lori's specific uses of the compounds are given in Table 4.

Table 4
Lori's Use of the Compounds in 2002

E-mail week 9

1. Aber viellen Leute lieben New York, weil gibt es verschiedene Lueten und Kulturen darin. Nur von neugierigung, haben Sie die Schwarzen Wald gesehen.

2. Yoga ist einfach prima! Ich intereßiere mich dafür, aber gemacht es schädlich nicht.

E-mail week 11

3. Ich haße Zensur! Wann man etwas zensiert, ist das schrecklich! Was denken Sie darüber, und was denken Sie über Indianer?

4. Wann man etwas zensiert, ist das fürchbar! Was denken Sie darüber, und was denken Sie über Indianer und Eskimos?

E-mail week 13

5. Ich glaube, dass konnen wir zuerst über Ausländer im Amerika sprechen, und dann über Ausländer in Deutschland sprechen, und dann verglichen sie mit einander. Was fühlen Sie darüber? Linda ist heute krank, ich muss mit ihr das diskutieren.

In example 1 in Table 4, Lori uses *darin* "there-in" anaphorically to reference the proper noun "New York." In example 2, she correctly uses *dafür* "there-for" in combination with *sich interessieren für* "to be interested in" in order to anaphorically reference the noun "yoga." This vocabulary item was stressed in class in preparation for the learners' first electronic contact with their keypals. Next, Lori uses *darüber* "there-over" twice in the phrase "Was denken Sie darüber?" ("What do you [formal] think about it?"). It should be noted, however, that this same phrase is rendered pragmatically inappropriate with her selection of the pronoun *Sie* instead of *du*. Lori's fifth and final use for the semester is an incorrect use of *darüber*. In sum, Lori's range of use is small (three different compounds), she does not use the compounds cataphorically, and the majority of her anaphoric uses index single-noun phrases as opposed to larger units, which is the preferred structure among the NSs (see Appendix 3).

In fall 2003 Lori used a total of seven *da*-compounds in 6499 words of e-mail correspondence. Her rate of *da*-compound use in these data was 1.08 per 1000 words. Lori's specific uses of the compounds in 2003 are given in Table 5.

In example 1 in Table 5, Lori uses the compound *darauf* inappropriately because it should substitute for the noun phrase *ihre Meinung* "your opinion"

Table 5
Lori's Use of the Compounds in 2003

E-mail week 9

1. Den Brief Anfangen and Abschnitten ist egal. Es kommt darauf an ihre Meinung. Du kannst schreiben auf Englisch oder Deutsch, wenn du willst!

E-mail week 10

2. It would be the same time we chat on teusdays only on thursdays instead. Was meinst du darüber? Es ist schwer, eine Zeit zu finden

3. Ich habe gesagt, dass ich OK sein werde, ob meine Kinder einen Freund oder eine Freundin hat. Ich stimme damit überein! Kinder, wie alle Leute, werden tun, was sie wollen, trotz des Gesellschaft.

E-mail week 12

4. Denkst du etwas darüber? Wenn du willst, sag es.

5. Wenn ihr wollt, bitte denkt an die Themenbereiche und lasst mich kennen, was ihr interessiert euch sich dafür. Ich möchte an etwas arbeiten, wofür ihr sich euch auch interessierten.

E-mail week 13

6. Ich hoffe, dass du und Heidi ein Thema finden konnen, dass ihr euch dafür interessieren.

E-mail week 15

7. Ihr könnt etwas heraustragen, ihr könnt etwas hineinstellen, meine Deutsche korrigieren, und auch mein Zitat ins Schluss integrieren, außerdem euere Meinungen darüber.

---

instead of co-occur with it. This particular error occurs a number of times in Lori's L2 discourse. It is especially noteworthy because the compounds are introduced as "pronoun substitutes" in Dippmann and Watzinger-Tharp (1987), the only other substantive instruction that Lori had received in *da*-compound use next to the corpus-based pedagogical intervention in 2003. In examples 2–4 Lori accurately uses two different compounds in order to reference anaphorically a larger unit or concept. She inaccurately uses *dafür* in examples 5 and 6 where she should have used *wofür* in her attempt to form a question with a reflexive verb in the second-person plural informal. In 7 she accurately uses *darüber* to anaphorically index a larger unit or concept (although the phrase in which it occurs is not completely grammatical). In sum, Lori's range of use is small (four separate compounds) and she does not have any cataphoric uses; however, she does begin to index anaphorically larger units or concepts, a trend which seems to be in line with NS uses in the corpus under study.

Lori's reading log for the non-telecollaborative course in 2004 contained 35 entries for a total of 5754 words, roughly equivalent to the total number of words in both her 2002 and 2003 e-mail correspondence in the telecollaborative courses. While her initial four entries are dated, Lori does not date her reading log entries after February 2, 2004, but they do follow the chronological and thematic progression of the semester, which concluded on April 30, 2004. Lori's journal entries were of a high quality both linguistically and semantically: she received 98/100 points for entries 1–5; 100/100 points for entries 6–13; and 100/100 points for entries 17–35. The reading logs were assessed according to a number of explicit criteria, including length and frequency of entries, use of relevant vocabulary (e.g., *der Jude* "the Jew [male]," *die Jüdin* "the Jew [female]," *die Hitlerjugend* "the Hitler youth [an organization]," *die Schlaufe* "clasp of a neck scarf [part of the uniform of the Hitler youth]"), idiomaticity (*meiner Meinung nach* "in my opinion," *ich frage mich ob* "I wonder if"), depth of reflection, and intertextuality (i.e., relating characters' experiences to personal experiences or experiences reported in the news or in other literary texts).

The most striking aspect of Lori's reading log is the drastic increase in the frequency of her *da*-compound use. While the rate of compound use remains more or less the same between 2002 and 2003 (0.83 and 1.03 compounds per 1000 words, respectively), it increases to 5.74 compounds per 1000 words in the semester following the corpus-based pedagogical intervention. In addition, both the range and accuracy of her uses also increase. In 2002, she used three different compounds and in 2003 she used four. In 2004, in contrast, she uses a total of ten different compounds including the (inaccurate) neologism *dadort* as well as *dazu* "there-to" and *damit* "there-with," the most commonly occurring compounds for the NSs in 2002 as indicated in Appendix 1 (which was shown to Lori in the intervention). Most notably, Lori's first cataphoric use occurs midway through the semester in journal entry 23. Finally, Lori also successfully uses two *wo*-compounds in her 2004 reading log. The single most frequent mistake that Lori makes in her performance of the *da*-compounds involves the use of the object of the prepositional phrase for which the compound should substitute. On the other hand, Lori's compound use in 2004 indicates a diversification of syntax, which includes anaphoric reference to single nouns, objects of prepositions, and larger units as well as the single cataphoric use mentioned above. Lori's three-year *da*-compound use is summarized in Table 6.

Table 6
Summary of Lori's *da*-Compound Use

Year	Text	Total Words	Total E-Mails/ Entries	Average Words per E-Mail/Entry	Total Compounds	Per 1000 Words	Cataphoric Uses
2002	E-mail	6001	21	286	5	0.83	0
2003	E-mail	6499	17	382	7	1.08	0
2004	Journal	5754	35	165	32	5.74	1

Discussion of Lori's *da*-Compound Use

If one takes Lori's performance of the compounds in course 2 (the first telecollaborative course) as a baseline, it appears that the subsequent instruction in their use in courses 3 and 5, two non-telecollaborative courses, based on Turneaure (1987) and Dippmann and Watzinger-Tharp (1987), respectively, had little or no influence on her performance of them as evidenced in her telecollaborative interaction in course 6, the second telecollaborative course. Because courses 5 and 6 ran concomitantly, one could expect that substantive instruction in *da*-compound use in course 5 might influence Lori's performance of them in course 6. This, however, does not seem to be the case. Instead, Lori's exposure to the pedagogical intervention at the end of course 6, a data-driven intervention that was composed of examples of *da*-compound use from the telecollaborative process data produced in course 2, appears to influence dramatically her performance of the compounds with respect to both frequency and range as evidenced in her subsequent handwritten reading log in course 7, a non-telecollaborative course.

There are, however, several limitations to this interpretation. First, one might argue that the genres of e-mail correspondence and handwritten reading logs are not comparable and thus attribution of the demonstrated increase in *da*-compound use to the intervention is not valid. Indeed, corpus analysis has revealed that particular linguistic features cluster in particular genres (e.g., Biber, Conrad, and Reppen 1998). Second, it may be the case that *Friedrich* contained a large number of compounds and that this increase in the number of compounds to which Lori was exposed crossed the threshold of attentional saliency for Lori, which, in turn, resulted in a concentration of her developmental energies in this direction. To be sure, examination reveals a frequency of compound use in the text that appears to be higher than that of the NSs in the 2002 and 2003 e-mail correspondence.

On the other hand, several additional factors seem to suggest that there indeed might be a relationship between the corpus-based intervention and the subsequent increase in Lori's *da*-compound use in her 2004 reading log. First, a similar corpus-enabled intervention on her overuse of V in 2002 does appear to have had an influence on her appropriate use of T in 2003. These data are both in the genre of e-mail correspondence. Lori does not report any additional instruction in second-person pronoun use between fall 2002 and fall 2003.

Second, researchers investigating telecollaborative FL study have posited that the regular inclusion of NSs in tutored instruction will offer "a new level of dynamism and immediacy to pedagogical exchange" (Kinginger 2004, p. 101). Such dynamism comprises, among other things, both exposure to a broader range of FL discourse options than is typically the case in traditional classroom fare as well as a diversification of learners' epistemic roles in the classroom (Nystrand *et al.* 1997; see also Kern 1995, p. 466). These aspects of telecollaboration, it was suggested, might positively influence the development of linguistic and intercultural competence in the learner. In a series of articles, Kinginger (2000) and Belz and Kinginger (2003) provide quantitative evidence that participation in telecollaboration does indeed positively influence the appropriate use of T for U.S.

learners of French and German (see also Kern, 1998, p. 72; Kinginger and Belz 2005; Thorne 2003, pp. 50–51). In particular, these authors found that the development of T hinged on episodes of "peer assistance," i.e., explicit instruction in the socio-pragmatically appropriate use of T, on the part of the NSs. Despite the fact that such peer assistance typically consisted of the presentation of fragmentary and contradictory "rules-of-use" (Belz and Kinginger 2003, p. 623), students exhibited clear development with regard to T. This fact led Belz and Kinginger to suggest that "it was not necessarily the *information* given by the NS that afforded this development, but rather the *act of peer assistance itself*" (2003, p. 630; italics in the original). Although Lori's keypals offered such peer assistance in 2002, she reported in her interview that she did not recall being offered this assistance and surmised that she "must have missed it." The corpus-enabled intervention on her T/V use provided another form of peer assistance, however, a form that allowed Lori to examine her own patterns of use (see Seidlhofer 2002) in comparison to those of both her NS keypals and her U.S. classmates.

Third, Lori may have wished to maintain positive face in front of her *U.S. classmates*. Previous research on telecollaboration has indicated that L2 development appears to be hastened when learners interact with people who matter to them. Until now, such people have generally been taken to be the NS keypals. However, Lori's exposure to Appendix 3 provided her with a concrete example of her L2 performance relative the performance of her non-NS classmates, individuals whom she had had the opportunity to observe face-to-face on a regular basis. In conversation with the author, Lori stated that she felt embarrassed when she learned that she had not used many *da*-compounds in the course of the semester, especially when she saw that some of her classmates, Lisbeth and Grace in particular, had used them quite extensively.

The little-explored factor of social class in FL learning (e.g., Kubota 2003; Lin 2000) may have contributed to the sharp increase in Lori's use of the *da*-compounds following the pedagogical intervention in 2003. The social class differences between the learners in Lori's 2002 telecollaborative German course were striking. As mentioned, Lori hailed from a rural, working-class background. The same was true for her American partner Linda, who once related in a class discussion that she had lived for 10 years in a trailer.[7] In comparison, Grace, a linguistically talented member of Lori's class, was the daughter of a department head at Lori's university, while her American partner, Lisbeth, the most proficient learner in the course, was the daughter of a corporate executive. Lisbeth often reported on her various international trips in class discussions; in particular, she regularly spent her summers in Germany as well as other parts of Europe. In contrast, Lori related on a biographical survey that she has only once left her state, as mentioned, because she "did not have the money and [her] parents were never involved with [her] schooling." Lori explicitly referenced her working-class background in this fashion at numerous points in the semester in essays, e-mail correspondence, and in conversations with the author. For example, in the first draft of her web-biography, she wrote that she was the first person in her family to attend college. She referred to this experience as "*anstrengend*" or "taxing" because of all the "financial problems" university study entails and because of the "*viele Legalische Wörter*" or "many legalistic words" she had had to learn. Based on the author's semester-long observation of Lori's reactions to Grace and Lisbeth, it seems that these two learners represented "people who matter" for Lori. When she saw via exposure to Appendix 3 that these two socially and linguistically desirable classmates exhibited the best *da*-compound performance for the group, she may have aspired to mimic them.

It should be noted that the claim here is not that Grace and Lisbeth exhibited top *da*-compound performances *because* they come from upper-middle class backgrounds; indeed, a number of studies has revealed that students from lower socio-economic backgrounds perform just as well or better than students from higher socio-economic backgrounds with respect to FL learning (e.g., Holobow *et al.* 1987; Holobow, Genesee, and Lambert 1991; Thomaneck 1980; see also Gee 2005, pp. 153–165 for the linguistic agility of Sandra, a working-class teen). In point of fact, Jason, a 19-year-old son of a physician who had previously studied at a prestigious East Coast university and who reported in interview that keypal interaction wasn't really "that big of a deal" for him because he had already met so many German speakers on the various ski trips that he had taken to Switzerland, ranked at the bottom of Lori's class with regard to *da*-compound use (see Appendix 3). Instead, it is suggested that Lori's realization that socially desirable others (with respect to the category of class) outperformed her with regard to *da*-compound use may have motivated her to pay attention to this grammatical feature more than the potential realization that there are a large number of *da*-compounds in the text *Friedrich*. In the end, the question of whether or not the corpus-enabled compound intervention influenced Lori's subsequent compound use is an empirical one, open to further developmentally-based investigation.

One such investigation reports on the results of a corpus-based pedagogical intervention on learners' under-use of modal particles during the 2004 partnership (Belz and Vyatkina 2005; Belz, Vyatkina, and Hundley 2005). The results suggest a strong relationship between the intervention itself and learners' subsequent (and rather dramatic) development of MP use with regard to frequency, range, and accuracy. This intervention is regarded as "developmental" in the second sense because focused instruction was delivered in three successive stages based on data in *Telekorp* while the 2004 partnership was still in progress. Unlike in 2002 and 2003, available resources afforded the daily entry of telecollaborative interactions into *Telekorp* in 2004, which, in turn, enabled corpus-based developmental intervention in the second sense.

Conclusion

The findings of this study are particularly relevant to language program directors because they underscore the growing consensus that unmonitored telecollaborative activity may not afford the full potential of such "unprecedented access to . . . representatives of the linguistic communities under study" (Kinginger 2004, p. 101) for the development of L2 linguistic competence. In other words, it is simply not enough, in the main, to turn learners loose in native-speaking regions of cyberspace in order to influence their L2 linguistic development (see Hanna and de

Nooy 2003). Instead, they require the strict guidance of languacultural experts, i.e., teachers, as a number of researchers have maintained for some time (e.g., Müller-Hartmann 2005; O'Dowd and Eberbach 2004). The current chapter has outlined several ways in which FL teachers may capitalize on the Internet-mediated, longitudinal, and bilingual nature of telecollaboration in order to implement corpus-based, developmental pedagogical interventions in the telecollaborative classroom, interventions that may have substantial meaning for the development of L2 competence. In contradistinction to other textually oriented approaches to FL learning, a contrastive learner corpus approach can provide comparative information about aspects of proficiency such as frequency of occurrence and distribution across media and genre in addition to relative accuracy of use.

The current chapter suggests that in addition to the logistical, technical, and social aspects of Internet-mediated FL education, language program directors might also wish to consider educating pre- and in-service teachers with respect to the application of contrastive learner corpus analysis to telecollaborative learning. In the field of English language teaching, a number of learner and NS corpora are already available, which could serve to supplement classroom-based telecollaborative activity. The disadvantage, of course, is that learners work with unfamiliar data instead of with their own previously produced discourse as is the case with *Telekorp*. Another possibility is the construction of "small corpora" using commercially available relational databases (see Ghadessy *et al.* 2001), an undertaking that Ragan describes as both "attractive" and "realistic" (2001, p. 208) for classroom teachers of language. Using as few as 6,000 words per learner (see McCarthy 2004, p. 4), instructors may construct corpora of their own students' discourse, which can offer considerable insight into their L2 use.[8] In the alternative, FL teachers may provide learners in their courses with tutorials at the outset of the semester in how to construct their own personal corpora (Coniam 2004) using readily available databases. Following each telecollaborative interaction, individual learners could enter their own discourse into a personal database, which they might search in order to discover patterns of error as well as development in their evolving L2s. Such personal corpora may prove to be important mediators in dynamic forms of assessment where the emphasis is on the "emergence of novelty" (Lantolf and Poehner 2004, p. 53), e.g., the encounter or personal use of new FL forms in the context of situated, ongoing intercultural interactions with people who matter.

Notes

1. See Belz (2003, p. 2) for a definition of "telecollaboration" as it is used in this chapter. *http://llt.msu.edu/vol7num2/speced.html*. The telecollaborative partnerships under study consisted of four instructional phases. During phase I, the U.S. students prepared a bilingual website that consisted of (1) individual web-biographies designed to introduce each U.S. student to their future German netpals; and (2) group-authored texts explicating an aspect of local university life (e.g., school spirit, the Greek system). Phase 2 was characterized by electronically-mediated transatlantic interaction on students' mutual reading of parallel texts (see Kinginger *et al.* 1999). In phase 3, the participants completed a website, which contained a critical essay on a topic that arose out of their semester-long engagement with the parallel texts. During the final phase,

the German students, pre-service English teachers, engaged with their instructor in intensive reflection on critical incidents that occurred in phases 2 and 3.

2. For two more recent reviews of Internet-mediated FL education (including intercultural education) see Kern, Ware, and Warschauer (2004) and Thorne and Payne (2005).

3. All data from *Telekorp* examined in this chapter are taken from asynchronous e-mail interactions. Synchronous chat data are also archived in *Telekorp* but for reasons of simplicity the focus here is on e-mail.

4. Borkin and Reinhart explain the pragmatic difference in the following way: "*excuse me* . . . is a formula to remedy a past or immediately forthcoming breach of etiquette or other light infraction of a social rule on the part of the speaker . . . *I'm sorry* . . . is an expression of dismay or regret at the unpleasantness suffered by the speaker and/or the addressee" (1978, p. 61).

5. Fourty-six uses of *Sie* were referential in nature in 2002, while two were metalingual; in 2003 there was one referential use and one meta-lingual use (e.g., an apology for using V in which the word *Sie* was used).

6. Other learners experienced other interventions based on their individual needs as assessed via (contrastive) learner corpus analysis as well as instructor observation.

7. This revelation was motivated by a course reading in which a German exchange student reported his surprise upon learning that his American host family lived in a trailer in northern Florida.

8. In spring 2005, Nina Vyatkina used this methodology in third-semester German courses at *Penn State University*.

References

Abrams, Zsuzsanna. 2003. The Effect of Synchronous and Asynchronous CMC on Oral Performance in German. *The Modern Language Journal* 87(2): 157–167.

Agar, Michael. 1994. *Language Shock: Understanding the Culture of Conversation*. New York: William Morrow.

Allwright, Dick. 2005. From Teaching Points to Learning Opportunities and Beyond. *TESOL Quarterly*, 39: 9–31.

Bardovi-Harlig, Kathleen. 1999. Exploring the Interlanguage of Interlanguage Pragmatics: A Research Agenda for Acquisitional Pragmatics. *Language Learning* 49(4): 677–714.

Barron, Anne. 2003. *Acquisition in Interlanguage Pragmatics*. Amsterdam: Benjamins.

Bauer, Beth, Lynne deBenedette, Gilberte Furstenberg, Sabine Levet, and Shoggy Waryn. 2005. The *Cultura* Project. In *Internet-mediated Intercultural Foreign Language Education*, edited by Julie A. Belz and Steven L. Thorne, 31–62. Boston, MA: Thomson Heinle.

Belz, Julie A. 2003a. From the Special Issue Editor. *Language Learning & Technology* 7(2): 2–5. *http://llt.msu.edu/vol7num2/speced.html*

———. 2003b. Linguistic Perspectives on the Development of Intercultural Competence in Telecollaboration. *Language Learning & Technology* 7(2): 68–117. *http://llt.msu.edu/vol7num2/belz/default.html*

———. 2005a. Telecollaborative Foreign Language Study: A Personal Overview of Praxis and Research. In *Proceedings of the Symposium on Foreign Language Distance Education and Distributed Learning*, edited by David Hiple and Irene Thompson. Honolulu: National Foreign Language Resource Center.

———. 2005b. A Microgenetic Case Study of the Relationship Between Sociopragmatic, Pragmalinguistic, and Grammatical Development in German as a Foreign Language. Manuscript in preparation.

_____. 2005c. Corpus-driven Characterizations of Pronominal *da*-compound Use by Learners and Native Speakers of German. *Die Unterrichtspraxis/Teaching German* 38(1): 43-59.

Belz, Julie A., and Celeste Kinginger. 2003. Discourse Options and the Development of Pragmatic Competence by Classroom Learners of German: The Case of Address Forms. *Language Learning* 53(4): 591-647.

Belz, Julie A., Jonathon Reinhardt, and Emily F. Rine. The Telecollaborative Learner Corpus of English and German (*Telekorp*) and the Issue of Time In Second Language Acquisition Research. Manuscript submitted for publication.

Belz, Julie A., and Nina Vyatkina. 2005. Learner Corpus Analysis and the Development of L2 Pragmatic Competence in Networked Intercultural Language Study: The Case of German Modal Particles. *Canadian Modern Language Review/Revue canadienne des langues vivantes* 62(1): 17-48.

Belz, Julie A., Nina Vyatkina, and Lisa Hundley. 2005. The Telecollaborative Learner Corpus of English and German (*Telekorp*): Applications for Materials Development, Pedagogical Intervention, and Developmental Analyses of SLA. Manuscript submitted for publication.

Biber, Douglas, Susan Conrad, and Randi Reppen. 1998. *Corpus Linguistics: Investigating Structure and Use*. Cambridge, UK: Cambridge University Press.

Biber, Douglas, and Randi Reppen. 1998. Comparing Native and Learner Perspectives on English Grammar: A Study of Complement Clauses. In *Learner English of Computer*, edited by Sylviane Granger, 145-158. New York: Longman.

Blake, Robert, and Eve Zystik. 2003. Who's Helping Whom?: Learner/Heritage Speakers' Networked Discussions in Spanish. *Applied Linguistics* 24(4): 519-544.

Borkin, Ann, and Susan M. Reinhart. 1978. Excuse Me and I'm Sorry. *TESOL Quarterly* 12(1): 57-69.

Brown, Roger, and Albert Gilman. 1960. The Pronouns of Power and Solidarity. In *Style in Language*, edited by Thomas Sebeok, 253-276. Cambridge, MA: M.I.T. Press.

Byram, Michael. 1997. *Teaching and Assessing Intercultural Communicative Competence*. Clevedon, UK: Multilingual Matters.

Byrnes, Heidi. 1986. Interactional Style in German and American Conversations. *Text* 2(1): 189-206.

Byrnes, Heidi, and Stefan Fink. 1987. *Wendepunkt*. Boston, MA: Thomson Heinle.

Chapelle, Carol. 2003. *English Language Learning and Technology: Lectures on Applied Linguistics in the Age of Information and Communication Technology*. Amsterdam: John Benjamins.

Chun, Dorothy. 1994. Using Computer Networking to Facilitate the Acquisition of Interactive Competence. *System: An International Journal of Educational Technology and Applied Linguistics* 22: 17-31.

Cobb, Tom. 2003. Analyzing Late Interlanguage with Learner Corpora: Quebec Replications of Three European Studies. *The Canadian Modern Language Review/La Revue canadienne des langues vivantes* 59(3): 393-423.

Coniam, David. 2004. Concordancing Oneself: Constructing Individual Textual Profiles. *International Journal of Corpus Linguistics* 9(2): 271-298.

Conrad, Susan. 1999. The Importance of Corpus-based Research for Language Teachers. *System: An International Journal of Educational Technology and Applied Linguistics*, 27(1): 1-18.

Delilse, Helga. 1986. Intimacy, Soidarity, and Distance: The Pronouns of Address in German. *Die Unterrichtspraxis/Teaching German* 19(1): 4-15.

Dewaele, Jean-Marc. 2004. *Vous* or *tu* ? Native and Non-Native Speakers of French on a Sociolinguistic Tightrope. *International Review of Applied Linguistics* 42(4): 383-402.

DiDonato, Richard, Monica Clyde, and Jacqueline Vansant. 2004. *Deutsch, na klar! An Introductory German Course*. 4th ed. New York: McGraw-Hill.

Dippmann, Gerda, and Johanna Watzinger-Tharp. 1987. *A Practical Review of German Grammar*. 2nd ed. Upper Saddle River, NJ: Prentice Hall.

Donahue, Frank, and Johanna Watzinger-Tharp. 2000. *Deutsch zusammen: A Communicative Course in German*. 3rd ed. Boston: Pearson Custom Publishing.

Donceva, Kostadinka. 1982. Zum syntaktischen Status des d-Pronominaladverbs als Korrelat. *Deutsch als Fremdsprache* 19(4): 221–224.

Dussias, Paola. 2005. Lexical and Morphological Development in Spanish-American Telecollaboration. In *Internet-mediated Intercultural Foreign Language Education*, edited by Julie A. Belz and Steven L. Thorne, 121–146. Boston: Thomson Heinle.

Fischer, Gerhard. 1998. *E-mail in Foreign Language Teaching: Toward the Creation of Virtual Classrooms*. Tübingen: Stauffenberg Verlag.

Folsom, Marvin. 1979. On the Demise of damit, etc. *Die Unterrichtspraxis/Teaching German* 12(1): 44–49.

Furstenberg, Gilberte, Sabine Levet, Kathryn English, and Katherine Maillet. 2001. Giving a Voice to the Silent Language of Culture: The *Cultura* Project. *Language Learning & Technology* 5(1): 55–102. *http://llt.msu.edu/vol5num1/furstenberg/default.html*

Fussell, Paul. 1983. *Class: A Guide through the American Status System*. New York: Summit Books.

Gee, James. 2005. 2nd ed. *Introduction to Discourse Analysis: Theory and Method*. London: Routledge.

Ghadessy, Mohsen, Alex Henry, and Robert Roseberry, eds. 2001. *Small Corpus Studies and ELT: Theory and Practice*. Amsterdam: Benjamins.

Granger, Sylviane. 1994. Learner Corpus: A Revolution in Applied Linguistics. *English Today* 10(3): 25–29.

———, ed. 1998a. *Learner English on Computer*. London: Longman.

———. 1998b. The Computer Learner Corpus: A Versatile New Source of Data for SLA Research. In *Learner English on Computer*, edited by Sylviane Granger, 3–18. London: Longman.

———. 2002. A Bird's-Eye View of Learner Corpus Research. In *Computer Learner Corpora, Second Language Acquisition, and Foreign Language Teaching*, edited by Sylviane Granger, Joseph Hung, and Stephanie Petch-Tyson, 3–33. Amsterdam: Benjamins.

———. 2003. The International Corpus of Learner English: A New Resource for Foreign Language Learning and Teaching and Second Language Acquisition Research. TESOL Quarterly 37(3): 538–546.

———. To appear. Learner Corpora. In *Corpus Linguistics: An International Handbook*, edited by Anke Ludeling, Merja Kytö, and Anthony McEnery. Berlin: Mouton de Gruyter.

Granger, Sylviane, Estelle Dagneaux, and Fanny Meunier. 2002. *The International Corpus of Learner English: Handbook and CD-ROM*. Louvain-la-Neuve, Belgium: Presses Universitaires de Louvain. *http://www.i6doc.com*

Granger, Sylviane, Joseph Hung, and Stephanie Petch-Tyson, eds. 2002. *Computer Learner Corpora, Second Language Acquisition and Foreign Language Teaching*. Amsterdam: Benjamins.

Granger Sylviane, and Stephanie Petch-Tyson, eds. 2003. *Extending the Scope of Corpus-Based Research: New Applications, New Challenges*. Amsterdam: Rodopi.

Granger, Sylviane, and Christopher Tribble. 1998. Learner Corpus Data in the Foreign Language Classroom: Form-Focused Instruction and Data-Driven Learning. In *Learner English on Computer*, edited by Sylviane Granger, 199–209. New York: Longman.

Halliday, Michael, and Ruqaiya Hasan. 1976. *Cohesion in English*. London: Longman.

Hanna, Barbara, and Julianna de Nooy. 2003. A Funny Thing Happened on the Way to the Forum: Electronic Discussion and Foreign Language Learning. *Language Learning & Technology* 7(1): 71–85. *http://llt.msu.edu/vol7num1/hanna/default.html*

Holobow, Naomi, Fred Genesee, and Wallace Lambert. 1991. The Effectiveness of a Foreign Language Immersion Program for Children from Different Ethnic and Social Class Backgrounds: Report 2. *Applied Psycholinguistics* 12(2): 179–198.

Holobow, Naomi, Fred Genesee, Wallace Lambert, Joseph Gastright, and Myriam Met. 1987. Effectiveness of Partial French Immersion for Children from Different Social Class and Ethnic Backgrounds. *Applied Psycholinguistics* 8(2): 137-152.

Johns, Tim. 2002. Data-Driven Learning: The Perpetual Challenge. In *Teaching and Learning by Doing Corpus Analysis. Proceedings of the Fourth International Conference of Teaching and Language Corpora*, edited by Bernhard Ketterman and Georg Marko, 107-117. Amsterdam: Rodopi.

Johns, Tim, and Philip King, eds. 1991. Classroom Concordancing. *English Language Research Journal* 4. Birmingham: University of Birmingham.

Kallmeyer, W. 1972. Verweisung im Text. *Der Deutschunterricht* 24(4): 29-42.

Kasper, Gabriele. 1985. Repair in Foreign Language Teaching. *Studies in Second Language Acquisition* 7: 200-215.

———. 2001. Classroom Research On Interlanguage Pragmatics. In *Pragmatics in Language Teaching*, edited by Kenneth Rose and Gabriele Kasper, 33-60. Cambridge: Cambridge University Press.

Kasper, Gabriele, and Kenneth Rose. Introduction. In *Pragmatics in Language Teaching*, edited by Kenneth Rose and Gabriele Kasper, 1-9. Cambridge: Cambridge University Press.

Kern, Richard. 1995. Restructuring Classroom Interaction with Networked Computers: Effects on Quantity and Characteristics of Language Production. *The Modern Language Journal* 79(4): 457-476.

———. 1998. Technology, Social Interaction, and FL Literacy. In *New Ways of Learning and Teaching: Focus on Technology and Foreign Language Education*, edited by Judith Muyskens, 57-92. Boston, MA: Thomson Heinle.

Kern, Richard, Paige Ware, and Mark Warschauer. 2004. Crossing Frontiers: New Directions in Online Pedagogy and Research. *Annual Review of Applied Linguistics* 24(1): 243-260.

Kinginger, Celeste. 2000. Learning the Pragmatics of Solidarity in the Networked Foreign Language Classroom. In *Second and Foreign Language Learning through Classroom Interaction*, edited by Joan Kelly Hall, 23-46. Mahwah, NJ: Erlbaum.

———. 2004. Communicative Foreign Language Teaching through Telecollaboration. In *New Insights into Foreign Language Learning and Teaching*, edited by Oliver St. John, Kees van Esch, and Eus Schalkwijk, 101-113. Frankfurt: Peter Lang.

Kinginger, Celeste, and Julie A. Belz. 2005. Socio-cultural Perspectives on Pragmatic Development in Foreign Language Learning: Microgenetic and Ontogenetic Case Studies from Telecollaboration and Study Abroad. *Intercultural Pragmatics* 2(4): 369-422.

Kinginger, Celeste, Alison Gourvés-Hayward, and Vanessa Simpson. 1999. A Tele-Collaborative Course on French-American Intercultural Communication. *The French Review* 72(5): 853-866.

Kubota, Ryuko. 2003. New Approaches to Gender, Class, and Race in Second Language Writing. *Journal of Second Language Writing* 12(1): 31-47.

Kutz, Daniel, and Susan C. Herring. 2005. Micro-Longitudinal Analysis of Web News Updates. *Proceedings of the Thirty-Eighth Hawai'i International Conference on System Sciences (HICSS-38)*. Los Alamitos: IEEE Press. *http://ella.slis.indiana.edu/ ~herring/news.pdf*

Lantolf, James P., and Matt Poehner. 2004. Dynamic Assessment of L2 Development: Bringing the Past into the Future. *Journal of Applied Linguistics* 1(1): 49-74.

Lee, Lina. 2004. Learners' Perspectives on Networked Collaborative Interaction with Native Speakers of Spanish in the U.S. *Language Learning & Technology* 8(1): 83-100.

———. 2005. Networked Collaborative Interaction: A Study of Native and Nonnative Speakers' Feedback and Responses. In *Internet-mediated Intercultural Foreign Language Education,* edited by Julie A. Belz and Steven L. Thorne, 147-176. Boston, MA: Thomson Heinle.

Lin, Angel. 2000. Lively Children Trapped in an Island of Disadvantage: Verbal Play of Cantonese Working-Class Schoolboys in Hong Kong. *International Journal of the Sociology of Language* 143: 63-83.

Lubrano, Alfred. 2004. *Limbo: Blue-Collar Roots, White-Collar Dreams.* Hoboken, New Jersey: John Wiley.

McCarthy, Michael J. 2004. Using a Corpus in Language Teaching. CALPER Professional Development Document CPDD 0410. The Pennsylvania State University, The Center for Advanced Language Proficiency Education and Research. *http://calper.la.psu.edu/publications.php*

Meraner, Rudolf. 1988. Satzverknüpfung durch Pronomen. Die Bedeutung des Pronomens im Text. *Der Deutschunterricht* 40(6): 69-83.

Moeller, Jack, Winnifred Adolph, Barbara Mabee, and Simone Berger. 2002. *Kaleidoskop: Kultur, Literatur und Grammatik.* 6th ed. Boston, MA: Houghton Mifflin.

Möllering, Martina. 2001. Teaching German Modal Particles: A Corpus-Based Approach. *Language Learning & Technology* 5(3): 130-151. *http://llt.msu.edu/vol5num3/mollering/default.html*

Möllering, Martina, and David Nunan. 1995. Pragmatics in Interlanguage: German Modal Particles. *Applied Language Learning* 6(1-2): 41-64.

Mühlhäuser, Peter, and Rom Harré. 1990. *Pronouns and People: The Linguistic Construction of Social and Personal Identity.* Cambridge: Blackwell.

Müller-Hartmann, Andreas. 2005. Learning How to Teach Intercultural Communicative Competence via Telecollaboration: A Model for Language Teacher Education. In *Internet-mediated Foreign Language Education*, edited by Julie A. Belz and Steven L. Thorne, 63-84. Boston, MA: Thomson Heinle.

Nesselhauf, Nadja. 2004. Learner Corpora and their Potential for Language Teaching. In *How to Use Corpora in Language Teaching*, edited by John Sinclair, 125-152. Amsterdam: John Benjamins.

———. To appear. Corpora and Language Teaching: What Learner Corpora Have to Offer. In *Linguistics, Language Learning, and Language Teaching*, edited by D. Allerton, C. Tschichold, and J. Weiser. Basel: Schwabe.

Norris, John. 2001. The Use of Address Terms on the German Speaking Test. In *Pragmatics in Language Teaching*, edited by Kenneth Rose and Gabriele Kasper, 248-282. Cambridge: Cambridge University Press.

Nystrand, Martin, Adam Gamoran, Robert Kachur, and Catherine Prendergast. 1997. *Opening Dialogue: Understanding the Dynamics of Language and Learning in the English Classroom.* New York: Teachers College Press.

O'Dowd, Robert. 2003. Understanding the "Other Side": Intercultural Learning in a Spanish-English E-mail Exchange. *Language Learning & Technology* 7(2): 118-144. *http://llt.msu.edu/vol7num2/odowd/default.html*

O'Dowd, Robert, and Karin Eberbach. 2004. Guides on the Side? Tasks and Challenges for Teachers in Telecollaborative Projects. *ReCALL* 16(1): 129-143.

Ortega, Lourdes, and Gina Iberri-Shea. 2005. Longitudinal Research in Second Language Acquisition: Recent Trends and Future Directions. *Annual Review of Applied Linguistics* 25: 26-45.

Pellettieri, Jill. 2000. Negotiation in Cyberspace: The Role of Chatting in the Development of Grammatical Competence. In *Network-Based Language Teaching: Concepts and Practice,* edited by Mark Warschauer and Richard Kern, 59-86. Cambridge: Cambridge University Press.

Poehner, Matt, and James P. Lantolf. 2003. Dynamic Assessment of L2 development: Bringing the Past into the Future. *CALPER Working Papers Series, No. 1.* The Pennsylvania State University, Center for Advanced Language Proficiency, Education and Research. *http://calper.la.psu.edu/publications.php*

Ragan, Peter. 2001. Classroom Use of a Systemic Functional Small Learner Corpus. In *Small Corpus Studies and ELT,* edited by Mohsen Ghadessy, Alex Henry, and Robert Roseberry, 207-236. Amsterdam: Benjamins.

Richter, Hans-Peter. 2001. *Damals war es Friedrich.* [Then it was Frederick.] 46th ed. München: dtv.

Schmidt, Richard. 1993. Consciousness, Learning, and Interlanguage Pragmatics. In *Interlanguage Pragmatics,* edited by Gabriele Kasper and Shoshana Blum-Kulka, 21–42. Oxford: Oxford University Press.

Scott, Mike. 2001. Comparing Corpora and Identifying Key Words, Collocations, and Frequency Distributions through the *WordSmith Tools* Suite of Computer Programs. In *Small Corpus Studies and ELT,* edited by Mohsen Ghadessy, Alex Henry, and Robert Roseberry, 47–67. Amsterdam: John Benjamins.

Seidlhofer, Barbara. 2002. Pedagogy and Local Learner Corpora. In *Computer Learner Corpora, Second Language Acquisition, and Foreign Language Teaching,* edited by Sylviane Granger, Joseph Hung, and Stephanie Petch-Tyson, 213–234. Amsterdam: John Benjamins.

Smith, Bryan. 2003. Computer-Mediated Negotiated Interaction: An Expanded Model. *The Modern Language Journal* 87: 38–58.

———. 2005. The Relationship Between Negotiated Interaction, Learner Uptake, and Lexical Acquisition in Task-Based Computer-Mediated Communication. *TESOL Quarterly* 39(1): 33–58.

Sotillo, Susanna. 2000. Discourse Functions and Syntactic Complexity in Synchronous and Asynchronous Communication. *Language Learning & Technology* 4(1): 82–119. *http://llt.msu.edu/vol4num1/sotillo/default.html*

Starke, Gunter. 1982. Weiterführende Nebensätze, eingeleitet mit Pronominaladverbien. *Deutsch als Fremdsprache* 19(4): 215–220.

Stemmer, Brigitte. 1981. Kohäsion im gesprochenen Diskurs Deutscher Lerner des Englischen. *Manuskripte zur Sprachlehrforschung* 18: 1–203.

Terrell, Tracy, Edwin Tschirner, and Brigitte Nikolai. 2002. *Kontakte: A Communicative Approach.* 4th ed. New York: McGraw-Hill.

Thomaneck, Jürgen. 1980. A Contrastive Sociolinguistic Analysis of Students of German as a Foreign Language. *International Review of Applied Linguistics in Language Teaching* 18(2): 135–138.

Thorne, Steven L. 2003. Artifacts and Cultures-of-Use in Intercultural Communication. *Language Learning & Technology* 7(2): 38–67. *http://llt.msu.edu/vol7num2/thorne/default.html*

Thorne, Steven L., and J. Scott Payne. 2005. Evolutionary Trajectories, Internet-Mediated Expression, and Language Education. *CALICO Journal* 22(3): 371–397.

Turneaure, Brigitte. 1987. *Der treffende Ausdruck: Texte, Themen, Übungen.* New York: W. W. Norton & Company.

Warschauer, Mark, ed. 1996. *Telecollaboration in Foreign Language Learning.* Honolulu: Second Language Teaching and Curriculum Center.

Wikipedia, The Free Encyclopedia. http://en.wikipedia.org/wiki/Blended_learning

Acknowledgments

This research is supported by a United States Department of Education International Studies and Research Grant (CFDA No.: 84.017A). I would like to thank Heidi Byrnes and other anonymous referees for their careful review of an earlier draft of this chapter. Their detailed commentary provided much food for thought and resulted in a thorough revision of this report; any remaining short-comings are mine alone. I would also like to express my gratitude to the focal learner, Lori, for her willingness to participate in this project and for her inspiring performance in the classroom.

Appendix 1

A Comparison of *da*-Compound Use by Native Speakers and Learners of German

da-compound	Raw Frequencies		Per 100,000 Words	
	Native Speakers	Learners	Native Speakers	Learners
dazu	26	4	39	9
damit	17	5	26	11 (5)
darüber	15	13	23	28 (1)
dafür	13	3	20	7
davon	12	11	18	24 (2)
dabei	9	2	14	4
darauf	9	3	14	7
daran	8	6	12	13 (3)
danach	6	6	9	13 (3)
darum	4	2	6	4
davor	3	0	5	0
dagegen	2	0	3	0
darin	2	4	3	9
dadurch	1	1	2	2
daraus	0	1	0	2
daneben	0	0	0	0
darunter	0	0	0	0
dazwischen	0	0	0	0
Total	127	61	191	132

Appendix 2

Structural Comparison of Top Five *da*-Compounds for Native Speakers and Learners

Structure	Raw Frequencies/ Percentage of the Time	
	Native Speakers	Learners
Anaphoric reference to a nominal phrase	15/76 = 20%	9/36 = 25%
Anaphoric reference to a prepositional phrase	5/76 = 6%	0/36 = 0%
Reference to a larger unit or concept	47/76 = 62%	9/36 = 25%
Anaphoric	31/76 = 41%	6/36 = 17%
Cataphoric	16/76 = 21%	3/36 = 8%
Verb-and-preposition combination	9/76 = 12%	17/36 = 47%
Unclear referent	0/76 = 0%	1/36 = 3%

Appendix 3

Frequencies of Individual Learners' Uses of Specific *da*-Compounds

Learner Name	Raw Frequencies of Individual *da*-Compounds	Raw Totals
Lisbeth	1 dadurch; 1 darum; 2 danach; 1 daran; 2 dabei; 5 davon; 1 damit; 3 dazu	16
Kendra	1 darauf; 2 davon; 2 damit; 1 dazu	6
Seamus	1 daraus; 1 darin; 1 danach; 2 daran; 2 davon; 1 damit	8
Grace	1 darin; 1 darum; 2 danach; 1 daran; 1 dafür; 4 darüber; 2 damit	12
Jenna	2 daran; 1 darauf; 1 dafür; 5 darüber; 2 davon	11
Lori	1 darin; 1 dafür; 3 darüber	5
Linda	1 darauf; 2 darüber	3
Jessie	1 darin	1
Jason, Jacob, Damon	None	0
Total		62

Epilogue
A Critical Look at Technologies and Ideologies in Internet-mediated Intercultural Foreign Language Education

Robert Train

Abstract

This chapter provides a critical perspective on the Internet-mediated intercultural projects presented in this volume. Internet-mediated intercultural foreign language education (a.k.a. telecollaboration) is presented as a site of critical intercultural discourse shaped and mediated by the technologies, ideologies, and practices that inform the complex ecology of foreign language education in general. The focus on the global term "education" is intended to conceptualize the ecological character of the endeavor, such that foreign language learning and second language acquisition are not viewed as separate from the teaching of foreign languages (i.e., instruction, pedagogy, curriculum) or from issues of sociocultural identity, educational policy, and teacher education. A critical reflexivity is outlined with special attention to the educational project of critical awareness of language, culture, community, and identity through intercultural interaction with peers. Some key ideologies of foreign language education are examined in socio-historical context with respect to the technologies and ideologies of standardization that have constructed the Native Standard Language as the dominant model for language, with its hegemonic implications for notions of culture, identity, and community in local, national, and global contexts. Ideologies of learner identity grounded in the concept of (Non)Native Speaker are critically discussed as contested sites of standardized and standardizing competence and language use (e.g., "communication," "negotiation," "interaction," and "error"). The possibilities for new intercultural conceptions of learner and teacher identity, expertise, and agency emerging in the telecollaborative practices described in this volume are considered.

Introduction

The chapters in this volume attest to the tantalizing possibilities for teaching, learning, and research afforded by the emerging practices of Internet-mediated intercultural foreign language education (ICFLE). These "telecollaborative" projects and the intercultural perspectives afforded by them display a refreshing sense of purpose and enthusiasm about what foreign language education (FLE) is, and perhaps even more important, an orientation toward what the multifaceted experience of teaching and learning of language and culture can be given the increasing availability of digital technologies. In its commitment to bringing added depth of understanding and meaning to the experience of foreign language (FL) learning, the body of work presented in this volume begins with the basic concern for moving beyond the limits of current practice in FLE.

Conscious of the pedagogical and research implications of ICFLE, these educators and researchers articulate learning and pedagogical goals that seek to expand the prevalent notions of cultural and linguistic knowledge, competence, and development. Language is conceptualized within an intercultural context that surpasses the traditional focus on micro-linguistic elements (e.g., grammar and vocabulary) to include more discourse-level perspectives, such as those gained through the analysis of learner corpora. The canonical notion of communication in FL pedagogy is reframed as a more meaningful, authentic, and problematic interaction between learners and native speakers (NSs). The role of culture is also re-conceptualized in order to break down monolithic notions and avoid reductionist approaches that foster cultural stereotypes (see Bauer *et al.*, this volume). This requires knowledge, skills, and sensitivities not generally included or available in traditional FL classroom settings, such as ethnographical techniques and perspectives and the ability to engage in culturally appropriate conversational styles in real time.

Taken together in their diverse approaches, these telecollaborative projects portray teaching and learning as an ongoing and dynamic process of reflecting and acting on what we do as FL teachers and learners—a sort of reflective and meta-reflective practice grounded in intercultural and meta-linguistic awareness. Working from the concept of intercultural competence, learners and teachers are guided toward developing the skills of discovery, interpreting, relating, and understanding that can lead to critical cultural awareness (Byram 1997; Müller-Hartmann, this volume) by which learners and teacher-learners begin to realize and relativize the cultural-situatedness and constructedness of their own way of seeing the world and the worldviews of others. These projects, as fundamentally intercultural, point us toward enlarging our views of what constitutes communities of practice (Wenger 1998) outside and on the margins of the traditional classroom. The evidence highlights the complex ecologies of these academic and professional communities of learners and teachers that are built on the vital tension between collaboration, learner autonomy, and intercultural conflict. Taking a critical stance toward national culture and stereotypical national identities, the educator-researchers of these chapters state their commitment to fostering more empowering identities for learners and teachers as "intercultural speakers" (Kramsch 1998) who negotiate over the course of a lifetime within and between the complex linguistic, sociocultural, and affective spaces of what Agar (1994) has called "languaculture" where "language" and "culture" are inseparable (see Belz and Thorne, this volume; Thorne, this volume).

As this volume amply demonstrates, telecollaboration as long-distance, intercultural class-to-class collaboration within academic settings brings Internet and videoconferencing technologies into FLE in ways that explore the emergent semiotic potentialities of multimedia, synchronous, and asynchronous modalities of communication. In this dynamic environment, or "ecology," both students and teachers engage in complex meaning-making processes that are not readily available in conventional classroom contexts with the largely standardized array of pedagogical materials and practices such as standardized textbooks. While navigating the margins of pedagogies and technologies, these telecollaborative endeavors are definitely not lost in cyberspace; instead, they are firmly anchored in the institutional priorities of university FLE with its concern for creating academic contexts for a more internationalized and intercultural educational experience for students. However, this volume also attests to a growing body of research (Belz 2005; Kramsch and Thorne 2002; Ware 2005; Ware and Kramsch 2005) pointing to a new set of educational demands, tensions, and concerns that ICFLE places on learners, teachers, and university language departments (see Schneider and von der Emde, this volume).

From a critical perspective, the crux of the issue is twofold. On the one hand, ICFLE is poised to provide students, teachers, program coordinators, and researchers with a space in which to "re-envision" (Ware and Kramsch 2005, p. 191) existing theories and practices of FLE. A central component of this sort of rethinking involves a critical awareness of what we do and how we conceptualize what we do in terms of a more critical and "responsive" pedagogy (Bowers and Flinders 1990). In such a pedagogy, we are aware and capable of responding in educationally constructive ways to the ecology of FLE with its complex relationships between classroom practices and the larger context of living in an increasingly global and conflicted post-9/11 world. In this sense, one must consider the ways in which ICFLE, as a newly constituted reflexive and self-reflexive field of action, transcends established boundaries to offer new possibilities, or "affordances," for learning, teaching, and research. On the other hand, it may well be the case that the intersection of ideologies and technologies that has shaped FLE to the present does not best serve the goals of a more intercultural FLE in new digital and global environments. From this standpoint, the emerging ICFLE is also in need of a critical discourse perspective that will examine some of its institutionalized ideologies of language, identity, and community, thus opening the way to allow researchers and educators to fulfill the promise of ICFLE. Therefore, one must inquire as to what extent these new telecollaborative approaches, grounded in the institution of FLE, reproduce the Native Standard Language (Train 2003), a complex constellation of hegemonic ideologies of language, (non)standardness, and (non)nativeness that have come to define the socio-historically and discursively constructed "realities" of language, culture, community, language use, and speaker identity inside and outside the classroom through ongoing processes of standardization. In the following sections, I move this critical awareness project forward by contextualizing telecollaborative pedagogies and technologies with respect to some of the ideologies surrounding the Native Standard Language (NSL) that inform FLE. These include ideologies of learner and teacher identity grounded in the concept of the NS and ideologies of language use surrounding communication and competence that shape the dominant notions of interaction in FLE.

In Search of the Critical and the Intercultural in Foreign Language Education

In order to examine the ideologies and technologies surrounding ICFLE, it will be necessary to find a critical place from which to speak because, as Reagan and Osborn have noted, the underlying ideological and cultural biases of FLE "remain unexamined and unaddressed" (2002, p. 8). While I agree that there is a relative lack of self-reflection with respect to the ideologies *qua* ideology that shape FLE (see, however, Ortega 1999; Pavlenko 2003; Train 2003; Valdés *et al.* 2003), there does exist a small but significant body of research that provides critical insights into the practices and theories prevalent in FLE (e.g., Kramsch 1987; Kramsch 1993). However, such critical perspectives have not been adequately incorporated into the lives of FL educators, students, and departments. With this situation in mind, I attempt to paint in rather broad brushstrokes one possible avenue to a critical understanding of ideology as a largely under-conceptualized component of FLE.

The general orientation that guides my discussion is that of *applied linguistics*, an interdisciplinary field that mediates between the theory and the practice of language acquisition, socialization, and use (Kramsch 2000). As a place of interdisciplinary reflection and investigation, applied linguistics offers a fittingly critical perspective on those very practices that are at the heart of ICFLE as outlined in this volume. An explicitly *critical* applied linguistics recognizes the need to "retain a constant skepticism, a constant questioning of the givens" (Pennycook 2001, p. 8) of what we do as researchers and practitioners, even with respect to such time-honored concepts as "communication" and "grammatical accuracy" (see Firth and Wagner 1997). A critical view also foregrounds the notions of discourse as social practice, which offer FL learners, educators, and researchers insights into telecollaboration as a site of *critical intercultural discourse* shaped and mediated by the technologies, ideologies, and practices that inform the complex ecology of FLE. The educational project proposed by proponents of critical discourse views of language involves various versions of critical language awareness (Fairclough 1992, 2001). According to Train (2003), a critical awareness of language-as-discourse involves

- an understanding of oneself as a speaker and learner of both the native language (L1) and the second or foreign language (L2);
- exploration of and engagement with individual and collective practices and ideologies (beliefs, attitudes, biases, prejudices) surrounding language broadly;
- an appreciation of variation as inherent in language, culture, and learning;
- the questioning of dominant linguistic and cultural knowledge and discourse (e.g., the NSL) and how they are constructed and represented;
- critical reflection on the tension and interplay that exist in language education between creative individual uses of language and conformity to institutionalized norms; and
- a transformative and empowering awareness of the sociocultural and discursive construction of speakers' identities and "realities" in a multilingual and multicultural world.

Recognizing that education should foster reflective stances toward language is consistent with a reflective approach to second and FL teaching as "one in which teachers and student teachers collect data about teaching, examine their attitudes, beliefs, assumptions, and teaching practices, and use the information obtained as a basis for critical reflection about teaching" (Richards and Lockhart 1994, p. 1). Reflective approaches also recognize the need for *critical* language teaching awareness (Train 2003, pp. 20–26; see also Gebhard and Oprandy 1999; van Lier 1996) in order to

- create an institutional space in which to explore and cultivate empowering professional identities for educators grounded in their expertise as bilingual and intercultural speakers that transcend the "native," "near-native," and "non-native" categories (Kramsch 1998; Rampton 1990);
- develop informed and reflective stances toward FLE as a socio-historically and discursively constructed set of practices; and
- empower educators to critically evaluate, question, and rethink the dominant policies, practices, and ideologies that have shaped FLE (e.g., correctness, accuracy, appropriateness, L2 exclusivity, communication, standards).

In addition, critical awareness of discourse must be expanded to embrace what Byram (1997, p. 34) calls *critical cultural awareness*—particularly in the context of telecollaboration where discourse is necessarily intercultural, as the chapters in the present volume amply demonstrate. Central to such an educational framework is a complex reflexivity between the learner, socialized into multiple discourses, ideologies, and practices associated with L1 culture (and more, in the case of multilingual learners), and the L2 speakers with their own complex array of cultural practices and experiences. This awareness of the positioning of self and other is also critical in its potential to transform the learner because the "relativisation of one's own and valuing of others' meanings, beliefs and behaviours does not happen without a reflective and analytical challenge to the ways in which they have been formed and the complex of social forces within which they are experienced" (Byram 1997, p. 35).

Telecollaboration: Discourse, Practice, and Ecology

For educators and researchers alike, telecollaboration is a particular type of learning environment that presents a number of challenges, not the least of which centers on the fundamental diversity of cultural backgrounds and communicative expectations that are involved in intercultural exchanges (Kern, Ware, and Warschauer 2004). A point of departure for the present discussion involves examining and rethinking what constitutes "language" and "the language" of FLE in the context of telecollaborative learning environments with their undeniable diversity and broader discursive contexts. In this respect, the notion of "discourse" is basic to critical approaches to language, culture, and identity (Foucault 1971; Gee 1996, 2005; Blommaert 2005) in which the traditional components (i.e., lexicon, syntax, morphology, phonology) and uses of language as well as speaker identities can no longer be understood in isolation from the diverse, multiple and complex sociocultural, political, and historical contexts that have constituted and been constituted through discourse. This discourse orientation recognizes that language cannot or should not be reduced to a set of formal and universal elements such as the "words and rules" that have been popularized as "the ingredients of language" (Pinker 1999).

Language-as-discourse posits a basic inseparability of culture and language. Drawing significantly from anthropological tradition, diverse interdisciplinary approaches agree that language is nothing if not cultural (see Agar 1994; Harris 1998; Kramsch 1998). This basic language-culture connection in discourse has been operationalized via interdisciplinary notions of "practice" (Bourdieu 2000; de Certeau 1984) and articulated variously in terms of "language as social practice" (Eckert 2000) and "language as cultural practice"(Schecter and Bayley 2002), with a focus on sociolinguistic and ethnographic methodologies that explore the multiple experiences of speakers as human being. The blending of the social and the cultural into the "sociocultural" has been appropriated by more socio-cognitively oriented, but no less interdisciplinary, approaches to language that treat discursive practices, particularly in Vygotskian perspective, as human activity with significant implications for language learning (Wertsch 1991). For example, ethnographic work on language and literacy has broadened the notions of content and culture by exploring classroom and household settings as "culturally mediated activity systems" that, in theoretical terms, shift attention to the complex "processes of how people live culturally" and move away from notions of culture that "assume that all members of a particular group share a normative, bounded, and integrated view of their own culture" (Moll 2000, p. 267).[1] This search for increasingly complex perspectives on culturality or socioculturality is central to an understanding of telecollaboration as intercultural discourse (Kiesling and Paulston 2005; Scollon and Scollon 2001) through which learners and teachers must confront the simplifying and standardizing notions of "the language" and "the culture" that are prevalent in FLE and in encounters between learners and NSs of the target language.

In considering telecollaboration in terms of intercultural discourse, the ecology metaphor is useful in rethinking language as fundamentally context-bound discourse and practice. In the earliest ecological accounts of language, "language ecology" is defined as "the study of interactions between any given language and its environment" (Haugen 1972, p. 325). More recent eco-linguistic views have expanded the idea of the interconnectedness of language with the world to a more discourse-oriented perspective on the complex role of language in constructing context, such that language both constructs the world and is constructed by it (e.g., Mühlhäusler 2003, p. 2).

Ecological views of language raise a set of crucial epistemological issues involving the social, cultural, and linguistic construction of reality (Berger and Luckmann 1989; Grace 1989). In short, discourse always poses the principle of relativity, most famously expressed in linguistic terms by Whorf's insight that our experiential world is a function of the human perceptual interface with both the external and internal environment of the human body (Lee 1996, p. 27). That is, our experience (as we subjectively apprehend it through our "cultural eyes") shapes and is shaped by our ways of talking and thinking about it.

Ecological perspectives (Barron, Bruce, and Nunan 2002; Kramsch 2002; Leather and van Dam 2002; van Lier 2004) have been useful in moving beyond purely cognitive views of learning (i.e., that learning takes place solely in the learner's mind and brain) to more semiotic views. In sum, learning is not separable from the learner's experience as a human being in the world. Moreover, learning requires the learner to be part of a larger context that makes learning possible and meaningful. If this is so for learning in general, it is unavoidably the case for intercultural FL learning, where each learner negotiates the complex cultures and identities that are part of being a speaker-reader-writer of different languages.

Critical Reflexivity

In addition to ecology and relativity, understanding telecollaboration as a site of intercultural discourse requires language educators, students, and researchers to address the important yet often neglected fact that language is fundamentally *reflexive* (Bauman and Briggs 2003; Lucy 1993; Taylor 2000). Reflexivity involves a set of meta-discursive practices that allow us, in Lucy's terms, "to use language to communicate about the activity of using language" (1993, p. 9). Although imaginings of language and culture are found in all languacultures, the reflexive properties of language are typically represented in mainstream linguistics as supplemental and inessential, as if language were somehow independent of the "reflexive discourse" that we use to talk about language and its everyday uses (Taylor 2000). This bias against explicitly addressing reflexivity is evident in FLE and SLA research (heavily influenced by the nativist assumptions of Chomskyan linguistics) in which language is assumed to be somehow "naturally" acquired. But from a discourse perspective it is clear that language acquisition is fundamentally social. As Taylor (1997) has argued, reflexivity is an important dimension of language and therefore should be explicitly incorporated into the study of language by linguists and, I would add, by language teachers and learners:

> It is by means of contextually embedded instances of normative meta-discourse—rather than by "unspoken agreements" or "tacit conventions"—that we establish language use as a normative form of behavior and impose and negotiate and contest the differential values and constraints that "we" in "our culture" place on linguistic phenomena. (Taylor 1997, p. 13)

In this sense, ICFLE and FLE in general must struggle against the ideological purging of explicit reflexivity from language as an object of study that is mirrored in FL textbooks and curricula that generally focus on linguistic form and "communication" with scant attention given to how speakers' discourse is constructed and reflected in language (see Belz, this volume). Telecollaboration in many respects pushes the notion of reflexivity in language to a new level of urgency as learners engage in complex intercultural interaction with speakers and their discourse norms (Belz and Kinginger 2003) in ways that are not generally possible in traditional FL classrooms.

While language is fundamentally reflective, it is the ways in which and to what ends humans reflect on language that is at stake. This elimination of messy reflexivity from the study of language has a long history that coincides with the formation of modern forms of consciousness and social organization, and with linguistic standardization. Already evident in Locke's work in 17th-century England, the action of abstracting and "purifying" language from society involved "a complex process of defining language in such a way that its social embeddedness could be construed as peripheral, pathological, and suppressible at the same time that a purified core could be elevated to the status of the privileged mode of generating knowledge" (Bauman and Briggs 2003, p. 36). Increasingly, critical strands of research have fostered awareness of the ideological presuppositions of linguistic and popular notions of language, thus prompting language professionals to begin examining their own meta-linguistic practices in relation to ideologies of language (Joseph and Taylor 1990). In telecollaborative FL instruction, learners and teachers must confront the social embeddedness of language practices, both their own and those of their native-speaker keypals, in the context of intercultural communication.

Ideology and Language Ideology

There are perhaps few terms that have had a more contentious history than *ideology*, which most often becomes reduced to a synonym for "false beliefs." The term "ideology" is used routinely in public discourse to discredit the beliefs of one's adversaries and to construct a set of oppositional positions between "us" and "them." However, the binary opposition of ideology to reality or truth does not go very far toward explaining how or why people think and act in certain ways—a tenet of ICFLE.

A more critical and ecological view conceptualizes the notion of "ideology" as both constitutive and reflective of a given socially constructed reality. This crucial conceptual and methodological issue in theorizing language and ideology can be expressed in the following terms: while ideology left unexamined and unquestioned can mask the sociocultural and historical contingency of "reality," the examination of ideology through a critical lens is powerfully revelatory of this same constructed view of the world (Hasan 1996). In this sense, ideologies are systems of belief and representation that both shape and are shaped by individual and collective ways of acting, interacting, knowing, evaluating, imagining, and being in the world. Ideologies are, in effect, *validity constructs* insofar as they make claims for a certain "reality" of the physical, social, symbolic, and affective world. As a validity construct, ideology is basic to the construction of the authority, relevance, and legitimacy of a given view of reality.

In the last several decades, a multidisciplinary view of *standard language* as an ideology has emerged (Lodge 1993; Lippi-Green 1997; Milroy and Milroy 1999; Silverstein 1996). Speakers of standard languages can be said to live in "standard language cultures" in which certain languages are believed to exist in standardized forms (Milroy 2001, p. 530). From the discourse perspective that I have outlined, the standard language provides a powerful, if not hegemonic, "normative metadiscourse" (Taylor 1997) that comments on the perceived reality of language in society by defining what counts as a/"the" language and profoundly shapes the discursive practices surrounding that constructed idea of language and speakers in a given context. A considerable body of research has also shown the standard language idea as being constructed by means of an ongoing sociopolitical, socio-cultural, and sociolinguistic process of *standardization* involving the codification and institutionalization of the dominant linguistic and cultural norms of privileged speakers in a given context (see Crowley 2003; Haugen 1966; Heath 1980; Joseph 1987; Lodge 1993; Milroy and Milroy 1999; Milroy 2001; Silverstein 1996).

In a effort to relate language ideology research to the concerns of FL educators and particularly those interested in telecollaboration, I explore the concept of the NSL (Train 2003) as a complex constellation of ideologies involving notions of language, (non)standardness, and (non)nativeness that have come to define the socio-historically and discursively constructed "realities" of language, culture, community, language use, and speaker identity inside and outside the classroom. From the standpoint of FLE, the study of language ideology in general and the NSL in particular highlights several important and interrelated issues. First, language is more than "language" in the narrowly construed structural account typical of mainstream Chomskyan linguistics. To recognize that ideology is part and parcel of language is to also acknowledge that language and culture are fundamentally inseparable. From there, it is possible to perceive the problematic relationship between what is thought to be "the language" and the complex language-culture practices as they can be observed in the variety and diversity of contexts of situation (Malinowski 1923) such as telecollaborative instruction. Second, language ideologies have both symbolic value and practical consequences for learner and teacher engagement and/or non-engagement in certain practices. Third, the constellation of attitudes and practices surrounding language that constitute language ideology are not isolated from other ideologies such as those concerning learning, teaching, technology, identity, culture, and community. Perhaps the most difficult and threatening point for educators, learners, and researchers is recognizing that language is "always and everywhere ideological" (Gee 1990, p. 104). Given the ubiquity of language in the lives of human beings, any account or description of language is always about more than "language" in a formal sense.

Telecollaboration, Native Standard Language, and Standardization

Standardization is the process of language-making by which elite and literate norms have come to define over time what constitutes "the language" of the empire, the nation, its citizens or subjects, and its schools. The standardization process confers privileged native-speakership on the users of the standard language. The standard language comes to be nativized as the putative native language of the educated members of society and becomes universalized and essentialized as the hegemonic "unitary language" (Crowley 2003; Gramsci 1975) of the larger national and/or international community of speakers. In the case of the most widely used of the European world ex-colonial languages, e.g., English, French, and Spanish, the discourse practices of a geographically and socially situated group (e.g., the royal court) in Castile or Ile-de-France or London were codified (i.e., inscribed in grammars and dictionaries), thus forming the basis of the universalized language of the kingdom and, later, the Empire. More recently, the polycentric standardization (Stewart 1968) of post-colonial prestige norms throughout the world has come to define "the Spanish language" or "the English language" with respect to a constellation of standard language practices attached to national and international identities linked together by a notion of global *Hispanidad*, *Francophonie*, or *World English* (Crowley 2003; Leith 1983; Lodge 1993; Mar-Molinero 1997; Watts and Trudgill 2002).

Telecollaboration and the Nation

An important point for telecollaborative pedagogies emerges quite clearly from the research on standardization: the practices attached to standard language constructs are very much tied to the imagining of human communities and identities around the concept of the *nation-state* (Anderson 1991). In early studies, the NSL construct was framed somewhat uncritically as being instrumental in overcoming the "problem" of linguistic diversity by creating "contrastive self-identification" (Fishman 1972) at the individual and societal levels between speakers of different languages within and between national borders. A critical discourse perspective, in contrast, foregrounds the ways in which standardization is instrumental in the discursive construction of the national identities (Wodak *et al.* 1999) that constitute and support the ideologies and technologies undergirding national communities, national languages, national literatures, and national cultures. From a critical perspective, however, the national unity embodied in standard languages cannot be disassociated from the troubling phenomena of ethnocentrism, xenophobia, racism, and purism (Bonfiglio 2002). In post-modern critical terms, the dynamic of "othering" and "selfing" has been problematized as an ideology of essentialism that is itself intertwined with the construction of "nativeness" and "authenticity" whereby "the attributes and behavior of socially defined groups can be determined and explained by reference to cultural and/or biological characteristics believed to be inherent to the group" (Bucholtz 2003, p. 400). For example, Jaffe has pointed out that the construct of "the French language" is an essentializing notion of the "one true, authenthic code associated with one authentic people" (1999, p. 121) conceived of in terms of nation. Education is part of this same ideological landscape of standardized notions of national identity, language, and culture:

> Schooling and teaching remain technologies of a nation . . . teaching remains about, within, and for the nation, tacitly about the protection and production of its Culture (and, by implication, its preferred ethnicities and races, languages, and codes) and committed to the production of its sovereign subjects. (Luke 2004, p. 24)

It is important in the context of telecollaborative pedagogies to underscore that the conjoining of education and technology has been basic to the standard imagining of a unitary language-culture-nation-self. For instance, the standardization of printing technologies in early modern Europe made possible the print languages (Anderson 1991) and print cultures (Eisenstein 1983) that are seen as central to national identities. The technological standardization of printing went hand in hand with increasingly standardized orthography and the diffusion of the first codifications or "grammars" of European national standard languages upon which FLE has been constructed (Auroux 1994; Joseph 1987; Train 2000).

The essentializing force of standardization presents a basic dilemma that is central to the telecollaboration projects described in this volume: how can learners, socialized to varying degrees into their standardized national Identity, Culture, and Language, with all the attendant ethnocentric baggage, "authentically" communicate and interact with the "foreign" NSs who in all likelihood also bring to the exchange their own culturally constructed pride and prejudice surrounding their sense of national Identity constructed to some degree in opposition to the Other? A recurring *leitmotif* in some research on telecollaboration is that technologically mediated pedagogies do not create an ecology of learning in which conflict and otherization magically disappear. Quite to the contrary, technology brings learners from both sides of the exchange into an environment in which discursively constructed conflict and misunderstanding is to some degree inevitable (see Scheider and von der Emde, this volume). For FL educators and students, a critical perspective on standardization offers a salutary challenge to the standardized imagining of language, culture, and identity in FLE, that is, a monolingual national community inhabited by putative NSs of the NSL. While recognizing the need to address very real normativity of the NSL, a critical take on standardization also problematizes the assumption of one-nation-one-language-one-culture-one-self as the *only* desirable model of community, language, culture, and identity.

Standardization, Variation, and Communication

Through the construction of a unitary notion of language-culture-community-identity, standardization constructs a standardizing view of the "reality" of language, culture, community, and identity in which diversity, and variability are seen as "problems" that can be ostensibly "solved," "managed," or "controlled" through standardization. This "language as problem" (Ruíz 1984) orientation that has guided much language policy in the world appears to be well integrated into SLA research and FLE (Train 2003). Standardization seeks to suppress variability in language that does not conform to the putative language-culture practices of educated adult native speaker-writers as codified in grammars. The standard language topos of "if it's not in the dictionary, it's not a word" can be seen as the "erasure" (Irvine and Gal 2000) of non-authorized lexical items from what is seen to constitute the valid "language." This powerful languaging and de-languaging effect exerted by standardization serves to define the standard language in opposition to practices of variation and language diversity. The inclusionary/exclusionary power of standardness extends to a broad range of discursive practices of variation and speaker identities that are positioned as "inadequate" or "deficient" with respect to the NSL:

- regional practices ("dialects")
- socio-economically or demographically situated practices ("minority language," "sociolects," "argot," "slang")

- situational, stylistic practices (informal registers)
- temporally situated practices (archaisms)
- inherent variability ("idiolect")
- bilingual and multilingual practices (code-switching, borrowing, contact languages)
- computer-mediated discourse ("Netspeak")
- second language learner practices ("interlanguage," "transitional competence," "approximative system," "error, " "non-native," "near-native," "native-like")

In framing linguistic diversity negatively, the NSL construct supports the marginalization and devaluing of bilingual, multilingual, and intercultural discourse practices that have been shown to be basic to telecollaboration. The question at hand is: to what extent do telecollaborative pedagogies participate in or work against powerful ideology?

As a basic concept and practice in FLE, "communication" looms large in telecollaboration. Much of the impetus for telecollaboration stems from the benefits both demonstrable and potential that are seen to accrue from communication between NS and non-native speaker (NNS). However, the intercultural discourse of telecollaboration has been shown to also involve intercultural misunderstanding (Belz 2003; Ware 2005) and conflict within the context of FLE as "global communicative practice" (Kramsch and Thorne 2002).

The common-sense view is to see "people just talking" according to the dominant notion of communication that assumes consensus and understanding between interlocutors. This view of communication is shaped by the NSL construct which, by virtue of its perceived uniformity, is perceived to possess superior communicative power. It is assumed to be the most "useful" and "efficient" variety of language within a nation due to its idealization as a vehicle for maximum communication (Ray 1963). The assumption that standardized language is necessary for efficient communication has extended to the dubious "deficit" view regarding non-standardized practices, critiqued by Labov (1972), whereby the standard language is seen as a requirement for the expression of cogent thought.

Standardized language, culture, and identity are increasingly yet problematically identified with global communicative practices. The "global" has long been associated with speaker participation in the national or world standard language-culture that is constructed in opposition to "local" varieties (e.g., Occitan with respect to French, Quechua to Spanish). Globalization has resulted in the somewhat misleading pluralization of the world standard language construct with concepts such as world Englishes. However, this globalness of world languages only exacerbates the tension among the various national Englishes or Spanishes undergoing pluricentric standardization and the non-standardized practices that in effect define them. As Monica Heller (1999, 2002) has convincingly demonstrated for the Canadian bilingual context of French and English, the ideology of the monolingual national standard language has morphed into an "ideology of commodification" that differentially values the language and culture practices of standard French over the diversity of observable practices among bilingual Canadians. In the globalizing ideology described by Heller, the school contributes to the notion of bilingualism as a commodity for exchange in an internationalized job market. But only a certain type of "parallel" or "double" bilingualism is valued, one in which the student is expected to "speak each 'language' as though it were a homogeneous monolingual variety" (Heller 2002, p. 48). In doing so, the school "promotes the socioeconomic advancement of one set of francophones," those who command the standard, "but marginalizes another set and narrows and normativizes the definition of what it means to speak French" (Heller 1999, p. 273). The same can be said of Spanish-as-a-foreign-language programs and heritage-language programs in the United States that for the most part seem to be increasingly focused on the job opportunities for Spanish speakers who have mastered the conventions of standardized Spanish.

Standardization as communicative efficiency has been linked to other ideologies of language use such as an ideology of correctness (Corson 2001; Leith 1983). The standardizing practice of European printers during the 14th to 17th century is difficult to separate from their role as the "inventors of *bon usage*" (Trudeau 1992). Correctness is seen as necessary for communication. "Non-standard" and/or "minority" practices such as Ebonics have been discursively constructed as threats to the communicative, political, and cultural unity of the nation. Models for "speaking and writing the language properly" have been diffused over the centuries through printed manuals, textbooks, and treatises on of any number of language-related topics including grammar, orthography, elocution, manners, public speaking, composition, style, and education (Watts and Trudgill 2002).

A critical stance toward standardization requires deep reflection and exploration on the part of educators as to the diversity and complexity of what literacy is and could be in FLE:

> Literacy is the use of socially, historically, and culturally situated practices of creating and interpreting meaning through texts. It entails at least a tacit awareness of the relationships between textual conventions and their contexts of use and, ideally, the ability to reflect critically on those relationships. Because it is purpose-sensitive, literacy is dynamic—not static—and variable across and within discourse communities and cultures. It draws on a wide range of cognitive abilities, on knowledge of written and spoken language, on knowledge of genres, and on cultural knowledge. (Kern 2000, p. 16)

This is a crucial point for telecollaboration where the discourse constructed through online interaction pushes the limits of what many educators would consider "correct" or "appropriate" uses of written language. However, as Bauer *et al.* (this volume) demonstrate in their *Cultura* project, the meaningful and skilled creation and interpretation of digital texts by students in a telecollaborative context constitutes literate practice. In this sense, telecollaboration can provide a space for "multimodal discourse" that incorporates "a new constellation of communicational resources" (Kress 2003, p. 9) into the standard print technologies.

Nativism and the Contested Sites of Competence, Authenticity, Expertise, and Agency

A significant and growing body of scholarship has problematized the concept of the NS as the most salient ideology of identity and language use connected to FLE (Valdman 1982; Rampton 1990; Kramsch 1997; Cook 1999; Belz 2002a, 2002b; Davies 2003; Train 2003). The need for new conceptualizations or re-imaginings of learner identity and competence has emerged as a central concern for ICFLE, as is demonstrated by the chapters in this volume (Belz; Schneider and von der Emde; Thorne).

The NS presupposes a *monolingual nativism* constructed in terms of standardized identities. The ideologically monolingual NS identity is bound to a homogeneous speech community in which NSs are assumed to "speak the same language" (Silverstein 1998). However convenient this monolingual nativism may seem, a critical perspective poses the fundamental normative question raised by these nativist assumptions: whose language? (Mey 1985). That is, whose linguistic practices, in what contexts, will be validated, and whose will be positioned *hors la langue*, thus falling outside the legitimating practices of the standardized norm with its putative community of NSs? The answer is contingent on historical and social context given that ideologies are never *hors contexte*. Through multiple re-contextualizations, ideologies reflect and shape shifting contexts of hegemony and dominance. Although the NSL may appear to represent a universal ideal of language, it is situated in the European context attached to the emergence of Western practices and technologies of literacy, education, and sociopolitical organization (e.g., nationalism, imperialism, and colonialism) that privileged the Graeco-Latin model of language (Joseph 1987) and its norm-bearers (Haugen 1966) embodied in kings, courtiers, and language professionals (scribes, printers). However, the locus of native-speaker normativity and cultural capital has repeatedly shifted, to use French as an example, from bourgeois revolutionaries, to the educated metropolitan urban middle class, to an emerging global elite socio-professional class of "symbolic analyists" (Reich 1991). Whoever and wherever the NS, the idealized and authoritative state of "the language" implies the construction and imposition of an idealized NS norm as the normative center (Bartsch 1987) of discourse practices, with the assumed internalization or nativization by speakers of the attitudes, behaviors, and affective stances attached to this norm.

The NS construct is fundamental to the pedagogizing, systematizing, and recontextualizing of knowledge (Bernstein 2000) of the NSL construct as a pedagogical hyperstandard (Train 2000) for the purposes of teaching the language to NNSs. The codified formal and appropriate communicative elements attributed to NSs come to constitute a set of pedagogical norms (Gass *et al.* 2002; Valdman 2000). Learner and teacher identity has been grounded in the ideologized concept of the NS as an educated monolingual speaker of the target language living in an ideologically homogeneous national culture. Still the learners are expected to conform to and, ideally, internalize the norm based on relatively little linguistic input and in a relatively reduced range of settings in which the language is presented.

A crucial issue for the present discussion is that the notion of NS has been, and continues to be, the implicit and explicit model for native competence in L1 as well as for ultimate attainment among learners. The nativist paradigm of competence has been at the center of much of what language researchers and educators have come to believe or disbelieve about language structure, use, and acquisition. The nativist conception of language was formulated as that of an "ideal speaker-listener, in a completely homogeneous speech-community" (Chomsky 1965, p. 3). Chomsky inherited and embraced the nativist view of language underlying the NS from the prescriptive tradition of grammarians who codified their idea of authoritative language practices (often conforming to their own) into national standard languages. In particular, Saussure offered nativists a scientific description of language based on an idealized state of "the language" (*langue*) that resembled the standard language, abstracted from the observable language practices (*parole*) of educated NSs, as represented by the linguist (Crowley 1990). The Chomskyan idealization of "competence" relegates the way people actually use language ("performance") to a theoretically unimportant status.

Much of the work of sociolinguistics and, more recently, corpus linguistics has been to question the homogeneity of the Chomskyan NS and to establish the social grounding of speakers' actual language practices in terms of variability correlating to social class, register, ethnicity, age, geography, and gender. Ethnographic and anthropological perspectives have come to focus increasingly on the very issues of sociocultural and interactional context (e.g., cultural knowledge, ideology, identity, local practice) that Chomskyan linguistics has attempted to banish, or at least marginalize, from the theory and study of language.

ICFLE must engage and contest the nativist focus on competence as formal accuracy and communicative appropriateness that is associated with an idealized NS and the NSL along with its concern for communicative efficiency. There is a considerable body of research in applied linguistics on what it means to know a language, particularly in terms of "the communicative competence" of second-language learners (Bachman 1990; Canale and Swain 1980; Canale 1983; Savignon 1972). In this context, the institutionalized normativity of the NSL is present in the notion of grammatical competence; that is, the degree to which the language learner has "mastered" (i.e., can accurately produce) the linguistic code. Grammatical competence is conceived of as one element within the larger communicative competence in which the language learner demonstrates the ability to use this grammatical competence in conjunction with sociolinguistic competence, discourse competence, strategic competence (Canale and Swain 1980), and pragmatic competence (Bachman 1990) in order to communicate appropriately according to the variable contexts in which language is used. But none of these competence models addresses the intercultural use of language in telecollaboration. Hence, the need for Byram's (1997) model of *intercultural* competence.

Telecollaboration as a site of *intercultural* discourse must also contend with the dominant paradigm in FLE and research in which the NS construct embodies the "monolingual bias" of SLA theory and FLE that "elevates an idealized "native" speaker above a stereotypical "non-native," while viewing the latter as a defective communicator, limited by an underdeveloped communicative competence" (Firth and Wagner 1997, p. 285), thus contributing to "the myth of the deficient communicator" (Belz 2002a). The ideology of (in)competence is discursively constructed through the term NS and its binary opposite, the NNS, along with a host of even murkier concepts: "near-native speaker" (see Koike and Liskin-Gasparro 1999; Valdés 1998), "the pseudo-native," or "quasi-native" speaker. The privileged competence and identity attributed to the NS raises questions as to the ultimate attainment of proficiency in an L2—whether discursively positioned NNSs can attain native-like proficiency, whether NNSs can become NSs, and why they would or would not want to, or have to.

An increasingly important body of research in applied linguistics throws into question the validity of the NS and the ideologically monolingual NSL as a suitable goal for competence in language learners (e.g., Belz 2002a, 2002b; Blyth 1995; Cook 1999; Kramsch 1997; Rampton 1990; Train 2003; Valdman 1982, 2000; Valdés and Figueroa 1996). The basic insight in this line of inquiry is that language learners, whether in the context of second-language, foreign-language, or heritage-language education, are not monolinguals, and therefore they do not, nor should they be expected to, speak, behave, or even think in exclusively monolingual ways. This critical perspective asserts that an understanding and valuing of the diverse bilingual or multilingual practices of language learners (such as code-switching, language-mixing, multilingual language play) are fundamental to language learning and therefore ought to be to incorporated into language education and pedagogy.

Intercultural education is well-positioned to challenge the hegemony of the NS and to re-appropriate and subvert the ideologies and discourses of nativism in ways that break down the binary native/non-native construct and highlight the value of being more-than-native. Rather than acquiescing to the ideological positioning of L2 learners as deficient, the "privilege of the non-native speaker" enables FL learners to "construct linguistic and cultural identities in the interstices of national languages and on the margins of monolingual speakers' territories" (Kramsch 1997, p. 368).

A basic premise of telecollaboration expressed in this volume is that "authentic" contact with NSs is desirable and beneficial in the development of language, as well as the skills of discovery and interaction required for intercultural learning. The notion of "authenticity" between learners and speakers of the target language must be examined in light of the ideological co-construction of NS and NNS (where one cannot appear to exist without the other) with respect to the NSL. The articulation of *authenticity* and *nativeness* of language, culture, and speakers is an attempt to discursively capture what might be called "the real language of real speakers." The question for ICFLE is: who will be the "real" speakers and how will they and their expertise be valued?

The salient point for ICFLE is to recognize that the notion of authenticity *inappropriately* privileges native-speaker use as the "proper language for learning" (Widdowson 1994, p. 387). In this respect, telecollaborative pedagogies must be attentive to the notion of *agency,* which designates the extent to which individuals and collectivities have a conceptual space for the understanding of themselves and acting upon that understanding. Telecollaboration should consciously question the ideologies of authenticity and nativeness attached to the NSL that create a very problematic, even paradoxical, sort of agency where speakers are seen as "empowered" *only* to the extent that they conform to the dominant NS norms. Intercultural FLE cannot be intercultural if a speaker's or teacher's nativeness and authenticity are seen as inherent qualities bestowed on speakers by right of birth or by the exceptional expertise of being able to "pass" as NS. Telecollaboration is well-placed to move beyond the predicament of (in)authenticity and (non)nativeness that positions the language learner as NNS who is an authentic foreigner and who is also expected to somehow act as native-like as possible.

The central concern that emerges for intercultural telecollaborative pedagogy and research is how to articulate a frame in which concepts of linguistic and cultural authenticity can be "resignified" (Kramsch, A'Ness, and Lam 2000) into a notion of agency, expertise, and identity that are not bound to the acquisition of authorized NSL practices as the sole means of empowering speakers, nor bound to the disempowering potential of the authentic NS. In the following sections, I explore each of the chapters in this present volume in terms of the themes discussed here. These chapters present a rich variety of perspectives on ICFLE. For that reason, I do not claim to comprehensively treat the positions and perspectives advanced in these articles.

Pedagogical and Praxiological Lessons from Internet-mediated Intercultural Foreign Language Education Research

In his chapter on research findings, pedagogical methods, and the theoretical frameworks of ICFLE, Thorne (this volume) makes the case, as I did at the beginning of my chapter, that all communication is intercultural (Scollon and Scollon 2001). Recognizing the fundamental interculturality of communicative activity is a step toward forging more responsive, and more responsible, FL pedagogies for students living in an increasingly complex world. This insight provides the basis for one goal of ICFLE: to "make visible and available the conceptual, linguistic, and cultural tools necessary for negotiating what is always and everywhere intercultural communication" (p. 23). The other goal of ICFLE articulated by Thorne is "to support the development of significant social relationships between persons who have been socialized into varying and varied languacultural viewpoints." Both goals problematize the notion that bi- and multi-lingual speakers merely shift between monolingual discourse systems. Rather, Thorne suggests that in an ecology of multiple codes, personal and collective histories, and the immediacy of talk-in-interaction, communication is an accomplishment assembled utterance by utterance. From this vantage point, the primary aspiration of FLE, and ICFLE in particular, is to enhance one's capacity to participate in such processes.

The *Cultura* Project

The fundamental issue for ICFLE addressed by the *Cultura* project (Bauer *et al.*, this volume) is that of conceptualizing and representing "culture" as both an element of human lives and as a pedagogical construct. The *Cultura* project takes as its starting point the premise that intercultural competence needs to become a much larger component of the language curriculum. This stems from the long-standing realization that the main focus of FL classes has been, and still is, on developing linguistic and communicative competencies. Despite a refocusing of curricular content toward the study of target cultures (as evidenced in the FL Standards), Bauer *et al.* observe that culture remains marginalized, often reduced to lists of facts or "culture capsules" that give a simplified and stereotyped picture of the other culture (p. 33). The *Cultura* project, in contrast, carefully avoids reducing cultural knowledge to capsules of discrete facts by encouraging students to explore both individual and socially constructed understandings of cultural phenomena. The *Cultura* exchange is integrated with classroom discussions and activities designed to encourage awareness of the culturally bound character of perceptions and values.

Cultura rejects the NSL ideology that reduces and systematizes language and culture into a unitary construct of "the language" and "the culture" that misrepresents, or fails to represent, or at best partially represents the observable complexity, diversity, and variability of the target language and culture. *Cultura* strives to "problematiz[e] national cultures from within and without" as learners and their partners experience first-hand the diversity of what it means to be a speaker of French, German, Russian, or Spanish through intercultural communication and questionnaires (p. 52). Culture is no longer limited to a generic and/or national culture attached to the national and/or global standard language and an abstract NS. Through the cultural self-reflections built into *Cultura*, learners are afforded a sense of agency and awareness as they cultivate "an increasingly complex sense of national identities and cultural heterogeneity" (p. 52).

Cultura raises another crucial question for ICFLE: what will be the terminology (or meta-discourse) we will use to talk about "culture" in ways that do not inadvertently support the NSL model? The *Cultura* project evokes the problematic metaphor of "understanding the inner core of another culture" as a way to talk about the "long process, akin to a journey on which one amasses pictures, words, impressions, fragments, and ideas, which one then tries to assemble into a coherent whole" (p. 34). While depth of cultural understanding is an important goal, it remains to be known whether cultures have an "inner core." This sort of meta-discourse seems very close to the traditional notion of an "essential" culture and identity that has been largely tied to unitary national cultures and identity. Moreover, one must ask whether the goal of constructing "a coherent whole" is a discursive residue of the very essentializing view of culture that an intercultural FLE and *Cultura* seek to avoid. This concern for a certain wholeness of representation of culture as seen from many sides and in many modalities is consistent with *Cultura*'s rejection of culture as monolithic. However, from a critical perspective that foregrounds socio-economic inequalities, the metaphorical coherence and wholeness of culture mask the complex, conflicted, and stratified character of culture (Hannerz 1992).

Learning How to Teach Intercultural Communicative Competence via Telecollaboration: A Model for Language Teacher Education

The evidence from ICFLE reported in this volume seems to suggest that students expect and assume that contact with the NS will lead to intercultural awareness and language proficiency (Müller-Hartmann, this volume,pp. 75–76). The researchers throughout the projects reported here remind educators and students that there is no single automatic, linear, or even predictable path of linguistic and cultural development in learners engaged in telecollaboration. Moreover, research that highlights the complexity, variability, and contextuality of intercultural learning deeply challenges the common-sense notion (in part, a legacy of audio-lingual methodologies grounded in behaviorism, and "natural" approaches attached to linguistic nativism) that somehow learners just acquire the language "naturally" when among NSs. The telecollaborative evidence suggests the need to educate students and teachers that learning involves much more than the metaphorical "contact" and "exposure" to contagiously authentic NSs.

In highlighting the complexity of language learning, ICFLE also brings out the complexity of the teachable, thus presenting the challenge of preparing teachers to be able to deal with global communicative practices that they and their students will encounter (Kramsch and Thorne 2002). Müller-Hartmann (this volume) addresses the need to develop language teachers' knowledge base of intercultural communicative competence (ICC) through experiential learning and model teaching. As in other intercultural telecollaborative situations, critical cultural awareness comes to the fore. In this case, "collaborative reflection" is seen as a way to lead student teachers to becoming reflective practitioners who will, in turn, guide their students in reflecting critically on their own practices. Following Tarone and Allwright (2005), shaping teachers' knowledge base is also seen as central to developing the practical and experiential knowledge that is crucial to becoming an expert teacher. Implicit in this position is the concept of teacher-as-learner, which in the ideological context of the NS-NSS relationship raises (again) questions regarding identity, expertise, and agency in the lives of teacher-learners as NSs, NNSs, or intercultural speakers.

Telecollaboration and Intercultural Student Ethnography

O'Dowd (this volume) brings technology to bear on the question of NS authoritative expertise and learner agency. O'Dowd recognizes the need for learners to become aware of the "dangers of over-generalizing" about the target culture based on the knowledge of a single or select group of NSs (O'Dowd, this volume, p. 101). Pedagogically, even a seemingly straightforward exchange about holidays has the potential for becoming a rich point, a learning moment, that also calls for a significant amount of thought and planning in order to support deeper intercultural learning, past the canonical "culture capsule" or "fact-based" approach to cultural knowledge critiqued by Bauer *et al.* (this volume). An effective strategy presented by O'Dowd is the use of carefully chosen "parallel texts" (readings, films, concepts) that attenuate the asymmetrical native-speaker-knows-all relationship, such that learners on both sides of the partnership have a common point of information and discussion. O'Dowd calls for "a framework of multiple perspectives" (Kern 2000, p. 258) in which learners critically evaluate information accessed from a variety of sources, such as their intercultural interlocutors, teachers, and texts. This approach could be enhanced by an explicitly critical discourse perspective in which one could envisage the incorporation of a "discourse-historical approach" (see Wodak *et al.* 1999; Wodak 2001) that "centers on political issues and seeks to integrate as many of the genres of discourse referring to a particular issue as possible, as well as the historical dimension of that issue" (van Leeuwen and Wodak 1999, p. 91).[2] Concretely, learners on both sides of the exchange could read contextualizing texts that might better situate some key discursive acts that appear in the learners' experiences and perspectives within larger discursively constructed ideologies of national identity and community. The integration of a discourse-historical approach would also give an explicit rationale to the shifting of pedagogical space in the FL curriculum to more intellectually substantive and more content-based material, while at the same time allowing for mainstream attention to language in communicative settings.

The application of ethnographical techniques and goals to ICFLE offers a promising pedagogical approach for addressing NS hegemony and breaking down the "stereotypical portraits" of the Other held by learners in telecollaboration (p. 96). From a discourse perspective, ethnography is crucial to a more practice-oriented critical intercultural FLE (see Barro, Jordan, and Roberts 1998; Roberts *et al.* 2001). It is also central to Byram's notion of the critical cultural awareness of the intercultural speaker, who, like an ethnographer, "can use a range of analytical approaches to place a document or event in context (of origins/sources, time, place, other documents or events) and to demonstrate the ideology involved" (Byram 1997, p. 63, quoted in O'Dowd, pp. 112–113). Hence, the ethnographer as a metaphor and ethnography as a technique for intercultural FL learning goes to the heart of the telecollaborative work described in this volume and elsewhere.

However, the language learner as ethnographer also raises the troubling question of the "objectivity" of the NS, the FL learner, and the teacher in observation and interaction. O'Dowd relates the comments of students (Katya and Lucie) in Germany regarding the inability of one of their American co-participants (Mary) to "to stay objective"(p. 107): "Her personal experience didn't allow her to discuss the topic objectively" (p. 103). The teacher-researcher seems to endorse the same idealized "scientific" objectivity of the ethnographer:

> [Mary's] comments show that she was unable to stand back and take a scientific approach to the exchange due to the emotional nature of the topics. Her experiences of the recent war in Iraq and her viewing of a film on gun control in the USA meant that she could not "talk about them more objectively." (p. 112)

However, it is precisely the assumption of *objective talk* and neutral observation that seems at odds with a critical cultural awareness that views all discourse as ideological, that is, historically and culturally constructed and contingent, grounded in a complex of worldview, values, attitudes, and social structures. An idealized view of ethnography (as not mediated by the participant observer's ideologies) appears to be operative as the researcher explains that

> learners need to see themselves more as young social scientists or ethnographers who are objectively researching the cultural context which influences and shapes the way their partners see the world. Their task is not to agree or disagree with their partners, but rather to learn more about their partners' world—and their own. (p. 116)

In this case, the educator-researcher seems to be grappling with the heuristic task of weighing the real benefits and difficulties of the intercultural telecollaborative project, while searching for "the ideal outcomes of intercultural contact" (p. 115):

> When learners become more conscious that their aim is not to debate with their partners but rather to understand how they experience their worlds and why this is so, then they may become more objective in their approaches and less willing to expect their partner to change all the stereotypes that they have of the target culture. (p. 115)

If any sort of "objectivity" is a goal or outcome, then one would wonder how "critical" the intercultural experience really is. Critical perspectives attempt to displace regimes of objectivity, authority, and authenticity by positing a certain inescapable and unstable subjectivity or subject-positioning of individuals in cultural and social context. In grappling with the dilemmas of intercultural learning and critical cultural awareness, we would be well served in considering Clifford's characterization of "participant observation" as a "dialectic of experience and interpretation," that involves "a continuous tacking between the "inside" and "outside" of events: on the one hand grasping the sense of specific occurrences and gestures empathetically on the other stepping back to situate these meanings in wider contexts" (1988, p. 34). This sort of critical relativism seeks to engage us with the ideologies that inform what we do and think, especially as "objective scientists" who observe culture and participate in it.

Morphological Development in Spanish-American Telecollaboration

In investigating the linguistic development of Spanish learners, Dussias (this volume) demonstrates the benefits of NS-NNS interaction via telecollaboration. Linguistic gains in this study were assessed by examining the transcriptions of Oral Proficiency Interviews (OPIs) that were conducted immediately before the learners began the telecollaborative sessions and shortly after the last session ended. Interestingly, the study's findings suggest that the documented linguistic gains (i.e., communication, fluency, and grammatical accuracy) "seem to readily transfer to spontaneous language production," as demonstrated by the OPI data (p. 142). Therefore, the study can be said to lend support to the claim (Sotillo 2000) that the type of language elicited in synchronous discussions reflects the complexity and characteristics of face-to-face interactions. This is a welcome finding, the strategic importance of which should not be dismissed. As one of the first studies to demonstrate quantitatively that there can be linguistic gains in telecollaboration, this sort of well-constructed research certainly makes a convincing "numbers" and "hard proof" case for the pedagogical value of computer-mediated intercultural courses and programs.

From a critical perspective, this examination of the linguistic consequences of computer-mediated communication between FL learners of Spanish and native Spanish speakers also raises a number of important questions as to how "communication" in telecollaboration is conceptualized as an area of SLA research and as pedagogical practice. In FLE, "communication" has become something of a shorthand for language use, grounded in an idealized competence (abstracted from actual communication) underlying systems of knowledge and skill required for communication, e.g., knowledge of vocabulary and skill in using the sociolinguistic conventions for a given language (Canale 1983). In mainstream iterations of SLA, the assumption of communication has been operationalized in terms of observable and analyzable "interaction" and "negotiation" between speakers. From a pedagogical standpoint, "meaningful and realistic interaction" has been one of the guiding principles for a communicative approach (Canale 1983, pp. 18–19). However, as Block has asserted, much SLA research labors under a "narrow and partial version of communicative competence" in which "the only subjectivity worthy of any in-depth discussion in SLA is that of NNS as "defective communicator" in contrast with NS as target identity" (2003, p. 80). For Block, the NS bias in the notion of communicative competence is one piece in the dominant SLA view based on a "tripartite view of language" in which (1) "language" is seen as rules of appropriate use (i.e., "communication") and linguistic competence (i.e., the formal system); (2) "tasks" are "what people do when speaking to one another," in keeping with the dominant Input-Interaction-Output (IIO) model the notion of "communicative task" comes to define interaction as "real" and "meaningful" because they reflect real world activity (2003, p. 68); and (3) conversational interaction as negotiation for meaning (NfM), which is seen as central to acquisition.

For the most part, the more SLA-oriented approaches to telecollaboration seem to acquiesce to the dominant paradigm critiqued by Block (2003). For example, it is pointed out that computer-mediated interaction (e.g., chat interactions and chat logs) can be an effective tool in helping learners to achieve higher levels of metalinguistic awareness and can furnish valuable linguistic material for aiding learners to "reflect on their interlanguage" (Dussias, p. 142). However, the operative notions of awareness and reflection in this SLA paradigm, as well as the benefits of online interaction, appear to be restricted to directing learners' attention to "noticing" the gaps that exist in their interlanguage grammar. Interaction is seen as the path to greater understanding of interlanguage as part of learning. This view, consistent with mainstream SLA research traditions, requires a notion of "error" as a driving force behind interaction, proficiency, and acquisition. Linguistic development is conceptualized as fewer errors (the attainment of grammatical accuracy) and "a decline in disfluency" (Dussias, p. 131). However, the error-focused data reveal little information as to the exact interaction and negotiation that might have led to increased fluency (or decline in disfluency). As an enduring legacy of the NSL, the focus-on-form goes along with the focus on error and (in)correctness as a basis for research. Despite the linguistic gains described, the data presented feel something like a chronicle of stubbornly persistent "non-target-like forms" that negatively position non-native learners as the locus of incorrectness. Moreover, evidence of bilingual and non-native discourse features (e.g., codeswitching, mixing strategies, and lexical innovation) appear to be characterized as deficiencies rather than as evidence for complex semiotic resources deployed by the learner.

While a reasonable source of data for L2 development in the context of the Dussias study, the use of the OPI as evidence of the transfer from computer-mediated communication to spontaneous language production remains problematic within a broader view of intercultural discourse. The "spontaneity," "complexity," and "interaction" reflected in the OPI are arguably severely constrained by the asymmetrical power relationship between interviewer and interviewee and the staged, monologic character of linguistic production (van Lier 1989). In short, the OPI does not take a social perspective on interaction that would recognize the intrinsically social nature of performance (McNamara 1997). The Native Standard Speaker view of language upon which the OPI is based (Valdés and Figueroa 1996) seems consistent with the reliance in the study on readily testable formal morphological (e.g., gender/number agreement, subject-verb agreement, tense/mood, *por/para*) and lexical elements, which are also among the linguistic features most readily codifiable in the standardized accounts of the-language-as-morphology-syntax-and-lexicon contained in grammars, dictionaries, and textbooks. It would appear that this study for all its qualities supports the rather narrow and asocial sense of context and language that has dominated much of SLA research and FLE (see Firth and Wagner 1997).

The critical intercultural discourse perspective I have outlined reframes communication in general and especially FL communication as intercultural communication (see Scollon and Scollon 2001). Language is always a complex affair that involves more than language structure to include the interplay of practice, ideology, and technology in language use. In particular, the use or multiple contextually dependent *uses* of language are interwoven with ideologies of standardized language structure, culture, identity, and community that have coalesced around the NS and NSL. The interaction between NSs and NNSs produced in telecollaboration should be considered in terms of the problematic and ideological character of intercultural communication. But even more to the point, educators and researchers should begin to recognize the uniqueness and specificity of the intercultural discourse of telecollaboration (see Belz, this volume) in its own right, not in the shadow of possible transfer to traditional pedagogical contexts.

Native and Nonnative Speakers' Feedback and Responses in Spanish-American Networked Collaborative Interaction

Research on networked collaborative interaction (Lee's term for "telecollaboration") seeks to explore the "negotiation for meaning and form" that is seen to play a crucial role in the development of language competence (Lee, this volume, p. 147). This formulation begs for a more critical stance toward the basic SLA tenets of "negotiation," "form," and "meaning" in the context of ICFLE. The underlying dominant notion of negotiation is that of "an activity through which L2 learners and interlocutors work together linguistically to repair or resolve impasses in communication and come to an understanding of each other's message meaning" (Pica 1996, p. 2). The premise is that through negotiation NSs and NNSs work together *linguistically*, and not *culturally*, to solve the communication problems and achieve understanding and meaning. This view discounts the basic fact of ICFLE that meaning is discursively constructed in complex *cultural* or *intercultural* contexts in which communication and understanding are far from inevitable outcomes given the complexity of global and local languages, cultures, communities, and identities. From a critical standpoint, the concept of negotiation must be framed with respect to the larger ideological contexts of intercultural communication in which the discourse of globalization is a discourse of power (Fairclough 2001, p. 207) grounded in profoundly unequal and asymmetrical relationships between the cultural and linguistic practices of human beings. In a world that is "increasingly interconnected and increasingly fragmented," it is important to realize, as Kramsch reminds us, "the term *culture* has replaced *nation* in the multinational corporate world of a globalized economy," leading us to believe that "all languages and cultures are equal and that all conflicts are only a "communication" problem within an otherwise established consensus on ultimate political and economic goals" (2002, p. 283). Echoing Cameron, Kramsch warns that the concept of intercultural communication "as it is currently used can be easily high-jacked by a global ideology of 'effective communication' Anglo-Saxon style, which speaks an English discourse even as it expresses itself in many different languages" (Kramsch 2002, p. 284).

The concept of negotiation in SLA studies has often focused on finding evidence of "corrective feedback" to learner "error." The value for SLA of negotiation-focused-on-feedback has become something of an article of interactional faith that has gone largely unexamined. This attention to feedback emerges in telecollaborative studies where the main goal is "to examine how both NSs and NNSs generate feedback and to what extent feedback is used to solve both linguistic and comprehension problems during NCI" (Lee, p. 152). In language pedagogy and SLA research, the role of feedback in negotiation has come increasingly to be seen in terms of "focus on form" (FonF), which "overtly draws students' attention to linguistic elements as they arise incidentally in lessons whose overriding focus is on meaning or communication" (Long 1991, pp. 45–46). Grounded in a narrow sense of context in which formal linguistic elements can be seen to "arise incidentally," FonF dismisses socially situated views of discourse that highlight the inseparability of linguistic structure from the ideologically shaped contexts of language use (Silverstein 1979).

The suggestion that awareness of form arises independently of language ideology seems highly implausible, particularly in the normative context of language education with its multi-millenary ideology of (in)correctness (Corson 2001; Leith 1983; Train 2000). In spite of the relatively recent emphasis in FLE and research on the communicative uses of language, questions arise as to how much "communication" is really going on in the classroom, and what is being communicated beyond the traditional focus on the (in)correctness of learners' linguistic production? From a curricular perspective, the NSL is associated with a restricted content that tends to focus on the standard language itself, whether as "grammar" (i.e., "focus of form," "accuracy," "structure," or explicit grammar instruction), "vocabulary" (i.e., lexical items isolated from meaningful discursive context), or "communication," with generally poorly integrated lessons on "culture." As Wilkinson (2001) has noted, FL curricula have given relatively little attention to teaching students how to recognize and use target language discourse norms, that is, the conventionalized ways of carrying on a conversation through turn-taking or shifting topics in a given situation. Awareness has emerged as central to the relationship of language use (communication, interaction, negotiation) to linguistic form and meaning. Corrective feedback is seen to foster learners' increased awareness of forms and pushes them to produce modified output that may lead to the development of learners' interlanguage (Lee, p. 149).

ICFLE could benefit from a more nuanced understanding of interaction in the context of ideologies of use. Critical questions include: What are the social meanings of feedback for NSs and learners? What are the affordances of and constraints on learner agency? How do NSs react to the agency of learners? Belz and Kinginger, for example, examine how learners develop "awareness of the social meanings of linguistic forms" (2003, p. 592) in telecollaborative partnerships. This "pragmatic awareness" reflected in "learner performance" develops toward approximation of the expert norm for interaction among peers. Interaction can be reframed in terms of studying the "normative order of talk" or "how talk is supposed to be organized" (Heller 2003, p. 253) in order to understand how inter-action in institutional settings (such as telecollaboration) produces knowledge about what is important in the world and how to act in it, how it produces and reproduces the moral order.

In FLE and SLA, the (non)native speaker is a binary categorization abstracted from the practices of actual speakers. As such, the NS becomes the norm-bearer (Haugen 1966) while the NNS is positioned as the bearer of error and the locus of "linguistic problems" at the morphosyntactic, semantic, and lexical levels and of "comprehension problems" related to meaning and comprehensibility (Lee, p. 152). The implied authority and infallability of the NS places the onus of prob-lem and error overwhelmingly on the NNS. True to linguistic nativism, the NS is the arbitrator of grammaticality and correctness. Moreover, the NNS is trapped into error through a standard research methodology that devises tasks that will elicit from the participants the provision and the use of corrective feedback through the negotiation of meaning and form (Lee, p. 153). The goal of "empow-ering learners to become active and effective language users" (Lee, p. 172) is pred-icated on the learners modifying their output in conformity to the NSL norm. From a critical perspective, however, the goal of learner empowerment can be seen as at odds with the positioning of learners and their production as problem-ridden, thus supporting teaching methodologies that focus on error, while leaving little room for appreciating the learners' engagement in the discursive making of com-plex intercultural meaning as intercultural speakers.

Codeswitching, for example, is framed as the best last resort to be used only in the interest of economy, conversational flow, or solving "linguistic or communica-tion problems" (Lee, p. 168). In another instance, the learner's clarification check, is in the form of a switch to L1 ("*pantalla*," "screen," "*correcto*"). This sort of clar-ification check "appears to have a positive short-term effect" on comprehension and vocabulary acquisition (Lee, p. 159). This apparent ambivalence as to the value of L1 and bilingual discourse practices also enters into the monolingual bias of language proficiency used to measure and characterize the NNS (dis)fluency, char-acterized as the (dis)appearance of non-native lexical innovation typified by codeswitching and mixing strategies in Dussias (this volume). Moreover, the cate-gorization of error types (Lee, p. 162) easily falls into reliance on the canonical "false cognates" (i.e., Spanish calques of English items) such as *realizar* for *darse cuenta de*, which have been constructed through NSL-based pedagogy, and which devalue bilingual discourse practices with respect to an idealized NS norm. For instance, it is not clear that all bilingual Spanish speakers in the United States sys-tematically distinguish *realizar* from *darse cuenta de*.

A critically informed view, grounded in ethnographic and sociocultural research, would offer a "language-as-resource" orientation (Ruíz 1984) in which the teacher also validates the "funds of knowledge" (Moll *et al.* 1992), i.e., the rich life experiences that the L2 learners bring with them as incipiently bilingual and intercultural speakers. From this perspective, codeswitching and language mixing are resources available to the learner (Belz 2002b; Blyth 1995), rather than a mark of NNS incompetence. This perspective explores the semiotic possibilities of inter-cultural discourse within the hybridity of computer-mediated discourse (see Baron 2000; Belz and Reinhardt 2004; Herring 2001).

Conflicts in Cyberspace: From Communication Breakdown to Intercultural Dialogue in Online Collaborations

Schneider and von der Emde (this volume) point out that telecollaboration under-lines the inadequacy of "communication" and "communicative competence" as organizing principles for FL study. These authors challenge the dominant notion of "successful communication" in the NSL model with its assumed consensus and understanding. Telecollaboration is reframed in terms of the inevitable inter-cultural misunderstanding (Belz 2003, 2005; Ware 2005; Ware and Kramsch 2005) and conflict that arises within the context of FLE as "global communicative prac-tice" (Kramsch and Thorne 2002). Rather than contriving strategies for avoiding conflict at all costs, Schneider and von der Emde establish a "dialogic paradigm" for making conflict and tension a valuable component of intercultural learning. This paradigm soundly rejects the standardizing essentialization of difference and marginalization of diversity of the unitary NSL construct in favor of an inter-cultural engagement within the Bakhtinian model of discourse. According to this model, and unlike the dominant SLA and pedagogical model, interaction and com-munication are (re)conceptualized in intercultural terms as a discursive engage-ment with an Other, "whether that Other is someone from a different culture and with a different language, or someone from within the same culture and language" (Schneider and von der Emde, p. 182). Moreover, dialogic conceptions of commu-nication emphasize that utterances are not merely the product of interlocutors, but in fact shape the interlocutors as well. This discursive tension also opens the door to an increased awareness of learner agency by insisting on the fundamental openness of linguistic utterances to interpretation, rather than supporting a nor-mative model of encoding and decoding utterances. Within this model of dis-course as fundamentally dialogic and intercultural, telecollaboration is also privileged as a site of multimodal discourse in which "speakers" display a broad range of semiotic resources to convey, interpret, and contest meaning (e.g., use of digital images such as the NRA symbol and U.S. flag). By heavily emphasizing "reflection and meta-reflection," Schneider and von der Emde characterize telecollaboration as a site of critical reflectivity, as I discussed earlier (p. 196).

In pedagogical terms, the chapter by Schneider and von der Emde emphasizes that telecollaboration provides an institutionalized academic environment in which "conflict" becomes intellectually engaging and meaningful. This focus on intellectually engaging and meaningful content within an exploratory and experi-ential framework is reflected in the project-based nature (see van Lier 2003; Warschauer 1995) of this telecollaborative course at Vassar and Münster. In the larger context of education in the United States, this conflict-as-content perspective is, to my mind, a much-needed antidote to the increasingly standardized and standardizing curricula and instruction (e.g., standards-based textbooks and instructional outcomes) in which knowledge, as well as teacher and learner identities, are increasingly subordinated to ideology-laden "conflict-less" content.

As the only chapter in this volume written from a literary and cultural studies perspective, Chapter 7 attests to the intellectual and institutional complexity of FLE at the level of university departments in which FLs are taught. University departments, inhabited by literary scholars, pedagogical specialists, and linguists of various stripes and sensibilities, embody diverse concerns and perspectives, all of which can contribute fruitfully to ICFLE. In terms of strategically engaging our students, our teacher colleagues, and administrators in telecollaborative projects, the "conflict" metaphor, however, could be accompanied by a framing of critical intercultural discourse as a unique place in which to explore the "rich points" (Agar 1994), those problematic and intriguing places in languaculture that beg for our attention, if only we learn how to notice and appreciate them (see also Belz 2005, p. 29).

At the Intersection of Telecollaboration, Learner Corpus Analysis, and L2 Pragmatics

Telecollaboration as a site of critical intercultural discourse offers expanded conceptions of competence that have hitherto been limited to the nativist assumptions present in linguistics and education. One case in point is the new *Telecollaborative Learner Corpus of English and German (Telekorp)* discussed in Belz (this volume) that comprises bilingual, Internet-mediated interactions among some 200 learners of German and English recorded during six years of telecollaborative partnerships (see also *http://www.personal.psu.edu/faculty/j/a/jab63/Telekorp.html*). As Belz states, the use of telecollaborative process data for the compilation of a learner corpus and the introduction of corpus-enabled results into the telecollaborative classroom in the form of data-driven learning may contribute to L2 development in general and to L2 pragmatic competence in particular. Challenging a reductionist NS-based notion of competence, *Telekorp* shows that competence is not restricted to the accuracy of particular forms but also encompasses frequency and distribution of use in larger discourse contexts over time. In broader sociolinguistic perspective, computer-assisted analysis of large corpora offers a way of revealing the norms of language use that are expressed in recurring collocations of words (Stubbs 2001). In this sense, corpus linguistics is concerned with not only what speakers can say, but also with what speakers do say (Stubbs 2001, p. 311). In terms of discourse-as-practice, corpus linguistics provides "new ways of studying linguistic routines: what is typical and expected in the utterance-by-utterance flow of spoken and written language in use" (Stubbs 2001, p. 316). From a critical perspective, learner corpora such as *Telekorp* provide a tangible space, supported by ample data, for critical awareness through the exploration and valuing of learner practices and at the same time also engagement with the normativity of target-language practices and the diversity of NS practices as represented concretely and quantitatively in the corpus.

In a very profound sense, the intersection of telecollaboration and learner corpus research described by Belz offers a transformative perspective for educators and researchers in ICFLE. This view shifts the focus in research and pedagogy from largely abstract and often nativist conceptions of *competence* to a more empirical account of the actual, observable *performance* of real speakers, both learner and native, in local contexts of use. Driven by data that is both qualitative (e.g., biographical surveys and retrospective interviews) and quantitative (e.g., frequency of use), this theoretical, methodological, analytical, and pedagogical approach significantly rethinks and reconfigures the standard SLA and FLE paradigms grounded in the NSL and NS model. In Belz' study, linguistic form and use (e.g., German second person pronouns, expressions of opinion, and pronominal adverbs) are attended to in an intercultural ecology where meaning is constructed through engagement with social and global issues (i.e., discourse norms, socioeconomic class) and local, interpersonal concerns. The project is also unique with respect to both the bilingual character of the pedagogical practices (e.g., both L1 and L2 use are validated) and linguistic data derived from them, which break down the rigidly monolingual paradigms of much L2 research and FLE. For all its impressive data and research implications, the approach advocated by Belz remains very teacherly and pedagogically grounded in the best sense of the terms. The teacher's role is that of an activist who does not shirk responsibility for student learning or the quality and meaningfulness of students' classroom experiences. As Belz states, "it is simply not enough…to turn learners loose in native-speaking regions of cyberspace" in order to facilitate linguistic, pragmatic, and/or intercultural development (p. 236). But unlike much traditional FL pedagogy, learners are provided with an institutional and educational space in which to begin to critically create empowering and validating bilingual identities. This is not an approach for the faint of heart. It offers a challenging and much-needed path for educators dedicated to exploring intercultural discourse in computer-mediated contexts.

Conclusion: The Hope of the Intercultural

Education and technology are, at their best, about hope for the future. Nearly a half century ago, at the juncture of print technologies and the emerging electronic technologies that are now commonplace, McLuhan heralded the electronic era with its "global village" as fundamentally different from the "typographic and mechanical age" of nations (1962, p. 31). Successive theories, reforms, and reformulations of teaching and learning have found much of their appeal in the promise of enhancing the educational experience of students, as in the case of the Foreign Language Standards that frames FLE in terms of communication in other languages, understanding of other cultures, connections with knowledge, insight into language and culture, and participation in multilingual communities at home and around the world (Phillips and Terry 1999). In conjoining technology and

FLE, telecollaborative pedagogies offer a future-facing approach to creating intercultural learning and teaching experiences for students and educators using
digital technologies that until recently were unavailable or inaccessible. This sense
of greater things to come is a fundamental perspective that has motivated my
critical account of some of the ideologies that inform the new Internet-mediated
approaches to FLE. In looking at telecollaboration as a site of critical intercultural
discourse, my central concern is that the content of the intercultural exchanges
presented in this volume, both as data to be studied in their own right and as a
heuristic for future pedagogical practice, can be seen through a larger and more
critical discourse-focused analytical lens. The contributions to this volume
vibrantly portray some of the 21st century's affordances for FLE, while at the same
time raise, tacitly or explicitly, many of the constraints that educators and learners
have inherited—enthusiastically, reluctantly, indifferently, or unwittingly—from
certain paradigms and practices anchored in the past and enduring in the present.
The critical view of ICFLE is also intended to offer, to borrow Freire and Freire's
(1994) term, a "pedagogy of hope," but, I hasten to add, not a blueprint for
the future.

    For all the changes in the ways of experiencing, understanding, and imagin-
ing the world that technologies and education have afforded human beings, a
salient point for my argument is the remarkable persistence of the standardized
notions of language, culture, community, and identity that were constructed
around and in conjunction with the technologies of print language and that have
been institutionalized in educational practices. From the perspective I've outlined,
FLE largely has been defined in terms of the ideological NSL and its attendant discourses, practices, and ideologies. As such, much of FLE has been a misdirected
struggle to control and marginalize variation and variability with respect to standardized models. And, I have tried to make the case that technology has served this
task quite well, from the printing presses that diffused standardizing orthogra-
phies and codified grammars of the NSL to later language-oriented technologies.
As for computer-mediated communication and the Internet, the jury is still out.
But, aside from the usual shrill protests of linguistic purists, there is not overwhelming evidence at this point that would indicate any serious threats to standard language practices coming from computer-mediated discourse (Crystal
2001), or at least not for the European alphabetic standard languages.

    The standard language construct will probably not disappear from either
society or schooling and, it must be said, no one including myself seriously asserts
that it should. Instead, what I am suggesting is that educators and researchers
recognize that the institution and practice of schooling is intertwined with the
ideologies of language, community, culture, and identity attached to what I have
called the NSL. By doing so, the way is opened for theories and practices of FLE to
become grounded in a deeper, more critical understanding of those basic ideologies, thus broadening the range of possibilities for new ways of thinking and doing.

    Critical research and pedagogical perspectives on language in the context of
FLE and computer-mediated discourse come in as a way to foster teachers' and
learners' critical awareness of the practices of standardization and variation. It has

been remarked that "the arrival of new, informal, even bizarre forms of language," such as those occurring in computer-mediated discourse, extends the range of our linguistic sensitivity and increases our awareness of the variability and normativity that is inherent in language (Crystal 2001, p. 242). Taking this a step further, this awareness of variety, diversity, and normativity must be "critical" in that speakers come to truly value the variability of language and culture practices through exploring, questioning, and reflecting on its complexity with respect to standard practices, rather than focusing on the marginalization of those variable practices, as has been the case. Education has paid lip service to issues of diversity but in order for "the "valuing" of language diversity to really count," as the late David Corson reminded us, "it needs to be carried out in a genuinely *critical* context" where language education is not conceptualized as an unproblematized *fait accompli*, but rather as "language critically acquired" and critically taught (2001, p. 77). Research into how language is used and imagined in the non-native, bilingual, and multilingual communities that are emerging in the context of the technologies of the 21st century is basic to this critical project because it places the practices of non-native, bilingual, multilingual, intercultural speakers who claim multiple identities at the center of FLE and asks us to question our practices and ideas about what languaculture is, how it is learned, how it is taught, and, ultimately, what it means to be an educated person.

Notes

1. A more detailed discussion of the relationship between language as social/cultural practice and sociocultural theory is developed from a sociolinguistic perspective in Train 2003.

2. Scollon and Scollon note that their term "discourse systems" is similar to Gee's influential notion of *Discourses*, defined as

    > ways of behaving, interacting, valuing, thinking, believing, speaking, and often reading and writing that are accepted as instantiations of particular roles (or "types of people") by specific groups of people, whether families of a certain sort, lawyers of a certain sort, bikers of a certain sort, business people of a certain sort, church members of certain sort, African-Americans of a certain sort, women or men of a certain sort, and so on through a very long list. Discourses are ways of being "people like us." They are "ways of being in the world," they are "forms of life." They are, thus, always and everywhere social and products of social histories. (Gee 1996, p. viii)

3. Discourse-historical analysis, grounded in critical discourse analysis, "perceives both written and spoken discourse as a form of social practice" (van Leeuwen and Wodak 1999, p. 91). The historical dimension of discursive acts is addressed in two ways in discourse-historical methodology: a) integration of all available information on the historical background and the original sources in which discursive "events" are embedded; and b) exploration of the ways in which particular types and genres of discourse are subject to diachronic change (van Leeuwen and Wodak 1999, p. 91). Ricento (2003) has skillfully employed this approach to describe the discursive construction of Americanism in the period from 1914 to 1925.

References

Agar, Michael. 1994. *Language Shock: Understanding the Culture of Conversation*. New York: William Morrow.

Anderson, Benedict R. 1991. *Imagined Communities: Reflections on the Origin and Spread of Nationalism*. Revised edition. London: Verso.

Auroux, Sylvain. 1994. *La révolution technologique de la grammatisation: Introduction à l'histoire des sciences du langage*. Liège: Mardaga.

Bachman, Lyle F. 1990. *Fundamental Considerations in Language Testing*. Oxford: Oxford University Press.

Baron, Naomi S. 2000. *Alphabet to Email: How Written English Evolved and Where It's Heading*. London and New York: Routledge.

Barro, Ana, Shirley Jordan, and Celia Roberts. 1998. Cultural Practice in Everyday Life: The Language Learner as Ethnographer. In *Language Learning in Intercultural Perspective: Approaches Through Drama and Ethnography*, edited by Michael Byram and Michael Fleming, 76–97. Cambridge: Cambridge University Press.

Barron, Colin, Nigel Bruce, and David Nunan, eds. 2002. *Knowledge and Discourse: Towards an Ecology of Language*. London: Longman.

Bartsch, Renate. 1987. *Norms of Language: Theoretical and Practical Aspects*. London and New York: Longman.

Bauman, Richard, and Charles Briggs. 2003. *Voices of Modernity: Language Ideologies and the Politics of Inequality*. Cambridge: Cambridge University Press.

Belz, Julie A. 2002a. The Myth of the Deficient Communicator. *Language Teaching Research* 6(1): 59–82.

———. 2002b. Second Language Play as a Representation of the Multicompetent Self in Foreign Language Study. *Journal of Language, Identity, and Education* 1(1): 13–39.

———. 2003. Linguistic Perspectives on the Development of Intercultural Competence in Telecollaboration. *Language Learning & Technology* 7(2): 68–99. *http://llt.msu.edu/vol7num2/belz/default.html*

———. 2005. Intercultural Questioning, Discovery, and Tension in Internet-mediated Language Learning Partnerships. *Language and Intercultural Communication* 5(1): 3–39.

Belz, Julie A., and Celeste Kinginger. 2003. Discourse Options and the Development of Pragmatic Competence by Classroom Learners of German: The Case of Address Forms. *Language Learning* 53(4): 591–647.

Belz, Julie A., and Jonathon Reinhardt. 2004. Aspects of Advanced Foreign Language Proficiency: Internet-mediated German Language Play. *International Journal of Applied Linguistics* 14(3): 324–362.

Berger, Peter L., and Thomas Luckmann. 1989. *The Social Construction of Reality: A Treatise on the Sociology of Knowledge*. New York: Anchor Books. Original edition, 1966.

Bernstein, Basil. 2000. *Pedagogy, Symbolic Control, and Identity: Theory, Research, Critique*. Lanham, MD: Rowman and Littlefield.

Block, David. 2003. *The Social Turn in Second Language Acquisition*. Washington, DC: Georgetown University Press.

Blommaert, Jan. 2005. *Discourse: A Critical Introduction*. New York and Cambridge: Cambridge University Press.

Blyth, Carl. 1995. Redefining the Boundaries of Language Use: The Foreign Language Classroom as a Multilingual Speech Community. In *Redefining the Boundaries of Language Study*, edited by Claire J. Kramsch, 145–183. Boston, MA: Thomson Heinle.

Bonfiglio, Thomas Paul. 2002. *Race and the Rise of Standard American*. Berlin and New York: Mouton de Gruyter.

Bourdieu, Pierre. 1979. *La Distinction, critique sociale du jugement*. Paris: Editions de Minuit.

———. 1982. *Ce que parler veut dire: l'économie des échanges linguistiques*. Paris: Fayard.

————. 2000. *Esquisse d'une théorie de la pratique*. Paris: Editions du Seuil. Original edition, 1972.

Bowers, C.A., and David J. Flinders. 1990. *Responsive Teaching: An Ecological Approach to Classroom Patterns of Language, Culture, and Thought*. New York: Teachers College Press.

Bucholtz, Mary. 2003. Sociolinguistic Nostalgia and the Authentication of Identity. *Journal of Sociolinguistics* 7(3): 398–416.

Byram, Michael. 1997. *Teaching and Assessing Intercultural Competence*. Clevedon, UK: Multilingual Matters.

Cameron, Debbie. 1998. What Has Gender Got to Do With Sex? In *Integrational Linguistics: A First Reader*, edited by Roy Harris and George Wolf. Oxford: Pergamon.

Cameron, Deborah. 1995. *Verbal Hygiene*. London: Routledge.

————. 2002. Globalization and the Teaching of Communication Skills. In *Globalization and Language Teaching*, edited by David Block and Deborah Cameron, 67–82. London: Routledge.

Canale, Michael. 1983. From Communicative Competence to Communicative Language Pedagogy. In *Language and Communication*, edited by Jack C. Richards and Richard W. Schmidt, 2–27. London: Longman.

Canale, Michael, and Merrill Swain. 1980. Theoretical Bases of Communicative Approaches to Second Language Teaching and Testing. *Applied Linguistics* 1: 1–47.

Chomsky, Noam. 1965. *Aspects of the Theory of Syntax*. Cambridge, MA: M.I.T. Press.

Clifford, James. 1988. *The Predicament of Culture: Twentieth-Century Ethnography, Literature, and Art*. Cambridge, MA: Harvard University Press.

Cook, Vivian. 1999. Going Beyond the Native Speaker in Language Teaching. *TESOL Quarterly* 33: 185–210.

Corson, David. 2001. *Language Diversity and Education*. Mahwah, NJ: Lawrence Erlbaum Associates.

Crowley, Tony. 1990. That Obscure Object of Desire: A Science of Language. In *Ideologies of Language*, edited by John E. Joseph and Talbot J. Taylor, 27–50. London: Routledge.

————. 2003. *Standard English and The Politics of Language*. 2nd ed. New York: Palgrave Macmillan.

Crystal, David. 2001. *Language and the Internet*. Cambridge, UK: Cambridge University Press.

Davies, Alan. 2003. *The Native Speaker: Myth and Reality*. Clevedon: Multilingual Matters.

de Certeau, Michel. 1984. *The Practice of Everyday Life*. Berkeley: University of California Press.

Eckert, Penelope. 2000. *Linguistic Variation as Social Practice: The Linguistic Construction of Identity at Belten High*. Oxford: Blackwell.

Eisenstein, Elizabeth L. 1983. *The Printing Revolution in Early Modern Europe*. Cambridge: Cambridge University Press.

Fairclough, Norman. 2001. *Language and Power*. 2nd ed. Harlow, UK: Longman.

————, ed. 1992. *Critical Language Awareness*. London: Longman.

Firth, Alan, and Johannes Wagner. 1997. On Discourse, Communication and (Some) Fundamental Concepts in SLA. *The Modern Language Journal* 81(3): 277–300.

Fishman, Joshua A. 1972. *Language and Nationalism: Two Integrative Essays*. Rowley, MA: Newberry House.

Foucault, Michel. 1971. *L'ordre du discours*. Paris: Gallimard.

Freire, Paulo, and Ana Maria Araújo Freire. 1994. *Pedagogy of Hope: Reliving Pedagogy of the Oppressed*. New York: Continuum.

Gal, Susan, and Judith T. Irvine. 1995. The Boundaries of Languages and Disciplines: How Ideologies Construct Difference. *Social Research* 62(4): 967–1001.

Garvin, Paul L., and Madeleine Mathiot. 1968. The Urbanization of the Guaraní Language: A Problem in Language and Culture. In *Readings in the Sociology of Language*, edited by Joshua A. Fishman, 365–374. The Hague: Mouton.

Gass, Susan, Kathleen Bardovi-Harlig, Sally Sieloff Magnan, and Joel Walz, eds. 2002. *Pedagogical Norms for Second and Foreign Language Learning and Teaching: Studies in Honour of Albert Valdman*. Amsterdam/Philadelphia: John Benjamins.

Gebhard, Jerry, and Robert Oprandy. 1999. *Language Teaching Awareness: A Guide to Exploring Beliefs and Practices*. New York: Cambridge University Press.

Gee, James P. 1990. *Social Linguistics and Literacies: Ideology in Discourse*. London: Falmer Press.

———. 1996. *Social Linguistics and Literacies: Ideology in Discourse*. 2nd ed. London: Taylor & Francis.

———. 2005. *An Introduction to Discourse Analysis: Theory and Method*. 2nd ed. London: Routledge.

Giroux, Henry A. 1981. *Ideology, Culture, and the Process of Schooling*. Philadelphia: Temple University Press.

Grace, George William. 1989. *The Linguistic Construction of Reality*. London: Routledge.

Gramsci, Antonio. 1975. *Quaderni del carcere*. Vol. 3. Turin: Einaudi.

Hannerz, Ulf. 1992. *Cultural Complexity: Studies in the Social Organization of Meaning*. New York: Columbia University Press.

Harris, Roy. 1998. The Integrationist Critique of Orthodox Linguistics. In *Integrational Linguistics: A First Reader*, edited by Roy Harris and George Wolf, 15–25. Oxford: Pergamon.

Hasan, Ruqaiya. 1996. The Ontogenesis of Ideology: An Interpretation of Mother Child Talk. In *Ways of Saying, Ways of Meaning: Selected Papers of Ruqaiya Hasan*, edited by Carmel Cloran, David Butt, and Geoffrey Williams, 133–151. London: Cassell.

Haugen, Einar. 1966. Dialect, Language, Nation. *American Anthropologist* 68: 922–935.

———. 1972. The Ecology of Language. In *The Ecology of Language: Essays by Einar Haugen*, edited by Einar Haugen, 325–339. Stanford: Stanford University Press.

Heath, Shirley Brice. 1980. Standard English: Biography of a Symbol. In *Standards and Dialects in English*, edited by Timothy Shopen and Joseph M. Williams, 3–32. Cambridge, MA: Winthrop Publishers.

Heller, Monica. 1999. *Linguistic Minorities and Modernity: A Sociolinguistic Ethnography*. London: Longman.

———. 2002. Globalization and the Commodification of Bilingualism in Canada. In *Globalization and Language Teaching*, edited by David Block and Deborah Cameron, 47–63. London: Routledge.

———. 2003. Discourse and Interaction. In *The Handbook of Discourse Analysis*, edited by Deborah Schiffrin, Deborah Tannen, and Heidi E. Hamilton, 250–264. Malden, MA: Blackwell.

Herring, Susan C. 2001. Computer-Mediated Discourse. In *The Handbook of Discourse Analysis*, edited by Deborah Schiffrin, Deborah Tannen, and Heidi E. Hamilton, 612–634. Oxford, England: Blackwell Publishers.

Hymes, Dell. 1972. On Communicative Competence. In *Sociolinguistics: Selected Readings*, edited by J. B. Pride and Janet Holmes, 269–293. Harmondsworth, UK: Penguin.

———. 1992. The Concept of Communicative Competence Revisited. In *Thirty Years of Linguistic Evolution*, edited by Martin Pütz, 31–58. Amsterdam: Benjamins.

Irvine, Judith T., and Susan Gal. 2000. Language Ideology and Linguistic Differentiation. In *Regimes of Language: Ideologies, Polities, and Identities*, edited by Paul V. Kroskrity, 35–83. Santa Fe, NM: School of American Research Press.

Jaffe, Alexandra. 1999. *Ideologies in Action: Language Politics on Corsica*. Berlin: Mouton de Gruyter.

Joseph, John E. 1987. *Eloquence and Power: The Rise of Language Standards and Standard Languages*. London: Pinter.

Joseph, John E., and Talbot J. Taylor, eds. 1990. *Ideologies of Language*. London: Routledge.

Kern, Richard. 2000. *Literacy and Language Teaching*. Oxford: Oxford University Press.

Kern, Richard, Paige Ware, and Mark Warschauer. 2004. Crossing Frontiers: New Directions in Online Pedagogy and Research. *Annual Review of Applied Linguistics* 24: 243–260.

Kiesling, Scott, and Christina Bratt Paulston, eds. 2005. *Intercultural Discourse and Communication: The Essential Readings*. Malden, MA: Blackwell.

Koike, Dale A., and Judith E. Liskin-Gasparro. 1999. What is a Near-Native Speaker? Perspectives of Job Seekers and Search Committees in Spanish. *ADFL Bulletin* 30(3): 54–62.

Kramsch, Claire J. 1987. Foreign Language Textbooks' Construction of Foreign Reality. *Canadian Modern Language Review/La Revue canadienne des langues vivantes* 44(1): 95–119.

———. 1997. The Privilege of the Nonnative Speaker. *PMLA* 112: 359–369.

———. 1993. *Context and Culture in Language Teaching*. Oxford: Oxford University Press.

———. 1998a. *Language and Culture*. Oxford: Oxford University Press.

———. 1998b. The Privilege of the Intercultural Speaker. In *Language Learning in Intercultural Perspective: Approaches through Drama and Ethnography*, edited by Michael Byram and Michael Fleming, 16–31. New York: Cambridge University Press.

———. 2000. Second Language Acquisition, Applied Linguistics, and the Teaching of Foreign Languages. *The Modern Language Journal* 84(3): 311–326.

———. 2002. In Search of the Intercultural. *Journal of Sociolinguistics* 6(2): 275–285.

———, ed. 2002. *Language Acquisition and Language Socialization: Ecological Perspectives*. London: Continuum.

Kramsch, Claire J., Francine A' Ness, and Eva W. S. Lam. 2000. Authenticity and Authorship in Computer-Mediated Acquisition of L2 Literacy. *Language Learning & Technology* 4(2): 78–104. *http://llt.msu.edu/vol4num2/kramsch/default.html*

Kramsch, Claire J., and Steven L. Thorne. 2002. Foreign Language Learning as Global Communicative Practice. In *Globalization and Language Teaching*, edited by David Block and Deborah Cameron, 83–100. London: Routledge.

Kress, Gunther R. 2003. *Literacy in the New Media Age*. London: Routledge.

Kroskrity, Paul V., ed. 2000. *Regimes of Language: Ideologies, Polities, and Identities*. Santa Fe, NM: School of American Research Press.

Labov, William. 1972. The Logic of Nonstandard English. In *Language and Social Context*, edited by Pier Paolo Giglioli, 179–215. Harmondsworth: Penguin Books.

Leather, Jonathan, and Jet van Dam, eds. 2002. *The Ecology of Language Acquisition*. Dordrecht: Kluwer.

Lee, Penny. 1996. *The Whorf Theory Complex: A Critical Reconstruction*. Amsterdam: John Benjamins.

Leith, Dick. 1983. *A Social History of English*. London: Routledge.

Lemke, Jay L. 1995. *Textual Politics: Discourse and Social Dynamics*. London: Taylor & Francis.

Lippi-Green, Rosina. 1997. *English with an Accent: Language, Ideology, and Discrimination in the United States*. London: Routledge.

Lodge, Anthony R. 1993. *French: From Dialect to Standard*. New York: Routledge.

Long, Michael. 1991. Focus on Form: A Design Feature in Language Teaching Methodology. In *Foreign Language Research in Cross-Cultural Perspective*, edited by Kees De Bot, Ralph B. Ginsberg, and Claire J. Kramsch, 39–52. Amsterdam: Benjamins.

Lucy, John A. 1993. Reflexive Language and the Human Disciplines. In *Reflexive Language: Reported Speech and Metapragmatics*, edited by John A. Lucy, 9–32. Cambridge: Cambridge University Press.

Luke, Allan. 2004. Two Takes on the Critical. In *Critical Pedagogies and Language Learning*, edited by Bonny Norton and Kelleen Toohey, 21–29. Cambridge: Cambridge University Press.

Malinowski, Bronislaw. 1923. The Problem of Meaning in Primitive Languages. In *The Meaning of Meaning: A Study of the Influence of Language upon Thought and of the Science of Symbolism*, edited by C. K. Odgen and I. A. Richards, 296-336. New York: Harcourt Brace Jovanovich.

Mar-Molinero, Clare. 1997. *The Spanish-Speaking World: A Practical Introduction to Sociolinguistic Issues*. London: Routledge.

McLuhan, Marshall. 1962. *The Gutenberg Galaxy: The Making of Typographic Man*. Toronto: University of Toronto Press.

McNamara, Tim F. 1997. "Interaction" in Second Language Performance Assessment: Whose Performance? *Applied Linguistics* 18(4): 446-466.

Mey, Jacob. 1985. *Whose language?: A Study in Linguistic Pragmatics*. Amsterdam: Benjamins.

Milroy, James. 2001. Language Ideologies and the Consequences of Standardization. *Journal of Sociolinguistics* 5: 530-555.

Milroy, James, and Lesley Milroy. 1999. *Authority in Language*. 3rd ed. London: Routledge.

Moll, Luis C. 2000. Inspired by Vygotsky: Ethnographic Experiments in Education. In *Vygotskian Perspectives on Literacy Research: Constructing Meaning through Collaborative Inquiry*, edited by Carol D. Lee and Peter Smagorinsky, 256-268. Cambridge: Cambridge University Press.

Moll, Luis C., Cathy Amanti, Deborah Neff, and Norma Gonzalez. 1992. Funds of Knowledge for Teaching: Using a Qualitative Approach to Connect Homes and Classrooms. *Theory into Practice* 31(2): 132-141.

Norton, Bonny, and Kelleen Toohey, eds. 2004. *Critical Pedagogies and Language Learning*. Cambridge: Cambridge University Press.

Ortega, Lourdes. 1999. Language and Equality: Ideological and Structural Constraints in Foreign Language Education in the U.S. In *Sociopolitical Perspectives on Language Policy and Planning in the USA*, edited by Thom Huebner and Kathryn A. Davis, 243-266. Amsterdam: Benjamins.

Pavlenko, Aneta. 2003. "'Language of the Enemy': Foreign Language Education and National Identity." *International Journal of Bilingual Education and Bilingualism* 6(5): 313-331.

Pennycook, Alastair. 2001. *Critical Applied Linguistics: A Critical Introduction*. Mahwah, NJ: Lawrence Erlbaum.

Phillips, June K., and Robert M. Terry, eds. 1999. *Foreign Language Standards: Linking Research, Theories, and Practices*. Lincolnwood, IL: National Textbook Company.

Pica, Teresa. 1996. Do Second Language Learners Need Negotiation? *International Review of Applied Linguistics* 34: 1-21.

Pinker, Steven. 1999. *Words and Rules: The Ingredients of Language*. New York: Basic Books.

Rampton, Ben. 1990. Displacing the 'Native Speaker': Expertise, Affiliation and Inheritance. *ELT Journal* 44: 338-343.

Ray, Punya Sloka. 1963. *Language Standardization: Studies in Prescriptive Linguistics*. The Hague: Mouton.

Reagan, Timothy G., and Terry A. Osborn. 2002. *The Foreign Language Educator in Society: Toward a Critical Pedagogy*. Mahwah, NJ: Lawrence Erlbaum.

Reich, Robert B. 1991. *The Work of Nations: Preparing Ourselves for 21st-Century Capitalism*. New York: Alfred A. Knopf.

Ricento, Thomas. 2003. The Discursive Construction of Americanism. *Discourse and Society* 14: 611-637.

Richards, Jack C., and Charles Lockhart. 1994. *Reflective Teaching in Second Language Classrooms*. Cambridge: Cambridge University Press.

Roberts, Celia, Michael Byram, Ana Barro, Shirley Jordan, and Brian Street. 2001. *Language Learners as Ethnographers*. Clevendon, UK: Multilingual Matters.

Ruíz, Richard. 1984. Orientations in Language Planning. *NABE Journal* 8: 15-34.

Rumsey, Alan. 1990. Wording, Meaning, and Linguistic Ideology. *American Anthropologist* 92: 346-361.

Savignon, Sandra. 1972. *Communicative Competence: An Experiment in Foreign-Language Teaching*. Philadelphia: Center for Curriculum Development.

Schecter, Sandra R., and Robert Bayley. 2002. *Language as Cultural Practice: Mexicanos en el Norte*. Mahwah, NJ: Lawrence Erlbaum.

Schieffelin, Bambi B., Kathryn Ann Woolard, and Paul Kroskrity, eds. 1998. *Language Ideologies: Practice and Theory*. Oxford: Oxford University Press.

Schiffman, Harold F. 1996. *Linguistic Culture and Language Policy*. London: Routledge.

Scollon, Ronald, and Suzanne Wong Scollon. 2001. *Intercultural Communication: A Discourse Approach*. 2nd ed. Malden, MA: Blackwell.

Silverstein, Michael. 1979. Language Structure and Linguistic Ideology. In *The Elements: A Parasession on Linguistic Units and Levels*, edited by Paul Clyne, William Hanks, and Carol Hofbauer, 193-247. Chicago: Chicago Linguistic Society.

———. 1996. Monoglot "Standard" in America: Standardization and Metaphors of Linguistic Hegemony. In *The Matrix of Language: Contemporary Linguistic Anthropology*, edited by Donald Brenneis and Ronald K. S. Macaulay, 284-306. Boulder, CO: Westview Press.

———. 1998. The Uses and Utility of Ideology: A Commentary. In *Language Ideologies: Practice and Theory*, edited by Bambi B. Schieffelin, Kathryn Aann Woolard and Paul Kroskrity, 123-145. Oxford: Oxford University Press.

Stewart, William A. 1968. A Sociolinguistic Typology for Describing National Multilingualism. In *Readings in the Sociology of Language*, edited by Joshua A. Fishman, 531-545. The Hague: Mouton.

Stubbs, Michael. 2001. Computer-Assisted Text and Corpus Analysis: Lexical Cohesion and Communicative Competence. In *The Handbook of Discourse Analysis*, edited by Deborah Schiffrin, Deborah Tannen and Heidi E. Hamilton, 304-320. Oxford, UK: Blackwell Publishers.

Tarone, Elaine, and Dick Allwright. 2005. Second Language Teacher Learning and Student Second Language Learning: Shaping the Knowledge Base. In *Second Language Teacher Education: International Perspectives*, edited by Diane J. Tedick, 5-23. Mahwah, NJ: Lawrence Erlbaum.

Taylor, Talbot J. 1997. *Theorizing Language: Analysis, Normativity, Rhetoric, History*. New York: Pergamon.

———. 2000. Language Constructing Language: The Implications of Reflexivity for Linguistic Theory. *Language Sciences* 22: 483-499.

Train, Robert W. 2000. Getting Past the Ideology of 'The Language': The Standardization of French and Spanish, and Its Implications in Foreign-Language Pedagogy. The University of California at Berkeley, unpublished doctoral dissertation.

———. 2003. The (Non)Native Standard Language in Foreign Language Education: A Critical Perspective. In *The Sociolinguistics of Foreign Language Classrooms: Contributions of the Native, the Near-native and the Non-native Speaker*, edited by Carl Blyth, 3-39. Boston, MA: Thomson Heinle.

———. 2003. Sociolinguistics and Language as Cultural Practice. *Journal of Sociolinguistics* 7(3): 432-442.

———. 2004. Review of Chomsky on Democracy and Education. *Teachers College Record* 106(2): 365-374.

Trudeau, Danielle. 1992. *Les inventeurs du bon usage (1529-1647)*. Paris: Minuit.

Valdés, Guadalupe. 1998. The Construct of the Near-Native Speaker in the Foreign Language Profession: Perspectives on Ideologies about Language. *Profession 1998*: 151-160.

Valdés, Guadalupe, and Richard A. Figueroa. 1996. *Bilingualism and Testing: A Special Case of Bias*. Norwood, NJ: Ablex.

Valdés, Guadalupe, Sonia V. González, Dania López García, and Patricio Márquez. 2003. Language Ideology: The Case of Spanish in Departments of Foreign Languages. *Anthropology & Education Quarterly* 34: 3-26.

Valdman, Albert. 1982. Français standard et français populaire: sociolectes ou fiction? *The French Review* 56(2): 218-227.

————. 2000. Comment gérer la variation dans l'enseignement du français langue étrangère aux Etats-Unis. *The French Review* 73(4): 648–666.

van Dijk, Teun A. 1998. *Ideology: A Multidisciplinary Approach.* London: Sage.

van Leeuwen, Theo, and Ruth Wodak. 1999. Legitimising Immigration Control: A Discourse-Historical Analysis. *Discourse Studies* 1(1): 83–118.

van Lier, Leo. 1989. Reeling, Writhing, Drawling, Stretching, and Fainting in Coils: Oral Proficiency Interviews as Conversation. *TESOL Quarterly* 23(3): 489–508.

————. 1996. *Interaction in the Language Curriculum: Awareness, Automony, and Authenticity.* New York: Longman.

————. 2003. A Tale of Two Computer Classrooms: The Ecology of Project-Based Language Learning. In *Ecology of Language Acquisition*, edited by Jonathan Leather and Jet van Dam, 49–63. Dordrecht: Kluwer.

————. 2004. *The Ecology and Semiotics of Language Learning: A Sociocultural Perspective.* Boston: Kluwer.

Varghese, Manka, Brian Morgan, Bill Johnston, and Kimberly A. Johnson. 2005. Theorizing Language Teacher Identity: Three Perspectives and Beyond. *Journal of Language, Identity, and Education* 4(1): 21–44.

Ware, Paige. 2005. "Missed" Communication In Online Communication: Tensions in a German-American Telecollaboration. *Language Learning & Technology* 9(2): 64–89. *http://llt.msu.edu/vol9num2/ware/default.html*

Ware, Paige, and Claire J. Kramsch. 2005. Toward an Intercultural Stance: Teaching German and English through Telecollaboration. *The Modern Language Journal* 89 (2): 190–205.

Warschauer, Mark. 2003. Demystifying the Digital Divide. *Scientific American* 289(2): 42–47.

————, ed. 1995. *Virtual Connections: Online Activities and Projects for Networking Language Learners.* Honolulu: Second Language Teaching and Curriculum Center.

Watts, Richard, and Peter Trudgill, eds. 2002. *Alternative Histories of English.* London: Routledge.

Wenger, Etienne. 1998. *Communities of Practice: Learning, Meaning, and Identity.* Cambridge: Cambridge University Press.

Wertsch, James V. 1991. *Voices of the Mind: A Sociocultural Approach to Mediated Action.* Cambridge, MA: Harvard University Press.

Widdowson, Henry G. 1994. The Ownership of English. *TESOL Quarterly* 28: 377–389.

Wilkinson, Sharon. 2001. Noticing Discourse: A Point of Departure for (Re)Designing the Conversation Course. *Foreign Language Annals* 34 (6): 523–533.

Wodak, Ruth. 2001. The Discourse-Historical Approach. In *Methods of Critical Discourse Analysis*, edited by Ruth Wodak and Michael Meyer, 63–94. London: Sage.

Wodak, Ruth, Rudolf de Cillia, Martin Reisigl, and Karin Liebhart. 1999. *The Discursive Construction of National Identity.* Edinburgh: Edinburgh University Press.

Woolard, Kathryn A., and Bambi B. Schieffelin. 1994. Language Ideology. *Annual Review of Anthropology* 23: 55–82.

Contributors

Beth Bauer (Ph.D., University of Pennsylvania) is Director of the Center for Language Studies and Senior Lecturer in Hispanic Studies at Brown University. She has published several articles on 19th-century Spanish literature and is the co-author, with Barbara Freed, of *Contextos: Spanish for Communication*. She teaches and supervises Spanish language courses at the intermediate and advanced levels, and has offered literature and culture courses at all levels, including graduate seminars on Spanish literature and on foreign language teaching methodology. In addition to a *Cultura* exchange with Mexico, her curricular initiatives include Spanish service-learning courses and a pilot Spanish Writing Center. Beth_Bauer@brown.edu

Julie A. Belz (Ph.D., University of California at Berkeley) is an Assistant Professor of German and Applied Linguistics and a Project Director at the Center for Advanced Language Proficiency Education and Research (CALPER) at Pennsylvania State University. She specializes in additional language learning and development, computer-mediated intercultural communication, interlanguage pragmatics, learner corpus analysis, discourse analysis, learner identity, language play, multilingual discourse, and literary accounts of language learning. Her publications appear in a variety of refereed journals including *Language Learning, The Modern Language Journal, The International Journal of Applied Linguistics, Language Learning & Technology, The Journal of Language, Identity, and Education*, and *Intercultural Pragmatics*. Julie conducts networked courses between the United States and Germany and oversees the establishment of *Telekorp*, a bilingual corpus of computer-mediated learner language. Her research has been supported by grants from the U.S. Department of Education. jab63@psu.edu

Lynne deBenedette (M.A., University of Michigan) is a Senior Lecturer in Russian at Brown University where she has coordinated the Russian language program since 1995. In addition to materials development, her interests include developing and assessing intercultural competence and the implications of Focus on Form research for the teaching of Russian. lynne_debenedette@brown.edu

Paola E. Dussias (Ph.D., University of Arizona) is Assistant Professor of Spanish, Linguistics, and Psychology at Pennsylvania State University. Her main research area focuses on sentence comprehension processes in bilinguals and second language learners. Her work on sentence parsing has been published in a number of volumes and journals, including *One Mind, Two Languages, The Handbook of Bilingualism, Studies in Second Language Acquisition*, and *The International Journal of Bilingualism*. She has also conducted research on the use of experimental techniques to study psycholinguistic processes involving code-switched utterances. Some of this work has appeared in *Revista Internacional de Lingüística Iberoamericana* and *Romance Phonology and Variation*. pdussias@psu.edu

Gilberte Furstenberg (*Aggrégation* in English at the University of Lille, France) is a Senior Lecturer in French at the Massachusetts Institute of Technology. She is the main author of two multimedia works: *A la Rencontre de Philippe*, a pioneering interactive fiction that has won national and international awards and *Dans un quartier de Paris*, an award-winning interactive documentary. She has been teaching French at M.I.T. for the last 25 years and started developing *Cultura* in 1997, thanks to an initial grant from the Consortium for Language Teaching and Learning and a subsequent one from the National Endowment for the Humanities. gfursten@mit.edu

Lina Lee (Ph.D., University of Texas at Austin) is an Associate Professor of Spanish and Coordinator of the Spanish Program at the University of New Hampshire, where she teaches both undergraduate and graduate courses, trains teaching assistants, and supervises foreign language interns. She teaches courses in applied linguistics, second language acquisition, and foreign language methods. She has published articles in the areas of oral proficiency testing, portfolio assessment, and Internet technologies for language learning in *Foreign Language Annals, Hispania, The CALICO Journal, System, ReCALL* and *NECTFL Review*. Lina is also the author of web sites for several Spanish textbooks. lina.lee@unh.edu

Sabine Levet (*Maîtrise de Lettres*, University of Paris–Sorbonne) is currently a Lecturer in French in Romance Languages and Comparative Literature at Brandeis University. She taught at M.I.T. from 1988 to 2001. She is one of the original developers of *Cultura*, with Gilberte Furstenberg (Massachusetts Institute of Technology) and Shoggy Waryn (Brown). She is the co-author, with Gilberte Furstenberg, of a teachers' guide and a student activities workbook for the French-language CD-ROM *Dans un quartier de Paris*, published by Yale University Press. Sabine has given numerous talks and workshops on the integration of technology into the foreign language curriculum and on the teaching and learning of culture, and has written articles about the development of tools for cross-cultural understanding. slevet@brandeis.edu

Andreas Müller-Hartmann (*Dr. phil.*, University of Osnabrück, Germany) is a Professor of Teaching English as a Foreign Language (TEFL) in the Department of English at the Pädagogische Hochschule Heidelberg, Germany. He teaches courses in American Studies and TEFL. He has conducted research and published books and articles on American cultural studies, qualitative research in the foreign language classroom, integrating technology into the EFL classroom, intercultural learning, and task-based language learning. He has recently co-authored a book on *Introduction to English Language Teaching* (2004) and co-edited a volume on *Task-based Language Learning and Teaching* (2004). Andreas.Mueller-Hartmann@ph-heidelberg.de

Robert O'Dowd (*Dr. phil.*, University of Duisburg-Essen, Germany) is a teacher of English and EFL Methodology at the University of León in Spain. He has written widely on the development of intercultural communicative competence through telecollaborative exchange. He is also a co-author of the *Log into English* software for Cornelsen Software in Germany. His current research interests include studying the role of virtual learning environments in foreign language education, telecollaboration, and task-based language learning. dfmrod@unileon.es

Sally Sieloff Magnan (Ph.D., Indiana University) is a Professor of French and Director of the University of Wisconsin-Madison Language Institute. She is also Editor of *The Modern Language Journal* and co-author of the first-year French textbook, *Paroles*, published by John Wiley and Sons. At Wisconsin, she oversees first- and fifth-semester French and co-directs the Interdisciplinary Second Language Acquisition Doctoral program. She has published widely in the AAUSC series, the Northeast Conference reports, in academic journals, and she has co-edited a book published by Benjamins Publishing Company. She teaches courses at the graduate and undergraduate levels in college teaching methods, second language studies, French language, and topics in French immigration. She received the honor of *Chevalier dans l'Ordre des Palmes Académiques* and several teaching awards. ssmagnan@wisc.edu

Jeffrey Schneider (Ph.D., Cornell University) is an Assistant Professor of German Studies at Vassar College. In addition to collaborating with his colleague Silke von der Emde on language learning and curriculum development, he is currently completing a book titled *Uniform Fantasies: Militarism, Masculinity, and Male Sexuality in Imperial Germany*. He also recently served as translator and consultant for the play *I Am My Own Wife* by Doug Wright, which won the 2004 Pulitzer Prize for Drama. JeSchneider@vassar.edu

Steven L. Thorne (Ph.D., University of California at Berkeley) is the Associate Director of the Center for Language Acquisition, Associate Director of the Center for Advanced Language Proficiency Education and Research (a National Foreign Language Resource Center), and Assistant Professor in Linguistics and Applied Language Studies at the Pennsylvania State University. His research addresses activity theory, additional language learning, and computer-mediated communication. Current and forthcoming publications include articles in *The Modern Language Journal, Language Learning & Technology, The CALICO Journal*, and a co-authored book titled *Sociocultural Theory and the Genesis of Second Language Development* (Oxford University Press, forthcoming in January 2006). sthorne@psu.edu

Robert Train (Ph.D., University of California at Berkeley) is an Assistant Professor of Spanish in the Department of Modern Languages and Literatures at Sonoma State University. He is also the Director of the Language and Culture Learning Center (www.sonoma.edu/forlang/lc2). His dissertation in Romance Philology dealt with *Getting Past the Ideology of 'The Language': The Standardization of French and Spanish, and Its Implications for Foreign-Language Pedagogy.* Train has published and lectured on the intersection of ideologies of language and language teaching, including the role of language-culture learning technologies in education. One of his current research projects studies the use of electronic bilingual journals in first- and second-year Spanish classes. His concern for promoting critical language awareness grew out of his years as a teacher in a public high school in the San Francisco Bay Area, where he taught Spanish and French to students from richly varied and largely bilingual backgrounds. robert.train@sonoma.edu

Silke von der Emde (Ph.D., Indiana University) is an Associate Professor of German Studies at Vassar College. In addition to her work on technology and language learning, she is the author of *Entering History: Feminist Dialogues in Irmtraud Morgner's Prose* as well as several articles on GDR literature, feminist theory, and German film. She is currently working on a book project on women, memory, and the "second German past." She is also co-directing a broad initiative at Vassar College on "History, Memory, and the Legacies of the Holocaust." vonderemde@vassar.edu

Shoggy T. Waryn (Ph.D., University of Iowa) is a senior lecturer at Brown University, where he teaches French language and French film. His interests range from media history, technology, and cross-cultural studies to online pedagogy and teaching. Before coming to Brown, Waryn worked for SmartPlanet.com and WebCT.com as a project manager and content provider. He is, with Gilberte Furstenberg (M.I.T.) and Sabine Levet (Brandeis), co-author of *Cultura* and has worked at Brown University on a Spanish and Russian version of the project with Beth Bauer and Lynne deBenedette. Shoggy_Waryn@brown.edu

AAUSC
The American Association of University Supervisors, Coordinators, and Directors of Foreign Language Programs

Purpose

Since its inception in 1980, the AAUSC has worked to:

- Promote and improve foreign and second language education in the United States

- Strengthen and improve foreign language curricula and instruction at the post-secondary level

- Strengthen development programs for teaching assistants, teaching fellows, associate instructors, or their equivalents

- Promote research in second language learning and development and on the preparation and supervision of teaching assistants

- Establish a forum for exchanging ideas, experiences, and materials among those concerned with language program direction

Who Can Join the AAUSC?

Membership in the AAUSC is open to anyone who is interested in strengthening foreign and second language instruction, especially, but not exclusively, those involved with multi-section programs. The membership comprises teachers, supervisors, coordinators, program directors, faculty, and administrators in colleges and universities that employ teaching assistants. Many members are faculty and administrators at undergraduate institutions.

How Do I Join the AAUSC?

Please fill out the following application for membership, and send it with annual dues to Robert Davis, or join online at *www.aausc.org*.

Dues (including yearly volume)

Regular .... $25.00/year, $40.00/two years
Student .... $15.00/year, $25.00/two years

Please make checks payable to:
Robert L. Davis, Secretary/Treasurer, AAUSC
Department of Romance Languages
University of Oregon
Eugene, OR 97403 USA
(541) 346-0956 phone
(541) 346-4030 fax
rldavis@oregon.uoregon.edu
www.aausc.org

AAUSC Application for Membership

New ❐   Renewal ❐

Name _____

School Address _____

_____

City _____ State _____ Zip _____

Telephone (work) _____

Fax _____

E-mail _____

Home address _____

City _____ State _____ Zip _____

Telephone (home) _____

Languages taught: Arabic ❐   Chinese ❐   ESL ❐

French ❐   Italian ❐   Japanese ❐   Portuguese ❐

Russian ❐   German ❐   Spanish ❐   Other ❐

Are you a: Teacher ❐   Program Director ❐

Dept. Chair ❐   Graduate Student ❐   Other ❐